Transgender China

Transgender China

Edited by
Howard Chiang

TRANSGENDER CHINA
Copyright © Howard Chiang, 2012.

All rights reserved.

First published in 2012 by
PALGRAVE MACMILLAN®
in the United States—a division of St. Martin's Press LLC,
175 Fifth Avenue, New York, NY 10010.

Where this book is distributed in the UK, Europe and the rest of the world, this is by Palgrave Macmillan, a division of Macmillan Publishers Limited, registered in England, company number 785998, of Houndmills, Basingstoke, Hampshire RG21 6XS.

Palgrave Macmillan is the global academic imprint of the above companies and has companies and representatives throughout the world.

Palgrave® and Macmillan® are registered trademarks in the United States, the United Kingdom, Europe and other countries.

ISBN: 978–0–230–34062–6

Library of Congress Cataloging-in-Publication Data

    Transgender China / edited by Howard Chiang.
       p. cm.
    Includes bibliographical references and index.
    ISBN 978–0–230–34062–6 (alk. paper)
       1. Transgenderism—China—History. 2. Transgender people—China—History. I. Chiang, Howard, 1983–

HQ77.95.C6T73 2012
306.76'8—dc23   2012031256

A catalogue record of the book is available from the British Library.

This book is printed on paper suitable for recycling and made from fully managed and sustained forest sources. Logging, pulping and manufacturing processes are expected to conform to the environmental regulations of the country of origin.

Design by Newgen Imaging Systems (P) Ltd., Chennai, India.

First edition: December 2012

10 9 8 7 6 5 4 3 2 1

Contents

List of Illustrations ... vii

Acknowledgments ... ix

Part I   Introduction

1. Imagining Transgender China
   Howard Chiang ... 3

Part II   Trans Figurations of History

2. How China Became a "Castrated Civilization" and Eunuchs a "Third Sex"
   Howard Chiang ... 23

3. Gendered Androgyny: Transcendent Ideals and Profane Realities in Buddhism, Classicism, and Daoism
   Daniel Burton-Rose ... 67

4. The Androgynous Ideal in Scholar-Beauty Romances: A Historical and Cultural View
   Zuyan Zhou ... 97

5. Transgenderism as a Heuristic Device: On the Cross-historical and Transnational Adaptations of the *Legend of the White Snake*
   Alvin Ka Hin Wong ... 127

Part III   Trans Locations of Culture

6. Begin Anywhere: Transgender and Transgenre Desire in Qiu Miaojin's *Last Words from Montmartre* (蒙馬牠遺書)
   Larissa N. Heinrich ... 161

7. Trans on Screen
   Helen Hok-Sze Leung ... 183

8	Writing the Body *Carlos Rojas*	199
9	Performing Transgender Desire: Male Cross-Dressing Shows in Taiwan *Chao-Jung Wu*	225
10	Transgenders in Hong Kong: From Shame to Pride *Pui Kei Eleanor Cheung*	263

Part IV Afterword

11	De/Colonizing Transgender Studies of China *Susan Stryker*	287

List of Contributors   293

Index   297

Illustrations

Figures

2.1	Drawing of an eunuch's castration	34
2.2	Instruments used for castration	36
2.3	Photo of a castrated boy	36
2.4	Medical images of Chinese eunuchs	40
2.5	Photographs of eunuchs	41
3.1	Lactating paragon of fraternal duty	77
3.2	"The Infant Manifests Its Form"	85
5.1	Production still from *New Legend of Madame White Snake*	149
7.1	Yan and Lily sitting together	192
7.2	Dieyi and Xiaolou	195
8.1	Ren Xiong, "Self-portrait"	200
8.2	Ma Liuming, "Dialogue with Gilbert and George"	206
8.3	Ma Liuming	208
8.4	Zhang Huan, "Weeping Angel"	210
8.5	Zhang Huan with prosthetic leg	211
8.6	Zhang Huan, "1/2"	213
8.7	Ma Liuming and Zhang Huan, "Third Contact"	220
9.1	Original appearance	239
9.2	Clear foundation, dark eye shadow, well-delineated eyebrows	239

9.3 Concealed tattoo, underhose, and bra   240
9.4 Wig, necklace, earrings, pins   240
9.5 Stage appearance   241
10.1 Joanne on the International Human Rights Day   277
10.2 Photo of the International Day Against Homophobia   277
10.3 Photo of Joanne speaking at a gender seminar   278

Tables

9.1 Some *fanchuan artists*' personal profiles   230
9.2 A feasible typology of male cross-dressing   248

Acknowledgments

This volume would not have been possible without the generous support from the following programs at Princeton University: Program in East Asian Studies, Shelby Cullom Davis Center for Historical Studies, Department of History, Program in the Study of Women and Gender (now the Program in Gender and Sexuality Studies), Program in History of Science, and the Department of English. I am especially grateful for the support of Benjamin A. Elman, chair of the Department of East Asian Studies and my dissertation co-advisor; Angela N. H. Creager, the director of Graduate Studies of the Program in History of Science in 2009 and my dissertation co-advisor; Daniel T. Rodgers, director of the Davis Center for Historical Studies in 2009; William C. Jordan, chair of the History Department in 2009; R. Marie Griffith, director of the Program in the Study of Women and Gender in 2009; and Claudia L. Johnson, chair of the English Department. I also warmly thank Ta-wei Chi, David L. Eng, Susan Naquin, Gayle M. Salamon, Tze-lan Deborah Sang, and Joan W. Scott for their participation in the conference that launched this volume, "Trans Ventures: Trans/Formations of Gender in Sinophone Culture," which was held in spring 2009 at Princeton University. I am grateful as well for the encouragement, advice, and patience of Brigitte Shull, Joanna Roberts, and Maia Woolner at Palgrave Macmillan. All of these individuals decided to place their trust in the efforts of a less-experienced scholar in the early production stages of this book. I hope the research findings presented in this anthology prove to be a meaningful investment of their time and faith in what I have tried to accomplish. Finally, I want to thank everyone who contributed to this project, but it is to the authors that this book is ultimately dedicated.

PART I

Introduction

CHAPTER 1

Imagining Transgender China

Howard Chiang

Sexologist Magnus Hirschfeld's *Die Transvestiten* (1910) and anthropologist Esther Newton's *Mother Camp* (1972) exemplify a rich tradition of scholarly thought and analysis on gender variance in the twentieth century.[1] Nonetheless, it was only in the last two decades that an explosion of academic interest in transgender topics became ever more pronounced. In the 1970s and 1980s, social, political, cultural, and intellectual trends paved the way for some transgender people to increasingly distance themselves from the women's movement and the gay and lesbian movement.[2] The emergence of queer studies as an umbrella field in the decade following these developments cultivated the growth and maturation of transgender studies.[3] Already in her seminal *Gender Trouble* (1990), philosopher Judith Butler used drag as a preeminent example to theorize the cultural performativity of gender, thereby reorienting women's studies beyond traditional concerns of feminist epistemology.[4] In *Female Masculinity* (1998), cultural theorist Judith Halberstam recentered women's relationship to masculinity, revealing a long-neglected undercurrent of Anglo-American literature and film.[5] Seven years later, the publication of *In a Queer Time and Place* (2005) enriched her problematization of the heteronormative alignment of sex and gender through the lens of subcultural practice.[6] This book has been deeply influential in establishing the centrality of transgender issues to queer studies.

Between *Gender Trouble* and *In a Queer Time and Place*, other important book-length contributions to the development of transgender studies include Vern and Bonnie Bullough's *Cross Dressing, Sex, and Gender* (1993), Judith Butler's *Bodies That Matter* (1993) and *Undoing Gender* (2004), Kate Bornstein's *Gender Outlaw* (1994) and *My Gender Workbook* (1998), Bernice Hausman's *Changing Sex* (1995), Leslie Feinberg's *Transgender Warriors* (1996), Zachary Nataf's *Lesbians Talk Transgender* (1996), Patrick Califia's *Sex Changes* (1997), Marjorie Garber's *Vested Interest* (1997), Riki Anne Wilchins's *Read My Lips* (1997), Don Kulick's *Travesti* (1998), Jay Prosser's *Second Skins* (1998), Viviane Namaste's *Invisible Lives* (2000), Joanne Meyerowitz's *How Sex Changed* (2002), and Henry Rubin's *Self-Made Men* (2003).[7] This early set of books laid down the theoretical and intellectual foundations for much of the transgender scholarship produced in the subsequent decade. More recent definitive books in transgender studies include David Valentine's *Imagining Transgender* (2007), Susan Stryker's *Transgender History* (2008), Patricia Gherovici's *Please Select Your Gender* (2010), Gayle Salamon's *Assuming a Body* (2010), and Genny Beemyn and Susan Rankin's *The Lives of Transgender People* (2011).[8] These newer studies demonstrate a remarkable measure of analytical sophistication and maturity, whether in terms of critical ethnography, synthetic history, clinically based psychoanalytic theory, materially grounded phenomenology, or social scientific empiricism.

Apart from monographic studies, the development of transgender studies, like the early phases of women's studies, has depended heavily on collaborative projects that brought together scholars and activists working independently on this marginal topic. The essays included in an early anthology called *PoMoSexuals* (1997), coedited by Carol Queen and Lawrence Schimel, bespeak the unique influence of postmodern theory on emergent critiques of gender dualism.[9] A formal joint endeavor in shaping the early contours of transgender studies first took place in 1998, when the leading journal in queer studies, *GLQ*, published its "Transgender Issue," guest edited by the trans activist-scholar Susan Stryker.[10] Meanwhile, other important voices challenging conventional sex dimorphism in social and cross-cultural settings came from such groundbreaking anthologies as *Third Sex, Third Gender* (1993), edited by Gilbert Herdt, and *Genderqueer* (2002), coedited by Joan Nestle, Riki Wilchins, and Clare Howell.[11] It was only by 2006, however, that the very first *Transgender Studies Reader*, coedited by Stryker and Stephen Whittle, appeared in print.[12] In the fall of 2008, a second set of critical essays devoted to transgender topics was published by the leading journal in gender studies, *Women's Studies Quarterly*.[13] And a recent collection of papers edited by Laurie Shrage, *You've Changed* (2009), took up the broader philosophical implications of sex reassignment.[14] By the beginning of this century, studies began to not only move away from, but also even challenge the "scientific" sexological framework that dominated most of the scholarship on nonnormative gender expressions in the previous century.[15]

Above all, these books and volumes have turned transgender studies into a semiautonomous, though in many ways highly contested, area of scholarly research. As David Valentine has noted, "The earliest use of transgender (in its institutionalized, collective sense) in U.S. activism dates no further than 1991 or 1992."[16] Despite the early 1990s rupture, the highly institutionalized and collective usage of the term "transgender" has important roots in the history of the feminist movement and the gay and lesbian movement, as well as in the historical dimensions of the categories of gender and sexuality. In the late nineteenth and early twentieth centuries, for example, a neat conceptual separation between male homosexual identity (erotic attraction) and overt effeminate behavior (gender expression) did not exist.[17] Sexologists loosely put masculine women, feminine men, same-sex desiring subjects, transvestites, and all sorts of gender variant people under the category of "inversion."[18] Furthermore, the distinction between "passing women," butches, and gender-normative same-sex desiring females had never been so clean and simple, but developed across the span of the entire twentieth century.[19] In the 1970s and 1980s, gay male activists pushed American psychiatrists to acknowledge the private nature of their sexual orientation, and antipornography and lesbian feminists condemned the public representation of female sexuality and nonnormative genders. Together, the gay activism in the aftermath of the DSM victory and the "sex wars" that eventually fractured the feminist movement began to define homosexuality *against what was visible* among gender/sexual subcultures.[20] These debates, in other words, began to distinguish the contemporary meaning of "transgender" from "homosexuality" by casting the former in terms of what the latter negated.[21]

By the 1990s, transgender studies came to be consolidated and widely recognized as an independent area of academic inquiry. Of course, debates ensued among activists, popular authors, academics, and other writers regarding what transgender precisely means (and the more general question of who fits into what categories has deeper historical ramifications in gay activism, feminism, and the civil rights movement). But with an expansive (even ambiguous), institutionalized, and collective notion of transgender, these actors nonetheless shared a commitment to advancing the political and epistemological interests of gender variant people. Moreover, as the twentieth century drew to an end, it seemed rather useful—and perhaps helpful—to distinguish the range of community, political, and intellectual work centered on trans folks from those centered on gays and lesbians. In the emerging field of transgender studies, transgender-identified scholars took the lead in breaking the ground of research;[22] contributors came from diverse disciplinary backgrounds with a heterogeneous set of theoretical, rhetorical, and methodological positions; and, most importantly, fruitful conversations have been largely enriched by self-reflexive insights on and a unique preference for novel interpretations of the meaning of embodiment, specifically, and the possible boundaries of human experience more broadly.[23] As Valentine puts it, "The capacity to stand in for an unspecified group of people is, indeed, one of the seductive things about 'transgender' in trying to describe a wide range of people, both historical and contemporary, Western and non-Western."[24]

Despite Valentine's promising remark, the considerable measure of enthusiasm that fueled the making of transgender studies has been confined mainly to North American and European academic circles. It logically follows that this area of scholarship is heavily oriented toward exploring Anglo-American society and culture. The only exception is the still growing literature that uses anthropological data on gender diversity to elucidate the limitations of Western-centric frameworks of gender dimorphism. But even here, the primary focus has been Native America and Southeast Asia.[25] Scholarly, activist, and creative work on transgender issues in Northeast Asia remains relatively scarce. With a few notable exceptions, gay and lesbian topics—alongside the translation of Western queer theoretical texts—continue to dominate critical studies of gender and sexuality in Taiwan, Hong Kong, and mainland China.[26] Particularly missing from the field of queer studies is a sustained critical engagement with Chinese transgender identity, practice, embodiment, history, and culture.

Recently, a number of Sinologists from different disciplines have begun to balance the analytical horizon of transgender studies. A China-centered perspective makes it possible to expand the scope of transgender scholarship in terms of historical nuance, cultural-geographical coverage, and methodological refinement.[27] It is in the spirit of providing this long overdue perspective that the present volume brings together these Sinologists for the first time. Although each chapter can be treated separately in its own right, they must also be taken together as a joint endeavor that explores the possibility (and potential limitations) of excavating a field of scholarly inquiry that we might assign the label of "Chinese transgender studies."

There is a consistent double bind in trying to consolidate a field under that name: the prospect of such an ambitious project brings with it key intrinsic perils or conceptual problematic. In the broadest sense, this merely echoes Susan Stryker's earlier comment that "the conflation of many types of gender variance into the single shorthand term 'transgender,' particularly when this collapse into a single genre of personhood crosses the boundaries that divide the West from the rest of the world, holds both peril and promise."[28] Although Chinese transgender studies promises to break new grounds and balance the existing insufficiencies in the broader field of transgender studies, it faces a politics of knowledge not unlike the set of problems it claims to exceed in the face of Western transgender studies. For instance, if the field of transgender studies was institutionalized only in the 1990s and, even more crucially, in North America, how can the category of *transgender* even with its widest possible definition, be applied to Chinese cultural and historical contexts? It should be added here that even in Western studies of transgenderism, scholars often traverse between treating the concept of gender as an analytical, thematic, topical, theoretical, historical, and epistemological category.[29] So the interest of venturing into new terrains of analysis is inherently fraught with questions of methodological assumption, categorical adequacy, and how they confound the fine line between research prospect and disciplinary closure. Independently and interactively, each of the following chapters reveals some of these major pitfalls and the corollary intellectual promises.

One way to imagine Chinese transgender studies is by adopting a focused definition of transgender to refer to practices of embodiment that cross or transcend normative boundaries of gender. This approach lends itself easily to identifying specific trans figures based on their self-representation, bringing to light concrete historical and cultural examples in which such identification occur, and stressing the importance of agency both in cultural production and with respect to the historical actors themselves who self-identify as trans. In "Gendered Androgyny," for instance, Daniel Burton-Rose takes a huge chronological sweep—over a period of nearly 25 hundred years—in isolating "concrete references to biological intersexuality as well as gender identities not necessarily paralleled in the physical body that did not conform to the available dominant categories." The examples that he uncovers in Buddhist, Daoist, and Classicist/Confucian sources serve as a pivotal reminder of the surprising fluidity of the gender and sexual ideations as depicted in these canonical Chinese texts. Perhaps there are scholars for whom some of these historical examples should be more appropriately absorbed into the category of gay. Yet, this preference bears striking similarity to earlier competing efforts in Western LGBT studies that only helped stabilize, rather than undermine, the field of transgender scholarship.[30] Burton-Rose carefully pitches his study as "an inoculation against superficial attempts to locate an indigenous transgender discourse in Chinese culture," but only so as "to enhance the potency of transgender and allied social movements."

In contrast, the chapter by Pui Kei Eleanor Cheung on "Transgenders in Hong Kong" offers a more contemporary perspective and marshals an even more identification-based approach to chart the structural transformations of the sociohistorical context in which trans individuals in Hong Kong have reoriented their subjectivity—from shame to pride. Even though general attitudes toward transgender people have become less negative and less hostile, many of Cheung's informants still experience great emotional distress and trauma on a daily basis, much of which could be attributed to the discriminations and prejudices that have survived from an earlier generation. The development of transgender subjectivity in Hong Kong corresponds to the Model of Gender Identity Formation and Transformation, or the "GIFT" model, which Cheung first delineates in her doctoral dissertation.[31] Like Burton-Rose, Cheung not only relies on a nominal notion of transgender to extend its analytical nuisance and possibility, but she also brings to light rare voices of Chinese transgender subjects that constitute a goldmine of thick ethnography.

In trying to imagine China in a transgender frame, Sinologists have famous examples with which to work. The area of Chinese culture in which cross-gender behavior has made the most prominent presence is none other than the theatrical arts. The best-studied example is perhaps the *dan* actors of traditional Peking opera. These actors start their professional training at a relatively young age and are the only qualified actors to perform the female roles in traditional Peking opera. Several scholars have explored in depth the historical transformation of their profession, social status, and popular image in the twentieth century.[32] In addition, although much has been speculated about the homoerotic subculture embedded within the broader social network of these opera troupes, we must not lose sight of the gendered implications of this male cross-dressing convention.[33] After all, the dan roles were traditionally played by men precisely because women were excluded from performing on the public stage.

Considering the important role of the theatrical arts in Chinese culture and history, the present volume sheds new light on some of its transgender dimensions. Here, the purpose is to move beyond the well-known dan figure by highlighting other explicit examples of cross-dressing in Chinese theatrical life. Chao-Jung Wu's chapter, "Performing Transgender Desire," does this by bringing us to the other side of the Taiwan Strait. Wu provides a systematic ethnographic analysis of the Redtop artists in Taiwan, a group of male cross-dressing artists who took the Taiwanese theatre culture by storm in the 1990s with their infamous *fanchuan* (cross-dressing) shows. Based on their public performances and personal interviews, Wu argues that the Redtop artists provide a most telling example of the cultural performativity of gender as theorized by Butler and others. The homosexual subculture that saturated the troupe's quotidian rhythms and structural underpinnings also troubles straightforward interpretations of the gender subversive acts as conveyed by the actors themselves, especially since these behavioral patterns were highly imbued with misogynist attitudes and hidden hierarchies of power relations defined around the normativity of gender orientation.

Of course, the identitarian method of transgender studies discussed so far raises important questions about the politics of representation, some of whose origins can be traced to an earlier generation of debates in gay and lesbian studies. What forms of practice or embodiment ultimately count and should get represented as authentically transgender? Who get to be singled out as full-blown trans figures? And whose voice has the authority to properly address or even "resolve" these issues? In light of the above examples, we might add, how do we avoid holding up the dan actors of Peking opera, the male impersonators of Yue opera, or the Redtop artists in Taiwan as "role models" or the ultimate yardstick for calibrating the degree of transgenderness in other examples of potentially subversive Chinese figures, histories, embodiments, and cultural and artistic productions?[34]

As scholars, activists, and others debate these questions in the United States and Europe, the reconfiguring of our analytical prism with a focus on China would invariably complicate the politics of queer representation and its underlying ideological and social agenda, as well as the practical and political implications. A main objective of this volume is precisely to make a critical intervention in unpacking these kinds of issues and debates. Any conceivable answer to the above set of questions would be inherently problematic in one way or another. Perhaps this squarely marks both the ugliness and flexibility of identity politics. Nevertheless, this should not prevent us from thinking more creatively about different ways of conducting Chinese transgender studies and how they might make broader impact on

Chinese studies, transgender studies, and other cognate fields of scholarly inquiry.

An alternative approach to Chinese transgender studies is by building on case studies of gender ambiguity or androgyny, rather than concrete examples of gender transgression. This method considers transgender practices not simply as the root of cultural identity, but also in terms of their relationship to broader circuits of knowledge and power. A surprising example comes from the chapter by Zuyan Zhou, who delves into a familiar genre of Chinese literature, namely, the scholar-beauty romances of the late Ming and early Qing periods. But unlike previous studies, Zhou highlights an underappreciated androgynous motif lurking in the otherwise renowned narrative of heteronormative romance between a *caizi* (talented scholar) and a *jiaren* (beauty). This literary genre often construes its protagonists as embodying the attributes of both genders (perfect combination of masculinity and femininity) to project a persistent ideal of androgyny. Contrary to the dominant interpretations of this androgyny craze, which tend to trace its origins to the gender fluidity of the broader historical and cultural context of the late Ming, Zhou explains the pervasive literary presentation of caizi's and jiaren's gender transgression in relation to the contemporaneous development of the cult of *qing* (sentiment), noting that such gender transgression instead "originates from literati scholars' recalcitrant impulses to assert their latent masculinity as institutionalized yin subjects."

Centering on the Beijing-based artist, Ma Liuming, Carlos Rojas's study carefully unravels the creative, social, and aesthetic expressions of Ma's androgynous embodiment. Along with Zhang Huan, Ma is a representative figure of a newly emerging group of Chinese performance artists whose work continues to subvert hegemonic constructs of gender and sexual identity. Rojas takes Butler's understanding of the iterative performativity of gender as a theoretical starting point and reflects more generally on the semiotics of corporeality—or the meanings and language of the body—based on a series of texts in the realm of cultural production, tracing the indigenous resources for Ma and Zhang's aesthetic creativity to the literary depictions of male homoromance in the Chinese opera field. Central to his study are the following questions: "How may subjects use their bodies to challenge the representational regimes within which they are embedded? What is the role of these semiotic systems in demarcating the systems' own conceptual limits?" In the examples found in Zhou's and Rojas's chapters, ideas and norms of gender are unsettled on the level of artistic genres—through manifestations of gender liminality that are embedded within the form of art (literature or performance), rather than appropriations of the completely opposite gender in public appearance.

The most radical approach to developing something that we might want to call Chinese transgender studies is perhaps by leaving behind Western-derived meanings of gender altogether—or at least problematizing them. This would make an important step in identifying and understanding Chinese "gender" variance on its own unexpected terms. By making a distinct departure from a "trans/gender" epistemology rooted in Western culture, we are also reconceptualizing our categories from a fundamentally global viewpoint. Helen Leung's chapter, for instance, begins with a conventional analysis of trans figures in Chinese cinema, but it ends with a radically suggestive interpretive strategy that restructures the very meaning of "trans" with respect to Chinese body modification practices. In "Transgenderism as a Heuristic Device," Alvin Wong focuses on the cross-historical adaptations of a famous Chinese story, the *Legend of the White Snake*. By following how this story "transgendered" across its adaptations in different cultural venues over time, Wong reveals the promise of these transhistorical variants to produce unruly moments of transgender articulation. If Wong's heuristic suggestion is based on historicity-crossing, Larissa Heinrich's chapter invites us to reconceptualize gender-crossing through the framework of literary genre-crossing. This innovative rendition of transgender aesthetic demands an inherently fluid definition of gender and demonstrates its concurrent transformative possibility across literary and geocultural divides. Finally, Howard Chiang's revisionist study of Chinese eunuchism offers a cautionary tale of the tendency to universalize transgenderism as a category of experience. He exposes the power, logic, and threshold of historical forces operating beyond the category's analytical parameters, especially in light of the modernist/nationalist bias of even the most reliable sources on Chinese castration. Taken together, these studies reorient the imagining of a transgender China by *not* assigning Western notions of gender and transgender an epistemologically and ontologically privileged position.

If cultural data from non-Western societies are useful for reflecting on Euro-American orderings of trans/gender, that certainly should not be the sole purpose of this book. Contributors did not simply collect "anthropological" data about China and report back to us what they found "out there" (although some of their work do engage with ethnography on the level of disciplinary practice). Even the familiar debates on the North American "berdache" or other "third sex/gender" people are oftentimes less about their experience, than about the theoretical preoccupations of Western academic discourses and identity politics.[35] Perhaps one of the major strengths of doing research on non-Western cultures, of which this anthology is an example, is the ability to capture a grid of knowledge and experience that exceeds the categorizations of gender, sexuality, and even transgender. Insofar as "the very constitution of the field of transgender studies *as* a field must remain a central question *in* the field," the findings of the present volume should be viewed as having some central bearing on the definition and practice of (trans)gender studies itself.[36] Again, what matters less is how Western (trans)gender theory or framework "works" in China, or whether or not it applies to a non-Western context. Yet precisely because transgender studies is enabled and complicated by the indeterminacy of such key concepts as gender, sexuality, and transgender, the studies that form this book point to different possibilities of transforming the field vis-à-vis the very reorientations of these concepts. And perhaps these potential transformations also have something to offer for the rethinking of area studies. For example, one of the underexplored areas in Chinese feminist studies and historiography that this book addresses concerns individuals who do not conform to—and practices that put pressure on—hegemonic norms of gender.

In the emerging field of queer Asian studies, scholars are envisioning an ever more expansive apparatus that could account for the myriad potentials and possibilities within cross-cultural configurations of gender and sexuality as they play out in Asia and elsewhere, in scholarly discourses, subcultural practices, grassroots movements, or otherwise.[37] Studies are leaving behind the homogenizing/heterogenizing debate on global identity categories,[38] looking for new avenues of research that transcend traditional disciplinary and methodological constraints,[39] and, above all, addressing and building new alliances across the globe to make post-Orientalist regimes of cross-cultural thinking possible.[40] If the animating force of transgender studies comes from a broad, collective, and always mutating definition of transgender, the view from China only makes the promise of transformation all the more meaningful to our imagination.

Notes

1. Magnus Hirschfeld, *Transvestites: The Erotic Drive to Cross Dress*, trans. Michael A. Lombardi-Nash (Amherst, NY: Prometheus Books, 1991); Esther Newton, *Mother Camp: Female Impersonators in America* (Chicago: University of Chicago Press, 1972).

2. David Valentine, *Imagining Transgender: An Ethnography of a Category* (Durham: Duke University Press, 2007), 29–65.
3. Susan Stryker, "Transgender Studies: Queer Theory's Evil Twin," *GLQ: A Journal of Lesbian and Gay Studies* 10, no. 2 (2004): 212–215.
4. Judith Butler, *Gender Trouble: Feminism and the Subversion of Identity* (New York: Routledge, 1990).
5. Judith Halberstam, *Female Masculinity* (Durham: Duke University Press, 1998).
6. Judith Halberstam, *In a Queer Time and Place: Transgender Bodies, Subcultural Lives* (New York: New York University Press, 2005).
7. Vern L. Bullough and Bonnie Bullough, *Cross Dressing, Sex, and Gender* (Philadelphia: University of Pennsylvania Press, 1993); Judith Butler, *Bodies That Matter: On the Discursive Limits of "Sex"* (New York: Routledge, 1993); Kate Bornstein, *Gender Outlaw: On Men, Women, and the Rest of Us* (New York: Routledge, 1994); Bernice Hausman, *Changing Sex: Transsexualism, Technology, and the Idea of Gender* (Durham: Duke University Press, 1995); Leslie Feinberg, *Transgender Warriors: Making History from Joan of Arc to Dennis Rodman* (Boston: Beacon Press, 1996); Zachary Nataf, *Lesbians Talk Transgender* (London: Scarlet Press, 1996); Patrick Califia, *Sex Changes: Transgender Politics* (San Francisco: Cleis Press, 1997); Marjorie Garber's *Vested Interest: Cross-Dressing and Cultural Anxiety* (New York: Routledge, 1997); Riki Anne Wilchins, *Read My Lips: Sexual Subversion and the End of Gender* (Ann Arbor: Firebrand Books, 1997); Kat Bornstein, *My Gender Workbook: How to Become a Real Man, a Real Woman, the Real You, or Something Else Entirely* (New York: Routledge, 1998); Don Kulick, *Travesti: Sex, Gender, and Culture among Brazilian Transgendered Prostitutes* (Chicago: University of Chicago Press, 1998); Jay Prosser, *Second Skins: The Body Narratives of Transsexuality* (New York: Columbia University Press, 1998); Viviane Namaste, *Invisible Lives: The Erasure of Transsexual and Transgendered People* (Chicago: University of Chicago Press, 2000); Joanne Meyerowitz, *How Sex Changed: A History of Transsexuality in the United States* (Cambridge: Harvard University Press, 2002); Henry Rubin, *Self-Made Men: Identity and Embodiment among Transsexual Men* (Nashville, TN: Vanderbilt University Press, 2003); and Judith Butler, *Undoing Gender* (New York: Routledge, 2004). Note that this list can only be selective rather than exhaustive. I have left out, for instance, Leslie Martin Lothstein, *Female-to-Male Transsexualism: Historical, Clinical and Theoretical Issues* (Boston: Routledge and Kegan Paul, 1983); and John Phillips, *Transgender On Screen* (New York: Palgrave Macmillan, 2006).
8. Valentine, *Imagining Transgender*; Susan Stryker, *Transgender History* (Berkeley: Seal Press, 2008); Patricia Gherovici's *Please Select Your Gender: From the Invention of Hysteria to the Democratizing of Transgenderism* (New York: Routledge, 2010); Gayle Salamon,

Assuming a Body: Transgender and Rhetorics of Materiality (New York: Columbia University Press, 2010); Genny Beemyn and Susan Rankin, *The Lives of Transgender People* (New York: Columbia University Press, 2011). See also Sally Hines, *TransForming Gender: Transgender Practices of Identity and Intimacy* (Chicago: University of Chicago Press, 2007); Lori B. Girshick, *Transgender Voices: Beyond Women and Men* (Hanover: University Press of New England, 2008); and Kate Bornstein and S. Bear Bergman, *Gender Outlaws: The Next Generation* (Berkeley: Seal Press, 2010).

9. Carol Queen and Lawrence Schimel, eds., *PoMoSexuals* (San Francisco: Cleis Press, 1997).

10. Susan Stryker, ed., "The Transgender Issue," special issue, *GLQ: A Journal of Lesbian and Gay Studies* 4, no. 2 (1998).

11. Gilbert Herdt, ed., *Third Sex, Third Gender: Beyond Sexual Dimorphism in Culture and History* (New York: Zone Books, 1996); Joan Nestle, Riki Wilchins, and Clare Howell, eds., *Genderqueer* (Los Angeles: Alyson Books, 2002).

12. Susan Stryker and Stephen Whittle, eds., *The Transgender Studies Reader* (New York: Routledge, 2006). See also Paisley Currah, Richard M. Juang, and Shannon Prince Minter, eds., *Transgender Rights* (Minneapolis: University of Minnesota Press, 2006); Mattilda, ed., *Nobody Passes: Rejecting the Rules of Gender and Conformity* (Emeryville, CA: Seal Press, 2006).

13. Susan Stryker, Paisley Currah, and Lisa Jeane Moore, eds., "Trans-," special issue, *Women's Studies Quarterly* 36, nos. 3–4 (2008). For more recent journal special issues, see Katharine Harrison and Ulricha Engdahl, eds., "Trans Gender Studies & Theories: Building Up the Field in a Nordic Context," special issue, *Graduate Journal of Social Science* 7, no. 2 (December 2010); "Race and Transgender Studies," special issue, *Feminist Studies* 37, no. 2 (Summer 2011).

14. Laurie J. Shrage, ed., *You've Changed: Sex Reassignment and Personal Identity* (New York: Oxford University Press, 2009). For a more recent edited volume, see Sally Hine and Tam Sanger, eds., *Transgender Identities: Towards a Social Analysis of Gender* (New York: Routledge, 2010).

15. This is all the more striking considering Valentine's claim that "the 'gender' that underpins 'transgender' and marks it as distinct from the 'sexuality' of mainstream gay and lesbian politics is one rooted in a sexological rather than feminist tradition." Valentine, *Imagining Transgender*, 59.

16. Valentine, *Imagining Transgender*, 34.

17. See, for example, George Chauncey, *Gay New York: Gender, Urban Culture, and the Making of a Gay Male World, 1890-1940* (New York: Basic Books, 1994). For the broader historiographical implications, see David Halperin, *How to Do the History of Homosexuality* (Chicago: University of Chicago Press, 2002).

18. Vernon Rosario, ed., *Science and Homosexualities* (New York: Routledge, 1997); Lucy Bland and Laura Doan, eds., *Sexology in Culture: Labeling Bodies and Desires* (Chicago: University of Chicago Press, 1998); Halberstam, *Female Masculinity*; and Jennifer Terry, *An American Obsession: Science, Medicine, and Homosexuality in Modern Society* (Chicago: University of Chicago Press, 1999).
19. Lillian Faderman, *Odd Girls and Twilight Lovers: A History of Lesbian Life in Twentieth-Century America* (New York: Penguin, 1991); Elizabeth Lapovsky Kennedy and Madeline D. Davis, *Boots of Leather, Slippers of Gold: The History of a Lesbian Community* (New York: Routledge, 1993); Meyerowitz, *How Sex Changed*; Lillian Faderman and Stuart Timmons, *Gay L.A.: A History of Sexual Outlaws, Power Politics, and Lipstick Lesbians* (New York: Basic Books, 2006); and Valentine, *Imagining Transgender*, 46.
20. On the history of American Psychiatric Association's decision to remove homosexuality from the Diagnostic and Statistical Manual of Mental Disorders (DSM), see Ronald Bayer, *Homosexuality and American Psychiatry: The Politics of Diagnosis* (Princeton: Princeton University Press, 1987). For a more recent reappraisal, see Howard Chiang, "Effecting Science, Affecting Medicine: Homosexuality, the Kinsey Reported, and the Contested Boundaries of Psychopathology in the United States, 1948-1965," *Journal of the History of the Behavioral Sciences* 44, no. 4 (2008): 300-318. On the feminist "sex wars," see, for example, Elizabeth Wilson, "The Context of 'Between Pleasure and Danger': The Barnard Conference on Sexuality," *Feminist Review* 13 (Spring 1983): 35-41; Ellen Willis, "Feminism, Morality, and Pornography," in *Powers of Desire: The Politics of Sexuality*, ed. Ann Snitow, Christine Stansell, and Sharon Thompsen (New York City: Monthly Review, 1983), 460-467; Ann Ferguson, "Sex War: The Debate between Radical and Libertarian Feminists," *Signs: A Journal of Women in Culture and Society* 10, no. 1 (1984): 106-112; Ilene Philipson, "The Repression of History and Gender: A Critical Perspective on the Feminist Sexuality Debate," *Signs* 10, no. 1 (1984): 113-118; Carol S. Vance and Ann Barr Snitow, "Toward a Conversation About Sex in Feminism: A Modest Proposal," *Signs* 10, no. 1 (1984): 126-135; and Lisa Duggan and Nan Hunter, *Sex Wars: Sexual Dissent and Political Culture* (New York: Routledge, 1995).
21. Valentine, *Imagining Transgender*, 53-57. See also Stryker, "Transgender Studies: Queer Theory's Evil Twin"; and Susan Stryker, "Transgender History, Homonormativity, and Disciplinarity," *Radical History Review* 100 (2008): 144-157.
22. Susan Stryker, "(De)Subjugated Knowledge: An Introduction to Transgender Studies," in *The Transgender Studies Reader*, ed. Stryker and Whittle, 1-17.
23. See Valentine, *Imagining Transgender*, 143-172.
24. Valentine, *Imagining Transgender*, 39.

25. Walter Williams, *The Spirit and the Flesh: Sexual Diversity in American Indian Culture* (Boston: Beacon Press, 1986); Serena Nanda, *Neither Man Nor Woman: The Hijras of India* (Belmont, CA: Wadsworth, 1990); Will Roscoe, *The Zuni Man-Woman* (Albuquerque: University of New Mexico Press, 1991); Sue Ellen-Jacobs, Wesley Thomas, and Sabine Lang, eds., *Two-Spirit People: Native American Identity, Sexuality, and Spirituality* (Urbana: University of Illinois Press, 1997); Sabine Lang, *Men as Women, Women as Men: Changing Gender in Native American Culture* (Austin, TX: University of Texas Press, 1998); Evelyn Blackwood and Saskia Wieringa, eds., *Female Desires: Same-Sex Relations and Transgender Practices across Cultures* (New York: Columbia University Press, 1999); Peter A. Jackson and Nerida M. Cook, eds., *Genders & Sexualities in Modern Thailand* (Chiang Mai, Thailand: Silkworm Books, 1999); Peter A. Jackson and Gerard Sullivan, eds., *Lady Boys, Tom Boys, Rent Boys: Male and Female Homosexualities in Contemporary Thailand* (New York: Harrington Park Press, 1999); Kulick, *Travesti*; Serena Nanda, *Gender Diversity: Cross-Cultural Variations* (Illinois: Waveland Press, 1999); Martin Manalansan and Arnaldo Cruz-Malave, eds., *Queer Globalizations: Citizenship and the Afterlife of Colonialism* (New York: New York University Press, 2002); Martin Manalansan, *Global Divas: Filipino Gay Men in the Diaspora* (Durham: Duke University Press, 2003); Megan Sinnott, *Toms and Dees: Transgender Identity and Female Same-Sex Relationships in Thailand* (Honolulu: University of Hawaii Press, 2004); Ara Wilson, *The Intimate Economies of Bangkok: Tomboys, Tycoons, and Avon Ladies in the Global City* (Berkeley: University of California Press, 2004); Gayatri Gopinath, *Impossible Desires: Queer Diasporas and South Asian Public Cultures* (Durham: Duke University Press, 2005); Gayatri Reddy, *With Respect to Sex: Negotiating Hijra Identity in South India* (Chicago: University of Chicago Press, 2005); Saskia Wieringa, Evelyn Blackwood, and Abha Bhaiya, eds., *Women's Sexualities and Masculinities in a Globalizing Asia* (New York: Palgrave Macmillan, 2007); and Kale Fajardo, *Filipino Crosscurrents: Oceanographies of Seafaring, Masculinities, and Globalization* (Minneapolis: University of Minnesota Press, 2011).

26. See, for example, Charlotte Furth, "Androgynous Males and Deficient Females: Biology and Gender Boundaries in Sixteenth and Seventeenth-Century China," *Late Imperial China* 9, no. 2 (1988): 1–31; Josephine Ho, ed., *Trans-gender* (Zhongli, Taiwan: Center for the Study of Sexualities, National Central University, 2003); Siu Leung Li, *Cross-Dressing in Chinese Opera* (Hong Kong: Hong Kong University Press, 2003); Fran Martin and Josephine Ho, eds., "trans/Asia, trans/gender," special issue, *Inter-Asia Cultural Studies* 7, no. 2 (2006); Tze-lan D. Sang, "The Transgender Body in Wang Dulu's *Crouching Tiger, Hidden Dragon*," in *Embodied Modernities: Corporeality, Representation, and Chinese Cultures*, ed. Larissa

Heinrich and Fran Martin (Honolulu: University of Hawaii Press, 2006), 98–112; Helen Leung, *Undercurrents: Queer Cultures and Postcolonial Hong Kong* (Hong Kong: Hong Kong University Press, 2008), 65–84; Eleanor Cheung, "GID in Hong Kong: A Critical Overview of Medical Treatments for Transsexual Patients," in *As Normal as Possible: Negotiating Sexuality in Mainland China and Hong Kong*, ed. Yau Ching (Hong Kong: Hong Kong University Press, 2010), 75–86.
27. The most poignant articulation of a "China-centered" approach to modern Chinese history can be found in Paul A. Cohen, *Discovering History in China: American Historical Writing on the Recent Chinese Past* (New York: Columbia University Press, 2010 [1983]).
28. Stryker, "(De)Subjugated Knowledge," 14.
29. An example is the disagreement on the historical and epistemological salience of gender in the history of transsexuality. See Hausman, *Changing Sex*; and Meyerowitz, *How Sex Changed*.
30. See, for example, Jonathan Ned Katz, *Gay American History: Lesbians and Gay Men in the U.S.A.*, rev. ed. (New York: Meridian, 1992 [1976]); and Feinberg, *Transgender Warriors*. The most famous example of this reclamation politics between lesbians and trans men is probably Brandon Teena. See Jacob Hale, "Consuming the Living, Dis(re)membering the Dead in the Butch/FTM Borderlands," *GLQ: A Journal of Lesbian and Gay Studies* 4 (1998): 311–328; and Judith Halberstam, "The Brandon Teena Archive," in *Queer Studies: An Interdisciplinary Reader*, ed. Robert J. Corber and Stephen Valocchi (Malden, MA: Blackwell, 2003), 159–169. For an overview of the border wars between butch lesbians and FTMs, see Valentine, *Imagining Transgender*, 151–153.
31. Pui Kei Eleanor Cheung, "Gender Variant People in Hong Kong: A Model of Gender Identity Formation and Transformation" (PhD thesis, University of Hong Kong, 2011).
32. Joshua Goldstein, "Mei Lanfang and the Nationalization of Peking Opera, 1912-1930," *positions: east asia cultures critique* 7, no. 2 (1999): 377–420; Li, *Cross-Dressing in Chinese Opera*; Joshua Goldstein, *Drama King: Players and Publics in the Re-Creation of Peking Opera, 1870-1937* (Berkeley: University of California Press, 2007); Wenqing Kang, *Obsession: Male Same-Sex Relations in China, 1900-1950* (Hong Kong: Hong Kong University Press, 2009), 115–144; John Zhou, "Crossdressed Nation: Mei Lanfang and the Clothing of Modern Chinese Men," in *Embodied Modernities*, ed. Heinrich and Martin, 79–97; Andrea S. Goldman, "Actors and Aficionados in Qing Texts of Theatrical Connoisseurship," *Harvard Journal of Asiatic Studies* 68, no. 1 (2008): 1–56; and Wu Cuncun and Mark Stevenson, "Speaking of Flowers: Theatre, Public Culture, and Homoerotic Writing in Nineteenth-Century Beijing," *Asian Theatre Journal* 27, no. 1 (2010): 100–129.

33. See, esp., Kang, *Obsession*, 115–144; and Wu and Stevenson, "Speaking of Flowers."
34. Jin Jiang, *Women Playing Men: Yue Opera and Social Change in Twentieth-Century Shanghai* (Seattle: University of Washington Press, 2009).
35. Valentine, *Imagining Transgender*, 157.
36. Valentine, *Imagining Transgender*, 172.
37. Dennis Altman, "Global Gaze/Global Gays," *GLQ: A Journal of Lesbian and Gay Studies* 3 (1997): 417–436; Peter Drucker, "Introduction: Remapping Sexualities," in *Different Rainbows*, ed. Peter Drucker (London: Gay Men's, 2000), 9–42; Chris Berry, Fran Martin, and Audrey Yue, eds., *Mobile Cultures: New Media in Queer Asia* (Durham: Duke University Press, 2003); Linda Garber, "Where in the World Are the Lesbians?" *Journal of the History of Sexuality* 14 (2005): 28–50; Afsaneh Najmabadi, "Beyond the Americas: Are Gender and Sexuality Useful Categories of Analysis?" *Journal of Women's History* 18 (2006): 11–21; Ara Wilson, "Queering Asia," *Intersections: Gender, History and Culture in the Asian Context* 14 (November 2006); Evelyn Blackwood, "Transnational Discourses and Circuits of Queer Knowledge in Indonesia," *GLQ: A Journal of Lesbian and Gay Studies* 14 (2008): 481–507; Fran Martin, Peter Jackson, Mark McLelland, and Audrey Yue, eds., *AsiaPacificQueer: Rethinking Genders and Sexualities* (Champaign: University of Illinois Press, 2008); Josephine Ho, "Is Global Governance Bad for East Asian Queers?" *GLQ: A Journal of Lesbian and Gay Studies* 14, no. 4 (2008): 457–479; Howard Chiang, "Empire of Desires: History and Queer Theory in an Age of Global Affect," *InterAlia: A Journal of Queer Studies* 3 (2008/2009); Peter A. Jackson, "Capitalism and Global Queering: National Markets, Parallels among Sexual Cultures, and Multiple Queer Modernities," *GLQ: A Journal of Lesbian and Gay Studies* 15 (2009): 357–395; Megan Sinnott, "Borders, Diaspora, and Regional Connections: Trends in Asian 'Queer' Studies," *Journal of Asian Studies* 69, no. 1 (2010): 17–31; Petrus Liu and Lisa Rofel, eds., "Beyond the Strai(gh)ts: Transnationalism and Queer Chinese Politics," special issue, *positions: east asia cultures critique* 18, no. 2 (2010); Yau, *As Normal As Possible*; Howard Chiang, ed., "Queer Transnationalism in China," topical cluster, *English Language Notes* 49, no. 1 (Spring/Summer 2011); Denise Tang, "Queer Asian Cultures," *Sociology Compass* 5, no. 8 (2011): 688–695.
38. See, for example, Fran Martin, "Getting Over It: Beyond the Hetero(genizing)/Homo(genizing) Divide in Transnational Sexuality Studies," *English Language Notes* 49, no. 1 (2011): 117–123. For the earlier debate on globalized gay identity in the China field, see Dennis Altman, "Rupture or Continuity? The Internationalization of Gay Identities," *Social Text* 48 (1996): 77–94; Lisa Rofel, "Qualities of Desire: Imagining Gay Identities in China," *GLQ: A Journal of*

Lesbian and Gay Studies 5, no. 4 (1999): 451–474; Dennis Altman, *Global Sex* (Chicago: University of Chicago Press, 2001); Lisa Rofel, *Desiring China: Experiments in Neoliberalism, Sexuality, and Public Culture* (Durham: Duke University Press, 2007).

39. Howard Chiang, "Sinophone Production and Trans Postcoloniality: Sex Change from Major to Minor Transnational China," *English Language Notes* 49, no. 1 (2011): 109–116; Howard Chiang and Larissa Heinrich, eds., *Queer Sinophone Cultures* (New York: Routledge, forthcoming).
40. On the implication of this effort for the field of Chinese studies, see Rey Chow, "Introduction: On Chineseness as a Theoretical Problem," *boundary 2* 25, no. 3 (1998): 1–24; Ien Ang, *On Not Speaking Chinese: Living between Asia and the West* (New York: Routledge, 2001); Shu-mei Shih, *Visuality and Identity: Sinophone Articulations across the Pacific* (Berkeley: University of California Press, 2007); Chu Yiu-Wai, "The Importance of Being Chinese: Orientalism Reconfigured in the Age of Global Modernity," *boundary 2* 35 (2008): 183–206; and Shu-mei Shih, "Theory, Asia, and the Sinophone," *Postcolonial Studies* 13, no. 4 (2010): 465–484.

PART II

Trans Figurations of History

CHAPTER 2

How China Became a "Castrated Civilization" and Eunuchs a "Third Sex"

Howard Chiang

I. Introduction

Although eunuchs had played an important role in the history of imperial China, it is surprising how little attention historians have paid to the actual measures of Chinese castration. Like footbinding, castration stands as one of the most important objects of Sinological criticism today. Both have come to represent powerful symbols of backwardness, oppression, despotism, and national shame in modern Chinese historiography. Starting in the early Republican period, cultural commentators often labeled late imperial China as a "castrated civilization" (被閹割的文明, *beiyange de wenming*), a characterization that perpetuated its more common perception as the "Sick Man of Asia" that emerged in the nineteenth century.[1] Simply put, observers, domestic and foreign alike, invoked the former trope to cast the practice of castration and the institution of palace eunuchs as pitfalls of dynastic China. But unlike the history of footbinding, Sinologists have remained considerably silent on the history of the castration operation itself. This chapter aims to move beyond this historiographical limitation. I approach eunuchism (the bodily state of castrated men), like other forms of embodiment, as a category of experience that needs to be historicized rather than foundational or uncontestable in nature.[2]

The distaste for eunuchs and the antipathy for the Chinese imperium became isomorphic during the peak of Western overseas imperial and colonial expansions.[3] In China's tremulous transition to a modern nation-state, men and women experienced profound changes in the prevailing norms and social conventions of gender. The civil service examination for men was formally abolished in 1905, but since the mid-nineteenth century, Western missionaries had created an increasing measure of educational opportunities for women.[4] As coastal cities such as Shanghai turned into global centers of cosmopolitanism, Chinese men and women adopted Western standards of fashion, and more women dressed in a way that would increasingly resemble the French and American "flappers" of the next generation.[5] The 1910s and 1920s were also a period when the cult of *qing* (情, sentiment) incorporated a foreign notion of free love, a kind of modern transformation that hinged on a new nationalist (even revolutionary) "structure of feeling" and reframed the meanings of marriage, the family, and the Chinese state for women.[6] In the decades surrounding May Fourth feminism, many reformers and revolutionaries voiced a pressing concern about patriarchal oppression, something they viewed as an intrinsic shortcoming of traditional (often dubbed "Confucian") Chinese culture. As castration, like footbinding, reflects the dominant perceptions of gender normativity at any given moment in time, the task of historicizing eunuchism requires us to be more cautious of its gendered implications, and its affiliation to what we might otherwise hasten to call "sex."

In an age of China's metaphoric portrayal as a castrated civilization, the perception of eunuchs as demasculinized "third sex" (第三性, *disanxing*) figures became increasingly common. However, historical standards of masculinity and femininity, and by extension emasculation and defeminization, on which such claims were purported shifted across time and place. As we will see, modern definitions of masculinity and femininity tend to be articulated within a Western biomedical lexicon and its cognate understandings of the human body. The absence of a Chinese word for sex until the 1910s suggests that the popular depiction of eunuchs as third sex people tells us more about our modern conceptual preoccupations than the historical experience of eunuchs themselves.[7] Before the emergence of the concept of sex, gender might be the more adequate category of analysis for understanding the meaning and practice of castration.[8] Rather than rendering eunuchs as third sex subjects who nominally defy the boundaries of male and female, this chapter offers a cautionary tale of the tendency to universalize transgenderism as an omnipresent rubric of historical experience. I explore the rise of the perception of China as a castrated civilization from the historical discourse that comprised eunuchism's demise, which occurred in tandem with the rise of the modernist notion that eunuchs are third sex figures and the adjacent equation of castration with emasculation. By problematizing the perception of eunuchs as transhistorical third sex subjects, I aim to expose the power, logic, and threshold of historical forces operating upon the eunuch embodiment, forces that ultimately contest the analytical value of absorbing all historic figures of gender liminality into the very category of transgender.

The emphasis on the masculinity of castration before the conceptual availability of sex revises the diverse scholarly literature on Chinese manhood that has drawn on legal, medicoscientific, family reform, homoerotic, theatrical, and diasporic examples.[9] It is perhaps worth noting that the gendered subjectivity of eunuchs has escaped the attention of contributors to the two pathbreaking volumes, *Chinese Femininities/Chinese Masculinities: A Reader* (2002) and *Asian Masculinities: The Meaning and Practice of Manhood in China and Japan* (2003), and of Kam Louie in his *Theorising Chinese Masculinity: Society and Gender in China* (2002).[10] If we borrow the queer theoretical insight of Judith Halberstam, who has narrated the first comprehensive history of female masculinity in Euro-American literature and film, we might be better equipped to entertain a more radical analytical separation of masculinity from men as fecund agents.[11] Chinese masculinity can thus be understood as neither a social extension of biological maleness nor the social meanings assigned to men per se, but a social relational indicator of a discursive cultural practice such as castration. This chapter's focus on the history of knowledge production about castration questions the naturalness assumed in previous studies regarding the immediate and productive relationship of men to manliness.

With respect to footbinding, historians have recently begun to revise its popular conception as a tool of gender oppression. In *Cinderella's Sisters* (2005), for example, Dorothy Ko shows that women as much as men participated in the perpetuation of this cultural practice with complex and nuanced historical agency.[12] That footbinding was often a marker of ethnic and national boundaries, a practice of concealment and adornment, and a sign of civility and culture before the nineteenth century betrays our modern explanations of it as a form of bodily mutilation, an "unnatural" practice, and a barbaric (even perverse) custom.[13] In a similar spirit, Angela Zito has demonstrated that twentieth-century discourses of the bound foot only reflect variations of its modernist fetishization, even thresholds of feminist theorization and intercultural displacements.[14] Taking cues from Ko and Zito, this chapter departs from outside the anticastration discourse, attempting to balance the historiographical condemnation of Chinese eunuchs. To bring to visibility the historicity of eunuchism and to situate castration in its proper historical and technical contexts, I will pay particular attention to how paradigms of masculinity changed over time, how the visual milieu reciprocated its politics and thresholds of cross-cultural translation, and the problem of narrating the historical experience of eunuchs based on the modern nationalist bias of our sources and informants. By reading against the grain, this chapter traces the formation of a textual and visual archive that documented the methods of Chinese castration, something that was distinctively absent before the nineteenth century and that, I suggest, directly led to eunuchism's social and cultural demise.

II. The Archival Problematic, and an Argument

Despite our best intentions, the reconstruction of an archive based on the sources available about Chinese castration is itself an inherently mediated and problematic project.[15] First, where do we end? If we assume that the metanarrative history of political change determines the metanarrative history of cultural transformation, we might conclude that the unequivocal demise of castration after the fall of the Qing empire in 1911 was a matter of course. However, even after the last Manchu emperor Puyi was expelled from the Forbidden City in 1924 by the warlord Feng Yuxiang, he was declared by the Japanese army as the Kangde emperor of the puppet state of Manchuria in 1934. As the Kangde emperor, Puyi was still surrounded by a dozen or so Chinese eunuchs.[16] When the Pacific War ended in 1945, these eunuchs did not suddenly just disappear altogether. Even in the postwar period, their bodies still served as a pivotal reminder of the past and their stories the lived experiences of castration, to both themselves and the global public. In October 1958, for instance, the Chinese government gathered the final cohort of eunuchs in Beijing and took a photo of them mixed in with Buddhist and Daoist monks. They were interviewed so that their oral histories could be officially transcribed, published, and circulated to a worldwide audience.[17] Even the death of the last surviving Chinese eunuch, Sun Yaoting, in 1996 might be a misleading signpost for where the story of Chinese castration ends.[18] This is because the afterlife of eunuchism in China—namely, the emergence of transsexuality in Sinophone communities—is indebted to the genealogical precursors discussed in this chapter, namely, factors that culminated in the thresholds of its beginning. Before we examine how the body morphology of eunuchs and transsexuals operate within shifting realms of scientific truth claims and geopolitics, our story must unravel the process whereby the normative regime of eunuchism lost its aura, meaning, and cultural significance.

Apart from the puzzling question of a precise endpoint, the reconstruction of the archive relies on the *type* of sources that are available. Here is where the parallel between footbinding's disappearance and castration's demise is most striking: the abundance of textual and visual sources from the nineteenth and early twentieth centuries almost always represents the bound foot and the castrated body by *exposing* them. This mode of representation runs against the very reason of their existence in Chinese history. After all, the naturalness of footbinding and castration depended on *concealing* the female and male bodies, because concealment links these customs to Chinese ideals of civility and culture (文, *wen*).[19] Therefore, upon reading the wealth of visual and textual documentations of the bound foot or the castrated body, the historian must avoid a telos of knowledge production that extracts a certain kind of historicity from these sources that lies beyond the hegemonic parameters of their existence. As Anjali Arondekar has reminded us in a different context, "Even though scholars have foregrounded the analytical limits of the archive, they continue to privilege the reading practice of recovery over all others."[20] It might be more useful to read the archival remains not as the ultimate arbiter of historical recuperation, but as "traces" of the past that enable alternative epistemological arrangements of the way the past and the present conjoin.[21] In other words, we must not retell a story about eunuchs that identifies with the kind of story that the sources themselves suggest at face value. What they leave us is not something to be "recovered," but something to be self-reflexively configured.[22]

Precise endpoints and the nature of the sources aside, the repository of "data" about Chinese castration is mediated by their availability. Three available "voices" unique to the historical period under consideration contributed to the making of this archive: Western spectators, eunuchs themselves, and members of the last imperial family. Together, the textual, photographic, and oral records they left behind disclose an increasing disparity between two registers of eunuchism as a mode of historical experience: on the macro level of global narration on the one hand, and on the micro level of individual embodiment on the other. My argument is that an antieunuch sentiment arose out of this growing disjuncture between a collective-public narration of nationalist teleology and a personal-private embodiment of preternatural corporeality. This nascent sensibility that casts the practice of castration and the existence of eunuchs as indicators of national shame and backwardness would reverberate through the rest of the twentieth century. As eunuchs' gender identity was evaluated anew in the modern era through the lens of Western biomedicine, China's association with the metaphor of a castrated civilization intensified over time. The period between the 1870s and the 1930s thus constituted a transitional phase when the castrated male body—much like women's bound feet and the leper's crippled body—seemed out of sync with the Chinese body politic at large.[23]

III. G. Carter Stent and the Formation of a Public Archive

The formation of an archive documenting the methods of Chinese castration marked a point of no return in the social and cultural demise of eunuchism in China. Textual descriptions of the operation highlight the fundamental difference between a natural male body and an altered, unnatural one. The first elaborate description of the method can be traced to an article by G. Carter Stent, published in the *Journal of the North China Branch of the Royal Asiatic Society* in 1877. This piece, called "Chinese Eunuchs," is arguably the earliest incidence of putting the steps involved in Chinese castration into printed words. The first textual objectification of the Chinese eunuch's corporeal experience thus came from the observation of an "outsider."[24]

Stent first read a version of his paper, which is more than 40 pages in length, before the Royal Asiatic Society on March 26, 1877. His opening sentence stamped the intention—and eventually the persistent significance—of his study, namely to bring something invisible to visibility, to crystallize a vague impression: "Much has been said and written about eunuchs at various times, but very little seems to be really known concerning them." "In fact," Stent continued, "everything relating to them is described so vaguely that one is almost tempted to believe that eunuchs exist only in the Arabian Night's Entertainments and other eastern tales, or in the imaginations of the writers, rather than actually belonging to and forming no inconsiderable portion of the human race."[25] Assigning Chinese eunuchs a textual status of reality, Stent's words epitomized the effort to expose the private experience of eunuchism in the public realm.

Neither opinions about the existence of eunuchs nor attacks on the tradition of castration were new to Chinese discourses. But the novelty of Stent's endeavor in making Chinese eunuchs a reality stems from its unambiguous Christian and Orientalist overtone. In his words, "Eunuchs are only to be found in eastern despotic countries, the enlightening influence of Christianity preventing such unnatural proceedings being practiced in the countries of those who profess it."[26] For Stent, the "unnatural proceedings" of castration in China reveal "at least one beneficial result of the spread of Christianity; for while we [Christian Westerners] are free from the baneful practice, it is a vile blot on less fortunate countries."[27] Similar to the discourse surrounding *tianzu* (天足, natural foot) in the antifootbinding movement, the significance of Stent's words lies in his explicit juxtaposition of China against a more enlightened West with an overt Christian justification.[28] However, Stent's assertion that Christianity and monogamy saved the West from the "unnatural proceedings" of castration is an erroneous interpretation, considering the important role played by the eunuchs in Byzantine history.[29] Defining China as one of the "less fortunate countries," Stent's project was unmistakably Orientalist in nature. It ultimately signaled the arrival of a rhetoric according to which China "lacked" the tools of narrating and recognizing its own deficiency, for which castration, like footbinding, typified an unnatural corporeal practice that was out of both place and time. As Yosefa Loshitzky and Raya Meyuhas have observed, "Eunuchs are perceived by the modern Western audience as grotesque rarities of the past that are associated with the 'otherness' of exotic cultures."[30] They have often been regarded as a "barbaric, archaic, and uncivilized phenomenon and therefore as an anachronism."[31]

The aspect of Stent's study that exerts the most lasting historiographic influence is not his missionary message, however, but his discussion of the operation of castration itself. To this day, his description of how, where, and by whom Chinese eunuchs were made remains the most cited reference on this topic since its first delivery in the 1870s. In fact, one would look in vain for a serious treatment of the subject that does not follow Stent's footsteps in one way or another. His words thus deserve quoting in full and a serious reappraisal.

> The place where men or boys are made eunuchs is just outside the inner Hsi-'hua gate (內西華門) of the palace, and within the imperial city. It is a mean-looking building, and is known as the Chang-tzu, 廠子, *the shed*. Within this building reside several men recognized by government, yet drawing no pay from it—whose duty consists in emasculating those who are desirous of becoming, or are sent to become—eunuchs.

These men are called tao-tzu-chiang, 刀子匠, "*knifers*," and depend entirely for their living on making eunuchs. They get a fixed sum—six taels—for every operation they perform on boys sent or brought to them, and for keep and attendance till the patients are properly recovered.

Grown up men desirous of becoming eunuchs, but who are too poor to pay the necessary fees, make arrangements with the "knifers" to repay them out of their salaries. But in any case the "knifers" dare not operate on them unless they (the candidates) have securities to vouch for their respectability.

The "knifers" have generally one or two apprentices to learn the profession; these are almost invariably members of their own families, so that the profession may be said to be hereditary.

When the operation is about to take place, the candidate or victim—as the case may be—is placed on a *kang* in a sitting—or rather, reclining position. One man supports him round the waist, while two others separate his legs and hold them down firmly, to prevent any movement on his part. The operating "knifer" then stands in front of the men—with his knife in his hand—and enquires if he will ever repent. If the man at the last moment demurs in the slightest, the "knifer" will not perform the operation, but if he still expresses his willingness, with one sweep of the knife he is made a eunuch.

The operation is performed in this manner:—white ligatures or bandages are bound tightly round the lower part of the belly and the upper parts of the thighs, to prevent too much haemorrage. The parts about to be operated on are then bathed three times with hot pepper-water, the intended eunuch being in the reclining position as previously described. When the parts have been sufficiently bathed, the *whole*,—both testicles and penis—are cut off as closely as possible with a small curved knife, something in the shape of a sickle. The emasculation being effected, a pewter needle or spigot is carefully thrust into the main orifice at the root of the penis; the wound is then covered with paper saturated in cold water and is carefully bound up. After the wound is dressed the patient is made to walk about the room, supported by two of the "knifers," for two or three hours, when he is allowed to lie down.

The patient is not allowed to drink anything for three days, during which time he often suffers great agony, not only from thirst, but from intense pain, and from the impossibility of relieving nature during that period.

At the end of three days the bandage is taken off, the spigot is pulled out, and the sufferer obtains relief in the copious flow of urine which spurts out like a fountain. If this takes place satisfactorily, the patient is considered out of danger and congratulated on it; but if the unfortunate wretch cannot make water he is doomed to a death of agony, for the passages have become swollen and nothing can save him."³²

This passage remains the most authoritative and influential source on the method of Chinese castration. However, for it to be treated as a trustworthy piece of primary evidence, presumably Stent would have to be present when one of such operations took place over the span of at least three days. The richness of his description is certainly remarkable, but its implicit claim of originality and validity is difficult to prove. In fact, this difficulty has not been sufficiently acknowledged in the existing literature, for almost all scholars of Chinese eunuchism have taken this passage for granted as a firsthand account of what actually happened during such an operation.

But what if Stent did not witness any of the castration surgeries? One can barely begin to imagine the historiographical implications if this were true, especially since Stent's text is indeed the earliest and most sophisticated documentation of how Chinese castration was performed.³³ Even if he did pay a visit to the "knifers" for just a single case of castration, did Stent stay for the entire duration (at least three consecutive days or longer)? In fact, his narrative would have us believe that he had personally observed at least two types of operation—successful and unsuccessful—to differentiate survival in the former case and potential death in the latter.

In a slightly different way, the content of Stent's words already betrayed their implicit claim of originality and validity. If the knowledge and skills required for performing castration were transmitted among "knifers" through hereditary apprenticeship, how was it possible for the operation to be described so openly by a Westerner in the first place? If part of the social integrity of the Chinese "knifers" came from maintaining a custom of oral instruction and personal demonstration, it seems highly improbable that a nonfamily or nonprofessional member, let alone a foreigner, would be allowed to witness the surgical protocol in such remarkable detail. An empirical proof of the existence of "the shed," where these operations were supposedly performed by the "knifers," would add a layer of validity to Stent's description. However, in their study of eunuchs in Qing and Republican China, scholars have pointed out that no discussion of the "knifers" could be found in the Qing palace archives.³⁴ As late as 1991, two urologists from Beijing Medical University still conceded that "most people, including urologists, do not have a clear understanding of what is actually done to a man or boy to produce an eunuch."³⁵

IV. Changing Paradigms of Masculinity

The exact procedure of castration is important because it essentially defines what makes someone a eunuch. The subtlety of Stent's emphasis that *both* the testes and the penis had to be removed for a surgical castration to be considered complete might escape the eyes of modern readers. The emphasis is subtle because this requirement sounds so natural to our ears. But as Gary Taylor has reminded us, if the ultimate purpose of castration is to impair a man's fertility, it is not necessary to destroy the penis but only the testes.[36] In fact, the earliest extant medical description of the operation, by the seventh-century Byzantine Greek physician Paul of Aegina, makes it clear that only the testicles, not the penis, were targeted by the techniques of contusion and excision.[37] Similarly, modern medical reappraisals of the operations performed on the European castrati singers indicate that only testicles were severed.[38] In his ambitious survey of the cultural history of the penis, David Friedman carefully incorporated a broad definition of the organ "not merely as the penile shaft and glass, but encompassing the testes, sperm, and all the other parts and products of the male genitalia."[39] This inclusive definition was fruitful for Friedman's undertaking precisely because the penile shaft had not always been the sole locus of biological masculinity since the beginning of Western civilization.

Indeed, Stent's discussion elicited polarized reactions from those who claimed to have had personal interactions with the palace eunuchs. Dong Guo, author of a pioneer 1985 study on the history of Chinese eunuchs, contended that Stent's account is outright erroneous.[40] According to his conversations with Peking palace eunuchs, "the key [to castration] is this: when someone is made a eunuch at a relatively young age, the procedure resembles the gelding of pigs by removing or protruding the testicles. This operation is at least not fatal, and because there is no major concern over bacterial infection from the cut, the person recovers in three to five days."[41] On the other hand, based on their physical examination of the last group of Chinese eunuchs conducted in the 1960s, two urologists from Beijing Medical University seconded Stent's observation: they confirmed that both the penis and the testes were detached from the eunuchs' bodies.[42] Though both were established on personal interactions with eunuchs, the discrepancy between verbal and visual evidence nonetheless left a historical residue of ambiguity surrounding the surgical parameters of castration. This exemplifies how "micro" accounts of eunuchoidal corporeality do not and *cannot* all subsume under "macro" narrations.

Recognizing this epistemic discrepancy, the urologists pointed out the popular "erroneous use of the term 'castration.'" "Although the Greek root of the word 'eunouchos' does indicate a castrated person," they explained, "the eunuch is not only castrated...'Emasculation' should be the right term to describe the procedure...We think it is better to define 'emasculation' as 'removal of external genitalia in man or boy', leaving 'castration' for removal of the testes."[43] This shift in conceptual preference from "castration" to "emasculation" highlights an important historical transformation in the biological definition of manhood: from a cultural regime of the scrotum to a regime of the penis. Between the sixteenth and twentieth century, the anatomical measure of manliness changed from whether a man has balls to whether a man has a big stick.[44] This fall of the scrotum and rise of the penis was accompanied by the process by which desire and libidinal pleasures replaced status and reproduction as the organizing principle for making sexual acts socially meaningful.[45] In late imperial China, the decline of the status-centered paradigm directly led to the increasing legal relevance of a gender-performance paradigm.[46]

One of the cultural forces that cemented the transformation from a scrotum-centered to a penis-centered regime of masculinity in Western Europe and America was the popularization of Freudian psychoanalysis in the early twentieth century. For Freud, castration anxiety was symptomatic of a psychogenic fear, or at least recognition, of "the lack of penis."[47] His most influential and controversial French disciple, Jacques Lacan, would subsequently prioritize the symbolic meaning of the phallus in lieu of the anatomical penis.[48] But the phallus is nothing but a figuration of the physical organ, a transcendental penis, so to speak, that extends rather than subverts its anatomical register.[49] To quote Taylor's astute insight, "Castration—in humanist Europe, as in previous human societies—attacked the scrotum. In twentieth-century psychoanalysis, by contrast, castration has been redefined as an attack on the penis."[50]

V. Medical Images as Proof and Evidence

In the 1890s, one of the foremost "pillars" supporting the characterization of Chinese castration more as an attack on the penis can be found in the reports of the American physician Robert Coltman (1862–1931). Born in Washington, Coltman received his medical training at Jefferson Medical College in Philadelphia. He was appointed Professor of Anatomy at the Imperial School of Combined Learning (Tongwen Guan, 同文館, which later became part of Peking

University) in 1896, Professor of Surgery at the Imperial University of Peking (later known as Peking University) in 1898, and personal physician to the Chinese royal family and surgeon at both the Imperial Maritime Customs and the Imperial Chinese Railways around that time.[51] Coltman was also known for his two books, *The Chinese, Their Present and Future: Medical, Political, and Social* (1891) and the more famous *Beleaguered in Peking: The Boxer's War Against the Foreigner* (1901), which reflected his reputation for being the first Westerner to reach the outside world during the siege of Peking by the Boxers.[52] In 1894, Coltman presented a hand-drawn image of the site of castration as it appeared on the body of one of his patients (figure 2.1). The expository text indicates that the image was produced by a Chinese assistant, a "xylographist."

Coltman included this image in an article called "Peking Eunuchs," which appeared in the *China Medical Missionary Journal* in 1894.[53] The article was intended as a follow-up on his earlier discussion of three eunuchs in the *Universal Medical Journal* in 1893.[54] Together, the two entries mentioned six Chinese eunuchs in total who visited Coltman for medical assistance. These eunuchs came to Coltman

CICATRIX OF EUNUCH.

* In reproducing the above, our Chinese xylographist has somewhat improved on the original sketch, with regard to geometrical nicety.—(ED.)

Figure 2.1 Drawing of an eunuch's castration site from Coltman (1894)
Source: Robert Coltman, "Peking Eunuchs," *China Medical Missionary Journal* 8 (1894): p. 28.

mainly for the obliteration of the urethral orifice, because they all suffered from the closing up of the orifice, which led to urination problems. Based on the six cases of eunuchs whom he treated, Coltman observed that "The majority of the eunuchs here [in China] have penis and testicles removed entire."[55] This statement was remarkable to him, because, as Coltman himself conceded, he "never for a moment supposed the mutilation extended beyond the testicles."[56] We will revisit Coltman in greater detail below when we compare the Westerners' account and eunuchs' narration of their own castration experience. For now, suffice it to say that the textual descriptions and the image of castration that he presented helped (re)define Chinese castration specifically in terms of a penis-centered paradigm of masculinity.

Similar to Stent's justification of a superior West, Coltman expressed "disgust and contempt" toward his Chinese eunuch patients.[57] His final word on them was "Do such specimen of humanity deserve sympathy?"[58] If we were to read the castration experience of Chinese eunuchs through the lens of Coltman's papers, we might subscribe to the view that the castrated male body undoubtedly *needed* Western biomedical assistance. We might hasten to add that the enlightenment nature of Western medicine was a viewpoint acknowledged even by Chinese eunuchs themselves, as demonstrated by their very decision to turn to Coltman for medical assistance. However, it is interesting to note that this group of eunuchs all expressed a considerable measure of resistance to treatment by a Western doctor, even a prestigious one such as Coltman who became personal physician to the Chinese imperial family: none of them returned to Coltman after their first visit even if they were explicitly instructed to do so for health reasons and their own recovery assessment. Therefore, by exposing the eunuch's body, Coltman's medical reports on Chinese castration ultimately contributed to its demise. In reading these reports, one detects an unprecedented fracturing of the meaning and experience of eunuchism. The failed mutuality and reciprocation between the eunuchs and Coltman marked the rise of a disjuncture in the experience of eunuchs—a discrepancy between foreigners' totalizing condemnation and their own embodied selves.

An additional piece of "evidence" that construed Chinese castration as the removal of penis and not just the testicles came from another "outsider," Dr. Jean-Jacques Matignon (1866–1928). Matignon had been a physician to the French legation in Peking since 1894. Having established a high reputation among European colonial officials, Matignon was about to be made Knight of the Legion of Honor. The unfortunate news of his victimization in the "Peking Massacre," the

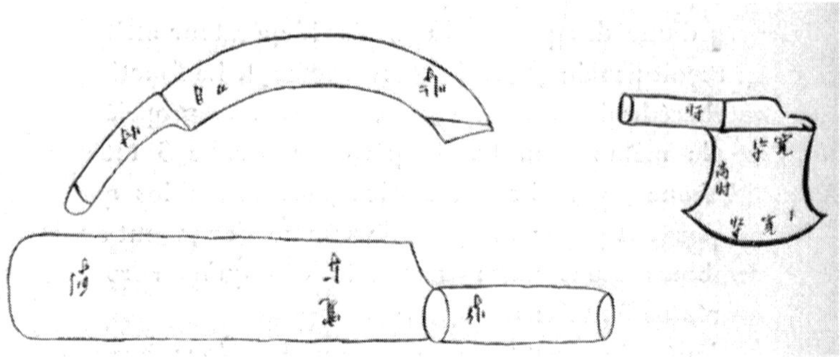

Figure 2.2 Instruments used for castration from Matignon (1896)

Source: Jean-Jacques Matignon, *Superstition, crime et misére en Chine: sourvenirs de biologie sociale* (Lyon: A. Storck & Cie, 1899), p. 182.

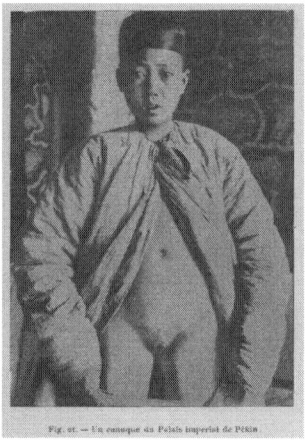

Figure 2.3 Photo of a castrated boy from Matignon (1896)

Source: Jean-Jacques Matignon, *Superstition, crime et misére en Chine: sourvenirs de biologie sociale* (Lyon: A. Storck & Cie, 1899).

Boxer Uprising, reached Europe in July 1900.[59] In 1896, Matignon offered an illustration of the surgical instruments used in castration (figure 2.2). Unfortunately, he did not indicate the source of these drawings, so it remains difficult to verify their originality and validity. He also obtained a photograph that exposes the naked body of a Chinese eunuch and reveals the physical site of castration (figure 2.3). In the article in which Matignon first published these images, which continue to be circulated widely today, he repeated Stent's earlier description of how castration was operated in China. In other words, Matignon was explicit in his intention in adding credibility to Stent's words with the new visual evidence he provided.[60]

This photographic proof of a Chinese eunuch's "lack of penis" makes it difficult for any viewer to deny its captured reality. The challenge is more conspicuous in Matignon's photograph than in Coltman's image. The difficulty largely stems from the indirect cultural labor of the photo, in which the unilateral viewing didactic turns the beholder's gaze into the object of the eunuch's gaze. As Michel de Certeau has put it, a compelling reading of cultural representation pays attention not only to "the production of the image," but also to the less obvious "secondary production hidden in the process of its utilization."[61] Or, in the words of Michael Taussig, "The image is more powerful that what it is an image of."[62] In the photograph presented by Matignon, the eunuch's reciprocal gaze forces anyone looking at his exposed body to surrender to an implicit operation of knowledge that, if neglected, would indicate a betrayal of his or her own eyes. To deny that the eunuch's corporeal experience was marked by "the lack of penis" would mean to disqualify the very spectatorial relationship (between the viewer and the seemingly uncensored record of the naked eunuchoidal body) that made the denial possible in the first place. On the eve of the twentieth century, Matignon's photo thus consolidated a visual layering of "truth" about Chinese castration—that it involved the elimination of male genitalia in its entirety. This ocular evidence added credence to Stent's earlier textual description, establishing the absence of both the penis *and* the scrotum as an indisputable reality in a castrated Chinese body from this point onward. It paved the way for twentieth-century discussions of Chinese castration to *forget* any eunuchoidal corporeality outside a penis-centered paradigm of masculinity.

The broader import of this amnesia cannot be overstated. The aforementioned cultural mechanics fundamental to its shaping were part of a global circuit of power relations, one that mediated the rise of Chinese medical photography in the late nineteenth century.[63] According to Sarah Fraser,

> Photography's role in shaping China's image from 1860 to 1900 is evident in the visual transformation of the Chinese subject of over a half-century of colonial intervention. In these shifts related to China's visual culture, the camera was an instrument of the contemporary practice to create types, classify peoples, and impose hierarchies upon the

world as it was being observed... By the turn of the century, the photographic lens was focused on larger statements about "the Chinese" and national character. Scenes of itinerant workers, destitute people, and military captives at the time of the Boxer Uprising reflect racial debates about the modern Chinese subject prevalent in international power relations.[64]

In her study of the translational politics of visualizing the Chinese, Larissa Heinrich has similarly pointed out that "in early medical photography in China we see the convergence of those colonial, commercial, ethnographic, and scientific ideologies that marked the indisputable entrance of the 'Chinese specimen' into global discourses of race and health."[65] Through its heterogeneous modes of circulation (e.g., archives, museums, private collections, and publications) and deployment of stylistics (e.g., the "before and after" clinical contrasting trope, portraiture, battlefield documentary, and erotic thematization), photographic images of the ill decontextualized and recontextualized Chinese identity by "representing supposedly specifically Chinese pathologies to a global medical community."[66] In the formative years of China's nation formation, the increasing popularity of clinical photography gave representational claims of Chinese pathology a new set of cultural valence and ideological relevance. The diseased ontology of the photographic specimen came to be absorbed by the very medium of its cultural production and naturalized as representative of the inherently pathological quality of Chinese empire and identity. Over the course of the nineteenth century, China was granted entrance into the global system of nation-states on the condition of being racially stereotyped as "the Sick Man of Asia" with growing intensity.[67]

The evolving relationship of the camera to its object of representation relied on, among other things, the circulation of certain medical beliefs about Chinese identity, which substantiated the "Sick Man" stereotype: in the nineteenth century, China was blamed for being the original home of the Bubonic plague, cholera, small pox, and, eventually, leprosy.[68] Through its photographic presence as medical specimens, the castrated male body joined the bound feet, the leper's crippled body, and other exotic corporeal "types" as exemplars of the material figuration of diseased embodiment peculiar to China. In this sense, Matignon's photograph could be viewed as a "confession of the flesh," whereby the penis-absent enuchoidal body displayed and circulated through it helped solidify an ideological portrayal of China as intrinsically deficient, problematic, and in need of Western (biomedical) assistance. Indeed, when we go back to Matignon's photo (figure 2.3), what we are looking at is less about "what is wrong with the eunuch," than about "what is wrong with China." Or to borrow Jacques Derrida's terms, the ghost of the penis affirms the spectral presence of the Eurocentrically commodified body; the *hauntology* of this absent presence revalues the global ontology and epistemology of *being* Chinese and knowing what Chinese is.[69]

How can the legacy of this (post)coloniality be evaluated? When we compare a set of photographs of eunuchs published in an English medical article in 1933 (figure 2.4) with images filed in the Qing palace archive (figure 2.5), we witness a distinct contrast in the operation of their epistemological claims. Although both images objectify the eunuch's body, the former carefully structures the viewer's position in the subjective terms of clinical (and, one not must forget, colonial) gaze.[70] As the object of this particular kind of gaze, the naked bodies of eunuchs constitute the pathological material ground on which the didactics of spectatorship was made possible in the first place. These unclothed bodies are intended to be compared, deciphered, and scrutinized in every minute detail, and such an attempt on the part of the viewer is comforted, or at least made less guilt-driven, by the artificial "blindfolding" of the patient's eyes, an epitome of twentieth-century medical photography. Unlike the eunuch in Matignon's photograph, the eunuchs in this photograph are stripped away of their ability to stare back at the person who is looking at them. Their anonymity thereby makes the power imbalance of this entire visual stimulation all the less threatening to the viewer. The images of eunuchs in the Qing palace archive, on the other hand, defy the foreigner's clinical and colonial spectatorship. The fully clothed body and the revealing eyes depict these young eunuchs in the normative terms of the native population, not an ostensibly mysterious, deficient object waiting to be investigated and treated according to the normative metrics of Western biomedicine.

The transformation in the power and epistemological claims of these images parallels Ruth Rogaski's insight regarding the conceptual transformation of *weisheng* in treaty-port China: what accompanied "a growing hegemony of biomedical approaches to health in the public discourse of Chinese elites" was "a concurrent acceptance of a picture of the Chinese people as inherently lacking when compared with Western-defined standards of health."[71] In the wake of what she calls hygienic modernity, the state launched an unprecedented public health campaign in which the meaning of weisheng moved away from a correlative cosmology of "guarding life," and

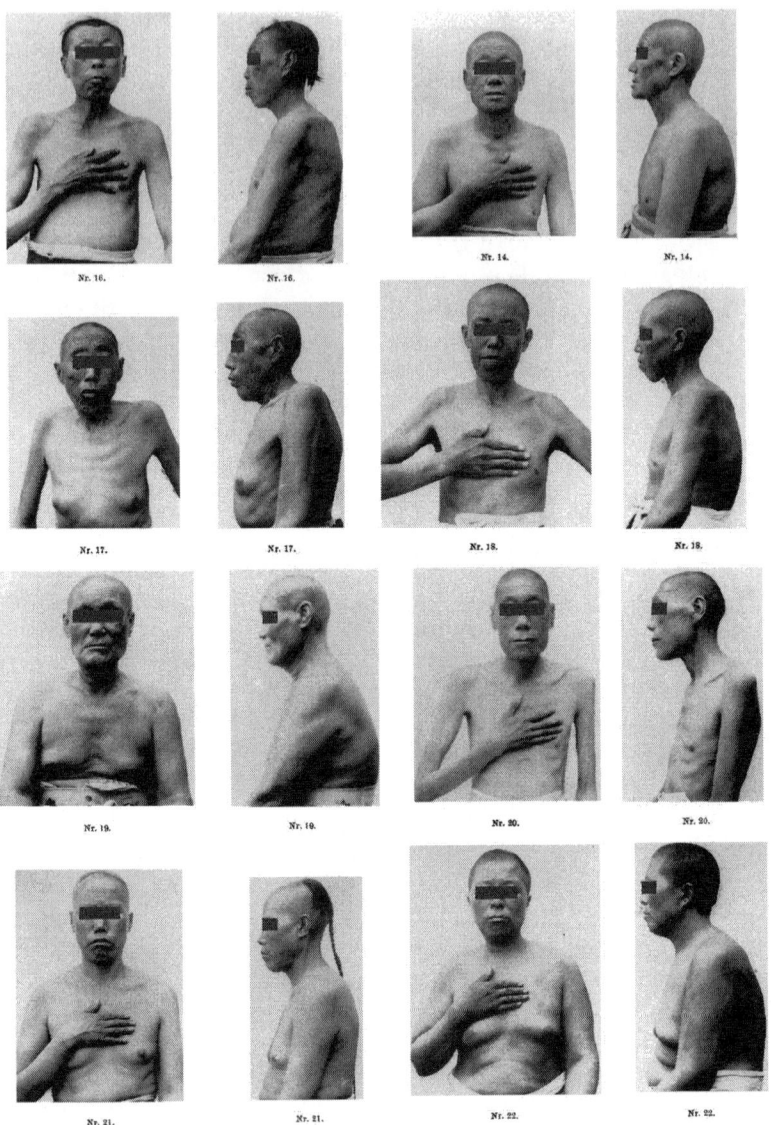

Figure 2.4 Medical images of Chinese eunuchs from Wilson and Roehrborn (1933)

Source: F. Wagenseil, "Chinesische Eunuchen," Zeitschrift für Morphologie und Anthropologie 32 (1933): 415–468, reprinted in Jean D. Wilson and Claus Roehrborn, "Long-Term Consequences of Castration in Men: Lessons from the Skoptzy and the Eunuchs of the Chinese and Ottoman Courts," *Journal of Clinical Endocrinology and Metabolism* 84, no. 12 (1999): 4324–4331, on p. 4329.

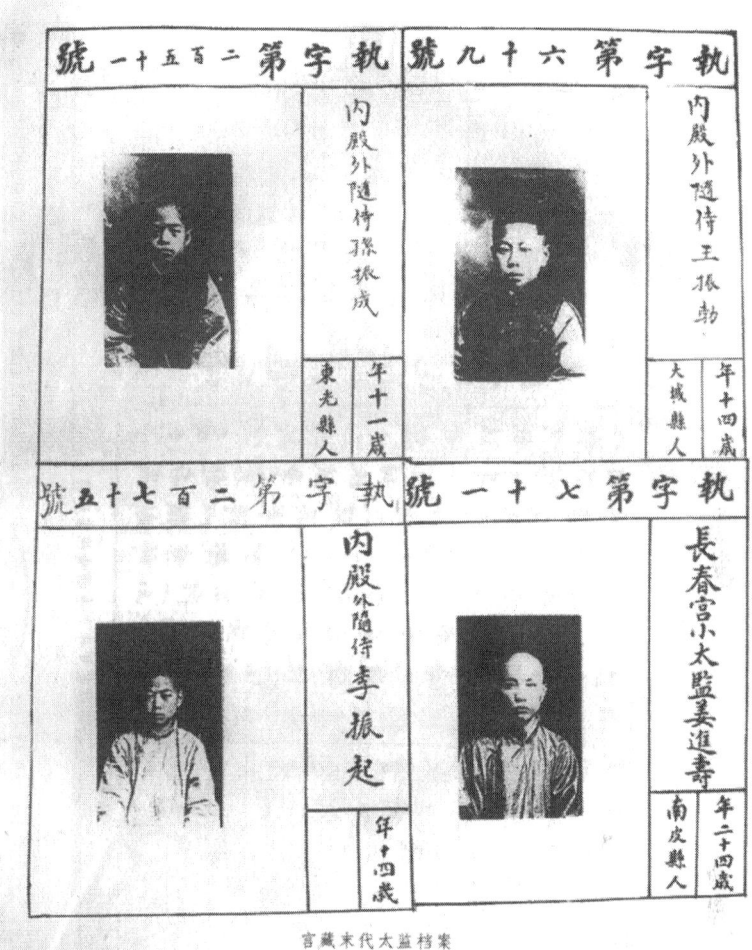

Figure 2.5 Photographs of eunuchs in the Qing Palace Archive
Source: Jia Yinghua (賈英華), *Modai taijian miwen: Sun Yaoting zhuan* (末代太監秘聞: 孫耀庭傳) (The secret life of the last eunuch: A biography of Sun Yaoting) (Beijing: Zhishi chubanshe, 1993). Reprinted with permission from Jia Yinghua.

toward an embrace of Western biomedical standards of health, disease, and cleanliness. Whether in the visual sphere of medical representation or in the conceptual domain of medical epistemology, imperialist circuits of power seized the Chinese body as an instrument for the production and validation of global knowledge claims about its inferiority. Nineteenth-century Western imperialism thus "left a brand on China," after which the image of China as a "castrated civilization" could be accepted, recycled, and even projected by the Chinese themselves.[72]

VI. From Missionary Narration to Eunuchs' Agency

Historians and other scholars have treated the accounts of Stent, Coltman, and Matignon as the bona fide source records of how castration was conducted in late Qing China, and have relied on them accordingly to reconstruct the presumed historical reality of the practice. For example, in his widely cited *Chinese Eunuchs* (1970), the only source Taisuke Mitamura drew on in describing how the operation proceeded in late imperial China was Stent's documentation.[73] In their renowned *History of Chinese Medicine* (1936), K. Chimin Wong and Wu Lien-teh renarrated Stent's description under the section on early Chinese surgery and reprinted Matignon's photograph that exposed a naked eunuch.[74] The entirety of Stent's article even made its way into the pages of one of the most humanist study of eunuchs to date, Charles Humana's *The Keeper of The Bed: A Study of the Eunuch* (1973).[75] A hand-drawn version of Matignon's photograph also appeared in Richard Millant's 1908 medical study of eunuchism, which treated the subject as a type of sexual perversion.[76] And these famous citations of Stent and Matignon represent only the tip of the iceberg. Even in his 1996 study of Ming-dynasty eunuchs, Henry Tsai still infers information about the castration operation in the early modern period from sources that are produced in the modern period, which always adopt a distinctively nationalist bias and are couched either in a scientific tone of objective observation or as an impassioned plea for abolition.[77]

Such detailed records as Stent's, Coltman's, and Matignon's were never committed in writing or visual imaging when castration was a widely accepted practice, because instructions for the practice were transmitted orally and demonstrated corporeally. Starting in the late nineteenth century, however, the availability of both textual and visual documentations regarding what castration entailed signaled the creation of new knowledge about eunuchs' bodies and new venues of its circulation. At the very least, this "repository" unveiled the secrecy surrounding the operation, transforming a private matter into something public. It is therefore reasonable that scholars of Chinese eunuchs have accorded Stent's account a high level of evidential authority, celebrating it as a rare piece of primary source about the practice. Similarly, Matignon's photograph continues to be circulated today as solid evidence for a regime of masculinity defined around the penis.

However, by bringing a corporeal practice as private as castration into the public domain, both Stent's textual description and Coltman's and Matignon's visualizations actually elevated, rather than diminished, the tension between the private and the public awareness of Chinese eunuchism. These foreigners' epistemic standardization of the castrated body in the public domain simultaneously made its personal relevance all the more invisible, silencing any corporeal embodiment of eunuchism that did not match their globalizing narrative. The development of the increasing irrelevancy of certain forms of corporeal experience thus went hand in hand with the collapse of eunuchism as a contested subject of experience. Their effort, in other words, constituted the first major step in making a practice as incendiary as castration one of the most *un*controversial issues in and out of China.

From this standpoint, what appears to be utterly inadequate about the existing literature on Chinese eunuchs is the one-sided meaning scholars have assigned and extrapolated from the act of castration—the permanent elimination of the biological reproductive capability of men. Here, it might be useful to borrow the insight of Nancy Rose Hunt from a different context (early twentieth-century Congo) to help us appreciate the significance of castration in Chinese history: namely, to "broaden our focus from reproduction narrowly defined in demographic and medical terms as fecundity and the birth of children, to social and cultural reproduction."[78] Insofar as our perception of the consequences of castration remains inside the framework of biomedical reproduction, the other half of the historical story completely escapes our attention: the castration of male bodies also *reproduces* eunuchs socially and culturally in imperial China.

To the extent that scholars have neglected the social and cultural reproductive aspect of castration, it could be said that they have implicitly behaved as passive agents of Western biomedicine in reinforcing its epistemic authority. Since the nineteenth century, the languages of Western reproductive anatomy and biology have provided both historians and historical actors an overt epistemic apparatus for privileging the biological consequence of castration to be the only indicator of its sociocultural function and reality.[79] As a result of this revaluation of its social-cultural reproductive meaning in a biomedical lexicon, the castrated male body easily became a third sex (sex as understood in the anatomical terms of Western biomedicine) and a sign for the inherently deficiency of the Chinese body, thereby enabling a cultural depiction of China as a castrated civilization that lacked virility.

To overcome this limited reading, we need to acknowledge the constructed nature of the bifurcation of Chinese castration as a mode of historical experience rather than renaturalizing it. On the level of personal-private experience, castration denotes a ritualized episode where the death of a man's biological fertility intersected with the birth of his new life as a eunuch. On the level of public-collective experience, castration represents a category that has marked both the elimination of its social and cultural reproductive role in history and the flattening of its epistemic significance to a biomedical one. In reducing the importance of castration to the realm of biology on both the macro and micro levels of historical experience, scholars have inevitably fallen short in handling the question of eunuchs' *agency* in their social and cultural reproduction.

VII. THE SOCIAL AND CULTURAL REPRODUCTION OF EUNUCHISM: DAILY EXPERTS

Whether we consider the scrotum to be the seat of male fertility or the penis the locus of male pleasure, the intended effect of castration on eunuchs is the deprivation of their power to breed biologically,. And that is it. They were not impotent in any other sense. Jennifer Jay, for instance, has shown that Chinese eunuchs retained an overtly "male" gender in aspiring to a traditional Confucian lifestyle: "From both the historical sources and the anecdotal reminiscences of Qing eunuchs, it seems that with very few exceptions, the Chinese eunuchs were without gender confusion at the time of castration, and after the operation they experienced physiological changes but no apparent shift in their gender identity and male-oriented role in society."[80] Many eunuchs got married, adopted children, or had kids before offering themselves to the imperial court, suggesting that their masculine social role remained intact as they continued to embrace Confucian family norms. Quite simply put, undergoing castration did not indicate, to them and to their surrounding community, a complete erasure of their masculine identity. More importantly, eunuchs also faced a greater degree of opportunity and power in comparison to other female servants (宮女, *gongnü*) inside the palace.[81] Indeed, the extent of their involvement in the political arena has been the predominant focus of Chinese historiography ever since their institutional lives were first systematically documented in 1769 in *The History of the Palace* (*Guochao gongshi*), a project commissioned by the Qianlong Emperor.[82]

But conventional wisdom tends to explain the politically corrupt activities of Chinese eunuchs as the result of their internalized anger and frustration with their lost manhood.[83] Gary Taylor might have a point here in inviting us to view the eunuch as "not a defective man but an improved one."[84] In imperial China, apart from the court officials, eunuchs were after all the people whom the emperor and his family trusted more than any other men. The tremendous political power Chinese eunuchs wielded extended beyond the bedchamber to the rest of the palace and, in well-known examples during the Tang and Ming dynasties, arguably throughout the Chinese empire.[85] Therefore, the political power of eunuchs should be interpreted less as an effect of their demasculinized subjectivity, than a definitive feature of their social and cultural sense of self as gendered through their abiding presence in Chinese history.[86]

Eunuchs could not reproduce biologically, but the practice of castration made their social and cultural reproduction possible. So even if it was not physically feasible for them to give birth to future generations of their own kind, eunuchs frequently took an active role in overseeing the nuts and bolts of castration, the single most important procedure that defined their identity. According to a lithograph from Shanghai in the late nineteenth century, when instances of self-castration occurred on the streets of late imperial Peking, eunuchs were the authorities to whom people often turned for assistance. The title of the lithograph is "How He Lost His Significance One Morning," and the textual description of the incident reads as follows:

> There once was a man named Tang who lived outside the Shunzhimen Gate in Peking. Though in his early twenties, Tang had already acquired the evil habit of gambling and on one recent occasion had lost all of his money. He had no place to flee to, nor any way to repay his debts.
>
> On the ninth of last month, Tang proceeded to the Changyu Pawnshop with the intention of obtaining two strings of cash by pawning a pair of short pants. The pawnbroker on duty told Tang that his pants weren't worth that much, and that he would have to add something more substantial if he hoped to obtain the desired amount. To this Tang replied, "But all I've got to my name are my balls (卵袋)!"
>
> "That would be just fine!" replied the pawnbroker with a laugh.

Tang walked away in a huff. When he got home, he sharpened his knife—which had a blade sharp enough to fell a kingdom—and returned to the Changyu Pawnshop. When he got there he removed all of his clothing and stood there as naked as when he was proceeded to turn himself into a sawed-off shotgun with a single energetic slash of his knife, losing enough blood in the process to float a pestle.

Tang passed out immediately, whereupon the pawnbroker, frightened out of his wits, rushed off to a local official's residence to find a eunuch who could come to Tang's rescue. On the way, he stopped at North City police headquarters to report the incident. Within minutes, the police had dispatched a runner to arrest the pawnbroker, and subjected him to a thorough questioning. Only through the intervention of an intermediary was he able to extract himself from a potentially burdensome lawsuit.

In the meantime, Tang had been carried home on a wooden plank, but he had lost so much blood that his life hung in a delicate balance. The proceedings described above cost the pawnshop some four hundred taels of silver.[87]

Late nineteenth-century lithographs have long been considered by historians as a creative source for the tangled social and cultural history of late Qing China.[88] This particular lithograph is no exception. First, Tang's choice of the word *ruandai*, which is translated here as "balls" but literally means an "egg bag," goes a long way to show that people had not always considered the bodily target of castration to be the entire male genital organ in late imperial China. This lithograph might in fact be the only visual representation of Chinese castration before Matignon's photograph. In the mid-nineteenth century, when the English word "testes" was translated into Chinese for the first time, the medical missionary Benjamin Hobson left no room for ambiguity when he remarked that the "outer kidney"—his terminology for the male gonad—was the organ responsible for "the generation of semen," and for "the change in voice and facial features alongside the elimination of reproductive power when castrated (閹之割之)."[89] In both examples, the message is clear: before the rise of the penis, the anatomical target of castration was the scrotum.

Moreover, the lithograph implies that when it came down to castration, eunuchs were the everyday experts whom people sought for advice. That "knifers" were not involved in this incident is reasonable, because they may have been located too deep inside Peking at the time to be a source of assistance, if they existed at all in light of Stent's account.[90] But for a health issue as serious as loss of blood, and potentially death, it is interesting to note that no physician is either mentioned in the expository text or present in the lithographic staging of this male-dominated event. Curiously enough, the individual who had the best view of what Tang actually excised from his body is the child located at the center of the drawing, and most certainly not the eldest man on the left who seems to focus more on Tang's upper body. If the lithograph is a tenable representation of common attitudes toward castration in late Qing society, one can infer from it that the preservation of castration as a cultural practice relied heavily on the role of eunuchs as a determinant agent in guiding its historical existence in China.

VIII. THE SOCIAL AND CULTURAL REPRODUCTION OF EUNUCHISM: SELF-NARRATION

Indeed, one of the most powerful ways through which eunuchs exerted a significant measure of agency in their social and cultural production was by narrating their own experience. This began arguably as early as when Stent was collecting materials for his study. He mentioned twice about the existence of native "informants."[91] Given the secretive impression that he gave of the system of "knifers" and "the shed," it would be only logical to assume that his account was based on information provided by other eunuchs, who would indeed be rather familiar with the practical measures involved in castration, at least more so than anyone else. Similarly, in Coltman's reports, all of the information about the actual castration experience were filtered and made accessible only through what the eunuchs said.[92] So the evidential status of foreigners' accounts is substantiated only when its epistemological function as a secondary, rather than a primary, source is adequately acknowledged.

But Chinese eunuchs did not narrate their experience only through the voice of "outsiders." Besides the textual and visual repository created by foreigners such as Stent, Coltman, and Matignon, additional historical information about the operation itself came from the personal recollection of late Qing eunuchs. According to Ren Futian and Chi Huanqing who were among the oldest surviving eunuchs in the twentieth century, the two most well-known places that offered professional services in castration prior to the 1890s were Biwu (Bi "the Fifth") and Xiaodao Liu ("pocket knife" Liu). Bi operated an establishment on Nanchang Street, whereas Liu's was located inside the Di'an Gate in the imperial city. "Each season," Ren and Chi explained, "they supplied the *Neiwufu* [Imperial Household Department] forty eunuchs. Together the two families were responsible for all the formal procedures pertinent to castration."[93]

According to Ren and Chi, "registration" with Bi or Liu was the first step required of parents who wished to turn their boys into palace eunuchs. In turn, the boys would be "examined—for his appearance, conversational skills, intelligence, and genital organ (done with his pants on)—and admitted only if considered appropriate." Although Bi and Liu "had many years of experience and the necessary utilities," Ren and Chi insisted that "the overall experience remained painful for the subject of operation, since they possessed neither pain relievers nor adequate medicinals that would help stop the bleeding. Antiseptic preparation was done simply by heating up the surgical knives with fire."[94] Committed to print almost a century apart, Ren and Chi's discussion of Bi and Liu seem to provide solid evidence for the "knifers" described by Stent.

However, their words verify Stent's account only by increasing, rather than decreasing, the distance he first established for the historical experience of castration between a personal realm of embodiment and a public domain of collective memory. Evident from this example, eunuchs themselves participated in the archival rendering of the "knifers" as primary operators of Chinese castration. This historiographic substantiation adds another layer of complexity to the historian's task, to quote medievalist Gabrielle Spiegel, of "solicit[ing] those fragmented inner narratives to emerge from their silences."[95] For any eunuch whose castration experience deviated from this global narrative would require additional explanation and narrative space for inclusion. One of the most popular alternative routes to serving in the palace, for instance, was voluntary castration (*zigong*, 自宫), a category that included self-castration.

More prevalent in the Ming dynasty, self-castration became illegal under early Qing law. The lessons from Ming eunuchs' political corruption were difficult to ignore, so up to the second half of the eighteenth century, Qing emperors made it illegal for civilians to castrate themselves, which simultaneously curbed the number of available eunuchs. However, the legal codes that imposed death penalty for voluntary castration were not strictly enforced throughout the first hundred years or so of Qing rule. In June 1785, the Qianlong Emperor took a step further in loosening the codes to allow the Imperial Household Department to accept individuals who offered themselves after voluntary castration.[96] Actually, this only reflected the strictness of the regulations imposed on eunuchs by early Qing rulers, which facilitated the decline in the formal supply of eunuchs and the growing number of eunuchs who fled. At one point Qianlong even promoted a policy of eunuch illiteracy.⁹⁷

Famous late Qing eunuchs whom the court admitted as a result of voluntary castration include Zhang Lande (more popularly known as Xiaode Zhang), Ma Deqing, and the last Chinese eunuch who died in 1996, Sun Yaoting.⁹⁸ To be sure, persons born with ambiguous or dysfunctional genitalia were categorized by physicians as "natural eunuchs" (*tianyan*, 天閹) and recommended for service in the imperial court as a typical solution. But in most cases of voluntary castration or zigong, the father was the person who performed the operation. Such was the experience of Ma Deqing, one of the last surviving Chinese eunuchs in the twentieth century:

> When I was nine, roughly in 1906, one day my father succeeded in persuading me to lie on the bed and castrated me with his own hands. That was a really agonizing and scary experience. I can't even recall the exact number of times I passed out. I've never been willing to discuss the incident with anyone, not because I'm shy, but because it was way too painful...
>
> Think about it: in those years, neither anesthesia, needles, nor blood-flow prevention medicines were widely available...consider the kind of pain inflicted on a restless kid by holding him down on the bed and cutting his *yaoming de qiguan* ["organ for life"] from his body! Every single vein was connected to my heart, and, with the kind of pain involved, I almost puked it out. Ever since, my reproductive organ and I became two separate entities.
>
> After the surgery, it was necessary to insert a rod at the end of the surgical opening. Otherwise, if the wound seals up, it becomes impossible to urinate and will require a second surgical intervention...Seriously, [in those years,] the meds applied to facilitate the healing of the wound were merely cotton pads soaked with white grease, sesame oil, and pepper-powder. Changing and reapplying the meds was always a painful experience.
>
> I remember I was on the dust *kang* ["depository"] all the time, and my father only allowed me to lie on my back. Sometimes I wished to move a bit when my back started to sore, but how could I? Even a mild stir would bring up extraordinary pain from the cut.⁹⁹

Similar in function to Ren and Chi's account, Ma's recollection of his childhood castration actually confirms aspects of the operation first described by Stent. Most notably, both Ma and Stent mention the kang on which castration was operated and the postsurgery necessity to place a rod inside the main orifice to secure successful future urination. From the lithograph to Ma's life narrative, then, eunuchs actively monitored the details of what it took to become and live as a eunuch, historically and historiographically—that is, in both historical real time and as vanguards of their own body history.

However, it is worth stressing that whereas "knifers" or professional castrators took the center stage in previous documentations of the operation, their role was replaced by Ma's own father in his reminiscence of his childhood castration experience. This is one of the most significant parallels between footbinding and castration in Chinese history: the cultural survival of both practices entailed a homosocial environment in the occasion and demonstration of their corporeality. Footbinding was a custom conducted by women and on women; castration was a practice performed by men and on men. But whether mothers bound the feet of their daughters, fathers castrated their sons, or male "knifers" operated on boys, neither footbinding nor castration should be understood as a timeless, spaceless practice with a universal *raison d'être*. In discussing the actual measures involved in castration and the degrading ways in which they were treated by the imperial family, the stories Chinese eunuchs told of themselves ultimately joined the public repository developed by European "outsiders," constituting the second major step in defining their own bodies as templates for national histories.

In the waning decades of the Qing dynasty, Chinese eunuchs' self-narrations and Western spectators' observations converged most tellingly in the Coltman reports. Recall that Robert Coltman, a personal physician to the Chinese imperial family, reported treating six Chinese eunuchs in Peking and—based on his experience—provided an image of the castration site of one of his patients (figure 2.1). Coltman revealed a transformation in his feelings toward eunuchs from "sympathy" to "disgust and contempt."[100] In the two articles he published in the *Universal Medical Journal* and the *Chinese Medical Missionary Journal* in the 1890s, Coltman admitted that this transformation may be explained by his realization that a surprisingly high number of Chinese eunuchs, at least during the late Qing period, actually castrated themselves. In all of the cases he reported, the patients did not merely undergo voluntary castration, but they became eunuchs through the more specific measure of self-castration. In 1894, Coltman wrote: "I am now fully convinced, that many of the eunuchs employed in and about the palace, *have made themselves so*, for the purpose of obtaining employment."[101] In light of the later personal recollections of eunuchs as discussed above, one might assume that self-castration was rather rare, and most voluntary castrations were carried out by their father. On the contrary, Coltman's reports presented evidence for the prevalence of self-castration in the last decades of eunuchism's existence.

One of Coltman's patients, over 50 years of age and who went to him "for the obliteration of the urinary meatus," was once with the Tongzhi Emperor and, after the death of the emperor, took service with the seventh prince. This eunuch "stated that at twenty-two years of age, he being married and the father of a year old girl baby, resolved to seek employment in the palace. He secured a very sharp *ts'ai-tao-tzu*, and with one clean cut removed his external organs of generation entire."[102] Coltman also operated on a eunuch 32 years of age, "who emasculated himself eighteen months ago." "This man," according to Coltman, "is a large framed sturdy fellow who could earn a good living in any employment requiring strength, but he deliberately emasculated himself for the purpose of getting an easy position in the Imperial employ."[103] Interestingly, some eunuchs castrated themselves to spite their fathers. One of his patients, 16 years old, "had an elder brother who had been made an eunuch at an early age, and was in service at the imperial palace. Knowing that his father depended on him (his second son) for descendants to worship at his grave, this lad, after a quarrel with his father, on the 23d of March, took a butcher-knife and cut off his penis close to the symphysis pubis."[104] Another eunuch, aged 22, cut off his penis and testicles "with a razor," explaining that "he was the only son of this father, and having had a quarrel with him, he had, to spite him, thus deprived him of all hopes of descendants at one blow—the dearest hope known to an elderly China-man."[105] To stress the relatively high incidences of self-castration in the late Qing, Coltman concluded that "many able bodied men voluntarily submit to the operation by others, and *not a few* perform it upon themselves."[106]

These examples confirm a number of the crucial insights that we have drawn thus far regarding the history of the demise of Chinese eunuchism: the foregrounding of the penis in the biomedical (re)definition of masculinity with respect to Chinese castration, the separation of the eunuchs' masculine subjectivity in the social sphere (as husbands, fathers, and sons) from the (gendering) effect of the castration operation itself in the realm of embodiment, the crucial role of foreigners—especially Western doctors—in relating the castration experience of Chinese eunuchs to a global community of observers, and the self-narration of eunuchs, though often conveyed through the voice of foreign informants, as a cornerstone in the shaping of twentieth-century common understandings of their own experiential past.

IX. The Abolishment of the Imperial Palace Eunuchs System

Adding to the public discourse on the corporeal experience of castration sustained by Western commentators and eunuchs themselves, members of the imperial family completed the process of turning the eunuchoidal body into homogenous anchors of anticastration sentimentality. Strictly speaking, there was no anticastration movement comparable to the antifootbinding movement that acquired a national urgency in the final years of the nineteenth century. The eunuchs system was simply terminated when the last emperor, Puyi, decided to do so. Puyi's ad hoc explanation for his decision, supplemented by the detailed recollection of his cousin Pujia, thus brought an end to the social and cultural production of Chinese eunuchs. Once the eunuchs system was abolished, the cultural existence of castration also came to a halt in China.[107] With Puyi and his relatives' autobiographical words printed and circulated globally, Chinese eunuchism became a truly historical experience.

According to Puyi, his main motivation for expelling palace eunuchs came from a fire incident inside the Forbidden City during the summer of 1923. By then, more than a decade had passed since Sun Yat-sen inaugurated a new republic. Puyi and the imperial family were nonetheless protected by the "Articles of Favorable Treatment of the Emperor of Great Qing after His Abdication" (清帝退位優待條件), an agreement reached between his mother Empress Dowager Longyu, Yuan Shikai, who was then the general of the Beiyang Army in Beijing, and the provisional Republican government in Nanjing. The articles guaranteed Puyi and his family the right to continue residence in the Forbidden City and ownership of Qing treasures, as well as a $4 million stipend a year and protection of all Manchu ancestral temples. Under these conditions, Puyi retained his imperial title and was treated by the Republican government with the protocol and privileges attached to a foreign monarch. Hence, the overthrown of the Qing dynasty did not end the institutionalization of eunuchs immediately. The corporeal experience of Chinese eunuchs existed almost a quarter into the twentieth century, as the demand for them survived with the imperial family in Peking.

Still relying on their service and loyalty at the time of the fire, Puyi mainly held eunuchs responsible for the incident. The fire swept across and destroyed the entire surrounding area of Jianfu Palace (建福宮) at the northwest corner of the Forbidden City, including Jingyixuan (靜怡軒), Huiyaolou (慧曜樓), Jiyunlou (吉雲樓), Bilinguan (碧琳館), Miaolianhuashi (妙蓮花室), Yanshouge (延壽閣), Jicuiting (積翠亭), Guangshenlou (廣生樓), Nihuilou (凝輝樓), and Xiangyunting (香雲亭).[108] The timing of the event coincided with Puyi's effort in cataloguing his official assets. Indeed, Jianfu Palace stored most of his valuables, including the wealthy repertoire of antiques, paintings, pottery, and ceramics collected by the Qianlong emperor. One day when he came upon (and was astonished) by a small portion of Qianlong's collection, he asked himself: "How much imperial treasure do I actually possess? How much of it is under my awareness, and how much of it has slipped through my fingers? What should I do with the entire imperial collection? How do I prevent them from being stolen?"[109] Ever since the founding of the republic, Puyi and members of his extended family had confronted repeated reporting of theft. The frequency of palace robbery rose rapidly by the early 1920s, which fed into an increasing recognition of the value of the Qing collection of artistry and material goods on the global market. In hoping to control the situation, Puyi decided to tabulate and document his inventory at Jianfu Palace. "On the evening of 27 June 1923," Puyi recollected, "the same day when the project was just underway, the fire took off, and everything was gone, accounted for or not."[110]

Puyi formally abolished the palace eunuchs system on July 16, 1923, only 20 days after the fire incident. In the words of his cousin, Pujia, who had been taking English classes with him since 1919, "the fire undoubtedly had a direct bearing on [this decision]."[111] Pujia recalled that after what happened to Fujian Palace, many eunuchs were interrogated, and Puyi learned from the interrogations about their previous success in stealing and selling his possessions. "And according to the fire department," Pujia added, "the crew smelled gasoline when they first arrived at the palace. When Puyi heard about this, he became even more confident in his accusation that eunuchs started the fire in order to cover up what they had stolen from Fujian Palace."[112] Initially met with great resistance from his father, uncles, wife, and other imperial family members, Puyi eventually won them over when he insisted: "If the palace is on fire again, who's willing to take the responsibility?"[113]

Interestingly, Puyi himself revealed a completely different reason for terminating the imperial employment of eunuchs. Although he realized how rampant theft was inside the palace, he was more concerned about his life than his possession. Not long after the Fujian

Palace incident, another fire was indeed started right outside his own bedchamber, Yangxingdian. Given how badly he treated eunuchs, Puyi's real motivation, therefore, came from his growing suspicion that eunuchs actually tried to kill him for revenge.

Moreover, Pujia suggested that Puyi's decision to end the eunuchs system was also shaped by the influence of their English teacher, Reginald Johnston. In 1923, Johnston informed Puyi about eunuchs smuggling treasures out of the palace and selling them in antique shops. As an "outsider" and a non-Chinese, Johnston was able to remind Puyi constantly and frankly of the rampant corruption of his palace eunuchs.[114] In addition, Puyi was quite explicit about his admiration and respect for Johnston.[115] It is reasonable to assume that part of Puyi's motivation for disbanding the palace eunuchs can be attributed to the way he was moved by his teacher's attitudes toward things Chinese.

But whether it is due to Puyi's own paranoia, frustration with palace theft, or intentional self-refashioning and self-Westernization under Johnston's influence, the historical reasons for getting rid of the eunuchs system are minimally concerned with how eunuchs felt or how they were treated. The elimination of eunuchism in China proceeded on one precondition: the transfer of historiographic agency from eunuchs themselves to members of the imperial family, especially the last emperor Puyi. With respect to castration, the historiographic distance between a public domain of collective memory and a private realm of individual embodiment was so firmly in place by the 1920s, that even when we are confronted with the concrete reasons and motivations for discontinuing eunuchism, a cultural system with two thousand years of history in China,[116] the reasons and motivations bear zero relevance to the actual embodied lives of castrated men. Eunuchism and castration are perceived as backward, oppressive, shameful, and traditional not because they impose violence onto men's bodies, not because they punish men corporeally, not because they hurt men's psychological well-being, and not because they demonstrate inflicted cruelty of the flesh: these are not the *real* reasons why eunuchism and castration elicit negative attitudes in Chinese nationalist sentimentality. Eunuchism and castration sound "bad" because they bring to sharp focus a host of social values—lagging behindness, oppression, shame, tradition, and even disregard for human rights—that gives Chinese civilization a history on the platform of the globe. When one enters this global platform to reflect on China's past, one essentially risks neglecting the personal voices of those castrated servants who lived closer than anyone else to the epicenter of that history.

X. Conclusion

From the Self-Strengthening to the May Fourth era, whereas the antifootbinding movement was built on the rhetorical power of newly invented categories such as tianzu ("natural foot") and *fangzu* ("letting foot out"), the demise of eunuchism depended on the collapse of the saliency of already existing categories such as tianyan ("natural eunuch") and zigong ("voluntary castration"). The annihilation of the relevance of these categories in Chinese culture thus carved out a space for new conceptual ontologies to be associated with the practice of sex-alteration, such as transsexuality. Viewed from this perspective, both eunuchism and transsexuality are categories of experience whose historicity is contingent rather than foundational or uncontestable.[117]

My implicit argument has been that before we enter the history of transsexuality in postwar Sinophone culture, it is necessary to consider its genealogical preconditions. The critical reflections on the meaning and value of evidence throughout this chapter are attempts to demonstrate "the possibility of examining those assumptions and practices that excluded considerations of difference in the first place." They ask and highlight "questions about the constructed nature of experience, about how subjects are constituted as different in the first place, about how one's vision is constructed—about language (or discourse) and history."[118] Insofar as the accounts analyzed above can be treated as representative of the social reality of castration in late Qing and Republican China, each of them moved from being a form of evidence operating on the level of individual embodiment to a source type functioning on the level of global historical narration. Surprisingly, they stand in for all that we know about how castration was actually operated in the past three millennia. As such, historiographically speaking, this textual and visual archive not only exposes the castrated body of the eunuchs in the public sphere, but also conceals its existence in the personal historical realm. I have adopted a very specific strategy to reading the archive assembled in this chapter: by "underscore[ing] the grids of intelligibility within which claims of both presence and absence have been asserted and questioned."[119] This method of archival problematization brings us closer to, rather than blinding ourselves from, the core issues of proof, evidence, and argumentation that define the historian's task.

The discursive effect of the sources laid out in this chapter belongs to the global episteme of historical narration, and is occasioned outside the pulses of men's embodied lives. Just like tianzu or fangzu are "'gigantic' categories formulated from a vintage point outside the concerns and rhythms of the women's embodied lives," the perpetual dissonance between the public records of Chinese castration and the varied private experiences of eunuchs in the past *becomes constitutive of* a nationalist sentiment that considers Chinese castration backward, traditional, shameful, and oppressive.[120] As a truly historical specimen, the castrated male body has come to appear completely out of sync with the Chinese body politic at large. When news of the "discovery" of the first Chinese transsexual eventually came from postcolonial Taiwan, her glamour saturated the lingering culture of a "castrated civilization."[121] The birth of a "corpus style" is predicated upon another's death.

Notes

1. Wu Guozhang (吳國璋), *Beiyange de wenming: Zhongguo taijian wenhualun* (被閹割的文明: 中國太監文化語) [Castrated civilization: On the culture of Chinese eunuchs] (Beijing: Zhishi chubanshe, 1999); Chen Cunren (陳存仁), *Beiyange de wenming: Xianhua Zhongguo gudai chanzu yu gongxing* (被閹割的文明: 閒話中國古代纏足與宮刑) [Castrated civilization: On footbinding and castration in ancient China] (Guilin: Guangxi Normal University Press, 2008). On "the Sick Man of Asia," see Larissa N. Heinrich, *The Afterlife of Images: Translating the Pathological Body between China and the West* (Durham: Duke University Press, 2008); Michael Keevak, *Becoming Yellow: A Short History of Racial Thinking* (Princeton: Princeton University Press, 2011); and Carlos Rojas, *The Sick Man of Asia: Diagnosing the Chinese Body Politic* (Cambridge: Harvard University Press, forthcoming). The "castrated civilization," therefore, must be historically contextualized on a par with other relevant images of China in the early twentieth century, such as "Yellow Peril" and "the sleeping lion." See Jing Tsu, *Failure, Nationalism, and Literature: The Making of Chinese Identity, 1895–1937* (Stanford: Stanford University Press, 2005), 88–96; Yang Ruisong (楊瑞松), *Bingfu, huanghuo yu shuishi: "Xifang" shiye de zhongguo xingxiang yu jindai Zhongguo guozu lunshu xiangxiang* (病夫、黃禍與睡獅:「西方」視野的中國形象與近代中國國族語述想像) [Sick man, yellow peril, and sleeping lion: The images of China from the Western perspectives and the discourses and imagination of Chinese national identity] (Taipei: Chengchi University Press, 2010).

2. Michel Foucault, *The History of Sexuality, Vol. 1: An Introduction*, trans. Robert Hurley (New York: Vintage Books, 1990); Joan Scott, "The Evidence of Experience," *Critical Inquiry* 17, no. 4

(Summer 1991): 773–797; David Halperin, *How to Do the History of Homosexuality* (Chicago: University of Chicago Press, 2002).
3. World historians have designated the period between the mid-nineteenth century and the First World War "the age of high imperialism." See Scott B. Cook, *Colonial Encounters in the Age of High Imperialism* (New York: Harper Collins, 1996).
4. Jessie Gregory Lutz, *China and the Christian Colleges, 1850–1950* (Ithaca, New York: Cornell University Press, 1971).
5. On the emergence of Shanghai as a global cosmopolitan center in the early twentieth century, see Meng Yue, *Shanghai and the Edges of Empires* (Minneapolis: University of Minnesota Press, 2005); Marie-Claire Bergere, *Shanghai: China's Gateway to Modernity*, trans. Janet Llyod (Stanford: Stanford University Press, 2009); and Jeffrey N. Wasserstrom, *Global Shanghai, 1850-2010: A History in Fragments* (New York: Routledge, 2009). On women's fashion in Republican China, see Eileen Chang, "A Chronicle of Changing Clothes," trans. Andrew Jones, *positions: east asia cultures critiques* 11, no. 2 (2003): 427–441; Anotnia Finnane, *Changing Clothes in China: Fashion, History, Nation* (New York: Columbia University Press, 2008). On American flappers, see Joshua Zeitz, *Flapper: A Madcap Story of Sex, Style, Celebrity, and the Women Who Made America Modern* (New York: Three Rivers Press, 2006). On flappers in France, see Whitney Chadwick and Tirza True Latimer, eds., *The Modern Woman Revisited: Paris between the Wars* (Piscataway, NJ: Rutgers University Press, 2003).
6. Haiyan Lee, *Revolution of the Heart: A Genealogy of Love in China, 1900–1950* (Stanford: Stanford University Press, 2007); Susan Glosser, *Chinese Visions of Family and the State, 1915–1953* (Berkeley: University of California Press, 2003); Tze-lan D. Sang, *The Emerging Lesbian: Female Same-Sex Desire in Modern China* (Chicago: University of Chicago Press, 2001).
7. On the emergence of the conceptual equivalent of "sex" in China, see Howard Chiang, "Why Sex Mattered: Science and Visions of Transformation in Modern China" (Ph.D. dissertation, Princeton University, 2012), Chap. 2; Leon Rocha, "*Xing*: The Discourse of Sex and Human Nature in Modern China," *Gender and History* 22, no. 3 (2010): 603–628. On "third sex," see Shi Kekuan (施克寬), *Zhongguo huanguan mishi: renzao de disanxing* (中國宦官祕史：人造的第三性) [The secret history of Chinese eunuchs: The man-made third sex] (Beijing: Zhongguo xiju chubanshe, 1988); Wang Yude (王玉德), *Shenmi de disanxing—Zhongguo taijian* (神秘的第三性—中國太監) [The mysterious third sex: Zhongguo taijian] (Hong Kong: Minchuang chubanshe, 1995).
8. Joan W. Scott, "Gender: A Useful Category of Historical Analysis," *American Historical Review* 91, no. 5 (1986): 1053–1075. On the significance of Scott's argument for Chinese historiography of

gender, see Gail Hershatter and Wang Zheng, "Chines History: A Useful Category of Gender Analysis," *American Historical Review* 113, no. 5 (2008): 1404–1421.
9. Matthew Sommer, *Sex, Law, and Society in Late Imperial China* (Stanford, CA: Stanford University Press, 2000); Everett Zhang, "Switching between Traditional Chinese Medicine and Viagra: Cosmopolitanism and Medical Pluralism Today," *Medical Anthropology* 26, no. 2 (2007): 53–96; Everett Zhang, "The Birth of Nanke (Men's Medicine) in China: The Making of the Subject of Desire," *American Ethnologist* 34, no. 3 (2007): 491–508; Susan Glosser, *Chinese Visions of Family and the State, 1915-1953* (Berkeley: University of California Press, 2003); Cuncun Wu, *Homoerotic Sensibilities in Late Imperial China* (London: Routledge, 2004); Wenqing Kang, *Obsession: Male Same-Sex Relations in China, 1900–1950* (Hong Kong: Hong Kong University Press, 2009); Wenqing Kang, "Male Same-Sex Relations in Modern China: Language, Media Representation, and Law, 1900-1949," *positions: east asia cultures critique* 18, no. 2 (Fall 2010): 489–510; Giovanni Vitiello, *The Libertine's Friend: Homosexuality and Masculinity in Late Imperial China* (Chicago: University of Chicago Press, 2011); Wu Cuncun and Mark Stevenson, "Speaking of Flowers: Theatre, Public Culture, and Homoerotic Writing in Nineteenth-Century Beijing," *Asian Theatre Journal* 27, no. 1 (Spring 2010): 100–129; and David Eng, *Racial Castration: Managing Masculinity in Asian America* (Durham: Duke University Press, 2001).
10. Susan Brownell and Jeffrey N. Wasserstrom, eds., *Chinese Femininities/Chinese Masculinities: A Reader* (Berkeley: University of California Press, 2002); Kam Louie and Morris Low, eds., *Asian Masculinities: The Meaning and Practice of Manhood in China and Japan* (London and New York: Routledge, 2003); Kam Louie, *Theorising Chinese Masculinity: Society and Gender in China* (Cambridge: Cambridge University Press, 2002).
11. Judith Halberstam, *Female Masculinity* (Durham: Duke University Press, 1998).
12. Dorothy Ko, *Cinderella's Sisters: A Revisionist History of Footbinding* (Berkeley: University of California Press, 2005).
13. Dorothy Ko, "The Body as Attire: The Shifting Meanings of Footbinding in Seventeenth-Century China," *Journal of Women's History* 8, no. 4 (1997): 8–27.
14. Angela Zito, "Bound to be Represented: Theorizing/Fetishizing Footbinding," in *Embodied Modernities: Corporeality, Representation, and Chinese Culture*, ed. Fran Martin and Larissa Heinrich (Honolulu: University of Hawai'i Press, 2006), 21–41. See also Angela Zito, "Secularizing the Pain of Footbinding in China: Missionary and Medical Stagings of the Universal Body," *Journal of the American Academy of Religion* 75, no. 1 (2007): 1–24.

15. The "archive" I am referring to here does not correspond to a physically existing archive. Rather, it refers to a repository of sources that I have collected that recount information about the castration operation as performed in late Qing China.
16. Aixinjueluo Puyi (愛新羅覺 溥儀), *Wo de qianbansheng* (我的前半生) [The first half of my life] (Beijing: Qunzhong chubanshe, 1981).
17. Ma Deqing (馬德清) et al., in *Wan Qing gongting shenghuo jianwen* (晚清宮廷生活見聞) [Life in Late-Qing Imperial Palace], ed. Zhongguo renmin zhengzhi xieshang huiyi quanguo weiyuanhui wenshi ziliao yanjiu weiyuanhui (中國人民政治協商會議全國委員會文史資料研究委員會) (Beijing: Wenshi ziliao chubanshe, 1982).
18. Seth Faison, "The Death of the Last Emperor's Last Eunuch," *New York Times*, December 20, 1996.
19. Ko, "The Body as Attire," 10.
20. Anjali Arondekar, "Without a Trace: Sexuality and the Colonial Archive," *Journal of the History of Sexuality* 14 (2005): 10–27, on 12.
21. Anjali Arondekar, *For the Record: Sexuality and the Colonial Archive in India* (Durham: Duke University Press, 2009).
22. My discussion of the archive is critically inspired by Michel Foucault, *The Order of Things: An Archaeology of the Human Sciences* (New York: Vintage Books, 1973); Jacques Derrida, *Archive Fever: A Freudian Impression*, trans. Eric Prenowitz (Chicago: University of Chicago Press, 1995); Carolyn Steedman, *Dust: The Archive and Cultural History* (New Brunswick: Rutgers University Press, 2002); and Ann Laura Stoler, *Along the Archival Grain: Epistemic Anxieties and Colonial Common Sense* (Princeton: Princeton University Press, 2008).
23. On the antifootbinding movement, see Ko, *Cinderella's Sisters*, Chaps. 1–2. On the leper's crippled body in the era of Chinese national modernity, see Angela Leung, *Leprosy in China: A History* (New York: Columbia University Press, 2009), Chap. 4.
24. G. Carter Stent, "Chinese Eunuchs," *Journal of the North China Branch of the Royal Asiatic Society* 11 (1877): 143–184.
25. Stent, "Chinese Eunuchs," 143.
26. Stent, "Chinese Eunuchs," 143.
27. Stent, "Chinese Eunuchs," 143.
28. Ko, *Cinderella's Sisters*, 16.
29. See Elizabeth James, ed., *Women, Men and Eunuchs: Gender in Byzantium* (New York: Routledge, 1997); Shaun Tougher, ed., *Eunuchs in Antiquity and Beyond* (Swansea: Classical Press of Wales, 2002); Kathryn M. Ringrose, *The Perfect Servant: Eunuchs and the Social Construction of Gender in Byzantium* (Chicago: University of Chicago Press, 2003); Kathryn Ringrose, "Eunuchs in Historical Perspective," *History Compass* 5, no. 2 (2007): 495–506; and Myrto

Hatzaki, *Beauty and the Male Body in Byzantium* (New York: Palgrave Macmillan, 2009), 86–115.
30. Yosefa Loshitzky and Raya Meyuhas, "'Ecstasy of Difference': Bertolucci's The Last Emperor," *Cinema Journal* 31, no. 2 (1992): 26–44, on 31.
31. Loshitzky and Meyuhas, "'Ecstasy of Difference,'" 34.
32. Stent, "Chinese Eunuchs," 170–171.
33. The only exception might be the passage documented in Chen, *Beiyange de wenming*, 81. However, I have not been able to locate this historical source.
34. Melissa S. Dale, "With the Cut of a Knife: A Social History of Eunuchs during the Qing Dynasty (1644-1911) and Republican Periods (1912-1949)" (PhD Dissertation, Georgetown University, 2000), 37; Liu Guojun (劉國軍) in Zhang Yaoming (張躍銘), *Zhanggong huanguan quanshu: Lidai taijian mishi* (掌宮宦官全書: 歷代太監密史) [The secret histories of eunuchs throughout the dynasties] (Harbin: Heilongjiang renmin chubanshe, 1996), 1690.
35. Wu Chieh Ping and Gu Fang-Liu, "The Prostate in Eunuchs," in *EORTC Genitourinary Group Monograph 10: Eurological Oncology: Reconstructive Surgery, Organ Conservation, and Restoration of Function*, ed. Philip H. Smith and Michele Pavone-Macaluso (New York: Wiley-Liss, 1990), 249–255, on 254.
36. Gary Taylor, *Castration: An Abbreviated History of Western Manhood* (New York: Routledge, 2000), 85–109.
37. J. Lascaratos and A. Kostakopoulus, "Operations on Hermaphrodites and Castration in Byzantine Times (324-1453 AD)," *Urologia internationalis* 58, no. 4 (1997): 232–235.
38. Enid Rhodes Peschel and Richard E. Peschel, "Medical Insights into the Castrati in Opera," *American Scientist* 75 (1987): 581–582.
39. David M. Friedman, *A Mind of Its Own: A Cultural History of the Penis* (New York: Penguin Books, 2001), 4.
40. Dong Guo (東郭), *Taijian shengyai* (太監生涯) [The life of eunuchs] (Yonghe City: Shishi chuban gongsi, 1985), 21.
41. Dong, *Taijian shengyai*, 22 (see also 12).
42. Wu and Gu, "The Prostate in Eunuchs."
43. Wu and Gu, "The Prostate in Eunuchs," 254–255.
44. Taylor, *Castration*, 46–47.
45. Michel Foucault, *The History of Sexuality, vol. 1: An Introduction*, trans. Robert Hurley (New York: Vintage, 1990 [1976]; Jeffrey Weeks, *Sex, Politics and Society: The Regulation of Sexuality since 1800* (London: Longman, 1981); Carroll Smith-Rosenberg, *Disorderly Conduct: Visions of Gender in Victorian America* (New York: Alfred A. Knopf, 1985); John D'Emilio and Estelle B. Freedman, *Intimate Matters: A History of Sexuality in America* (New York: Harper & Row, 1988); Sharon Ullman, *Sex Seen: The Emergence of Modern Sexuality in America* (Berkeley: University of California Press, 1997); Arnold

Davidson, *The Emergence of Sexuality: Historical Epistemology and the Formation of Concepts* (Cambridge: Harvard University Press, 2001).
46. Matthew H. Sommer, *Sex, Law, and Society in Late Imperial China* (Stanford: Stanford University Press, 2000).
47. Sigmund Freud, "The Passing of the Oedipus Complex," *International Journal of Psychoanalysis* 5 (1924): 419–424. For an account of the relevance of female castration to the development of psychoanalysis, see Carla Bonomi, "The Relevance of Castration and Circumcision to the Origins of Psychoanalysis: 1. The Medical Context," *International Journal of Psychoanalysis* 90 (2009): 551–580.
48. See Jacques Lacan, *Écrits: A Selection*, trans. Alan Sheridan (New York: W. W. Norton & Co., 1977).
49. For feminist endorsements of Lacan over Freud, see especially Jane Gallop, *Reading Lacan* (Ithaca: Cornell University Press, 1985), 20–21.
50. Taylor, *Castration*, 91.
51. "Dr. Robert Coltman, Royalty's Friend, Dies; Was Physician to the Former Imperial Family of China, Where He Lived for Forty Years," *New York Times*, November 5, 1931, 23.
52. Robert Coltman, *The Chinese, Their Present and Future: Medical, Political, and Social* (Philadelphia: F. A. Davis, 1891); Robert Coltman, *Beleaguered in Peking: The Boxer's War Against the Foreigner* (Philadelphia: F. A. Davis, 1901).
53. Robert Coltman, "Peking Eunuchs," *China Medical Missionary Journal* 8 (1894): 28–29.
54. Robert Coltman, "Self-Made Eunuchs," *Universal Medical Journal* (November 1893): 328–329.
55. Coltman, "Self-Made Eunuchs," 329.
56. Coltman, "Peking Eunuchs," 28.
57. Coltman, "Peking Eunuchs," 28.
58. Coltman, "Peking Eunuchs," 29.
59. "Obituary: J. J. Matignon," *British Medical Journal* 2, no. 2065 (1900): 268.
60. Jean-Jacques Matignon, "Les eunuchen in Peking," *Arch Clin Bordeaux* 5 (1896): 193–204, reprinted in Jean-Jacques Matignon, *Superstition, crime et misére en Chine: souvenirs de biologie sociale* (Lyon: A. Storck & Cie, 1899).
61. Michel de Certeau, *The Practice of Everyday Life*, trans. Steven Rendall (Berkeley: University of California Press, 1984), xiii.
62. Michael Taussig, *Mimesis and Alterity: A Particular History of the Senses* (New York: Routledge, 1993), 62.
63. Larissa N. Heinrich, "The Pathological Empire: Early Medical Photography in China," *History of Photography* 30, no. 1 (2006): 26–37.
64. Sarah E. Fraser, "Chinese as Subject: Photographic Genres in the Nineteenth Century," in *Brush and Shutter: Early Photography in China*, ed. Jeffrey W. Cody and Frances Terpak (Los Angeles, CA: Getty Research Institute, 2011), 91–109, on 106.

65. Larissa N. Heinrich, *The Afterlife of Images: Translating the Pathological Body between China and the West* (Durham: Duke University Press, 2008), 76.
66. Heinrich, *The Afterlife of Images*, 105.
67. On the evolving politics of "the Sick Man of Asia," apart from Heinrich, *The Afterlife of Images* (2008), see also Yang, *Bingfu, huanghuo yu shuishi* (2010); Keevak, *Becoming Yellow* (2011); and Rojas, *The Sick Man of Asia* (forthcoming).
68. Carol Benedict, *Bubonic Plague in Nineteenth-Century China* (Stanford: Stanford University Press, 1996), 166; François Delaporte, *Disease and Civilization: The Cholera in Paris* (Cambridge, MA: MIT Press, 1986); Larissa N. Heinrich, "How China Became 'the Cradle of Small Pox': Transformations in Discourse, 1726-2002," *positions: east asia cultures critique* 15, no. 1 (2007): 7–34; Angela Leung, *Leprosy in China: A History* (New York: Columbia University Press, 2009).
69. Jacques Derrida, *Specter of Marx: The State of the Debt, the Work of Mourning, and the New International*, trans. Peggy Kamuf (New York: Routledge, 1994).
70. This colonial gaze, strictly speaking, is not identical to the kind of clinical gaze described by Foucault. For Foucault's historicization of the Western medical gaze, see Michel Foucault, *The Birth of the Clinic: An Archaeology of Medical Perception* (New York: Vintage, 1994). For important critiques of Foucault's colonial blind spot, see, for example, Ann Laura Stoler, *Carnal Knowledge and Imperial Power: Race and the Intimate in Colonial Rule* (Berkeley: University of California Press, 2002).
71. Ruth Rogaski, *Hygienic Modernity: Meanings of Health and Disease in Treaty-Port China* (Berkeley: University of California Press), 9.
72. See James Hevia, "Leaving a Brand on China: Missionary Discourse in the Wake of the Boxer Movement," *Modern China* 18, no. 3 (1992): 304–332; James Hevia, "Looting Beijing: 1860, 1900," in *Tokens of Exchange: The Problem of Translation in Global Circulations*, ed. Lydia H. Liu (Durham: Duke University Press, 1999), 192–213; and James Hevia, *English Lessons: The Pedagogy of Imperialism in Nineteenth-Century China* (Durham: Duke University Press, 2003). See also Lydia Liu, *The Clash of Empires: The Invention of China in Modern World Making* (Cambridge: Harvard University Press, 2004).
73. Mitamura Taisuke, *Chinese Eunuchs: The Structure of Intimate Politics*, trans. Charles A. Pomeroy (Rutland, VT: Charles E. Tuttle, 1970), 28-35.
74. K. Chimin Wong and Wu Lien-teh, *History of Chinese Medicine: Being a Chronicle of Medical Happenings in China from Ancient Times to the Present Period*, 2nd ed. (Shanghai: National Quarantine Service, 1936), 232-234.
75. Charles Humana, *The Keeper of the Bed: A Study of the Eunuch* (London: Arlington, 1973), 125–153.
76. Richard Millant, *Les Eunuches à travers les ages* (Paris: Vigot, 1908), 234.

77. Shih-shan Henry Tsai, *The Eunuchs in the Ming Dynasty* (Albany, NY: State University of New York Press, 1995).
78. Nancy Rose Hunt, *A Colonial Lexicon: Of Birth Ritual, Medicalization, and Mobility in the Congo* (Durham: Duke University Press, 1999), 32.
79. See, for example, Benjamin Elman, *On Their Own Terms: Science in China, 1550-1900* (Cambridge: Harvard University Press, 2005), Chaps. 8 and 11; Benjamin Elman, *A Cultural History of Science in Modern China* (Cambridge: Harvard University Press, 2006), Chap. 4; Heinrich, *The Afterlife of Images*; Yi-Li Wu, *Reproducing Women: Medicine, Metaphor, and Childbirth in Late Imperial China* (Berkeley: University of California Press, 2010); and Chiang, "Why Sex Mattered," Chap. 2.
80. Jennifer W. Jay, "Another Side of Chinese Eunuch History: Castration, Adoption, Marriage, and Burial," *Canadian Journal of History* 28, no. 3 (1993): 459–478, on 466.
81. By a greater degree of opportunity and power, I am referring to explicit/legal opportunities and power. One could argue that it was still possible for *gongnü* to exercise some kind of de facto political power implicitly, such as based on their ties to powerful female figures inside the palace. On the role of eunuchs in the Qing court, see Evelyn Rawski, *The Last Emperors: A Social History of Qing Imperial Institutions* (Berkeley: University of California Press, 2001), 162–166.
82. Yu Minzhong (于敏中), ed., *Guochao gongshi* (國朝宮史) [A history of the palace during the Qing period], 5 vols. (Taipei: Taiwan xuesheng shuju, 1965); Qing Gui (慶桂) et al., ed., *Guochao gongshi xubian* (國朝宮史續) [A supplemental history of the palace of the reigning dynasty], reprint ed. (Beijing: Beijing guji chubanshe, 1994).
83. See, for example, Shi, *Zhongguo huangguan mishi: renzao de disanxing*, 8–12; Zou Lü鄒律, *Lidai mingtaijian miwen* (歷代名太監祕聞) [The secrets of famous eunuchs] (Tianjin: Tianjin renming chubanshe, 1988), 306; Gu Rong (顧蓉) and Ge Jinfang (葛金芳), *Wuheng weiqiang—gudai huangguan qunti de wenhua kaocha* (霧橫帷牆—古代宦官群體的文化考察) [A study of the culture of ancient eunuchs] (Shanxi: Shanxi renmin jiaoyu chubanshe, 1992), 316–354; Tang Yinian (唐益年), *Qing gong taidian* (清宮太監) [Qing palace eunuchs] (Shenyang: Liaoning University Press, 1993), 5; Yan Dongmei (閻東梅) and Dong Cunfa (董存發), *Ren zhong yao—wan Qing quanjian zhi mi* (人中妖—晚清權監之謎) [Monsters among humans: The riddle of late-Qing powerful eunuchs] (Beijing: China Renmin University Press, 1995), 3–6; Wang, *Shenmi de disanxing*, i; Zhang, *Zhanggong huangguan quanshu*, 6; Xiao Yanqing (肖燕清) in Zhang, *Zhanggong huangguan quanshu*, 1901. See also the negative depiction of eunuchs in Han Suolin (韓索林), *Huangguan shanquan gailan* (宦官擅權概覽) [An overview of the power of eunuchs] (Shenyang: Liaoning University Press, 1991 [1967]); Du Wanyan (杜婉言), *Zhongguo huanguanshi* (中國宦官史) [History of Chinese eunuchs] (Taipei: Wenjin

chubanshe, 1996); Zhang Yunfeng (張雲風), *Zhongguo huanguan shilui* (中國宦官事略) [Matters regarding Chinese eunuchs] (Taipei: Dadi, 2004); Wang Shounan (王壽南), *Tangdai de huanguan* (唐代的宦官) [Tang-dynasty eunuchs] (Taipei: Commercial Press, 2004); Shiniankanchai (十年砍柴), *Huangdi, wenchen he taijian: Mingchao zhengju de "sanjiaolian"* (皇帝,文臣和太監: 明朝政局的"三角戀") [The emperor, scholar officials, and eunuchs: The triangular relationship of the political situation in the Ming dynasty] (Nanning: Guangxi Normal University Press, 2007); Wang Jingzhong (汪靖中), *Wugen zhi gen: Zhongguo huanguan shihua* (無根之根: 中國宦官史話) [The roots of the rootless: History of Chinese eunuchs] (Beijing: Dongfang chubanshe, 2009).

84. Taylor, *Castration*, 38.
85. Wang, *Shenmi de disanxing*, 60–94, 115–155; Tsai, *The Eunuchs in the Ming Dynasty*; David Robinson, *Bandits, Eunuchs, and the Son of Heaven: Rebellion and the Economy of Violence in Mid-Ming China* (Honolulu: University of Hawai'i Press, 2001); Wang Sho, *Tangdai de huanguan*; Zhang Chengxiang (張承祥), "Wan Ming huanguan Feng Bao zhi yanjiu" (晚明宦官馮保之研究) [Research on the late Ming eunuch Feng Bao] (MA thesis, National Central University, 2006); Shiniankanchai, *Huangdi, wenchen he taijian*.
86. Historians today continue to have a difficult time in resisting the appeal of the trope of "emasculation," despite their critical positioning of their analyses of Chinese eunuchs. See, for example, Melissa Dale, "Understanding Emasculation: Western Medical Perspectives on Chinese Eunuchs," *Social History of Medicine* 23, no. 1 (2010): 38–55; Christine Doran, "Chinese Palace Eunuchs: Shadows of the Emperor," *Nebula: A Journal of Multidisciplinary Scholarship* 7, no. 3 (September 2010): 11–26.
87. Don J. Cohn, *Vignettes from the Chinese: Lithographs from Shanghai in the Late Nineteenth Century* (Hong Kong: Chinese University of Hong Kong Press, 1987), 36–37.
88. See Cohn, *Vignettes*; Wu Yoru (吳有如) et al., ed., *Qingmuo fushihui: Dianshizhai huabao jingxuanji* (清末浮世繪:《點石齋畫報》精選集) [Late Qing Lithographs: Best Collections of *Diunshizhai huabao*] (Taipei: Yuanliu, 2008).
89. Benjamin Hobson, *A New Treatise on Anatomy* (1851), section on 外腎 (*waishen*, "outer kidney"). See Howard Chiang, "Why Sex Mattered: Science and Visions of Transformation in Modern China" (PhD dissertation, Princeton University, 2012), Chap. 2.
90. Stent, "Chinese Eunuchs," 170–171.
91. Stent, "Chinese Eunuchs," 171, 181.
92. Coltman, "Self-Made Eunuchs"; Coltman, "Peking Eunuchs."
93. Ma Deqing et al., in *Wan Qing gongting shenghuo jianwen*, 224.
94. Ma Deqing et al., in *Wan Qing gongting shenghuo jianwen*, 225.

95. Gabrielle M. Spiegel, "The Task of the Historian," *American Historical Review* 114, no. 1 (2009): 1–15, on 15.
96. Mei Xianmao (梅顯懋), *Luori wanzhong: Qingdai taijian zhidu* (落日晚鍾: 清代太監制度) [The system of Qing-dynasty eunuchs] (Shenyang: Liaohai chubanshe, 1997), 139.
97. Dale, "With the Cut of a Knife," 27.
98. On Zhang: Zou, *Lidai mingtaijian miwen*, 292–303, on 294 (account through taiyi); Yang Zhengguang (楊爭光), *Zhongguo zuihou yige taijian* (中國最後一個太監) [The last eunuch in China] (Beijing: Qunzhong chubanshe, 1991), 6–22, on 14; Yan and Dong, *Ren zhong yao* 107–133, on 108; Xiao Yanqing (肖燕清) in Zhang, *Zhanggong huanguan quanshu*, 1903–1907. On Ma: Ma Deqing et al., in *Wan Qing gongting shenghuo jianwen*. On Sun: Jia Yinghua (賈英華), *Modai taijian miwen: Sun Yaoting zhuan* (末代太監秘聞: 孫耀庭傳) [The secret life of the last eunuch: A biography of Sun Yaoting] (Beijing: Zhishi chubanshe, 1993); Ling Haicheng (凌海成), *Zhongguo zuihou yige taijian* (中國最後一個太監) [The last eunuch in China] (Hong Kong: Heping tushu, 2003), 17–21.
99. Ma Deqing et al., in *Wan Qing gongting shenghuo jianwen*, 222–223.
100. Coltman, "Peking Eunuchs," 28.
101. Coltman, "Peking Eunuchs," 28 (emphasis mine).
102. Coltman, "Peking Eunuchs," 28.
103. Coltman, "Peking Eunuchs," 29.
104. Coltman, "Self-Made Eunuchs," 329.
105. Coltman, "Self-Made Eunuchs," 328–329.
106. Coltman, "Peking Eunuchs," 29 (emphasis mine).
107. See also Pujie's recollection in Pujia (溥佳) and Pujie (溥傑), *Wan Qing gongting shenghuo jianwen* (晚清宮廷生活見聞) [Life in Late-Qing Imperial Palace] (Taipei: Juzhen shuwu, 1984), 304–306. This statement requires further qualification. In the context of this chapter, "castration" is used in this sentence as a synonym for "eunuchism" as it relates to the Chinese imperium polity. There is a growing trend within the contemporary transgender community in the West to advocate/normalize castration ideation (e.g., "male-to-eunuch" instead of "male-to-female"). I thank Susan Stryker for pointing this out to me. See Richard J. Wassersug and Thomas W. Johnson, "Modern-Day Eunuchs: Motivations for and Consequences of Contemporary Castration," *Perspectives in Biology and Medicine* 50, no. 4 (2007): 544–556; Thomas W. Johnson, Michelle A. Brett, Lesley F. Roberts, and Richard J. Wassersug, "Eunuchs in Contemporary Society: Characterizing Men Who Are Voluntarily Castrated," *Journal of Sexual Medicine* 4 (2007): 940–945; Michelle A. Brett, Lesley F. Roberts, Thomas W. Johnson, and Richard J. Wassersug, "Eunuchs in Contemporary Society:

Expectations, Consequences and Adjustments to Castration," *Journal of Sexual Medicine* 4 (2007): 946–955; Lesley F. Roberts, Michelle A. Brett, Thomas W. Johnson, and Richard J. Wassersug, "A Passion for Castration: Characterizing Men Who Are Fascinated with Castration," *Journal of Sexual Medicine* 5 (2008): 1669–1680.

108. Puyi, *Wo de qianbansheng*, 148; Pujia and Pujie, *Wan Qing gongting shenghuo jianwen*, 22.
109. Puyi, *Wo de qianbansheng*, 147.
110. Puyi, *Wo de qianbansheng*, 148.
111. Pujia and Pujie, *Wan Qing gongting shenghuo jianwen*, 28.
112. Pujia and Pujie, *Wan Qing gongting shenghuo jianwen*, 31–32.
113. Pujia and Pujie, *Wan Qing gongting shenghuo jianwen*, 32.
114. For Reginald Johnston's own account of his interaction with Puyi during this period, see Reginald Fleming Johnston, *Twilight in the Forbidden City*, 4th ed. (Vancouver: Soul Care Publishing, 2008 [1934]).
115. Puyi, *Wo de qianbansheng*.
116. Yuan Qu (遠樞), *Diyici huanguan shidai* (第一次宦官時代) [The first era of eunuchs] (Taipei: Yuanliu, 1999).
117. Here I am drawing on the notion of historicizing experience discussed in Scott, "The Evidence of Experience."
118. Scott, "The Evidence of Experience," 777.
119. Arondekar, "Without a Trace," 26.
120. Ko, *Cinderella's Sisters*, 68.
121. On the history of the first Chinese transsexual, see Howard Chiang, "Sinophone Production and Trans Postcoloniality: Sex Change from Major to Minor Transnational China," *English Language Notes* 49, no. 1 (2011): 109–116; Chiang, "Why Sex Mattered," epilogue.

CHAPTER 3

Gendered Androgyny: Transcendent Ideals and Profane Realities in Buddhism, Classicism, and Daoism

*Daniel Burton-Rose**

In his seminal *Imagining Transgender: An Ethnography of a Category,* David Valentine observes that "in both scholarly and activist work the use of transgender as a category of analysis and action restricts the possibilities of explaining gender variance as much as it enables it."[1] During his fieldwork in New York City in the late 1990s, Valentine writes repeatedly of encountering people designated as transgender by social workers and academics who reject the relevance of the label to their persons or, particularly among people of color sex workers, had never even heard the word.[2] If this is the case in one of the world's great metropolises of gender-bending and queer activism, years after the term transgender had entered common circulation, how much more problematic is the retroactive deployment of this term across a broad range of cultures and locales?

I accept that placing oneself on a continuum of others who have faced similar difficulties and celebrated similar triumphs is a powerful means of asserting one's presence. This move has already been initiated in the transgender rights social movement by Leslie Feinberg in *Transgender Warriors* (1996). Yet such claiming of individuals for categories they could not have recognized flattens the range of human experience and elides the diversity of the concepts of sex, gender, and sexuality.

In this chapter, I survey motifs relating to strains within gender regimes that butted against or destabilized a strict male-female dichotomy over a period of nearly 25 hundred years. I attempt not to pin current conceptions of transgender identities upon temporally and geographically remote Others, but to explore cases in which the physical form or sexual orientation of people was perceived as presenting a threat to a gendered social order. I investigate concrete references to biological intersexuality as well as gender identities not necessarily paralleled in the physical body that did not conform to the dominant categories—that is, which were considered "neither male nor female." By use of the term "gendered androgyny" in the title, I indicate a particular interest in unpacking the sex roles upon which ostensibly gender-neutral ideals are predicated and which they often compound rather than transcend. By examining metaphors that could have been realized as a philosophical and spiritual idealization of gender integration or have remained latent and untapped in "the well-supplied warehouses of official ritual"[3]—i.e., gender-ambiguous imagery in the classical canon that could have been deployed by later adherents of this tradition, but which was not.

I attempt to be sensitive to categories of gender as they would have been relevant to the people who experienced them. Accordingly, I do not employ the term transgender in regard to any period before which it was coined, instead using a range of concepts such as sex change and androgyny that leave more room for the diversity of the practices under scrutiny. I focus on concepts related to gender, sex change, and claims of transcendence of sex and gender in the three classical canonical traditions of China: Buddhist, Classicist ("Confucian"), and Daoist, as well as in Inner Alchemy (*neidan* 內丹), a dynamic hybrid of all three. I cover material dating from the first millennia BC to the Ming and Qing dynasties (1368–1911), introducing some of the most prominent motifs of sex change and androgyny in Chinese culture while aspiring to chronological clarity.[4] With this spatial and temporal range, a detailed examination of each case in its own cultural milieu is not possible. Rather, for the purposes of this volume I have deemed it most important to identify a wide range of examples to invite further consideration of what light a transgender studies lens might or might not be able to shed on them in the future.

In reviewing one of the first English-language studies of homosexuality in Chinese history Charlotte Furth, the eminent social historian of gender and medicine in late imperial China, warned: "Compensatory history is scholarship in a hurry."[5] By pointing out the grim social realities that often underlaid female devotees' desire for sex change or male meditators' ostensible honoring of the feminine principle, I have attempted here not compensatory history but an inoculation against superficial attempts to locate an indigenous transgender discourse in Chinese culture. This is not a gesture of hostility toward contemporary activists thirsty for historical examples from which to draw strength, but rather an attempt to enhance the potency of transgender and allied social movements by providing a means to vaccinate against monodimensionalism, thus hopefully circumventing the cyclical crises of infatuation and disillusionment that result from uncritical romanticization of diverse peoples and cultures. Indeed, by attempting to illumine the social conditions in which gender transgressive imagery flourished, I seek to show both the difficulty and the power of an "utopistic" dream of gender fluidity within societies whose hierarchies necessitate gender oppression destructive to all involved. Such issues remain vital to the transgender movement, particularly regarding its uneasy relations with feminism.[6]

"Non-Males" and "Non-Females" in the Early Buddhist Community

A social category in the early Buddhist community disruptive to sexual dimorphism and the male-female gender dichotomy was that of *paṇḍaka*. Leonard Zwilling writes that the word itself is "of obscure origin but that ultimately may be derived from *apa* + *aṇḍa* + *ka*, 'without testicles.'" He continues: "*Paṇḍaka* and its synonyms are to be interpreted metaphorically as we do in English when it is said of a weak or pusillanimous person that he (or even she) 'has no balls.'"[7] A disinclination to act according to prescribed gender norms prompted a metaphorical desexing of the offender's body.

Paṇḍaka was a clearly delineated category subdivided into five types corresponding to Brahmanical medical and legal treaties. The categories "share[d] the common quality of... 'lacking maleness.'" Zwilling elaborates: "Even as early as the period of the *Atharva Veda*, *paṇḍakas* were viewed as a distinct group, different from ordinary males and females, and apparently transvestite. The *Vinaya*, in fact, goes so far as to distinguish sexual activity between normative males from sexual relations between a socially normative male and a *paṇḍaka*."[8] Bernard Faure adds: "both hermaphroditism—a kind of hypersexuality—and impotence—a 'hyposexuality'—were seen as characteristic of the *paṇḍaka*, and as such, were threatening and/or despised."[9]

Early Buddhist monastic codes (vinaya) explicitly excluded those judged to be sexually deviant, including the androgynous, asexual, and those with an aversion to the opposite sex.[10] The logic was that cenobites "must be capable of performing sexually while controlling their desire to do so."[11] The "control" clause is at least as significant as that of "capable." The early accounts of third-sex people in the monastic community often portray them as possessing destabilizing sexual appetites. For example, the *Mahāsāṅghika Vinaya* tells of a monk caught fondling another monk after lights out. When brought before the Buddha, Śākyamuni asks him who he is. Faure relates:

> The monk responds, "I am a princess." Then the Buddha asks him/her what kind of woman he/she is. The monks [*sic*] says, "I go both ways. I am neither man nor woman," and then explains that he/she became a monk because he/she heard that monks needed wives and he/she wanted to help out. This is followed by a long passage about how unmanly men should not be allowed into the saṅgha.[12]

The five types of paṇḍaka were translated into Chinese as the "Five Types of Non-males" (*Wu zhong bu nan* 五種不男 or *Wu bu nan* 五不男). The relevant entries from the Digital Dictionary of Buddhism read:

> (1) 扇搋 *saṇḍha* (*saṇḍha paṇḍaka*); by birth impotent. (2) 留拏 *rugṇa* or *ruṇḍa paṇḍaka*; "maimed," i.e. emasculated males. Also written 犍黃門. (3) 砂梨沙掌拏 *īrṣyā* (*īrṣyā paṇḍaka*); those whose sexual desires are only aroused by jealousy. (4) 半擇迦 *paṇḍaka* are eunuchs[13] in general, but in this category are described as hermaphrodites. (5) 博叉 *pakṣa* (*pakṣa paṇḍaka*); impotent during one-half of the month.[14]

This schema prompted a parallel categorization for women, the "Five Types of Non-females" (*Wu zhong bu nü* 五種不女 or *Wu bu nü* 五不女). These are: the conch (*luo* 螺), the striped (*jin* 筋), the drum (*gu* 鼓), horned (*jiao* 角), and the pulse (*mai* 脉). This typology had wide-ranging influence on Chinese culture, where it reached beyond the ken of Buddhism into canonical medicine, with Li Shizhen 李時珍 (1518–1593) using the exact same terminology in his *Systematic Materia Medica* (*Bencao gangmu* 本草剛目) published in 1596.[15] The persistence of this classificatory system over a millennia and a half and across the Central Asian Himalayan divide demonstrates the continued presence of people who did not fit in to a strict sexual dichotomy. Simultaneously, it illustrates the need professionals—from cenobite lawmakers to classically trained physicians—felt to classify and thereby contain them. As in the early Buddhist community, there was a place in late imperial China for those who were neither male nor female, but it was in a discretely circumscribed box.

Conversations with Māra

Despite their importance as monastics and patrons, female Buddhists have continually been subjected to gender discrimination from the earliest days of the community. Debates over the possibility of attaining enlightenment in female form have caused sex change—instantaneously or over the course of reincarnations—to be a central issue in the lives and practices of female devotees throughout the history of Buddhism.

One of the earliest textual records of a challenge to the terms of this debate occurs in the "Suttas of the Sisters" chapter of the *Saṃyutta Nikaāya*.[16] As Alan Sponberg explains the incident: "One day Māra, the Buddhist personification of doubt and temptation," appeared to Somā, the daughter of the chaplin of Bimbisāra and one of the most famous disciples of Śākyamuni,

> as she was resting under a tree, taunting her with the conventional belief of women's limited intelligence and spiritual capacity... Recognizing the trap, Somā banishes Māra with a confident affirmation of the strength of her meditative concentration and wisdom.[17]

The "banishment" is prompted by Somā's retort:

> To one for whom the question doth arise:
> Am I a woman, or
> Am I a man, or what not am I then?
> To such a one is Māra fit to talk.[18]

Here the Buddhist path to enlightenment is open to women on the condition that they do not speak of gender as such: not of their femininity nor of a third category to which women would belong if they were no longer classified as women. We thus have one of the historical Buddha's original disciples wrestling with the radical inclusiveness of the founder's vision by asserting a refusal *not* to wrestle with it.

Pure Lands: Boys' Clubs or Open Admission?

Chinese Pure Land (*jingtu* 淨土) practices required that women be reborn as men to gain access to a range of celestial paradises.[19] This exclusivity was a Chinese innovation: in the Indian paradises devoted to Akṣobhya, there is no prohibition on females. Rather, "men and women are born in the normal manner, but without any impurity or suffering on the mother's part," while this birth itself "does not result from ordinary sexual intercourse."[20] The question I would like to examine is to what extent the androcentric prejudices of Pure Land Buddhism encouraged fantasies of sex change in female devotees.[21]

By the advent of Kumārajīva's 鳩摩羅什 AD 406 translation of the *Scripture of the Lotus Blossom of the Fine Dharma*, more commonly known in English as the *Lotus Sutra* (*Miaofa lianhua jing* 妙法蓮華經; Sanskrit *Saddharmapuṇḍarīka-sūtra* T. 262.9.1c–62b),[22] there is a clear prohibition on female attainment as such. In this most popular of Buddhist scriptures in China (and Korea and Japan), while holding court, Buddha retains the bodhisattva Prajñākūta so that he might meet the deity Mañjuśrī, who was then returning from a successful conversion mission in the depths of the sea. Prajñākūta asks Mañjuśrī if, by means of the *Scripture of the Blossom of the Fine Dharma*—the same text of which this episode forms a part—any had been able to achieve Buddhahood. Mañjuśrī replies that indeed there is such a one, "the daughter of the dragon King Sāgara, whose years are barely eight."[23]

The bodhisattva Prajñākūta is skeptical:

> I have seen the Thus Come One of the Śākyas throughout incalculable kalpas tormenting himself by doing what is hard to do, piling up merit and heaping up excellence, seeking the Path of the bodhisattva and never resting. When I look at the thousand-millionfold world, there is no place, not even the size of a mustardseed, where the bodhisattva did not cast away body and life for the beings' sakes, and only then did he achieve the Way of bodhi. I do not believe that this girl in the space of a moment directly and immediately achieved right, enlightened intuition.[24]

The *nāga* princess (*long nü* 龍女; Sanskrit *nāgakanyā*) materializes before the bodhisattva, performs obeisance, stands off to the side, praises the Buddha and states her intention to aid suffering beings as well. Buddha's divinized disciple Śāriputra then steps in.[25]

> You say that in no long time you shall attain the unexcelled Way. This is hard to believe. What is the reason? A woman's body is filthy, it is not a Dharma-receptacle. How can you attain unexcelled bodhi? The Path of the Buddha is remote and cavernous. Throughout incalculable kalpas, by tormenting oneself and accumulating good conduct, also by thoroughly cultivating the perfections, only by these means can one then be successful. Also, a woman's body even then has five obstacles. It cannot become first a Brahmā god king, second the god Śakra, third King Māra, fourth a sage king turning the Wheel, fifth a Buddha-body. How can the body of a woman speedily achieve Buddhahood?[26]

In reply the nāga princess offers up a precious gem to the Buddha, who promptly accepts it.²⁷ "With your supernatural power you shall see me achieve Buddhahood even more quickly than that!" the princess declares. "At that time," the narration continues:

> The assembled multitude all saw that dragon girl in the space of an instant turn into a man, perfect bodhisattva-conduct, straightaway go southward to the world-sphere Spotless, sit on a jeweled lotus blossom, and achieve undifferentiating, right, enlightened intuition, with thirty-two marks and eighty beautiful features setting forth the Fine Dharma for all living beings in all ten directions.²⁸

The passage concludes: "The bodhisattva Wisdom Accumulation [Prajñākūta], as well as Śāriputra and all the assembled multitude, silently believed and accepted."²⁹

Burton Watson cites this passage as proof that the "revolutionary doctrines" of this scripture "operate in a realm transcending all petty distinctions of sex or species, instant or eon."³⁰ Yet as for "petty distinctions of sex," our impression is just the opposite: the bodhisattva Prajñākūta and Śāriputra discriminate against the nāga princess on the basis of her sex (if not her species!), but does giving up that sex to prove her achievements undermine or confirm discrimination? Rather, is not her action an acknowledgment that a female body is indeed too filthy to serve as a vessel for the attainment of Buddhahood? She must cast it off to join the cosmic boy's club; for centuries afterwards female devotees sought to model their transcendent ambitions on hers.

The tale of the nāga princess provided support for women who bucked the gender ideologies of imperial China. Wu Zetian 武則天 (624–705), founded her own dynasty, the Zhou 周 (690–705), reigning as the "August Thearch" (*huangdi* 皇帝), a term only applied to men before and since. Wu drew upon the dragon princess's refutation of the assertion that a woman could not become a Buddha or a king, lavishly funding a mural of this key scene in Dunhuang cave 331.³¹ She also quite literally became a Buddha by claiming for a three-and-a-half-month period from 694–695 that she herself was Maitreya.³² Yet Wu did not so much abandon her female existence to assume the air of a man to rule, as she challenged the male prerogative of rulership. She thereby thwarted the precedent in which a woman could rule as dowager through a male relative but never openly herself. The gender transgressive imagery available in Buddhism served as a weapon in her arsenal.

From at least the seventh century on there was a consistent strain within Chinese Buddhism, particularly Chan, that asserted "gender differences make no difference to attaining enlightenment."³³ Its adherents regularly drew upon the nāga princess episode and that of the abbotess of Moshan 末山, Liaoran 了然. The latter, in dialogue with a male student, described herself as having "neither male nor female marks (*xiang* 相)." The student retorted: "Why doesn't she transform herself?" to which the abbotess replied, "She is not a spirit, nor a ghost. What would you have her become?" and thereby provoked his enlightenment.³⁴

The *Lotus Sutra* in which the dragon princess tale emerged was also the impetus for the popularization of the bodhisattva Avalokiteśvara in China and his transformation into the Goddess Guanyin, the so-called Goddess of compassion who is one of the most widely worshipped deities in China from medieval times to the present. Indeed, though the two bear no connection in the scripture, the Dragon Princess begins appearing as one of Guanyin's attendants beginning in the twelfth century.³⁵

Despite Guanyin's celebrated sex change from the Tang dynasty (618–907) on, there is clearly no instance in which she is worshiped for this power. Rather, in one of her most popular manifestations, that of the White-robed Guanyin, as Yü Chün-fang puts it, she is "a fertility goddess who nevertheless is deprived of sexuality."³⁶ Though Guanyin includes promises of sexual access to men within the domain of her *upāya*istic practices (i.e., means of conversion appropriate to the object of attempted conversion), she rarely delivers consummation, and unlike in Japan—as with, for example, the monk Shinran (1173–1263)—she is not first known to those she converts in this manner as a male deity.³⁷

Androgynous Ideals in Tibetan Buddhism

Sponberg provides a helpful framework in which to analyze the tension between transcending and reifying gender boundaries in Buddhism. He categorizes attitudes toward women and the feminine in the first millennium or so of Buddhism into "soteriological inclusiveness," "institutional androcentrism," "ascetic misogyny," and "soteriological androgyny."³⁸ The first he understands as closest to the praxis of the early Buddhist community. It is the view "that one's sex, like one's caste or class (*varṇa*), presents no barrier to attaining the Buddhist goal of liberation from suffering."³⁹

Institutional androcentrism, in contrast, appears in the *vinaya* particularly. It betrays an anxiety not with the potential of women as spiritual practitioners but with the accommodation of the nascent cenobitic community to a society that demanded that women be placed under male control.[40] Ascetic misogyny—in this schema—is more "defensively hostile in tone,"[41] reflecting the characterization of women into the quintessential obstacle for the presumptively male renunciant.

Soteriological androgyny "formulated the goal of Buddhist practice psychologically as a dynamic state of non-dualistic androgynous integration."[42] Sponberg concedes that this perspective "did not become fully articulated, in the written literature at least, until sometime after the sixth or seventh century CE," thus "significantly post-dating" the other perspectives enumerated. The texts and practice traditions in which it does find expression, moreover, "are not part of the core tradition shared by all forms of Buddhism."[43]

> The innovation of this attitude lies in its dramatic revalorization of the feminine—its reassessment of the soteriological relevance not just of the feminine, in fact, but of socially defined gender characterizations in general, a reevaluation of all those qualities and expectations culturally ascribed to male and female... Rather than simply seeing sexual and gender differences as irrelevant and ultimately insignificant, this fourth attitude takes a more actively positive stance... Differences are acknowledged as provisional, as not ultimately real, and they are further affirmed as potentially powerful means of soteric transformation.

Sponberg continues:

> The underlying assumption expressed in this view is that all beings, to differing degrees, consciously or unconsciously, manifest the full range of characteristics conventionally identified as gender specific. Certain psychological characteristics are conventionally distinguished as feminine or masculine, but the emphasis is on the soteriological potential of those differences rather than on the social limitations they often reflect. Femininity and masculinity are seen as dialectically interactive modes of all human existence—mutually complementary and equally essential to the ideal state, a state of androgynous integration.[44]

This attitude, first seen in clear relief in Indo-Tibetan Vajrayāna beginning in the seventh century, redefines essentialist gender categories as it reifies gender essentialism.[45]

In the Vajrayāna school, the female and male-identified qualities of insight and skillful means (*upāya*) or compassion (*prajña*) respectively were deified then caused to copulate with "sexual union representing the androgynous ideal."[46] Sponberg warns:

> We should be careful not to overidealize what we find here. The potential for a truly androgynous soteriology based on an attitude of equivalence undoubtedly is great in light of this development; but we should ask how much of that potential in fact as been realized in practice. Who, we might well wonder, has really benefitted the most from this revolution in Buddhist soteriology? In theory the shift to an androgynous ideal should have undermined the repression of female spiritual practice sanctioned by the androcentrism and misogyny of the monastic establishment.[47]

Put differently, what is liberating to women or transgendered people in a schema designed for men struggling with conflicts arising from institutionalized sexual repression? My answer is, without deliberate redeployment, nothing.

Harbringers of Imperial Disaster

What of China before Buddhism first arrived in the Latter Han dynasty (25–220 CE)? The *Shijing* 詩經, the collection of folk ballads dating roughly from the eleventh to the seventh centuries BC,[48] which Classicists claimed as their exclusive domain in the early imperial period, contains one line that suggests integrating dichotomous gender characteristics in one person. A variation on a refrain in the poem "Jiong zhuo" 泂酌 (*Mao* #251) declares: "The triumphant and concordant lordling is/Father and mother of the people." 愷悌君子, 民之父母. This inspired some degree of commentary, with Jia Yi 賈誼 (200–169 BC) elaborating on the traits of the ideal ruler: "He causes the people to have the reverence of a father and to have the intimacy of a mother [toward him]. When he is like this, then he can be father and mother of the people. If not the pinnacle of virtue, who can be like this?"[49]

This line is most intriguing as a remnant of a path not taken. Although we get lactating paragons of filial piety and fraternal duty (figure 3.1)[50] as well as cross-dressing scholar romances[51] in the late imperial period, for most of its existence the Classicist tradition plays gender cop more than gender outlaw. Yet, we should be wary of uncritically accepting Classicists's own self-presentation and note that

Figure 3.1 Lactating paragon of fraternal duty from Liang Yannian 梁延年, ed., *Shengyu xiang jie* 聖諭像解 (The Sacred Edict, Illustrated and Explained), 1681. Reproduced courtesy of Princeton University's Gest East Asian Library.

"vocational"[52] Classicists had private devotional practices (including Buddhism and Inner Alchemy) that could nurture aspects of their psyches left thirsty by orthodox ritual.

For early medieval Classicists, gender disruptions were classifiable under cosmological portents. Although slighted by official histories, official historians still saw it as their duty to record these events as materially relevant to the condition of the empire. Robert Ford Campany, drawing on the theorist of religious studies Jonathan Z. Smith, characterizes the efforts of these "historians of the strange" (as Pu Songling 蒲松齡 [1640–1715] would describe himself over a millennia later than Campany's primary subjects), as "locative" rather than "utopian." These terms are defined as: "a joyous celebration of the primordial act of ordering as well as a deep sense of responsibility for the maintenance of that order through repetition of the [cosmogonic] myth, through ritual, through norms of conduct, or through taxonomy" versus a schema in which "liminality becomes the supreme goal rather than a moment in a rite of passage."[53]

Gan Bao 干寶 (d. 336), court historian of the Eastern Jin dynasty (AD 317–420), is an exemplar of this profile and the author of the earliest surviving collection of anomaly accounts (*zhiguai* 志怪) in anything like its original form.[54] Although at the time Gan Bao composed *Soushenji* 搜神記 Buddhism had already been in China for well over a century, the text shows remarkably little influence from the most important social developments in contemporary Yangzi Delta: the introduction of Buddhism and Celestial Master Daoism.[55] The entries in *Soushenji* are attentive to sex changes and gender boundary disruption with, by my count, 17 of the 464 entries in the standard reconstituted edition addressing such transgressions. Classified like Borges's apocryphal Chinese encyclopedia, the categories suggested to me by the text are:

> Cosmongonic Myths: 340
> Clothing:[56] 154 (men and women embracing one another's dress, causing disorder in the empire); 180; 187 (loss of gender differentiation evinced in sandal style); 188 (entire country imitates hairstyle of palace women's quarters, bringing disaster to the empire); 193; 214
>> Intersex: 195
>> Male pregnancy: 349
>> Sex change: 115, 130*[57] (in birds); 145; 158* (in birds); 196; 300
> Zoological (including insects and birds): 130* (birds); 158* (birds); 182, 333 (insects)

The tales from Gan Bao's work most relevant to sex change in humans are as follows:

> A Male Becomes a Female (145)
> During the Jianping reign period of Aidi [of the Western Han, 6-2 CE], a man transformed into a woman in Yuzhang. She married and bore one child. Chen Feng of Chang'an said: "For the *yang* to change into *yin* will bring about destruction, the end of the lineage: it is an omen of mutual self-destruction." One explanation said: "The person who became a wife and bore a child will skip one generation, then [posterity]

will be cut off." For this reason, when Aidi died, Pingdi was destroyed [after succeeding him], and then Wang Mang usurped the throne.[58]

哀帝建平中,豫章有男子化為女子,嫁為人婦,生一子。長安陳鳳曰:「陽變為陰,將亡;繼嗣,自相生之象」。一曰:「嫁為人婦,生一子者,將復一世,乃絕。」故後哀帝崩,平帝沒,而王莽篡焉。

One Person, Two Reproductive Organs (195)

During the year of Emperor Hui [of Qin], in the capital of Luo[yang] there was a person with both male and female organs, both of which were functional. Furthermore this person was by nature enthusiastically lascivious.

The empire suffered from military disorder [i.e., insurrections] because of the disordering of male and female influences (*qi*), and monstrous physical forms were made.[59]

惠帝之世,京、洛有人,一身而男女二體,亦能兩用人道,而性尤好淫。天下兵亂,由男女氣亂,而妖形作也。

A Girl of Anfeng Becomes Male (196)

During [Qin] Huidi's Yuankang reign period, there was a female child in Anfeng named Zhou Shining who, having attained the age of eight, gradually transformed into a male. Having reached the age of seventeen or eighteen, her male influences (*qi*) were complete, yet the transformation of her female form had not been fulfilled, nor had the male form disappeared. [This person] took a wife, but did not conceive children.[60]

惠帝元康中,安豐有女子,曰周世寧,年八歲,漸化為男。至十七八,而氣性成。女體化而不盡,男體成而不徹,留妻而無子。

Throughout his work, Gan Bao's narrative voice is strongly moralizing. Entry 300, which is concerned with defining the proper form of *qi* circulation in the cosmos and evidence of its disruption, contains the clearest statement of the author's principles:

> The movement of things in response to change follows constant ways, and it is only when things take a wrong direction that injurious anomalies appear. Thus, when the lower body grows where the upper should, or the upper grows in place of the lower—these are contrary energies. If a human begets a beast or a beast begets a human—this is *qi* in chaos. When a man becomes a woman or a woman becomes a man, it is *qi* transposition.[61]

The text continues:

> Males and females do not each possess the androgynous ability to transform and engender the way primal energy can; nostrils are not fit places for gestation. Things consecrated to the Dao should not be used by lesser beings.[62]

Any disruption of clear gender boundaries—be it as minor as a change in sandal style or as significant as a sex change resulting in children—was considered troubling and potentially disastrous. As with the classifiers of "non-males and non-females" in the early Buddhist community, Classicists were clearly distressed whenever fashion or biology failed to conform to their idealized celestially sanctioned order.

Church Daoism

Conceived of as an idealized anti-Confucianism that flourished on the margins of orthodox society, an amorphous Daoism has often been treated by scholars and popular writers alike as too laid back to trouble itself with gendered repression. The historical reality is, not surprisingly, less clear-cut. In terms of gender ideologies, Daoism is perhaps best conceived of as the "good cop" to Classicism's "bad cop," reinforcing dichotomous ideals in a subtler but equally profound manner.

"Church Daoism," the "indigenous high religion of China" in Anna Seidel's phrase, began when Laojun, or "Lord Lao," descended to Zhang Daoling 張道陵 in the mountains of the Kingdom of Shu to reveal the divine covenant governing the Way of the Celestial Masters (*Tianshidao* 天師道). The traditional date for this occurrence is AD 142.

In part due to its persistent rejection of (ostensibly) celibate monasticism, Celestial Master Daoism in its formative period did not suffer from the same misogyny as Buddhism. As early as the Northern Wei dynasty (AD 386--534) Daoists composed texts in imitation of the Buddhist vinaya.[63] Buddhist and Daoist institutions and cenobites appear to have been spoken of in tandem in official discourse from the early Tang on,[64] but the Celestial Master order did not initially adopt celibate guidelines. The first major order to do so was the Complete Perfection Teachings (Quanzhen jiao 全真教), which came into existence in the disordered period that preceded the Yuan dynasty. Yet, according to Vincent Goossaert, even at their peak in the Qing only 10 percent of priests lived in abbeys.[65] Women held positions of leadership and advanced to the same level as men, with the exception that they seem to have been unable to hold the ultimate hereditary position of the Celestial Master himself. Laojun's most famous composition, the *Daodejing*, already contained a strong advocacy of feminine principles, with its valorization of the "Valley Spirit" (*gu shen* 谷神) and the "Mystic Feminine" (*xuan pin* 玄牝).[66] While the *Daodejing* itself was never the most important text for the Church, its persistence and availability throughout the imperial period inevitably influenced the values of Daoist clergy and laymen.

Of the Three Teachings, Daoism has inspired the most rapturous praise from contemporary scholars for its gender values. The most unrestrained accolade appears in the volume of *Science and Civilisation in China* devoted to Inner Alchemy, in which Joseph Needham and his partner Lu Gwei-Djen waxed: "And how profound a truth lay hid in this exaltation of the feminine qualities and virtues to the highest place, perhaps nothing less than the key to all human social evolution in its sublimation of intra-specific aggressiveness."[67] There is clearly more of the authors' projection here than any social or textual reality in any period of Chinese history. Clarke Hudson comments curtly on the passage: "Needham's view that inner alchemists essentially aim to maximize yin is colored by his love of the *Daodejing* and his love of peace, and is not objectively accurate." Hudson elaborates:

> Readers who assume a strong continuity between the *Daodejing* and medieval Daoism may assume that medieval Daoists must therefore also seek to balance yin and yang, or exalt the yin. But this is not true. Medieval Daoists are essentially devoted to personal salvation from this world of decay and death, of imperfection and dissatisfaction. The cultivation of health and holism through balancing yin and yang is but the first step on their path to salvation, which ultimately leads beyond the realm of yin and yang to the purer realm of the One *Qi*, Great Ultimate, Limitless, or Dao (also equated with the heavens, celestial deities, and cosmogenesis). And this One *Qi* is yang. Because yang is "pure," "high," and associated with "life," while yin is "impure," "low," and associated with "death," the purer, higher realm of eternal life is marked "yang" relative to the sublunar, mortal realm, which is "yin." Thus, while the harmonization of yin and yang, or cultivation of yin, may play some role in the practices of medieval Daoism, usually these Daoists would ultimately be aiming for a state of pure yang.[68]

As with Sponberg on the Vajrayāna school, Hudson reminds us that the idealization in meditative regimens may conceal values opposite to those they seem to betray at first glance.

Inner Alchemy Prefigured: The Infant as Early Daoist Body God

The most striking gender-bending imagery in Daoism contrasts starkly with female Buddhist devotees fervently praying to be reborn as men. In the male pregnancy motif, the adept is enjoined to visualize a child within his or her body. The first reference to an inner embryo occurs in the *Xiang'er* commentary to the *Laozi* 相爾老子注 (Dunhuang Stein 6852), which most modern scholars accept as an early production of the Celestial Masters.[69]

The *Xiang'er* commentary condones visualizations of body gods, but objects to visualization of the Dao itself as having a constant form and location. Those who say "nurturing the [transcendent] embryo and refining the physical form should be like making clay into pottery" 培胎練形當如土為瓦時 are teaching "false arts" and sowing "false deceptions" that "should not be adopted" as "to act upon them is the height of delusion."[70] We know from this that there were communities in the Latter Han dynasty that implemented a reading of the *Laozi* as a guide for physiospiritual transformation, and that concentration on an incipient body within their own played a major part in their practices. The transcendent embryo thus predates not only the advent of Inner Alchemy, which likely is not named as such until the Song,[71] but the Highest Purity (*Shangqing* 上清) revelations of AD 364–370 in which it plays such an important part in iconography,[72] often depicted suspended on a cloud above a meditating adept.

The first appearance as a body god of what would become the Infant (*ying'er* 嬰兒) of Inner Alchemy is testified quite early in the Daoist religious tradition. The Infant appears in *The Central Scripture of the Most High Lord Lao* (*Taishang Laojun zhongjing* 太上老君中經), also called the *Central Scripture of Laozi* (*Laozi zhongjing* 老子中經) and the *Jade Calendar of the Pearly Palace* (*Zhugong yuli* 珠宮玉曆 DZ 1168), which according to Kristofer Schipper "may well be the most ancient treatise of Daoist lore of the universe which has come down to us in a complete form."[73] Possibly of Latter Han dynasty provenance,[74] the teachings of this text are "entirely centered around the vision of the Infant."[75]

In the text, an "Infant" (*chizi* 赤子: literally, "ruddy baby") is the hierogonic progeny of the Yellow Old (Man) of the Central Pole (*Zhongji Huanglao* 中極黃老[76] or the Perfected Central Yellow [*Zhong huang zhenren* 中黃真人]) and his spouse the Jade Woman of Mysterious Radiance of Great Yin (*Taiyin xuanguang yu nü* 太陰玄光玉女 or the Pure Woman [*Su nü* 素女]). The importance of this child is evident in the fact of it being the only body deity to be named in the older, *Outer portion of the Most High Vistas of the Yellow Court Jade Scripture* (*Taishang huangting waijing yu jing* 太上黃庭景外玉經 DZ 332),[77] where he is identified as the Perfected Child-Cinnabar (*Zi dan zhenren* 子丹真人). He is nourished, in the *Central Scripture*, by the adept's circulation of qi through the viscera.

The relevant portion of the scripture reads:

> I am the child of the Tao. The human being has me too, but it is not the individual "I". I am right there, at the canal of the stomach, facing south, sitting on a bed of jade and pearls, under a canopy of yellow clouds...My mother at my right; she carries me in her arms and feeds me; my father stands at my left to teach and protect me. ...[I] Zidan of Primal Yang am nine-tenths of an inch high. When you think of me, then make me become on equal height with your body.[78]

In the *Central Scripture*, this new body created by the adept is indestructible: "Your body is of equal height with Heaven and Earth. The ten-thousand things of Heaven and Earth cannot attack you without all the gods from Heaven and Earth knowing it. Thus your body with its four limbs cannot be hurt. If it hurts or itches, the gods know it too."[79] The transcendent body that male and female devotees could produce within themselves made possible a self-promotion into the celestial realm. Like female Buddhist adepts wishing to become Buddhas, this meditation technique promised autodivinization.

In section 20 of the *Inner* portion of the *Yellow Court Scripture*, we first see instructions on the creation of the "embryo transcendent"[80] (*taixian* 胎仙, section 1) along lines common in Inner Alchemy: that is, a "transformation body" for "long-life" achieved in part by the cessation of seminal emission:

> By coagulating the essence and fostering the womb, you will generate a body by transformation; by detaining the embryo and causing the essence to stop, you will live a long life.[81]
> 節精育胞化生身 留胎止精可長生

In these texts, the Crimson Child is housed in the Cinnabar Field (lower and middle in the *Central Scripture*, upper in the *Yellow Court Scripture*). These would be conflated in Inner Alchemy, so that the Infant became synonymous with the Golden Elixir refined in this location in the adept's body. Visualization practices centered on imagining a child in devotees' bodies are remarkably consistent over the nearly two millennia of the Daoist creed. In mythology the deity Laozi himself is the product of autogenesis. As an informant in Taiwan explained to Schipper in the 1970s:

In the matrix, he [Laozi] sang sacred texts for eighty-one years. Thereupon he was born out of the left armpit of mother Li. At birth he had white hair which is why he was called the "old child."...As to his reincarnation in the womb of mother Li, one must know that it was he himself who transformed his body from nothingness into the shape of mother Li, so was to return into his own matrix; there was never any other mother Li. People today are not aware of this fact and say that the Old Lord came [from the outside] to place himself in mother Li's womb. In fact, it was not at all like that![82]

As Schipper summarizes: "Laojun is the body of the Dao before birth; Laozi is the Old Child and the Old Master of this world."[83] In this schema there is an explicit move to coopt female generative powers for male practitioners, a strategy that expands the gendered possibilities of men while undermining the biological prerogatives and associated essentialized qualities of women.

THE ORDERED WORK

Inner Alchemy is inextricably linked with Church Daoism but should not be carelessly conflated. A product of the selective combination of correlative cosmology, cults to transcendents (*xian* 仙), Learning of the *Changes* (*Yi xue* 易學), liturgical Daoism, Lao-Zhuang thought, canonical medicine, laboratory alchemy (*waidan* 外丹), Learning of the Principles/Learning of the Way (*Li xue* 理學/*Dao xue* 道學; i.e., Song dynasty Classicism), as well as Three Teachings thought and cults that came into its own in the Song dynasty, one of Inner Alchemy's greatest debts to Daoism is the centrality of the Infant in its program of transcendence. Fabrizio Pregadio cautions that despite the dramatic similarities with the Inner Alchemical practices that follow, we should not simply equate early Daoist meditational regimes with the self-conscious Inner Alchemy of the Song dynasty. Indeed, the dedivinization of body gods is one of the defining elements of Inner Alchemy. As Pregadio puts it: "the notion of generating an inner embryo is not a *neidan* innovation," while reminding that "[t]he image of the embryo changes according to the understanding of neidan itself."[84] Inner Alchemy is also very much a Dao-Buddhist hybrid, with the explicit goal of many late imperial texts being to "become a transcendent, become a buddha" (*cheng xian cheng fo* 成仙成佛).[85]

Of all Inner Alchemical works *Principles of the Innate Disposition and the Lifespan* (*Xingming guizhi* 性命圭旨 1615; hereafter *Principles*) contains the clearest depiction available of the process by which one

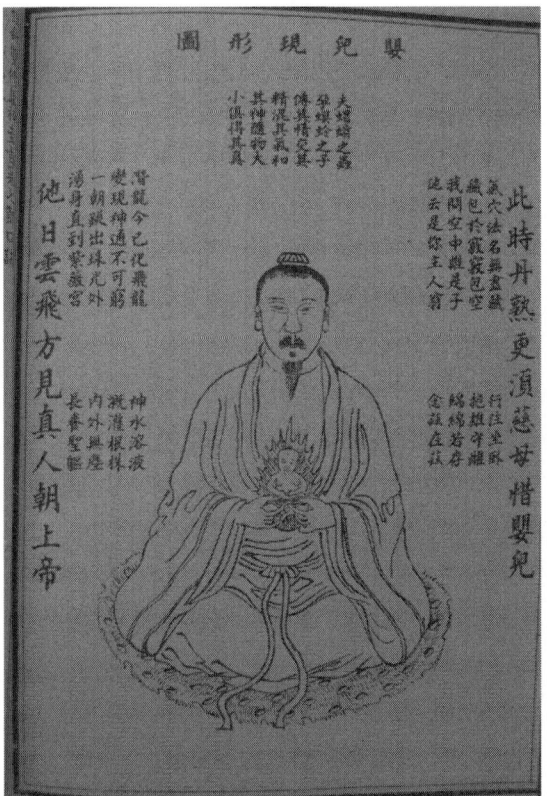

Figure 3.2 "The Infant Manifests Its Form" from *Xingming guizhi* (1615). This illustration from edition contained in Ding Fubao's 丁福保 *Daozang jinghua lu* 道藏精華錄 (Essential flowers of the daoist canon), 1922. Reproduced courtesy of Princeton University's Gest East Asian Library.

gestates and nurtures the "holy embryo" (*shengtai* 聖胎) or "transcendent embryo" (*xian tai* 仙胎), "the Infant" (figure 3.2), and the pure "*yang* spirit" (*yang shen* 陽神). These images should not cause us to lose sight of the fact that the most important transformation defies depiction: the changing over of one's entire being from our postnatal state of growth and decay to an atemporal realm in which there is neither birth nor death.

To create this inspired replica, one first synthesizes pure yin and pure yang in the atemporal, rather than mundane state. This is the end of a reversion exercise achieved by extracting the essence from the trigrams *li* 離 and *kan* 坎, which represent yin within yang and yang within yin respectively. These purified energies are then caused to "copulate" (*jiaogou* 交媾)—the word is unabashedly sexual, though not particularly erotic—in a cauldron located in the practitioner's lower abdomen. The gestation occurs over 10 lunar months—that is, completed cycles of the circulation of inner substances, the means by which one strips one's self of yin impurities and creates a perfect, pure yang body. This is then birthed out the sinciput[86] and nurtured for three more years before it achieves independence. Once it does so, the new body can be multiplied infinitely.

Sexing Sexlessness

In Inner Alchemy, female cultivators can embark upon the same path of transcendence as men, but to do so they must first change their bodies into male bodies by flattening their breasts and cutting off menstruation.[87] The primary difference is in the first stage of practice, in which women refine blood into qi, rather than refining essence (*jing*), which is conflated with semen. This is consistent with the Chinese medical motto "In women regard blood as the ruler" (*nüzi yi xue wei zhu* 女子以血為主). Thus the slogan is "Refine the blood to transform it into *qi*" (*lian xue hua qi* 煉血化氣), rather than "Refine the [seminal] essence to transform it into *qi*" (*lian jing hua qi* 煉精化氣). This leads to the cessation of menstruation, which is called "decapitating the red dragon" (*zhan chilong* 斬赤龍). A regimen of breast massage combined with breathing and visualization exercises results in the diminishment of the breasts. Taken together, this causes the female adept's body to become "like that of a man's" (*ru nanzi yipan* 如男子一盤).[88] Just as men's penises should shrink and detract as they advance on the path of transcendence,[89] so too should women regain a prepubescent body whose greater proximity to the cosmic origin is evinced by its lack of sexual differentiation.

Consistent with the Inner Alchemical process for men, women also conceive the "holy" and "transcendent embryo."[90] This is not depicted in the single body chart depicting a female cultivator in the late imperial period. But two rare images of a female adept producing the transcendent infant body and bodies occur in the 1890 set of 22 paintings commissioned by Gao Rentong 高仁峒 (1841–1907), abbot of the White Cloud Monastery in Beijing.[91] These paintings, funded by a female patron to honor the folk Goddess Niangniang 娘娘,[92] are primarily based on images in *Principles*.[93]

The upper half of the fifteenth painting, "The Yang Spirit Manifests Its Appearance" (*Yangshen xian xiang* 陽神現像) shows the Goddess and her seated, meditating replicant suspended on a five-hued cloud above her. The twenty-fifth, "Dividing the Self in Responsive Transformation" (*Fen shen gan hua* 分身感化), reveals the multiplication by five of the replicant selves.[94] Significantly, the female practitioner is *not* depicted with an infant inside her abdomen, but she does have proof of the latter fruits of this process hovering above her, a common motif from the Song dynasty on in illustrations accompanying the Shangqing scriptures.

Thus, women in the late imperial period regained access to the descendants of the meditational techniques they practiced as equals in the early Celestial Masters community. Yet in the later iteration, the ostensibly equal access path to transcending gender while transcending the mundane was predicated on a twofold denigration of themselves: first for possessing an impure yin nature as women, second for containing impure yin elements as a person.

Conclusion

My findings indicate that throughout the broad spatial and temporal range explored, there was a continual pressure on gender classifications, dichotomous and otherwise. That individual subjects did not succeed in transcending the limits of their time should not surprise us. What is more heartening is that so many felt the impetus to attempt to do so. In demarcating boundaries they revealed the existence of those who did not fit into the favored options, creating other devalued categories to contain these troubling identities and make them less disruptive. The development of meditational techniques for men aimed at integrating a sundered psyche reveals the psychological cost of adherence to the gender binary model, yet fundamentally accommodates rather than transcends it. Chinese traditions have produced a rich storehouse of gender integrating symbolism, but the wealth of the storehouse indicates just how difficult life was for the people who did not fit the socially condoned model of sexual division. In our own advocacy of a society with freedom of sexual orientation and gender identification, we should not lose sight of the profane realities that undergirded earlier attempts to escape the straightjacket of gender ideologies.

Notes

* I am grateful to Howard Chiang for helping to orient me within the field of transgender studies and to Meghan Fidler for suggesting structural improvements to this piece. Andrea Castiglioni, Douglas Gildow, and Elena Valussi responded generously to an eleventh hour request for feedback. I regret that I was not able to take all their suggestions into account in the present chapter.

1. David Valentine, *Imagining Transgender: An Ethnography of a Category* (Durham, NC: Duke University Press, 2007), 17.
2. For instance, Valentine, *Imagining Transgender*, 3–6, 17–18, and 21.
3. Eric Hobsbawm, "Introduction: Inventing Traditions," in *The Invention of Tradition*, ed. Eric Hobsbawm and Terence Ranger (Cambridge: Cambridge University Press, 1983), 6.
4. This obviously entails a risk of overreaching. For an earlier article of similar ambition and perhaps related pitfalls, see Alex Wayman, "Male, Female, and Androgyne: Per Buddhist Tantra, Jacob Boehme, and the Greek and Taoist Mysteries," in *Tantric and Taoist Studies in Honour of R.A. Stein*, ed. Michel Strickmann (Brussels: Institut Belge des Hautes Etudes Chinois, 1983).
5. Charlotte Furth, Review of *Passions of the Cut Sleeve: The Male Homosexual Tradition in China*, by Bret Hinsch, *Journal of Asian Studies* 50, no. 4 (1991): 912.
6. "Utopistics" is the neologism coined by Immanuel Wallerstein to indicate not "dreams of heaven that could never exist on earth," but plausible alternative futures. Immanuel Wallerstein, *Utopistics: Historical Choices of the Twenty-first Century* (New York: The New Press, 1998), 1–2.
7. Leonard Zwilling, "Homosexuality as Seen in Indian Buddhist Texts," in *Buddhism, Sexuality, and Gender*, ed. José Ignacio Cabezón (New York: State University of New York Press, 1992), 204.
8. Zwilling, "Homosexuality," 205.
9. Faure continues: "The same is true for castration, although the condemnation of the latter was in some cases attenuated by its ascetic motivations." Benard Faure, *The Red Thread: Buddhist Approaches to Sexuality* (Princeton, NJ: Princeton University Press, 1998), 77.
10. Faure, *The Red Thread*, 73.
11. Faure, *The Red Thread*, 77.
12. Faure, *The Red Thread*, 77, n. 37. See also Zwilling, "Homosexuality," 205. Zwilling relates a similar episode from the *Paṇḍukavatthu* section of the *Makāvagga* with the difference that (at least in translation) the pronoun by which the *paṇḍaka* is referred is not problematized. Zwilling, "Homosexualty," 207–208.
13. "Eunuch" is a problematic translation, as it indicates a practice not current in early India.
14. Digital Dictionary of Buddhism (hereafter DDB) 般荼迦.
15. On which see Charlotte Furth, *A Flourishing Yin: Gender in China's Medical History, 960–1665* (Berkeley: University of California Press, 1999), 54–55. Charlotte Furth, "Androgynous Males and Deficient Females: Biology and Gender Boundaries in Sixteenth- and Seventeenth-Century China," *Late Imperial China* 9 no. 2 (1988)

should also be consulted. On Li's relation to natural history more broadly, see Carla Nappi, *The Monkey and the Inkpot: Natural History and Its Transformations in Early Modern China* (Cambridge: Harvard University Press, 2010).
16. Vol. 1: 128–135. Cited in Alan Sponberg, "Attitudes towards Women and the Feminine in Early Buddhism," in Cabezón ed., *Buddhism, Sexuality, and Gender*, 9.
17. Sponberg, "Attitudes," 9.
18. Sponberg, "Attitudes," 9.
19. More precisely, Chinese Pure Land practices required that everything—from insects to domestic animals to women—be reborn as men. "Pure Land" is a Chinese neologism retroactively applied to some Mahāyāna beliefs and practices in India; the phrase *jingtu* itself may be a productive mistranslation: Jan Nattier, "The Realm of Akṣobhya: A Missing Piece in the History of Pure Land Buddhism," *Journal of the International Association of Buddhist Studies* 23, no. 1 (2000): 73–74 n. 6.
20. Nattier, "Akṣobhya," 82.
21. These can be searched for in the Taishō Canon by the phrases "Transform into a male" (*biancheng nanzi* 變成男子) and "Transform from a woman into a man" (*zhuan nü cheng nan* 轉女成男), which, when not directly referencing the nāga princess episode, usually appears in women's prayers to be reborn as men. Particularly relevant in this regard is the illustrated *Scripture on the Buddha's Decree on Changing from a Woman's Body* (*Foshuo zhuan nüshen jing* 佛說轉女身經) translated in 1195, on which see Kyoto National Museum and The Institute of Oriental Manuscripts of the Russian Academy of Sciences, *Shiruku Rōdo moji o tadotte: Roshia tankentai shūshū no bunbutsu* (シルクロード文字を辿って: ロシア探検隊収集の文物) [On the trail of texts along the Silk Road: Russian expeditions discoveries of manuscripts in Central Asia] (Kyoto: Kyōto Kokuritsu Hakubutsukan, 2009), 176–177.
22. The earlier *Zhengfahua jing* 正法華經 (T. 263.9.63–133) of Dharmarakṣa 法護 was largely ignored after Kumārajīva's more graceful translation.
23. Leon Hurvitz, trans. *Scripture of the Lotus Blossom of the Fine Dharma* (New York: Columbia University Press, 1976), 199. All translations from the Chinese follow Hurvitz.
24. Hurvitz, *Scripture*, 200.
25. Eugene Wang warns of Śāriputra: "By our modern standards, he must have been an obnoxious misogynist or male chauvinist." See Eugene Wang, *Shaping the Lotus Sutra: Buddhist Visual Culture in Medieval China* (Seattle: University of Washington Press, 2005), 141.
26. Hurvitz, *Scripture*, 200–201.
27. This jewel is a gender signifier: "Each Nāga princess was believed to carry a priceless jewel on her head which male Nāgas did not possess."

Diana Paul, *Women in Buddhism: Images of the Feminine in Mahāyāna Tradition* (Berkeley: University of California Press, 1985 [1979]), 186.
28. The Sanskrit accentuates the gender change: "Then at the time the daughter of the nāga king Sāgara showed herself in the presence of all the world and before the eyes of the elder Śāriputra, *with her female faculties suppressed and male faculties displayed*, herself become a bodhisattva." Hurvitz, *Scripture*, 379, emphasis added. Compare to Paul's translation of the same passage: "Then, at that instant in time, before the Elder Śāriputra and the entire world, *king Sāgara's daughter's female organs vanished, and the male organ became visible.*" Paul, *Women in Buddhism*, 189, emphasis added.
29. Hurvitz, *Scripture*, 201.
30. Burton Watson, trans. *The Lotus Sutra* (New York: Columbia University Press, 1993), xix.
31. Reproduced in Wang, *Shaping*, 141.
32. The classic study of this legitimization campaign is: Antonio Forte, *Political propaganda and ideology in China at the end of the seventh century: inquiry into the nature, authors and function of the Dunhuang document S.6502, followed by an annotated translation* (Kyoto: Scuola Italiana di Studi sull'Asia Orientale, 2005).
33. Miriam Levering, "The Dragon Girl and the Abbes of Mo-Shan," *Journal of the International Association of Buddhist Studies* 5 no. 1 (1982): 22.
34. Levering, *Dragon Girl*, 28.
35. Chün-fang Yü, "P'u-t'o Shan: Pilgrimage and the Creation of the Chinese Potalaka," in *Pilgrims and Sacred Sites in China*, ed. Susan Naquin and Yü Chün-fang (Berkeley: University of California Press, 1992), 163.
36. Yü, "P'u-t'o Shan," 172. Yü explains the sex change in the following way: "Miracles and pilgrimage traditions probably provided the initial impetus. Art and literature then promoted and popularized them. I suggest that each major form of the feminine Guanyin was originally anchored in one specific place, connected with one life story, and depicted with one type of iconography." On this subject see also Rolf Stein, "Avalokiteśvara/Kouan-Yin: Exemple de Transformation d'un Dieu en Déesse," *Cahiers d'Extrême-Asie* 2 (1986). For an elaboration of the most important pilgrimage site linked to the White-robed Guanyin, see: Yü, "P'u-t'o Shan."
37. For instance, Yü, "P'u-t'o Shan," 166–169. Faure adds: "In her infinite compassion and her desire to convert beings by adapting to their passions, Guanyin even condones homosexual love, as in the Japanese story of the old monk who, after having lived three years in perfect love with his novice, was stricken with grief at the youth's premature death. During the funerary wake, Kannon appears to him under the guise of the beloved novice, and reveals that he/she had taken human form in order to reward him for a virtuous life (!)" Faure, *The Red Thread*, 20.

38. Sponberg, "Attitudes," 8.
39. Sponberg, "Attitudes," 8.
40. Sponberg, "Attitudes," 13–18.
41. Sponberg, "Attitudes," 19.
42. Sponberg, "Attitudes," 24–25.
43. Sponberg, "Attitudes," 25.
44. Sponberg, "Attitudes," 25.
45. Sponberg, "Attitudes," 26–27.
46. Sponberg, "Attitudes," 27.
47. Sponberg, "Attitudes," 28.
48. Michael Loewe, "Shih Ching 詩經," in *Early Chinese Texts: A Bibliographical Guide*, ed. Michael Loewe (Berkeley: University of California Press,1993), 415.
49. 使民 有父之尊, 有母之親. 如此而后可以為民父母矣. 非至德其孰能如此乎. I am indebted to the discussion of this line in Charles T. Sanft, *Rule: A Study of Jia Yi's* Xin shu (Dissertation: Münster University, 2005), 60–64. I slightly alter his translation. Interestingly, the same phrase, "father and master of the people," continued to be employed in modern Japan, describing the Meiji emperor's own ideal conception of his role (albeit in stereotyped classical language). Donald Keene, *Emperor of Japan: Meiji and His World, 1852–1912* (New York: Columbia University Press, 2002), 140 and 302.
50. Discussed in Furth, *A Flourishing Yin*, 221. For more on this period, see: Furth, "Androgynous Males and Deficient Females," 1–31. Liang Yannian 梁延年, ed., *Shengyu xiang jie* 聖諭像解 (The Sacred Edict, Illustrated and Explained), 1681, contains two images of lactating men with accompanying anecdotes: j. 2: 19a–20a (nursing his deceased stepmother's daughters) and j. 2: 21a–b (nursing his deceased brother's son). Lactating men imply not only gender transgression but a different version of the capabilities of sexed bodies. Compare to Caroline Walker Bynam, *Jesus as Mother: Studies in the Spirituality of the High Middle Ages* (California: University of California Press, 1984).
51. Roland Altenburger, "Is It Clothes that Make the Man? Cross-Dressing, Gender, and Sex in Pre-Twentieth-Century Zhu Yingtai Lore," *Asian Folklore Studies* 64, no. 2 (2005). For androgyny and late imperial literature see: Zuyan Zhou, *Androgyny in Late Ming and Early Qing Literature* (Honolulu: University of Hawai'i Press, 2003) and Zhou's contribution to the present volume.
52. The phrase is that of Romeyn Taylor, who describes the official religion of the Ming dynasty as "the vocational religion of the literati." Romeyn Taylor, "Official Religion in the Ming," in *The Ming Dynasty, 1368–1644*, ed. Denis Twitchett and Frederick W. Mote, vol. 8, part 2 (Cambridge: Cambridge University Press, 1998), 848.
53. Quoted in Robert Ford Campany, "Two Religious Thinkers of the Early Eastern Jin: Gan Bao and Ge Hong in Multiple Contexts," *Asia*

Major 3rd series 18, no. 1 (2005): 179–180. See also: Robert Ford Campany, *Strange Writing: Anomaly Accounts in Early Medieval China* (Albany: State University of New York Press, 1996), 12–14.

54. Although "the textual history of the [*Soushenji*] is among the most complicated of all the anomaly accounts... over ninety percent of the 464 items in today's text are attested in extant Six Dynasties commentaries, Tang and early Song collectanea." Campany, *Strange Writing*, 55–56.
55. Campany, "Two Religious Thinkers," 2005: 183.
56. Compare to non-gender boundary disrupting clothing focused entries, items 213 and 223.
57. Asterisk (*) indicates entries listed under more than one category.
58. Translation adapted from Kenneth J. DeWoskin and J. I. Crump, *In Search of the Supernatural: The Written Record* (Stanford, CA: Stanford University Press, 1996), 76.
59. Translation adapted from DeWoskin and Crump, *In Search*, 95.
60. Translation adapted from DeWoskin and Crump, *In Search*, 95.
61. DeWoskin and Crump, *In Search*, 143.
62. DeWoskin and Crump, *In Search*, 144.
63. Richard Mather, "K'ou Ch'ien-chi and the Taoist Theocracy at the Northern Wei Court," in *Facets of Taoism: Essays in Chinese Religion*, ed. Holmes Welch and Anna K. Seidel (New Haven: Yale University Press, 1979), 111.
64. Jacques Gernet, *Buddhism in Chinese Society: An Economic History from the Fifth to the Tenth Centuries*, trans. Franciscus Verellen (New York: Columbia University Press, 1995), 131, 140, 141, 145, 212, 226, 256, 281, 284, 287, 290, and 304.
65. Vincent Goossaert, "Quanzhen, What Quanzhen? Late Imperial Taoist Clerical Identities in Lay Perspective," paper presented at the International Symposium on Quanzhen Daoism in Modern Chinese Society and Culture, University of California, Berkeley, Nov. 2–3, 2007, 2.
66. Interestingly, in *Daodejing* verse 15 William Boltz has identified "one of the uncommon cases where we can detect the conscious shifting of meaning away from a sexual image to one apparently perceived as a benign non-sexual one." The passage in both Mawangdui manuscripts is: *nü yi zhong zhi xu sheng* 女以重之徐生, "taking a hold of the female and 'bestirring' (=impregnating) her, she slowly generates life." In all received versions, "the image of pregnancy has been completely eradicated." William G. Boltz, "Manuscripts with Transmitted Counterparts," in *New Sources of Early Chinese History: An Introduction to the Reading of Inscriptions and Manuscripts*, ed. Edward Shaughnessy (Berkeley: Institute of East Asian Studies, 1997), 279–280.
67. Joseph Needham and Lu Gwei-Djen, *Science and Civilisation in China, Chemistry and Chemical Technology, Spagyrical Discovery*

and Invention Part V: Physiological Alchemy (London: Cambridge University Press, 1983), 54.
68. Clark Hudson, "Spreading the Dao, Managing Mastership, and Performing Salvation: The Life and Alchemical Teachings of Chen Zhixu" (PhD dissertation, Indiana University, 2007), 258–259.
69. Schipper objects that "the style, the tone, and the theology are quite different" from that of Celestial Master ecclesia. He speculates that it could date "possibly from as early as the first century A.D." Kristofer Schipper and Franciscus Verellen, eds., *The Taoist Canon: A Historical Companion to th*e Daozang (Chicago: University of Chicago Press, 2004), 77. Stephen Bokenkamp, who has translated the extant fragment (Stephen R Bokenkamp, *Early Daoist Scriptures* [Berkeley: University of California Press, 1997], 78–148) calls the text "authentically early" (59), and notes eight points at which he believes *Commandments and Admonitions for the Family of the Dao* (*Dadaojia lingjie* 大道家令戒 DZ 789.12a–19b) reveals a knowledge of the *Xiang'er* commentary. *Commandments and Admonitions* contains an internal pronouncement dating itself to a particular day in AD 255. It is one of only a handful of surviving texts from the original Celestial Masters community.
70. Quoted in Bokenkamp, *Early Daoist*, 92.
71. Often in texts claiming to be of the Tang: see Farzeen Baldrian-Hussein,"Inner Alchemy: Notes of the Origin and Use of the Term *Neidan*," *Cahier d'Extrême-Asie* 5 (1989): 90. James Robson informs me that he has been able to date some of these texts to the Tang.
72. Also predating Shangqing are testaments to a latter idea associated with the Inner Alchemical reproduction process, that of "dividing the physical form" (*fen xing* 分形), which appears in both Ge Hong's *Master Who Embraces Simplicity* (*Baopuzi*; problematically translated by James R Ware, *Alchemy, Medicine and Religion in the China of A.D. 320: The Nei P'ien of Ko Hung (Pao-p'u tzu)* [Cambridge, MA: M.I.T. Press, 1966]) and the *Traditions of Divine Transcendents* (*Shenxian zhuan*; impressively translated by Robert Ford Campany, *To Live As Long As Heaven and Earth: A Translation and Study of Ge Hong's Traditions of Divine Transcendents* [Berkeley: University of California Press, 2002]).
73. Kristofer Schipper, "The Inner World of the Lao-Tzu Chung-Ching 老君中經," in *Time and Space in Chinese Culture,* eds. Huang Junjie and Erik Zürcher (Leiden: Brill, 1995), 115.
74. On dating see Schipper, "Inner World," 118–119.
75. Schipper, "Inner World," 124.
76. This "Huang-Lao," though suggesting the poorly understood Warring States philosophical school, has not been decisively related to it by scholars.
77. Based on phonological reconstruction, this text likely originated in the Celestial Master Community before the flight from Hanzhong 漢中 in the Northwest to, eventually, the Eastern Jin kingdom in the

Southeast. The oldest extant copy is a reproduction of a rubbing of a stele written by Wang Xizhi 王羲之 (303–379) in 337. There is also a Tang stele.
78. Translated in Schipper, "Inner World," 124.
79. Translation adapted from Schipper, "Inner World," 124.
80. Or "immortals in embryonic state"—see Fabrizio Pregadio, "Early Daoist Meditation and the Origins of Inner Alchemy," in *Daoism in History: Essays in Honour of Liu Ts'un-Yan*, ed. Benjamin Penny (New York: Routledge, 2006), 142—ancestors reborn in heaven through the application of dedicated progeny. Inverted, these characters are the "transcendent embryo" (*xian tai*) of Inner Alchemy.
81. Translated in Pregadio, "Early Daoist," 139.
82. Kristofer Schipper, *The Taoist Body*, trans. Karen Duval (Berkeley: University of California Press, 1993), 122. I have silently amended Wade-Giles to Pinyin throughout this paper.
83. Schipper, *Taoist Body*, 125.
84. Pregadio, "Early Daoist," 139, 138.
85. For example, in *Principles of the Innate Disposition and the Lifespan* (on which see below) the apotheosis is depicted as both "Flying Ascension" and "Confirmation as Vairocana." On this text, see Daniel Burton-Rose, "Integrating Inner Alchemy into Late Ming Cultural History: A Contextualization and Annotated Translation of *Principles of the Innate Disposition and the Lifespan (Xingming guizhi* 性命圭旨) (1615)" (MA thesis, University of Colorado, 2009).
86. That is, the crest of a skull; the area that is the fontanel in infants before the cranial plates expand and meet, corresponding to the ultimate yang point on the body, the cavity of One Hundred [Yang Channel] convergences (*bai hui* 百會).
87. This sexist inequality was only confronted within the Internal Alchemical tradition in the early twentieth century by Chen Yingning, who emphasized differentiation from the atemporal realm rather than a deficiency of yang as the original cause of human mortality. On Chen see Xun Liu, *Daoist Modern: Innovation, Lay Practice, and the Community of Inner Alchemy in Republican Shanghai* (Cambridge: Harvard University Press, 2009). For more on female Daoist cultivation practices see: Elena Valussi, "Men and Women in He Longxiang's *Nüdan hebian*," *Nan nü: Men, Women & Gender in Early & Imperial China* 10, no. 2 (2008): 242–278; Suping Li 李素平, *Nü shen nü dan nü dao* 女神女丹女道 (Beijing: Zongjiao wenhua chubanshe, 2004) and Sara Neswald, "Rhetorical Voices in the Neidan Tradition: An Interdisciplinary Analysis of the 'Nudan Hebian' (pref. 1906) Compiled by He Longxiang (fl 1900-1906)." (PhD dissertation, McGill University, 2007).
88. Fu Jinquan 傅金銓, *Nügong lian ji huandan tu shu* 女功煉己還丹圖書, in *Nüdan hebian* 女丹合編, ed. He Longxiang 賀龍驤 (Chengdu:

Er'xian an, 1906), 3a. The last character seems an error for the orthographically similar *ban* 般.

89. "Relevant terms include: *suogui* 縮龜 (retraction of the turtle[-head]), *guisuo buju zhi jing* 龜縮不舉之景 (scene in which the turtle[-head] retracts and does not rise), *mayin cangxiang* 馬陰藏相 (the horse's nether-region hides its marks)." Hudson, "Spreading," 352 n. 459.
90. For instance, Fu, *Nügong,* 7a.
91. For more on Gao see Vincent Goossaert, *The Taoists of Peking, 1800–1949: A Social History of Urban Clerics* (Cambridge: Harvard University Asia Center, 2007), esp. 172–175.
92. She is more grandly titled "Primordial Mistress of the Azure Mists, Divine Transcendent Holy Mother of the Eastern Peak" (*Dongyue taishan tianxian shengmu bixia yuanjun* 東岳泰山天仙聖母碧霞元君) and commonly referred to as "Taishan Niangniang" (*Taishan niangniang* 泰山娘娘) or "Venerable Mother of Taishan" (*Taishan laomu* 泰山老母). Zhongguo daojiao xiehui 中国道教协会, ed., *Daojiao shenxian huaji* 道教神仙畫集 (Beijing: Huaxia chubanshe, 1995), 110.
93. A comparative table is provided in Xun Liu, "Visualizing Perfection: Daoist Paintings of Our Lady, Court Patronage, and Elite Female Piety in the Late Qing," *Harvard Journal of Asiatic Studies* 64, no. 1 (2004): 67.
94. Reproduced in Zhongguo daojiao xiehui, *Daojiao shenxian huaji,* 118 and 121.

CHAPTER 4

The Androgynous Ideal in Scholar-Beauty Romances: A Historical and Cultural View

*Zuyan Zhou**

As a human inclination to cross the culturally demarcated gender-division, transgender in Chinese culture also finds expression in the phenomenon of androgyny, where a subject's recalcitrant impulses against cultural imperatives prompt him/her to move back and forth across the gender-division with great freedom, thus formulating an identity that encompasses both the masculine and feminine principles. In the literature of late imperial China, the phenomenon of androgyny is most prominent in scholar-beauty romances that flourished during the late Ming and early Qing period. Like actors and actresses in traditional Chinese theater, heroines in that genre often don male garments masquerading as men and moving freely between genders in the game of courtship. One most interesting case can be traced to the early Qing romance *Renjian le* (Happiness in the human world), which creates a *caizi* (talented scholar) and a *jiaren* (beauty), both endowed with androgynous inclinations.

The heroine of the fiction has two names: Zhuangzhu (a pearl on the palm) and Yinan (suitable to be a male), pertaining to the two parts of her gender identity. Having dressed in male clothes since her childhood, been educated with Confucian classics, and often accompanied by a "boy"—her maid in disguise—the girl deports perfectly like a man; and "his" dashing carriage beguiles numerous beauties to send over matchmakers to seek an ideal union. To avoid troubles, the family moves away and she has to occasionally return to her native sexual role. Thereafter, "if anyone knows she is a 'male,' she will meet him as Yinan; if anyone knows she is a female, she will emerge as Zhuangzhu. Changing her gender like a chameleon, she puzzles everyone who meets her."[1]

Not only is androgyny inscribed in the jiaren's name and bearing, but it also characterizes the mode of her courtship. Impressed by her poetry, Ruqi, a talented scholar, deeply admires "his" talents. The scholar is then invited to visit the beauty's house where he is received by her, cross-dressed as a man. Yinan tells Ruqi that the poetry is, in fact, composed by "his" younger sister, and "he" happily serves as a matchmaker for Ruqi and "his sister," who is—of course—none other than herself. Thereafter, Yinan switches back to her native feminine identity of Zhuangzhu; and the romance winds up with a happy union between the scholar and the beauty. The active role that the jiaren plays in courting the caizi indicates her adoption of a male mode of behavior in a culture where boudoir confinement is the norm, a heretic gender stand that is also projected in the male garment she puts on. Thus, she personifies the ideal of androgyny, which is defined by Cynthia Secor as "the capacity of a single person of either sex to embody the full range of human character traits, despite cultural attempts to render some exclusively feminine and some exclusively masculine."[2] And the psychological impetus for her gender deviation perfectly matches Carolyn Heilbrun's perceptive observation that "androgyny seeks to liberate the individual from the confines of the appropriate."[3]

The beauty's androgynous drift is mirrored symmetrically in the scholar, a man with extraordinary beauty, as well as inscribed in his name and titles. The first part of his name, *Ru*, is made of two parts, meaning respectively "water" and "female," whereas the second part *qi* usually refers to a vessel. If we ignore the normal meaning of ru as "you" in classical Chinese, by taking its ideographical connotations, then the name actually means "a female organ." This feminine implication is reinforced by the two parts comprising his title, *hu* and *lian*, both bearing a jade radical, which often appears in Chinese women's names, hence carrying unmistakable feminine import. More accurately, his gender identity is inscribed in a second title, *Xiuhu* (embroidery tiger), which he chooses after the late Ming literati celebrity Tang Bohu (1470–1523), his personal idol. Since needlework in imperial China was an exclusive female avocation and "tiger" is a conventional trope for masculinity, the title signals an incorporation of opposite gender attributes in his identity. Interestingly, just as Yinan's gentlemanly bearing induces female attention, Ruqi's feminine beauty courts male aggression. The son of the prime minister jails him in his house and forces him to be both his sister's husband and his *longyangjun* (male sex partner), thus seriously treating him as "a female organ." It is in rejecting this role of prostitute/concubine that his latent masculinity surfaces. Ruqi sneaks out of the palatial prison; and when the prime minister again presses him into the unwanted marriage after he becomes a pawn in the bureaucracy under the sway of the latter's authority, he asks for a temporary withdrawal from the court in resistance to the invasion of power, thus affirming his tiger personality. In his oppression by the patriarchal power, Ruqi is reduced to a marginal man, hence sharing the same marginal position with women in the patriarchal power structure. In asserting his latent virility as a marginal/feminized man, he, just like Yinan, personifies androgyny in his gender stance.

The gender freedom traced above in *Renjian le* stands out as a prominent feature of scholar-beauty romances, while Yinan and Ruqi may be viewed as exemplary caizi and jiaren in that genre. Dramatically exaggerated, protagonists of this genre often embody perfect combination of masculinity and femininity, functioning like personification of androgyny. The genre consciously endows its protagonists with opposite gender attributes to project its vision of androgyny. This chapter will explore the historical and cultural dimensions of this literary phenomenon. I will argue that in the cultural context of the late Ming, the androgyny craze in scholar-beauty romances may be viewed as a reflection of the social changes, ideological upheaval, and political agitation that destabilized the traditional gender dichotomy in Chinese culture. Underlying the pervasive literary presentation of caizi's and jiaren's gender transgression throb literati scholars' andric impulses to defy their yin status in the traditional gender paradigm. In the following pages, I will delineate several aspects of late Ming culture that may have contributed to the prominent phenomenon of androgyny in scholar-beauty romances.

Obfuscation of Male-Female Division: Gender Fluidity in Late Ming Culture

In the background of caizi's and jiaren's free movement between genders lurks a trend in the late Ming of gradual disintegration of traditional gender roles in social life owing to multiple forces in its culture. The flourishing commerce, a surplus of wealth, widespread education, rising individualism, prevailing hedonism, and the cult of qing (feeling, emotion, or affection) all contributed to the blurring of the traditional division between the two sexes. Among these cultural factors, the cult of qing, in particular, has been singled out as a pivotal cause for the emergence of feminine male characters in the literature during this period.[4] In fact, this powerful trend may have contributed to the feminization of the male culture as a whole, as I will argue below.

The gender ambiguity in late Ming culture is manifest most publicly in men's lives. The late Ming was a time when homosexuals were visible in different classes and regions, a phenomenon that could not be culturally disassociated with the cult of qing. Male prostitution was popular and even cohabitation of male couples appeared to be an accepted institution.[5] The presence of homosexuality was particularly prominent in literature, revealing its forcible impress on literati consciousness. Associated with the popularity of homosexuality is the widespread expression of homoeroticism. In social life, donning colorful and effeminately fancy clothes became fashionable among some scholars.[6] In Chapter 30 of *The Scholars* Wu Jingzi (1701–1754) presents a theatrical competition among those who play dan (female) roles; the exclusive male gender of the organizer, the female impersonators, and the audience gives us a glimpse at the male fascination with homoeroticism. The acceptance of public homosexuality and homoeroticism extended into early and mid-Qing.

The gender inversion of patriarchal culture is also reflected in the feminization of literati's aesthetic and literary tastes. Late imperial China witnessed a change in the aesthetics guiding masculine beauty, as revealed in paintings and literature. Robert van Gulik aptly observes that "instead of the middle-aged bearded men of the Tang and Song periods, ardent lovers in Ming paintings are more often depicted as young men without beards, moustaches or whiskers"; the removal of these male features inevitably feminizes their visage, with the result that their faces become largely indistinguishable from those of women.[7] Accordingly, in Chinese literature, along with what Martin Huang calls the shift of novelistic focus form "public life to private life," its setting from battlefields to bedchambers,[8] the rough-hewn heroes of the *haohan* category in traditional Chinese novels—as Keith McMahon indicates—are eclipsed by men of feminine beauty, the *fengliu* type.[9] Men became so feminine in literary presentation that, as Sophie Volpp observes in her study of the characterization of a male wife in a story by Li Yu (1611–ca. 79), "natural femininity becomes attracted to young boys rather than women."[10]

Correspondingly, Ming calligraphy reveals ascendancy of the yin spirit, as the cultural chronicler Xie Zhaozhi (1567–1624) remarks, "In our age, more scholars practice soft strokes than firm strokes."[11]

The scripts of the Ming master Wen Zhengming (1470–1559), as William Willetts observes, are "suggestive of the soft and the feminine—fairies flying among the clouds and dancing on the waves—rather than the dragon-like and tiger-like qualities," the yang spirit latent in the brushwork of the Tang master Liu Gongquan (778–865).[12] Under the stimulation of qing, as Kang-I Sun Chang points out, late Ming witnessed a revival of *ci*, a poetic genre of emotional intensity; the feminine style of its *wanyue* school became a ready vehicle for literati to purge their effusive emotion.[13] Similarly, late Ming theater was dominated by the feminine spirit of the Southern School. The mainstream of late Ming theater was *kunqu*, a dramatic form noted for its soft tunes, delicate music, mellifluous singing, and ornate poetic lines; its effete strains lent a striking contrast to the sonorous and vigorous *zaju*, a form popular in the preceding Yuan dynasty. A salient feature of the kunqu stage at this period was its dominance by dramas of romance (*wenxi*) over plays of military feats (*wuxi*), which signals the ascendance of feminine impulses in Chinese theater. Since kunqu is generally regarded as an aristocratic genre composed by and mainly serving scholars, its feminine features mirror literati's feminine taste. The fact that in Wu Jingzi's aforementioned fictional presentation of a theatrical contest, all player are female impersonators reveals the feminization of the taste of its organizer as well as the literati audience. The effeminacy of Ming-Qing theater was thrown into relief by the double-feminization of female impersonators, who assumed female roles on the stage and often offered sexual services offstage.

In her study, Maram Epstein attributes the feminization of male characters in Ming-Qing fiction to the cult of qing because, as she argues, with the deep cultural association between qing and yin, "the feminine enjoyed a privileged position" in the aesthetic of the cult of qing. Male characters, therefore, "adopted feminine personae as part of their nonconformist performance of authenticity."[14] Given the powerful and pervasive influence of the cult of qing in late Ming society, we are tempted to extend its association with the feminization of male characters in literature to the feminization of the male culture as a whole. In the ambience of cultural valorization of qing, the feminine inclinations that the male culture seems to embrace in theater, poetry, calligraphy, dressing fashion, and aesthetic tastes may be—at least partially—attributed to the "privileged position" that "the feminine enjoyed" in the antihegemonic movement of the cult of qing. As an intrinsic component of the cult of qing, the feminization of the male culture may be viewed as literati's subconscious expression of the "authentic" in defiance of orthodoxy. Despite its gynic appearance, therefore, it carries andric implication.

Concurrent with the feminization of the patriarchal culture is the masculinization of women. Scholarship in recent two decades has abundantly demonstrated the widespread female literacy in gentry households, the female literary networks, and the extensive publication of female poetry, which all point to the obliteration of the intellectual distinction between sexes, which is held as ideal in traditional Chinese ideology.[15] Some even indicate the compatibility of talent with virtue in the late Ming conception of womanhood.[16] Although female literacy was cultivated in late imperial period originally to facilitate women's conformism and to enhance their value in the marriage market, it inevitably stimulated romantic sentiments, political enthusiasm, and individualistic impulses, which—in turn—bred cross-gender behavior. Catalyzing female literacy was the glamorous courtesan, the moral paragon and cultural icon in the late Ming. Talented in poetic skills, active in romantic pursuit, and heroic in political actions, the courtesan embodied in a woman the most admirable male qualities, incarnated female potential for companionate relationship, and epitomized the late Ming ideal of androgyny.[17]

In religious practice, female deities began to replace their male counterparts as idols of worship;[18] and some women assumed leading roles in religious communities.[19] The ascendant masculine impulses in women may also have contributed to a marked increase of jealous wives in domestic life, which partially accounts for the prominent presence of shrews in the literature of this period (Wu 363–382). Meanwhile, flourishing commerce often obliged merchants to stay away from home for extended periods, leaving household management to their wives; the authority that women wielded in such families fostered independence, leading to aberration from traditional womanhood. Stimulated by the prevailing hedonism, women's views on sex became more open and active. In a popular song entitled "Stealing," which Feng Menglong (1574–1654) supposedly collected from women, the persona assuming a female voice chants: "In the past only men decoyed us; in this new age we women seduce men."[20] Although the suspicion about the authenticity of the personal voice assumed in such folk songs and the belief in literati's possible manipulation of such lines expressed in Western scholarship may reduce their social relevance, they adumbrate—at least—an emerging female consciousness for gender inversion in courtship.[21] Women's psychological captivation by the active mode of courtship finds expression in the strong empathy they expressed for Du Liniang, the valiant pursuer of love in Tang Xianzu's (1550–1616) masterpiece *The Peony Pavilion*, which won immense popularity among female readers and performance audiences in the late Ming and early Qing. Accordingly, a well-known drama composed by Li Yu is titled *Women Pursue Men* (*Feng qiu huang*). With women's awakened libido energy seeking an outlet, the conventional boudoir confinement began to relax, at least in some areas. Commenting on women's behavior during the Jiajing regime (1522–1567), a scholar writes: "[in the past] they were deeply secluded, never making an appearance; they either made wine or weaved clothes." "Nowadays they dress like prostitutes, make acquaintances with old women, moving in and out of the house with heads held high, as if they were not different from men."[22] Such a phenomenon, though maybe only occasionally visible in society, contributes to the conception of gender movement in scholar-beauty romances.

Even in martial arts, a privileged domain of men, some women excelled. The well-known female commander Qin Liangyu (1584–1648) devoted her lifetime to military services. Her small army of 3,000 soldiers turned out to be so powerful that the area surrounding her hometown was the only region free from molestation by the late Ming peasants' rebellion. Her courage outshone many male generals and won the highest honor from the emperor, who lamented the lack of a single man with her valor to suppress the rebellion.[23] Qin was by no means the only woman active in the late Ming military arena; a number of women took up arms as Ming loyalists. One female warrior even donned a man's uniform in combat. In the sixteenth-century anti-Japanese war, female commanders in the armies of the Guangxi region were also celebrated for their valor and courage. Xu Wei (1521–1602), a participant of the war himself, composed a group of poems to glorify them.[24] Female excellence in martial arts may account for the emergence, during the Wanli regime (1573–1619), of several full-length fictions dramatizing the military careers of General Yang's family, which crystallized in *The Popular Tales of General Yang's Family* (*Yangjiajiang yanyi*). Though deriving its sources from the antecedent materials in the Song and Yuan dynasties, the late Ming fictions are noted for their graphic portrayal of 12 female members of the Yang family, all dedicating their military services to safeguarding the motherland. The division between men and women became so obscured that occasionally each sex crossed over it, masquerading as the other, using cross-dressing as expediency in emergent situations.[25]

Marginal Men's Intensified Yin Consciousness and Sentimental Affinity to Extraordinary Women

While the gender fluidity in late Ming society provides a relevant cultural context for the prominent presence of androgyny in literature, its celebration in scholar-beauty romances is more personally related to the gender preference of the male authors, for the genre—as generally believed—are essentially male productions. Not only caizi's gender position, but also jiaren's may be intrinsically related to literati authors' treasured values and ideals. Marginal men and women—as the above discussion on *Renjian le* indicates—can often share an identical gender position in patriarchal culture, a perception that has also been incorporated into the contemporary feminist theory: What determines one's gender is not his sexual identity, but his social/political/ideological position.[26] This feminist insight applies well to premodern Chinese culture, in which men were institutionally relegated to a yin position in front of the ruler, since Dong Zhongshu (179–104 BC.) applied the metaphysical terms, yin and yang, in designating human gendered relation.[27] Scholars' yin consciousness tends to be intensified when they experience an alienation complex, alienation from the court, orthodoxy, and prevailing conventions. From the mid-Ming onward, such a yin consciousness became more palpable in literati writings when, unsurprisingly, scholars constantly compared themselves to women.

Literati's political alienation in the Ming was partly attributable to the diabolic interference into politics of eunuchs, such as Liu Jin (1451–1510) in the mid-Ming and Wei Zhongxian (1568–1627) in the late Ming. In expressing their frustration under the sway of eunuchs' tyranny, scholar-officials often resorted to the figure of a concubine and a wife deserted by the emperor in self-reference, indicative of their intensifying awareness of their marginal/"feminine" identity. In the corpus of the eminent scholar Wang Yangming (1472–1529), for instance, there is a group of five poems under the rubric "Lamentations of a Deserted Wife," in which he compares himself to an abandoned wife of the ruler, after he was first jailed and then sent to political exile for his involvement in a campaign to expel Liu Jin from the court.[28]

Not only were officials frustrated in their political career constantly aware of their "concubine" status, but also were scholars who experienced setbacks in their career advancement. Ming-Qing was a period when the civil service examinations became extremely competitive, leaving many talented scholars rankless after a lifelong futile struggle. As a consequence, literati experienced intensified political and social marginality, which engendered in them sentimental kinship with women. The analogy between a woman and an unwanted official, a deep-rooted cultural conceit established when Qu Yuan initiated the *xiangcao meiren* (flower and beauty) tradition, struck a responsive chord and aroused acute poignancy in the psyche of many Ming-Qing literati.

A prominent case is that of Xu Wei (1521–1593), a talented scholar who was regarded by Yuan Hongdao (1568–1610) as "our contemporary Li Bai and Du Fu," but failed nine times in examinations.[29] Such excruciating experiences inevitably bred a sense of marginality and an emotional affinity with women. Thus, in his poems he repeatedly compares literati scholars in career advancement to palace ladies waiting for the emperor's patronage, and compares those failing in examinations to country girls who have lost their youthful color and still remain single.[30] In his lament over personal anxiety constantly audible in his writings, Yuan Hongdao catches the "wailing of a widow in the night."[31] Yet, a literatus' feminized identity is never identical to that of an ordinary woman; growing up in Confucian society, a man can never fully obliterate his duty-bound obligation to society from his consciousness. The coexistence of this masculine yearning for social service and literati's feminized social status enables Yuan Hongdao not only to catch the "wailing of a widow" in Xu Wei's writings, but also to discern "a royal air" (*wangzhe qi*), a dignified spirit to which "ordinary women subordinate to others can never expect to aspire."[32] It is this mettlesome spirit, lofty aspiration, and the "grief of a hero who has no lord to whom to devote his loyalty" that make the marginalized literati temperamentally comparable only to those females with masculine (heroic) spirit, the *nüzhong zhangfu* (female hero) of one type or another.[33]

It is not surprising that Xu Wei reveals fascination with gender-crossing women in his writings. He highly praises a lady who, upon the breaking out of a rebellious riot, dons a man's clothes in masquerade as a magistrate to confront the situation and pacify the insurgence;[34] he applies the term *nü zhangfu* to praise a woman with superior morality.[35] Hua Mulan, the archetype of Chinese androgyne, so captivates him that not only does he repeatedly adopt her image when referring to extraordinary women, he also writes a play to eulogize her. The motif of androgyny is even more prominent in his play *Nü zhuangyuan* (Women principal graduate), in which a female transvestite comes first in the imperial examination and rules with great competency as a ranking official. The obsession with nüzhong zhangfu revealed in Xu Wei's writings may mirror the gender fluidity in late Ming culture delineated above; more likely, it registers his conscious or subconscious identification with the female heroes, or women with male gender attributes, who provide a literary vehicle to vicariously gratify his own stifled masculine ambition as a marginal man. Such shared gender identity, sentimental affinity, and literary transference may also characterize the relationship between the literati authors of scholar-beauty romances, most of them marginal/"feminized" men who failed to pass civil service examinations, and the caizi and jiaren that they create in the genre, a point to be further discussed below. Xu Wei's masculine aspiration and his valorization of the andric, as seen in his application of *zhangfu* to extraordinary women, point to another late Ming cultural dimension that may have contributed to the androgyny craze in a more significant way: the unsuppressed masculinity of marginal men.

Ascendance of Yang Impulses in Institutionalized Yin Subjects

In *Renjian le*, Ruqi's valiant resistance to the sexual aggression from the power center demonstrates a marginal/feminine man's affirmation of masculinity, hence an "androgynous" stance. In the larger context of Ming culture, this can also be viewed as an inscription in literature of the ascendance of yang impulses in literati subjects, notwithstanding their institutionalized yin status, a tendency that gained momentum particularly in the late Ming when a native version of individualism was thriving in Chinese society.

In molding their gender identity, scholars were inevitably influenced by Confucianism, the institutionalized ideology and the basis of their education. While Confucianism stipulates the need for one's submission to authority, according to Dong Zhongshu's influential gender paradigm of human relationship, it endorses the right of the subordinate to challenge the authority, should the latter prove unworthy and inadequate. Thus latent in the feminine veins of the personal identity it promotes is a masculine drive to which it subscribes and affirms one's inner autonomy.[36] The virile will to defend self-independence vis-à-vis a despotic autocracy grows into a moral compulsion in Mencius, Confucius's eminent apostle, who valiantly questions the absolute authority of the monarch and unabashedly claims the reciprocity between the ruler and the subject.[37] In Mencius's thinking, courage—particularly the courage to adhere to one's moral vision—becomes a quintessential quality of a Confucian gentleman. In addition, he expresses this view in the gendered images of "concubine" and "hero" that left lasting impact on Chinese scholars' conception of gender in the course of history, the Ming in particular.

To convey contempt for men's lack of authenticity, Mencius labels their submissive compliance and slavish demeanor "the way of the concubine" (*qiefu zhidao*).[38] On the other hand, he applies the term *da zhangfu* in reference to his ideal hero, a "great man" with an impeccable moral outlook and indomitable will power. The moral fiber of such a Confucian paragon is so strong that he is "above the power of riches and honors to make dissipated, of poverty and force to make bend."[39] The frequent presence of these gendered terms in Ming scholars' writings, as shown below, bespeaks Mencius's tremendous influence on the literati culture of the Ming.

Opening Huang Zongxi's (1610–1695) famous intellectual history *Mingru xuean* (Case studies of the Ming Confucians), one is impressed by the ubiquitous presence of Mencius's name in literati's speeches. When Chen Xianzhang (1428–1500), the distinguished pioneer of the School of the Mind, read of the ideal personality of "the people of the heaven" (*tianmin*) in *Mencius*, he exclaimed that such people were the very models for the literati scholars of his time.[40] Worship for Mencius reaches such an extent that occasionally he is even valorized over the sage master Confucius. Gu Xiancheng (1550–1612), a leader of the Donglin Party, for instance, highly exalts Mencius for bringing righteousness into prominence in the Confucian discourse—a value that inspired many Ming scholars in political confrontation—and apparently contributing to the ascendance of yang impulses in literati identity.[41]

Ming dynasty was notorious for the tyranny of the monarchy. Confronted with the mounting despotism of the court, Ming scholars constantly derived masculine energy from *Mencius* to offset their institutionalized yin status in formulating a more balanced identity. In such gender construction, the Mencian icon da zhangfu serves as a moral paragon. In the early Ming, this can be seen in scholars' defiant resistance to the emperor Zhu Yuanzhang's (1328–1398) attempt to remove Mencius's image from the Confucian temple, for the sage was viewed as a potentially subversive force for his unmasked attack on political tyranny.[42] Braving the risk of death, a scholar Qian Tang protested against the emperor's move, despite the ruler's open warning against such protests. Sending his death-defying challenge to the emperor, Qian declared: "If I die for Mencius, I will die in glory."[43] In placing himself "above the power of force to make bend," Qian proves himself a bona fide Mencian da zhangfu, an icon he apparently worshiped and one with whom he was even ready to identify through martyrdom.

Ming history records numerous cases of scholar-officials' valiant affirmation of virility in their death-defying challenge to imperial tyranny. Another well-known case in the early Ming period was Fang Xiaoru's (1357–1402) martyrdom in refusing to draft an usurpation rescript. Summoned by the Yongle emperor (r. 1403–1424) to draft an edict to justify his usurpation, Fang repeatedly refused to appear in the court. When finally forced to go, he put on mourning clothes and wailed in the court. Pressed to write, he threw the brush onto the ground and cried: "I cannot draft this edict, even if I have to die."[44] With his dauntless courage and unadulterated integrity, Fang Xiaoru exemplified the yang spirit of the Mencian da zhangfu. Huang Zongxi thus takes him as the "spiritual father for the Ming scholars,"[45] whereas Wang Fuzi (1619–1692) exclaims, "Alas! With Fang Zhengxue's death, the species of Chinese scholars is extinct."[46] A national idol of the Ming dynasty, Fang Xiaoru left tremendous impact not only on shaping Ming scholars' identity, but also on late Ming/early Qing literature, serving as a prototype for caizi in scholar-beauty romances.

A prominent case can be traced to the early Qing fiction *Kuaishi zhuan* (A tale of gratifying souls) whose hero, called Changqi (constant wonder), is nicknamed "Huzi" (beard), for he wears a heavy beard, an eminent badge of masculinity. The nephew of an upright scholar who was executed for keeping the writings of Fang Xiaoru, Changqi kills the informant to avenge his uncle. After escaping from the prison he castrates himself, masquerades as a eunuch, and travels to a small neighboring country, and rallies an army to march on the Chinese border. The slogan that he raises for the mutiny is "to vindicate Fang Xiaoru," which is finally endorsed by the emperor in an appeasement endeavor. The hero's physical castration of his body signifies a renunciation of his gender association with patriarchy as well as his affinity to the feminine and the marginal, which is further projected in his identification with a weak, small country located on the border of the central kingdom, a geographical figure for political marginality. It is in this female/marginal (yin) position that he vociferates in a lion's roar to vindicate men's masculinity (yang) in political life; thus, he personifies the political stand of androgyny in our definition of the term. The triumph of his campaign dramatically presented in the fiction not only celebrates the virility of a marginal man, but also points to Fang Xiaoru's role as a fictional model for caizi's characterization and a spiritual inspiration for literati authors in conceiving scholar-beauty romances.

Fang Xiaoru's andric spirit is carried on, and spelt out more verbally, in the action and words of Luo Yifeng (fl. late fifteenth century) during the Chenghua regime (1465–1487), a period noted for ascendance of eunuchs' power. As a candidate in the imperial examination to present a strategy for the emperor in the court, he cited the flowing lines from the Song master Cheng Yi (1033–1107) to admonish the sovereign: "During the day a ruler should devote more time to meeting his ministers; he should spend less time with eunuchs and his consorts." When a court official endeavored to take away the second part of the line to avoid offending the emperor, he insisted on keeping it for cautionary effects. Later, when the emperor planned to keep a ranking official Li Wenda in the court during the latter's mourning period, in apparent violation of the code of filial piety, Luo presented a remonstrance to challenge the imperial plan, and was consequently deposed.

Not only did Luo Yifeng demonstrate virility in his deeds, but he also expressed captivation to masculinity in the following remarks that may serve as a verbal testimony to the ascendance of yang impulses in subjects' psyche in the Ming:

> I am virile by nature, hence I am attracted to masculine souls. Such attraction is hard to explain in words, like the feeling of a hungry and thirsty man when he longs for food. If I cannot get such a man as my permanent companion, I respectfully befriend him...My worship for virility comes from my nature... Mencius says: "I am skillful in nourishing my vast, potent passion-nature. It is exceedingly great and exceedingly strong; it fills up all between heaven and earth. With such nature one is above the power of riches and honors to corrupt, of poverty and mean conditions to make swerve from principle, and of power and force to make bend. Such a man of uttermost sincerity and utmost virility may be called a *da zhangfu*."[47] What I worship most is the virility in Mencius' words.[48]

In Huang Zongxi's observation, the Mencian da zhangfu that Luo presents here is nothing less than a truthful portrayal of his own personality.[49] With his transcendent and virile character, Luo never echoes others' words or bends his will in his life. Thus, in *Mingru xuean* Huang honors him as "a master for the Ming scholars," ranking him side by side with such lustrous figures as Fang Xiaoru and Wang Yangming.[50]

In late Ming, marginal men's affirmation of masculinity can be probably seen most prominently in the lives of official Hai Rui (1512–1587) and monk Daguan (1544–1604). In his well-known memorial "On Safety" (Hai 217–221), Hai Rui blames the Jiajing Emperor (r. 1522–1566) for many social vices prevalent at the time. Legend goes that before submitting the remonstrance, he bought a coffin and sent all servants home in anticipation of death. Hai Rui's heroism is matched in the Wanli period by Daguan, an eminent monk who ventured into the realm of politics and lost his life. In response to his disciples' and friends' advice against his risky trip to the capital to save another monk, Deqing, and to resist the emperor's tax policy, Daguan made the following reply that later became quite well-known: "At the time when I cut my hair, I felt as if I had already cut off my head."[51] He was subsequently persecuted by the Shenzong emperor (r. 1573–1619) during his stay in the capital. Venerated as "an eminent religious master" by Shen Defu (1578–1642) in his influential unofficial history *Wanli yehuo bian*, monk Daguan contributed significantly to the upsurge of yang energy in marginal scholars in late Ming culture.[52]

The marginal scholars' growing masculinity vis-à-vis political tyranny in the Ming period traced above provides a revealing context for the androgynous ideal celebrated in scholar-beauty romances, particularly, for the characterization of caizi in that genre. As a prominent feature of the genre, caizi—like all the politically alienated scholars in the Ming history discussed above—is always presented as a marginal man, a feature that is suggested by a common epithet that designates his identity, *luonan gongzi* (a literatus in distress). In *Renjian le*, this "distress" takes the form of Ruqi's imprisonment in the house of the prime minister. The hero's resistance to the sexual invasion in that work points to another feature of the genre: the confrontation between the marginal man and the power source that appears nearly in every work of scholar-beauty romances, although oftentimes such a confrontation is unfolded in the realm of politics, similar to the historical cases traced above. The romance is, therefore, often set in a time when a diabolical power—such as Yan Song (1480–1567), Wei Zhongxian (1568–1627), and Jia Sidao (1213–1275)—rides roughshod over the bureaucracy, marginalizing the scholars and stimulating their masculine action. Heroes in "Yuanyang pu" (The record of a union) and *Meng zhong yuan* (Union in a dream) both risk deposition to impeach Yan Song; protagonists in *Yuanyang pei* (A union of mandarin ducks), *Hongmei ji* (Mistress and maid), and *Tiehuaxian shi* (A romance of sward-flower immortal) all take actions to combat Jia Sidao. Just like the da zhangfu in Ming history, caizi personify androgyny with their assertion of yang impulses as yin subjects. As products of marginal men, the genre provides a literary vehicle for literati authors to vicariously affirm their andric urgings, which might have been suppressed in their real lives and yet they yearn to assert it through art. In a way, the ascendant yang impulses in institutionalized yin subjects—strongly throbbing in the Ming culture—are artistically fictionalized and enthusiastically celebrated in this genre.

Eremitism as an Expression of a Marginal Subject to Avow Andric Impulses

In addition to political activism, marginal scholars' masculine impulses also find outlet in political seclusion. In *Renjian le*, for instance, Ruqi's valiant resistance to the sexual aggression from the prime minister's family takes the form of his temporary withdrawal from the court. In fact, seclusion, as a component of caizi's characterization, appears in many works of this genre. The eremitic undercurrent of scholar-beauty romances—in a way—mirrors the hermetic inclination popular among Ming literati scholars, and it also carries an androgynous association in its gender implication.

Although Confucianism mandates that scholars should devote themselves to politics to uphold the Way, it encourages seclusion when moral order fails to prevail, or, the acceptance of marginal status to affirm one's integrity/inner virility. Unconditional espousal of seclusion is promoted by the Daoist philosophy, which also expresses it in more explicitly gendered terms. In the Daoist classic the *Laozi*, a Daoist sage is presented as someone "who understands masculinity and yet reserves femininity."[53] Although these words are often believed to imply advice to the ruler to uphold the virtues of humility and flexibility as an avenue to the dominant status, it points to the gender principle embraced and developed by the adherents of the Daoist tradition in fashioning their hermetic identity: to accept marginal/"female" status through reclusion to affirm one's personal autonomy/masculinity. In Daoist tradition an illustrating case can be traced to Zhuangzi, the legendary character in the book that bears the title of his name, who declined the ruler's invitation to govern the entire domain of his kingdom in favor of a carefree life of fishing in a river. Rationalizing his decision through a self-referential metaphor, Zhuangzi remarked that he preferred to be an ordinary tortoise, "alive and dragging its tail in the mud," rather than the sacred one, "dead," "wrapped up in a box," and "stored" in the emperor's ancestral temple.[54] Zhuangzi's tenacious adhering to the "mud"—the mother earth, an archetypal symbol of yin, which connotes social/political marginality—is thus motivated by a compulsion to keep alive his personal autonomy and inner virility. By adopting a yin mode of life to affirm his yang impulses, Zhuangzi exemplifies the Daoist ideal of androgyny inherent in Laozi's teaching, just as Mencius plays the pivotal role in highlighting the masculine aspect of Confucianism. In their study of psychology and sex roles, therefore, Alexandria G. Kaplan and Mary Anne Sedney observes: "Within the religious teaching of the East, androgyny is achieved in isolation from society. Those seeking enlightenment through intermingling feminine and masculine impulses need to withdraw from society, to seclude themselves in order to seek personal fulfillment."[55] Such a perception bears on the gendered associations of eremitism celebrated in scholar-beauty romances and the hermetic trend in Ming culture.

Scholars' antagonism to the decadent court during the Ming, particularly after mid-Ming, triggered a trend of seclusion. Prominent scholars during this period often demonstrated spiritual defiance in willfully estranging themselves from the power source to defend personal autonomy. A well-known case can be traced to the life of Tang Xianzu, a talented scholar who repeatedly failed in the civil service examination. In the late 1570s, the grand secretary Zhang Juzheng (1525–1582), in an attempt to hoodwink the world into believing his son's validity as a principal graduate (*zhuangyuan*), repeatedly connived to make Tang a study companion to his son by implicitly promising his success in the metropolitan examination. Tang's resistance to Zhang's first attempt brought catastrophe to his examination. Categorically declining Zhang's second offer, he remarked: "I dare not follow, or I will lose my chastity as a virgin."[56] Later, after Tang entered officialdom he again declined patronage by other two grand secretaries, the most powerful men in the court.

Tang's self-identification with a virgin, a rhetoric device that is also often used in scholar-beauty romances, carries a gender implication that can be associated with androgyny. In the power structure of patriarchy, the virgin—for having not yet succumbed to male domination—stands as a symbol of both political marginality and spiritual virility. Tang's rhetoric reveals both a keen awareness of his social marginality and spiritual alienation as a man of integrity defiantly asserting personal will under the sway of a decadent oligarchy. To accept his role in the political conspiracy would be tantamount to acquiescence to a spiritual rape and to compliance with the "way of the concubine." To further guard his "virginity," Tang later withdrew from the court after his remonstrance to the emperor spelled a disaster to his political career.

On top of political alienation, Ming scholars' longing for spiritual freedom also contributed to their lethargy over and disillusion with officialdom. Frustrated by his role as a magistrate and yet yearning for public reputation as a Confucian scholar, Yuan Hongdao repeatedly shuffled between officialdom and seclusion; suffocated by the repressive ambience of official life, Wen Zhengming (1470–1559) gave up his position in the imperial academy; estranged from his superiors and longing to pursue his personal interest, Li Zhi handed in his official cap. While the talented painter Dong Qichang (1555–1636) dallied with an official career briefly before taking protracted retirement in the "hermitage of arts," He Xinyin (1517–1579), Wong Longqi (1498–1583), and Qian Xushan (1497–1574)—the outstanding thinkers in the School of the Mind—either refused to sit for or quitted the imperial examination in protest against orthodoxy. The talented scholar Chen Jiru (1558–1639) even burned his scholar's robe at the age of 29 to demonstrate his determined rejection of officialdom. Willard Peterson observes in his study that a sample of every fifth biographical entry in Huang Zongxi's *Mingru xuean* shows that nearly a third of the men did not take examinations, did not serve, or lived most of their adult lives in some form of private retirement.[57] Small wonder, as Chen Wanyi indicates, Su Shi (1037–1101), the Song literatus with a penchant for seclusion, became a cultural celebrity in the late Ming period.[58]

In embracing political marginality/femininity to affirm personal autonomy/masculinity, literati scholars were modeling an androgynous identity, which may be sentimentally and spiritually related to their admiration for gender-crossing women, with whom they share a similar gender stand. In his writings Li Zhi, for instance, repeatedly exalts a female Buddhist Danran with whom he often conferred on religion. As study on Buddhism indicates that, compared with a male adept, a religious woman with her closer ties to the family often has to overcome more obstacles "in extricating herself from the familial context."[59] To pursue the Buddhist path, therefore, Danran had to possess stronger willpower than a man did. In praise of such andric propensity, Li Zhi takes her as her father's "son," and calls her a "prominent man" (*dashi*) and a "gentleman hermit" (*chushi zhangfu*).[60] Viewed in light of marginal scholars' propensity to rhetorically identify with women during this period, Li Zhi's praise of

Danran as a "gentleman hermit" may imply self-aggrandizement for the radical stand he himself took: in leaving the court and residing in a monastery to maintain the self-autonomy of a da zhangfu, he embraced a politically marginal/female position—symbolically on a par with Danran—and became a "female gentleman hermit" himself.

As literary inscription of literati culture, Ming scholars' eremitic inclinations also find expression in scholar-beauty romances, where the archetypal Chinese eremite Tao Yuanming (376–427) figures pervasively as a spiritual inspiration. The narrator in *Tiehuaxian shi* explicitly states that its hero, Cai Qizhi, follows the footsteps of the Jin hermit to hand in his seal when he feels his unbending disposition at odds with the bureaucratic superiors. In the second tale of *Zhenzhu bo* (Pearl ship), the hero chants Tao Yuanming's renowned line, "how can I bend my waist for five bushels of rice," before withdrawing from the court. In embracing political marginality, caizi in this genre reveals keen awareness of their feminized identity; hence they constantly compare themselves to women. Yet, just like Tang Xianzu in history, they feel inclined to identify not with ordinary women, but virtuous women defending virginity, in whom they apparently see a mirror image of their eremitic selves in guarding political integrity. In *Hudie mei* (A butterfly matchmaker), for instance, when an elder persuades three young scholars to serve the newly established Sui dynasty by comparing them to "virgins" who have never pledged allegiance to any ruler and hence are different from the "married women," the officials of the previous dynasty, the three men reply in unison:

> "You are right, sir, but we are afraid that women with vision would rather remain spinsters in their boudoirs until the declining age, than trust their virginity to disgraced men to humiliate their parents."
> (Nanyue daoren 720)

In seeking seclusion, therefore, caizi are consciously taking a gender stand identical to that of jiaren defending virginity. The analogy becomes so striking when we consider in the genre jiaren's collective antipathy to palace service: the heroines in *Tiehuaxian shi* and *Dingqing ren* (A tale of loyal love) both attempt to plunge themselves into river to dodge a life in the harem, whereas the heroine in *Qiao Lianzhu* (A union ingeniously arranged) first tries to cut her hair to convert to religion—and later goes through a mock nuptial ceremony with another girl—to shun palace service. While the scholars decline office, the beauties dodge palace enrollment: in their concerted refusal to identify with the power center, they affirm their masculinity by embracing political marginality.

Almost as a rule in the genre, caizi and jiaren descend from the lines of retired officials or secluded dissenters, from whom they inherit a transcendental outlook. While following the generic pattern, caizi always pass the official examinations with flying colors and enter officialdom; they share a propensity to withdraw instantly or after a brief period of service, which is always conveyed in a generically favored term *jiliu yongtui* (to retreat while one is on the crest of the wave). When withdrawal does not happen, the narrative tends to stop abruptly at the point of caizi's entry into the bureaucracy, as if once he identifies himself with the power source and loses his marginal status, his thematic mission is fulfilled. Even after he has entered officialdom, caizi may still face the confrontation with the power source, as elite power figures tend to press newly crowned zhuangyuan into marrying their daughters, a plot that not only appears in *Renjian le*, as mentioned above, but also in *Huanzhong zhen* (Truth in mirage) and *Fenghuang chi* (Phoenix pond). The marginalized scholar caizi, therefore, is forever at war with an overlord. It is in his resistance to power and his eremitic propensities that his latent masculinity surfaces. Perceptible behind caizi's image, therefore, are the two trends in literati culture traced above, scholars-officials' confrontational stance in politics and their spiritual affinity to the hermetic mode of existence. In his characterization, therefore, is inscribed scholars' avowal of unsuppressed virility as marginal men, that is, their ideal of androgyny.

Literati's Defiant Assertion of Virility in Ideological Confrontation

In *Renjian le*, Yinan's free movement between the two genders and the active role she plays in courting the man of her heart, as dramatic shows of her androgynous personality, are intrinsically related to the cult of qing, which—in a way—reflects literati's assertion of virile impulses in ideological confrontation, as shown in the following discussion.

Along with their defiant stand in political confrontation, late Ming scholars' surging masculine impulses also find expression in their challenge to the hegemonic Cheng-Zhu orthodoxy, which was turning ever more suppressive and antihuman in social practice, and revealed growing artificiality and hypocrisy. The widening gap between its rigid moral dogmas and its advocators' amoral behavior led to scholars' further disillusionment with orthodoxy. A case in the upper echelon can be found in Zhang Juzheng, the grand secretary and imperial tutor during the Wanli regime, who imposed on the young emperor a rigid standard of personal conducts but was found posthumously to have been living in luxury, accepting bribery, and abusing power.[61]

Underlying scholars' ideological confrontation is their revulsion against the suppression of human desire and love, which is embedded in orthodoxy and encapsulated in the cultural imperative that one should "extinguish desire (*renyu*) to uphold the heavenly principle (*tianli*)," a dogma that was preached by some followers of the Song Neo-Confucian School of the Principle. Although such dichotomous approach to desire and principle was meant to enhance human morality, it was often given excessively rigid interpretation in government-promoted orthodox discourse and, hence, "abused" in social practice to suppress basic human desire. In Ming-Qing society, this led to the convention of widow chastity, and—in some extreme cases—widow martyrdom and fiancé chastity; and it obviously clashes with the thriving liberal sentiments in the literati culture. It is to resist such morbid orthodoxy in assertion of personal authenticity that the latent andric impulses surface in literati's psyche. This can be seen in the case of Xia Tingmei (fl. seventeenth century), an obscure farmer who became a member of the leftist Taizhou School in the School of the Mind. In the following lines, Xia raises a hue and cry against the Song antithetical treatment of *li* and *yu*:

> Who divided heavenly principle and human desire? If you ponder over this question, you will find yourself enlightened and confused in terms. If you are enlightened, human desires are heavenly principle; if you are not enlightened, even heavenly principle becomes human desire.[62]

Such argument against li-yu antithesis is quite common in late Ming liberals' writings; what distinguishes Xia Tingmei from others is that he spells out the gender stance of such a confrontational view clearly in the following remarks: "To be a *da zhangfu*, one has to follow the authenticity of his mind and act only according to his authentic will. To be swayed and led by worldly conventions and other's behavior is the way of the concubine."[63] It is clear that for the left-wing of the School of the Mind, the Mencian idol of da zhangfu had turned into a paragon of strong willpower, serving as a fountainhead of courage when they questioned orthodoxy.

Xia's above use of Mencian terminology may reflect the influence of Wang Gen (1483–1540), a pioneer of the Taizhou School, who adopted similar language when he stressed the vital importance of self-reliance and designated men's "dependence on the world" as "the way of the concubine."[64] The masculine fiber of the late Ming anti-conventional stance is probably nowhere more graphically presented than in Huang Zongxi's following portrayal of the Taizhou School:

> Scholars [in this school] can often fight dragons and snakes with bare hands...They can no longer be bound by the orthodox...They have turned heaven and earth upside down. Before them there was no precedent; after them there will be no equals.[65]

The association of spiritual independence with the male gender-valuation of the da zhangfu, inherent in Wang Gen's, Xia Tingmei's, and Huang Zongxi's above quotes, lies behind many late Ming scholars' perception of the gender identity that they were fashioning in their confrontation of orthodoxy. In Yuan Zhongdao's words, "A *da zhangfu* should conduct himself with utmost freedom, taking delight in his own leisure. How can he follow others in tears and laughter, letting other thread his nose [like an ox] and control his head [like a horse]?"[66] Similarly, Li Zhi takes the independent-minded souls who protect others as "great men," and those who seek protection from others as "petty men."[67] He laughs at himself for parroting others' words in his youth, like a dog following others' suit barking at a shadow; and he prides himself for having finally grown from a "dwarf" into a "giant" (his version of da zhangfu) in his old age.[68]

In ideological confrontation, late Ming da zhangfu often demonstrate their spiritual virility in their moral courage to affirm the validity of human desire, for the suppression of which orthodoxy lies at the core of the decadent marital conventions that grant marital decision to the senior generation and deprive those involved the right to pursue love. Thus, with great courage He Xinyin (1517–1579) writes, "The mind cannot do without desire," although he immediately cautions against an unrestrained indulgence in sexual desire.[69] In a similar vein, Li Zhi validates the selfish nature of human beings.[70] The masculine gender implication of late Ming liberals' defiant assertion of human desire/love is more clearly spelt out in a poem composed by Tang Yin (1470–1526), entitled "Sitting Silently in Front of the Burning Incense." In the poem, Tang Yin first expresses the suspicion that people's mouths did not often match their hearts when they spoke, for the sexual drive that had been viewed as a basic human need in ancient time was taken as a shame in his time. He then cautions the world to listen to him: "All men are inevitably going to die. A *da zhangfu* is someone who in death can face his living identity without shame."[71] In the minds of late Ming liberals, such as Tang Yin, apparently, the moral courage to admit one's sexual desire becomes a defining quality of the great man. Such perception, indeed, may well have inspired He Xinyin's affirmation of human desire and Li Zhi's defense of men's selfish nature; it serves as an ideological foundation for the emergence of the cult of qing.

In recent Western discussion of the cult of qing, scholars have recognized the antihegemonic nature of the movement. In defiantly asserting the legitimacy of human desire, the pioneers of the cult of qing demonstrates a considerable amount of courage, although the cult "progressively lost" its "transgressive edge" as it unfolded and integrated itself in literati culture.[72] It is not surprising that in their writings, late Ming liberals often exalt women who cross gender restrictions in active pursuit of love, for, historically, sexual desire had been more severely repressed in Chinese women. As personification of the virile will of marginal subjects in confrontation of the decadent orthodoxy, such nü zhangfu share a similar gender stance, as well as a common cause, with the recalcitrant thinkers of the late Ming period, hence winning their special respect and admiration.

The two idols of female heroes most ardently celebrated in late Ming literati culture are Zhuo Wenjun and Hongfu, one a widow of the Han dynasty (206 BC –AD 220) who broke loose from the bondage to the inner chamber to elope with the man of her heart, the other a Tang *chuanqi* heroine who masquerades as a man to gain entrance into the chamber of her chosen man. In the late Ming perception, Wenjun and Hongfu, in liberating themselves from the confines of their prescribed femininity, not only exemplify the androgynous stance in courtship, but also demonstrate a marginal subject's virile will in defiance of established conventions. Hence, the tale of Hongfu was repeatedly adapted to dramatic versions during the Ming, and it appeals immensely to Tang Xianzu, who annotates Zhang Fengyi's (1527–1613) drama *The Tale of Hongfu* and writes an inscription for Zhang Taihe's *Hongfu*. Similarly, Li Zhi praises Hongfu for her "peerless intelligence" in spotting a worthy man.[73] With equal ardor, Tang Xianzu expresses admiration for Zhuo Wenjun, whom he ranks side by side with the emperor: "Emperor Wu of the Han stands out among the dignitaries; Zhou Wenjun distinguishes herself among the commoners."[74] Li Zhi, likewise, exalts Wenjun's courage for eloping with her lover in "achieving a great deal at the expense of minor humiliation."[75]

Such celebration of transgressive female androgynes was inevitably frowned upon in the patriarchal order. Li Zhi's support of Zhuo Wenjun's heretic position later was cited as a crime in a memorial sent in by his opponent, leading to his arrest, and ultimately to his martyrdom in prison. Although Tang Xianzu was not so severely persecuted, his celebration of women's gender deviation in love and courtship also courted censure from the orthodox. One friend reprimanded him for composing "excessively florid lines";[76] another reproached him for his obsession with drama.[77] Commenting on his position in composing *The Peony Pavilion*, Anthony Yu, therefore, applies the term "uttermost daring."[78] In initiating the antihegemonic cult of qing, the late Ming scholars, such as Li Zhi and Tang Xianzu, either paid a high price or demonstrated great courage. By taking a masculine stance as marginal subjects in confrontation of orthodoxy, these liberal-minded scholars were posing a gender position that can be termed androgynous, hence akin in spirit to the gender-crossing androgynes that they celebrate in their writings.

As mirror reflection of the late Ming liberal thinking, scholar-beauty romances also glorify the seditious souls of Wenjun and Hongfu, who constantly serve as role models and spiritual aspirations for heroines in their revolt against cultural restraints. In the late Ming story collection *Xihu erji* (Two collections about the West Lake), Zhuo Wenjun is deified as a fairy maid to the Queen Mother of the West;[79] the nuptial freedom that Wenjun pursues is taken as the supreme felicity of human life by the heroine of *Jiaohong ji*, a drama of the same period.[80] In the mind of Ruan Jianglan, the romantic hero in the first tale of *Zhaoshi bei* (A cup that illuminates the world), maidens and damsels in respective households should emulate the models of "sublime women and gallant females, such as Hongfu and Wenjun, who elope with the men of their hearts."[81] Indeed, the female aspirants for gender freedom mushrooming in this genre consciously follow the footsteps of the archetypal androgynes in molding their identity. Inspired by the antecedent of Zhuo Wenjun, Xueer, the heroine of *Wufeng yin* (Song of five phoenixes), invites her lover to cross the forbidden line of her boudoir to seal a connubial compact; emulating Hongfu's strategy, Miss Zhaohua, the heroine of *Liner bao* (Granting a prominent son as a reward), masquerades as a man to dodge an imposed marriage. The early Qing romance *Hudie mei* even unfolds a sequel to the master chuanqi tale of the Tang dynasty, where the Sui dignitary, Yang Su, acquires another unrivaled beauty after Hongfu deserts him to elope with her lover. But this concubine successor turns out to be another Hongfu, who swears a love oath to a scholar before involuntarily filling her position in Yang's harem and ultimately she—following Hongfu's footstep—unites with her lover without even losing her virginity. The figures of Hongfu and Zhuo Wenjun loom so large and emerge so pervasively in characters' dialogues, psychological activities, authorial prefaces, and interlaced poetry that one may almost sense the obsession of the genre with these archetypal androgynes.

As if in conscious emulation of Hongfu, a more dramatic mode of gender fluidity in the pursuit of love, cross-dressing, becomes a recurrent behavioral pattern in jiaren's lives in the genre, of which Yinan's chameleonlike characterization in *Renjian le* can be viewed as a unique derivative. Oftentimes, jiaren cross-dress as males setting out on a journey in search of the men of their dreams, or they go through a fake nuptial ceremony with another girl under male garments to dodge an unwanted marriage with a villain. In playing an active role to control their nuptial destiny, they adopt a masculine mode of courtship that is dramatically projected on the male garments they don. Such dramatic plots, traceable in *Baigui zhi* (A tale of white jade), *Chun Liu Ying* (A happy triangle), *Yu Jiao Li* (The romance of three ideal lovers), and many others, becomes a hallmark of scholar-beauty romances, and the most graphic demonstration of the androgynous ideal celebrated in the genre.

Yet, its artistic appeal notwithstanding, jiaren's dramatic action can find little support from historical records. Although critics have indicated that as a flourishing character type, jiaren can be viewed as a "by-product" of late Ming courtesan culture, embodying all its esteemed values, yet its relevance to social life remains questionable.[82] Although the expansion of the female sphere in late Ming society that "had begun to blur the centuries-old boundary between inner and outer spheres," as Dorothy Ko documented in her study, may have inspired literati authors to conceive jiaren's dramatic actions in the genre, it does not seem to serve as a historical correlate, for in Ko's discussion the shifting inner-outer boundary is largely attributed to the movements of tutors, travelers, courtesans, and career women, not virgin maidens.[83] Boudoir confinement may have relaxed a bit during this period, yet no cultural historian has claimed its breach as an accepted behavioral pattern in respectable families, not even in the Jiangnan area. While female cross-dressing was occasionally resorted to as a means of survival in war-torn zones, no record indicates its social use in courtship. The gap between social reality and literary presentation may suggest that the fervor of qing has inspired literati scholars to project a germinating social consciousness, or even subdued impulses, in a magnified form in literature to present their aspirations and ideal. In a certain way, women's "expanded sphere of activity" in the late Ming is fictionally augmented by literati imagination under the spur of qing to project their ideal of androgyny.

In light of scholars' aforementioned valiant assertion of human desire vis-à-vis orthodox suppression that constitutes the mainstream of the late Ming liberal thinking, the androgyny dramatically presented in jiaren's characterization may be intrinsically related to literati's androgynous stance in ideological confrontation. In the presentation of jiaren's active pursuit of love, we may sense literati authors' valiant intent to validate human desire and human love. The male garment on the beauty's body in the game of courtship may well signal literati authors' masculine spirit as marginal men defying the dominant ideology of the time.

In the above discussion, I have explored the historical and cultural dimensions of the androgynous ideal in scholar-beauty romances. While this literary phenomenon may owe its conception to the gender fluidity in Ming culture, ideologically, it originates from literati scholars' recalcitrant impulses to assert their latent masculinity as institutionalized yin subjects, hence reflecting their own androgynous position. Just like literati scholars in the Ming, caizi and jiaren adopt androgynous stance in the closely related domains of politics and ideology in their joint battles against established conventions and villainous power. Since the Mencian icon da zhangfu was appropriated and transformed by Ming scholars in their political/ideological confrontation into a source of courage, inspiration, and a role model, the rhetoric of da zhangfu and nüzhong zhangfu gains wide currency in scholar-beauty romances in designating heroes and heroines with wholesome gender identity. Viewed in the historical and cultural context of late Ming, the ideal of androgyny celebrated in scholar-beauty romances is, therefore, charged with a strong note of self-expression and self-aggrandizement. It is through the stylistically inflated and artistically idealized characterization of caizi and jiaren that literati scholars project their preferred values, liberal outlooks, and their ideal of androgynous personality. After the mid-Qing, when the Neo-Confucian left-wing thinking went out of vogue, the cult of qing lost its initial appeal, literati's sense of marginality eased, and the traditional concept of gender dichotomy regained its lost ground, androgyny as a symbolic mode for self-expression gradually lost its urgency in male literati's psyche as well as its popularity in their literary productions.

Notes

* This chapter is developed from, and partly based on, my book *Androgyny in Late Ming and Early Qing Literature* (Honolulu: University of Hawaii Press, 2003), see 9–11, 13–19, 26–30, 34–39, 98–99, 101, 106, and 108. I want to thank the editor for granting me the permission to use some materials in that book.

1. Tianhuazang zhuren (天花藏主人), *Renjian le* (人间乐) (Shenyang: Chunfeng wenyi chubanshe, 1985), 19.
2. Cynthia Secor, "The Androgyny Papers," *Women's Studies: An Interdisciplinary Journal* 2, no. 2 (1974): 139–141, on 139.
3. Carolyn G. Heilbrun, *Toward a Recognition of Androgyny* (New York: Alfred Knopf, 1973), x.
4. Maram Epstein, *Competing Discourses, Orthodoxy, Authenticity, and Engendered Meanings in Late Imperial Chinese Fiction* (Cambridge: Harvard University Asia Center, 2001), 118.
5. Bret Hinsch, *Passion of the Cut Sleeve: The Male Homosexual Tradition in China* (Berkeley: University of California Press, 1990, 11–38; Wang Shunu (王书奴), *Zhongguo changjishi* (中国娼妓史), reprint ed. (Shanghai: Shanghai shudian, 1992 [1934]), 225–230.
6. Fu Yiling (傅衣凌), *Mingdai jiangnan shimin jingji shitan* (明代江南市民经济试探) (Shanghai: Shanghai renmin chubanshe, 1963), 107.
7. Robert Hans van Gulik, *Sexual Life in Ancient China* (Leiden: E. J. Brill, 1961), 294.
8. Martin Weizong Huang, "Dehistoricization and Intertextualization: The Anxiety of Precedents in the Evolution of the Traditional Chinese Novel," *Chinese Literature, Essay, Review, Article* 12 (1990): 45–68, on 57.
9. Keith McMahon, *Causality and Containment in Seventeenth-Century Chinese Fiction* (New York: E. J. Brill, 1988), 51.
10. Sophie Volpp, "The Discourse on Male Marriage: Li Yu's 'A Male Mencius's Mother,'" *positions* 2, no. 1(1994): 113–132, on 129.
11. Xie Zhaozhi (谢肇淛), *Wu Zazu* (五杂俎), vol. 1 (Beijing: Zhonghua shuju, 1959), 198.
12. William Willetts, *Chinese Calligraphy: Its History and Aesthetic Movement* (Oxford: Oxford University Press, 1987), 133.
13. Kang-I Sun Chang, *The Late-Ming Poet Ch'en Tzu-lung: Crises of Love and Loyalty* (New Haven: Yale University Press, 1991), 41–68.
14. Epstein, Competing Discourses, 118.
15. Dorothy Ko, *Teachers of the Inner Chambers: Women and Culture in Seventeenth-Century* (Stanford: Stanford University Press, 1994).
16. Dorothy Ko, "Pursuing Talent and Virtue: Education and Women's Culture in Seventeenth-and Eighteenth-Century China," *Late Imperial China* 13, no. 1 (June 1992): 9–39, on 9; Kang-I Sun Chang, "Ming-Qing Women Poets and the Notions of 'Talent' and 'Morality,'" in *Culture and State in Chinese History*, ed. Theodore

Hunt, R. Bin Wong, and Pauline Yu (Stanford: Stanford University Press, 1997), 236–258, on 247.
17. Ko, *Teachers*, 274–90.
18. Yu Songqing (俞松青), "Ming Qing shiqi minjian zongjiao jiaopai zhong de nüxing" (明清时期民间宗教教派中的女性), *Nankai daxue xuebao* (南开大学学报) 5 (1982): 29–33.
19. Beata Grant, "Female Holder of the Lineage: Linji Chan Master Zhiyuan Xinggang (1597–1654)," *Late Imperial China* 17, no. 2 (December 1996): 51–76.
20. Feng Menglong (冯梦龙), *Ming Qing minge shidao ji* (明清民歌时调集) (Shanghai: Shanghai guji chubanshe, 1986), 299–300.
21. Shuhui Yang, *Appropriation and Representation: Feng Menglong and the Chinese Vernacular Story* (Ann Arbor: Center for Chinese Studies, University of Michigan, 1998), 36.
22. Gu Qiyuan, "Kezuo zhuiyu," cited in Xia Xianchun (夏咸淳), *Wanming shifeng yu wenxue* (晚明士风与文学) (Beijing: Zhongguo shehui kexue chubanshe, 1994), 48.
23. Zhang Tingyu (张廷玉), *Ming shi* (明史), vol. 23 (Beijing: Zhonghua shuju, 1974), 6944–6948.
24. Xu Wei (徐渭), *Xu Wei ji* (徐渭集), vol. 2 (Beijing: Zhonghua shuju, 1983), 363–365.
25. Tian Yiheng (田艺蘅), *Liuqing rizha* (留青日札) (Taipei: Guangwen, 1970), 98–100 and 141.
26. Toril Moi, *Sexual/Textual Politics: Feminist Literary Theory* (London & New York: Methuen, 1985), 166.
27. Dong Zhongshu (董仲书), *Chunqiu fanlu* (春秋繁露), in *Sibu congkan* (四部丛), vol. 10 (Shanghai: Shanghai shudian, 1989), 76.
28. Wang Yangming (王阳明), *Wang Yangming quan ji* (王阳明全集), vol. 1 (Shanghai: Shanghai guji chubanshe, 2006), 692.
29. Yuan Hongdao (袁宏道), *Yuan Hongdao ji jian jiao* (袁宏道集笺校), vol. 2 (Shanghai: Shanghai guji chubanshe, 2008), 746.
30. Xu, *Xu Wei ji*, vol. 1, 160; Xu, *Xu Wei ji*, vol. 3, 890.
31. Yuan, *Yuan Hongdao*, vol. 2, 716.
32. Yuan, *Yuan Hongdao*, vol. 2, p. 716.
33. Yuan, *Yuan Hongdao*, vol. 2, p. 716.
34. Xu, *Xu Wei ji*, vol. 2, 626.
35. Xu, *Xu Wei ji*, vol. 4, 1138.
36. Zhou Zuyan, "Aspiring to Be a *Da Zhangfu*: Masculinization in Late Imperial Chinese Literature," *Tankang Review* 35, no. 1 (2004 Autumn): 79–117, on 82–83.
37. Mencius, "The Works of Mencius," *The Four Books*, trans. James Legge (New York: Paragon Book Reprint Corp, 1966), 733.
38. Mencius, "The Works of Mencius," p. 650.
39. Mencius, "The Works of Mencius," p. 651.
40. Huang Zongxi (黄宗羲), *Mingru xuean* (明儒学案), vol. 1 (Beijing: Zhonghua shuju, 2008), 79.

41. Zhang Xuan (张萱), *Xiyuan wenjian lu* (西园闻见录), vol. 2, reprint ed. (Taipei: Huawen shuju, 1968 [1632]), 954.
42. Mencius, "The Works of Mencius," 734.
43. Zhang, *Ming shi*, vol. 13, 3982.
44. Zhang, *Ming shi*, vol. 13, 4019.
45. Huang, *Mingru xuean*, vol. 2, 1042.
46. Wang Fuzi (王夫子), *Chuanshan quan shu* (船山全书), vol. 10 (Changsha: Yuelu shushe, 1988), 93.
47. My translation of the quoted lines from *Mencius* is adapted from James Legge's translation, *The Works of Mencius*, 189, 190, and 265.
48. Huang, *Mingru xuean* vol. 1, 6.
49. Huang, *Mingru xuean* vol. 1, 6.
50. Huang, *Mingru xuean* vol. 1, 5–6.
51. Tang Xianzu (汤显祖), *Tang Xianzu quan ji* (汤显祖全集), vol. 2 (Beijing: Beijing guji chubanshe, 2001), 1079.
52. Shen Defu (沈德符), *Wanli yehuo bian* (万历野获编), vol. 3 (Beijing: Zhonghua shuju, 1997), 691.
53. Rhett Y. W. Young and Roger T. Ames, trans., *Lao Tzu Text, Notes, and Comments* (San Francisco: Chinese Materials Center, 1981), 154.
54. Burton Watson, trans., *The Complete Works of Chuang Tzu* (New York: Columbia University Press, 1986), 187–188.
55. Alexandria G. Kaplan and Mary Anne Sedney, *Psychology and Sex Roles: An Androgynous Perspective* (Boston: Little Brown, 1980), 75.
56. Tang, *Tang Xianzu quan ji*, vol. 3, 2581.
57. Willard J. Peterson, *Bitter Gourd: Fang I-Chih and the Impetus for Intellectual Change* (New Haven: Yale University Press, 1979), 5.
58. Chen Wanyi (陈万益), *Wanming xiaopin yu Mingji wenren shenghuo* (晚明小品与明季文人生活) (Taipei: Daan chubanshe, 1988), 1–36.
59. Grant, "Female Holder," 60.
60. Li Zhi (李贽), *Li Zhi wen ji* (李贽文集), vol. 1 (Beijing: Shehui kexue wenxian chubanshe, 2000), 171.
61. Frederick W. Mote and Denis Twitchett, eds., *The Cambridge History of China*, vol. 7 (Cambridge: Cambridge University Press, 1988), 515, and 528
62. Huang, *Mingru xuean* vol. 2, 721.
63. Huang, *Mingru xuean* vol. 2, 721.
64. Huang, *Mingru xuean* vol. 2, 711.
65. Huang, *Mingru xuean* vol. 2, 703.
66. Yuan Zhongdao (袁中道), *Kexuezhai ji* (珂雨斋集), ed. Yang Jialuo, vol. 2 (Taipei: Shijie shuju, 1965), 756.
67. Li, *Li Zhi wen ji*, vol. 1a, 53.
68. Li, *Li Zhi wen ji*, vol. 1b, 63.
69. He Xinyin (何心隐), *He Xinyin ji* (何心隐集) (Beijing: Zhonghua shuju, 1981), 40.

70. Li, *Li Zhi wen ji*, vol. 7, 358.
71. Tang Yin (唐寅), *Tang Bohu quan ji* (唐伯虎全集) (Beijing: Zhongguo shudian, 1985), 15–16.
72. Epstein, *Competing Discourses*, 79.
73. Li, *Li Zhi wen ji*, vol. 1, 182.
74. Tang, *Tang Xianzu quan ji*, vol. 2, 866.
75. Li, *Li Zhi wen ji*, vol. 3, 719.
76. Tang, *Tang Xianzu quan ji*, vol. 2, 1401.
77. Chen Jiru (陈继儒), "Mudan ting tici" (牡丹亭题辞), *Tang Xianzu yanjiu ziliao huibian* (汤显祖研究资料汇编), comp. Miao Xiaotong (毛效同), vol. 2 (Shanghai: Shanghai guji chubanshe, 1986), 855.
78. Anthony Yu, *Rereading the Stone: Desire and the Making of Fiction in Dream of the Red Chamber* (Princeton: Princeton University Press, 1997), 105.
79. Zhou Ji (周楫), *Xihu erji* 西湖二集 (Hangzhou: Zhejiang renmin chubanshe, 1981), 309.
80. Meng Chenshun (孟称舜), *Jiaohong ji* (娇红记) (Shanghai: Shanghai guji chubanshe, 1988), 18.
81. Zhuoyuanting zhuren (酌元亭主人), *Zhaoshi bei* (照世杯) (Shanghai: Shanghai guji chubanshe, 1985), 6.
82. Chang, *The Late-Ming Poet*, 11–13.
83. Ko, *Teachers*, 142.

CHAPTER 5

Transgenderism as a Heuristic Device: On the Cross-historical and Transnational Adaptations of the *Legend of the White Snake*

Alvin Ka Hin Wong

I. INTRODUCTION

Any project that attempts to read transgender meanings into Chinese histories and cultural representations will almost always encounter the following question: How do we "apply" an Euro-American theoretical and social category such as transgender to different national contexts? But even this obsession with the question of applicability assumes the coherence of the exporting term transgender, thereby relegating different forms of "Chinese" gender variance as simply the incomplete faces of an otherwise coherent field of knowledge. This chapter takes as its point of departure the unpredictability and speculative aspects of transgender subjectivities in the process of adaptation across genre, time, and space. I will first give a brief review of recent works in Chinese studies that touch on transgender topics before making the case for a cross-historical methodology that treats transgenderism as a heuristic open signifier.

In Chinese studies, scholars have begun to pay more systematic attention to transgender topics. For example, Wu Cuncun has discussed the gender and class hierarchies between male literati and young male actors who played the female dan roles in Peking opera in the Ming-Qing era.[1] Helen Hok-Sze Leung theorizes the cultural production of two modes of transgender subjectivities—transsexualism and transgender butch—in postcolonial Hong Kong cinema.² In her study of Wang Dulu's martial arts novel, *Crouching Tiger, Hidden Dragon* (1941), Tze-lan D. Sang proposes that the original text offers more ethnic, gender, and bodily transgressions than Ang Lee's cinematic adaptation allows.³

While I still insist on the importance of historicizing what transgender might mean in different periods of Chinese history, I also want to ask the more ambitious question of how similar categories of gender variance in Chinese history may brush against one another in what Walter Benjamin calls a historical materialist approach.⁴ In my constellational approach, I emphasize the productive potentials of a cross-historical methodology that places the transgender theoretical protagonist, *renyao* (人妖), at the center of analysis. In Chinese, the compound renyao literally means human prodigy; when separated into two words, *ren* literally means the human and *yao* the demon or evilness. In its modern colloquial Chinese usage, it often refers to lady boys and male transsexuals in Thailand. Renyao in its transphobic Chinese-speaking usage then bears the strongest link to the local Thai identity of the *kathoey*, which "has developed into a word used almost exclusively for males who prefer the female gender role, i.e., cross-dressers, transsexuals and varieties in-between. That is, *kathoey* has begun more and more to denote 'transgender.'"⁵ Given that part of the modern transphobic usage of renyao rests on its imagined horror that the binary opposites (the human and the demon) can coexist within a gender variant body, I will critically relate this demarcation of the human and the nonhuman in modern Chinese lexicon to earlier dichotomizing logics of the human and the demonic in Ming folklores. Specifically, after probing the subjection of feminine-demonic transgression in Feng Menglong's *Legend of the White Snake* (白蛇傳) written in the late Ming, I will demonstrate how modern literary and media adaptations of the legend reconfigure femininity as a mobile ground for imagining perverse sexuality and transgender femme subjectivity.

Briefly, the story is set in the years of Southern Song governed by Emperor Gaozong. Madame Bai, with a thousand years of magical power, incarnates as human and seduces a handsome young man named Xu Xuan (許宣). Her entrance into the human world is accompanied by another green fish demon, Qing Qing. In later versions of *The Legend*, Xu Xuan's name changes to Xu Xian, and the green fish becomes a green snake. In this didactic and moralist tale, Bai is narrated as an evil woman/demon who brings ill luck to Xu and poses threats to his life. The story ends with the powerful monk Fai Hai saving Xu's life and suppressing the two demons under the Leifeng Pagoda in West Lake. It concludes with a Buddhist, moralist tone: "Admonish the worldly people not to lust! A person filled with lust will be deluded by sex."[6]

The ren/yao division in Feng's text depends on a cosmological worldview of Confucian gender that subjugates the feminine as the demonic. I will trace the logic of feminine transgression as evident in the ending of Feng's text by examining how early Qing writer Pu Songling's story "Renyao" further substantiates the politics of feminine subjection in renyao representations: Pu tells a story of heterosexual male cross-dressing that results in a forced male-to-female sex change, mandated by a cuckooed husband who forces the punished cross-dresser to make do with the "wrong" gender and become his mistress. Situating the issue of feminine subjection in the intertwined context of these different renderings of renyao subjectivity and gender variance, I will then draw on recent work on same-sex relations in Republican China to situate the May Fourth writer Yu Dafu's story "Renyao" with respect to the broader cultural context in which the renyao transgender subject was pathologized. My reading finds that despite the introduction of Western sexology during this historical moment of colonial modernity, Yu's text actually opens up more complicated relationships between the renyao subject and the feminine in the sense that *both* the male narrator and his object of desire are ambiguously gendered and feminized. Subsequently, I turn to Li Bihua's 1986 Hong Kong novel *Qingshe* (*Green Snake*) and read it as an "unfaithful adaptation" because, unlike its predecessors, in this iteration of the *Legend* the green snake embodies a mobile form of femininity that is at once perverse and multidirectional in her pursuit of desire.

Finally, I end with the transnational visuality of the legend in the 1992 Taiwan TV series the *New Legend of Madame White Snake* produced by Cao Jingde, which I interpret as a text that manages different forms of femininity in its representation of female masculinity. I call the feminine expression of actress Yip Tung's embodiment of female masculinity in her portrayal of Xu Xian as the "transgender femme." Given the various historical periods and different Chinese-speaking geographies that this chapter concerns with, I want to clarify from the outset that the term renyao as deployed here does not indicate some preconceived notions of femininity and masculinity or an original emergence of the Chinese transgender. Although in Feng's text he never refers to Madame Bai as a "renyao" but simply as a yao (demon), renyao as a relational trope productively serves as a reading framework that indicates how the cosmological worldview of the human subject depends on the repudiation and disciplining of transgressive femininity that Bai embodies. Theorizing renyao as a relational term rather than a specifically confined sexual category of transgenderism then introduces femininity as a shifting and mobile formation as it relates to the diverse configurations of renyao in each of the texts examined here. Furthermore, I define femmeness as a transgender mode of expressing, embodying, and visualizing femininity that can reside in various gendered and sexed bodies. In particular, I will demonstrate the extent to which Cao's TV series creatively expresses hyperfemmeness in heterosexual form in the actress Angie Chiu's presentation of Bai while representing Yip Tung's cross-dressing performance in a male role that is less butch but more femme. Therefore, transgender femmeness illustrates a peculiar transgender configuration of a female body into a masculine body that, at the same time, does not forsake feminine qualities even in its corporeal embodiment of female masculinity. This again illustrates that female masculinity in its transgender form must be framed relationally to the engendering of femininity.

Above all, this cross-historical study insists that the category transgender concerns not only the applicability of Western theory in Chinese contexts; but, more provocatively, it can also serve as a heuristic lens through which one could see how a specific gender-variant term such as renyao mutates across Chinese cultural history and, indeed, "transgenders" in different forms of cultural production through the very processes of adaptation across the heterogeneous times and spaces of the Sinophone world.[7] It aims to show how transgender studies in Chinese and Sinophone contexts are as much about excavating and "recovering" specific transgender terminology such as renyao as they are about its *afterlife* in cultural translations across time and space. Consequently, a heuristic approach to transgenderism treats transgender as a historically open, speculative category.[8] It traces certain transgender protagonist such as the renyao across different sites of China and sees what kinds of friction and uncertainty may emerge as we theorize about transgender politics in a nonpredetermined fashion.

This cross-historical approach builds significantly on Carolyn Dinshaw's concept of "touching on the past," which is "a queer historical impulse, an impulse toward making connections across time between, on the one hand, lives, texts, and other cultural phenomena left out of sexual categories back then and, on the other, those left out of current sexual categories now."[9] While this chapter certainly takes up Dinshaw's call by demonstrating how modern adaptations of the tale queerly touch on the "original" text in the late Ming through temporal continuity, it also takes into account Wai Chee Dimock's proposal of "literature for the planet" by turning our attention to the wider span and durations of textual mutations in deep time across different spaces. Dimock writes, "Understood in this sense—as the temporal disunity among readers—relativity of simultaneity suggests that the continuum of literature is anarchic: impossible to regulate or police."[10] In this way, a heuristic method in tracking transgenderism across different times and places of Chinese and Sinophone cultures not only contributes to the immediate fields of Chinese literary studies, adaptation studies, and transgender studies; but the nonpredeterminate textual translations of the white snake tale also demonstrate that literature can disrupt the enforced boundary of nation-states and geopolitical regions, as well as the assumed temporal distinction between "pre-modern" and "modern" literature. Therefore, a cross-historical heuristic appreciates the dual senses of both textual continuity and disorganized temporality as we embark on this journey of tracing the surprising connections and missed connections between Chinese literary studies and transgender studies.

II. Moral and Gender Contentions

In one of the earliest attempts to fictionalize the folklore into literary form, late Ming scholar and bibliographer Feng Menglong wrote "Madame White Snake Jailed Eternally in the Leifeng Pagoda" (白娘子永鎮雷峰塔) in his *Jing Shi Tong Yan* (警世通言). Written in 1624, the text translated the story from folklore to vernacular Chinese. To trace the historical developments of the story, it is more productive to situate the text in the multiple moral contentions that conditioned the textual representation of gender and sexuality than assuming a single moral framework in Ming dynasty. In particular, the relationship between ren and yao, the human and the nonhuman, was not always structured in a binary in earlier folklores. For example, in Pan Jiangdong's encyclopedic compilation of research materials devoted to the legend, he cites the mythological belief that Chinese civilization creator Nuwa was often believed to embody a snake-body and a human face.[11] This example suggests that the fusion between human and nonhuman entities, perhaps the earliest example of ren/yao embodiment, did not immediately invite moral judgment. Instead, it was even glorified. Another earlier legend that might have inspired the thematic structure of the white snake legend appeared in a

500 chapter collection of stories in Song dynasty called *Taiping Guang Ji* (太平廣記) in AD 978. This version makes a rare example of the seduction genre because the demonic seducer actually incarnates in a male body and seduces a young girl, but the tale ends up reinforcing male heroism in which a knight shoots the snake demon to death, saves the girl, and marries her.[12]

In "From Folklore to Literature Theater," Whalen Lai underscores another dichotomy of morality at work within the genealogy of stories about man-God encounters in ancient Chinese legends in Han dynasty. Lai shows that not all encounters with the nonhuman are censored with moral conclusions. Within these encounters, meetings with the immortal gods are celebrated with fertility themes, while meetings with the devils are deemed as "unfortunate." Lai concludes, "So perhaps it is fitting that by Han, the romance of 'fortuitous encounter' with immortals was set apart from the horror of 'unfortunate run-in' with the devil."[13] Thus, within the genre of human romances with the nonhuman, this Han tradition creates another binary between the good and bad romances, where human (ren) encounter with demon (yao) is seen as unfortunate.

While Feng Menglong's canonization of the legend inherits the binary logics of good immortal versus bad devil that was already present in the Han traditional folklore, it nonetheless features a unique rhetorical strategy whereby feminine subjectivity is equated with the demonic, the deviant, and the abnormal, descriptions typically employed in modern condemnations of transgender subjects. Specifically, Feng utilizes literary techniques of *narrative reversal* in which qualities that mark Madame Bai as alluring, seductive, and beautiful all turn out to be improperly aggressive, psychically abnormal, and physically destructive to the male protagonist Xu Xuan. For instance, the third-person narrator describes Bai's beauty in a way that simultaneously highlights her demonic power: "Xu Xuan has always been an honest person, upon seeing this alluring woman whose beauty is like flower and like jade, accompanied by yet another pretty servant, his mind is uncontrollably aroused."[14] Shortly after, Bai introduces herself: "I am the sister from the Bai family, was married to Mr. Zhang; unfortunately he passed away, now buried in this Thunder Mountain range."[15] This short, introductory dialogue already marks Bai as an allegorical embodiment of the modern transgender renyao (human/demon) subject: this is not a "direct" transgender embodiment in the modern sense of gender transformation, but an "allegorical" renyao embodiment that parallels gender and moral transgressions. Bai embodies the alluring beauty that is humanly corporeal to Xu; yet, her beauty foreshadows the demonic power to destroy, thus implying her embodiment of destructive and deviant sexuality as well.

In addition to this literary description of Bai's renyao embodiment, Feng also organizes the moral implication of the story around a Confucian cosmological worldview that legitimates a hierarchical mapping of gendered subjects. This cosmological worldview is buttressed by the Buddhist tone of the ending, which stresses the importance of separating sexually transgressive bodies from normative "human" bodies. Specifically, Bai's embodiment of both human and demonic qualities, while initially posing threats only to Xu, progresses through the development of the story and becomes a danger to the cosmological social body at large. This is reflected in the text's narrative of feminine transgression, which dramatizes Bai's dangerous qualities on top of the story's narrative reversal. While Bai's gender identity remains feminine in her incarnation as a human being, she shifts from her role as a virtuous and compatible wife in a "companionate marriage" to an endangerment to Xu's masculine quality as a husband.[16] Specifically, when Xu is working as a clerk in a Chinese herbal shop in Zhenjiang, Bai suggests that they set up their own herbal shop. The narrator describes, "Since the opening of the herbal store, the transactions grew day by day, and Xu Xuan gains prosperously."[17] Here, Bai is still described as a compatible wife for Xu who helps him become successful while remaining a helper in his business. This companionate quality of Bai quickly transforms into an aggressively controlling power over him. In particular, when Xu gets special pardon from his previous misdemeanor and returns to Hangzhou, he becomes aware of Bai's identity as a demon ever since the monk Fai Hai warns him about her. Moreover, Bai introduces herself to Xu's sister and her husband even before Xu returns home. At this point, Xu begs for his life in front of Bai. Bai, realizing that her nonhuman identity is exposed, gives Xu a final warning: "I honestly tell you, if you listen to my words and stay happy with me, everything will be fine; if you remain suspicious with alternative thoughts, let me warn you that the whole city will be flooded with blood, everyone will be drown, and all will be dead for no reason."[18] Bai's alarming message to Xu shows that her feminine virtue as a compatible partner is conditional in the sense that her submission to Xu will only remain so if he recognizes her as a female human subject. Once Xu doubts her identity as a woman/human, Bai warns that she will cease being one as well by exerting her controlling power over him and bringing cosmic destruction to the world at large.

Bai's feminine transgression is occasioned by her nonhuman status as an animalistic demon, in contrast to the equally nonhuman but almighty power of the Buddhist monk Fai Hai. In this moment of the narrative, Xu Xuan visits the temple where Fai Hai serves as a highly ranked monk. Suddenly, a storm emerges in the ocean, and Xu sees a small boat fast approaching the shore with Bai and Ching Ching riding on it. Just when Xu decides to go home with Bai, Fai Hai shouts loudly and addresses Bai: "*Yechu* (業畜/demonic animal) What are you doing here?" The monk warns Bai again: "*Yechu*, how dare you come again and be improper, destroy the human civilization! This old monk especially comes for you."[19] Again, Feng's specific word choices stand out by marking Bai's status as a demonic female and transgressive subject, which is contrasted with Fai Hai's assumed proper subject position. First, *Yechu* is a specifically loaded Chinese phrase that is addressed to demons. Separated into two words, *Ye* often points to another phrase *zuiye* (罪業), meaning sinful deeds, while *chu* often refers to animals. The closest linking word to *chu* would be *chusheng*, meaning livestock in general.

The regulatory gendered consequence of this particular framing of Bai's subject position as demonic, animalistic, nonhuman, and improper can be better situated within the emergence of the Ming code of *lijiao* (proper teaching), which not only orders gender into binary framework of men and women, but more so through a hierarchical structure that implies the power relations between subject positions. As Kwang-Ching Liu and Richard Shek have noted, "The ethics of *lijiao* centered on the doctrine of Three Bonds—the obligation of child to parents, wife to husband, and official to monarch—which was expressed ritualistically in ancestor worship, marriage ceremonies, and the complex rites at the imperial court, including the sacerdotal exercises of the emperor himself."[20] Situating Fai Hai's policing of Bai's transgressive femininity allows us to read her as an allegory of gender transitivity in which she constantly fluctuates between statuses of the human and the demon, the submissive wife and the controlling partner. As someone who both deviates from humanness and transgresses proper lijiao in her direct challenge to higher authorities like her husband and the monk, Bai embodies a feminine transgression that can be read as a moral transgression contesting the Confucian cosmological order at large, which is resolved at the end of the story. Indeed, the moral lesson of the story is clearly spelled out by Fai Hai's suppression of Bai and Ching Ching under the Leifeng Pagoda and Xu's conversion to Buddhist ethics. Xu offers the last Buddhist chants: "Powerful monk helps me leave the earthly place, Iron tree leads to blossom and meets the spring; turning to next life and turn again, birth gives to rebirth . . . lust is emptiness and emptiness is lust, emptiness and lust must be clearly distinguished."[21] Consequently, the resolution of the story supports the Confucian cosmology with a strong Buddhist insistence of distinguishing lust from calm emptiness. This textual necessity to differentiate what is lust and what is the Buddhist way, of course, implies that the various gender transgressions and "improper" femininity of Bai's renyao embodiment must be distinguished from the orderly and proper ethics of humanity.

If Feng Menglong's rendition of the legend marks Bai as the exemplar of the renyao embodiment through its textual fixation of Bai's improper femininity with nonhumanity within a cosmological worldview of gender, Pu Songling, an early Qing writer who penned the story "Renyao"[22] in his *Liaozhai Zhiyi* (*Strange Tales from a Chinese Studio*), would further affix the embodiment of renyao into a preeminent category of transgenderism. Despite its more specific narration of a "sex change" incident, the story retains a moralizing logic of subjugating the feminine. In "Renyao," a man disguises himself as a woman to seduce another woman; his cross-dressing act was later discovered by the woman's husband, who then castrates the man and makes him his concubine instead. In Charlotte Furth's important study of men who become women, women who transform into men, and accounts of individuals with congenital intersexed conditions in literary and historical records, she shows that Pu's literary representation of renyao is based on an earlier story about Sang Ch'ung from Shansi, a man who was raised as a girl with bound feet, lived close to female quarters, and was known to "falsify" his gender to have sex with those women.[23] Thus, Pu's tale about cross-dressing and sex change actually still adheres to similar logics of hierarchical Confucian cosmology found in Feng's Ming text, because the woman's husband is positioned as the one who restores "order" by punishing another male cross-dresser and forcing him to take the feminine role. Wenqing Kang, in his overview of the appearances of renyao subjectivities in the Republican period, also notes Pu's emphasis of restoring normative gender even in a narrative about gender-crossings: "One might add that in classical records, gender transformations and male same-sex relations always seemed to be appropriated and subsumed within the framework of normative gender relations."[24]

If Pu's literary inflection of the Sang Ch'ung case substantiates rather than defies the subjugation of the feminine through the narrative's emphasis on "restoring" cosmological gender worldview that dichotomizes relationship between male and female, husband and wife, emasculated-turned-feminine and the masculine, how did the literary trope of renyao further develop into multiple categories of the transgender that are historically specific to Republican China (1911–1949)? In what ways did Western sexological division of gender binary, along with its concepts of homosexuality, heterosexuality, and pathology build on and extend earlier notions of renyao embodiment? How did notable May Fourth writers, such as Yu Dafu, respond to this transmutation of earlier tropes of feminine transgression (in Feng's text) and literary transgenderism (in Pu's text) by Western frameworks of gender and sexuality? In *Obsessions: Male Same-Sex Relations in China, 1900–1950*, Wenqing Kang argues that due to the New Culture Movement's general turn to science and revolt against Confucianism and feudalism, competing categories of sexual practices that were already present in earlier Chinese history were reevaluated anew under the scope of modern Western science.[25] While terms such as *tongxinglian'ai* (same-sex love) may be compatible with the then emerging idea of free love championed by May Fourth intellectuals, other categories such as renyao multiplied into numerous gender-crossing subjects that bear the sign of pathology. Kang elaborates the lists of pathologized gendered subjects: "Among those named as renyao were a sexually prematurely developed boy, crossdressers, intersex people who might have sex with both men and women, Peking opera *dan* actors, male prostitutes, and any men who behaved and dressed in a feminine fashion and had sex with other men. Early twentieth-century writers used the image of renyao as evidence of social and political crisis."[26]

While I agree with Kang that categories like renyao comprise a whole range of sexed and gendered subjects whose sexual orientations and gender roles may move constantly within and beyond the category of the transgender or same-sex relationships due to the very productive nature of sexual discourse that Foucault outlines in *The History of Sexuality*,[27] this multiplicity of pathologizing discourse on renyao still hinges upon the trope of the feminine as demonic in earlier Ming folklores. Indeed, the trope of demonic femininity was examined anew under the then emerging discourse of May Fourth literary humanism. The binary oppositions between the human and the nonhuman, modernity and traditionalism, and man and woman were under strong attacks by early May Fourth intellectuals such as Hu Shi and Chen Duxiu and later on reexamined under the literary modernism of Lu Xun, Yu Dafu, Ba Jin, and others. That is to say, humanism was posed as a question rather than assumed as a given in literary imaginations.[28] Specifically, Lu Xun's 1918 short story

"A Madman's Diary" most pointedly poses humanism as an ambiguous problem when the narrator who realizes that his brother is as cannibalistic as the other men in his village, asks: "How can a man like myself, after four thousand years of man-eating history—even though I knew nothing about it at first—ever hope to face real men?"²⁹

Here, Lu Xun equivocates feudal Chinese tradition and cannibalism symbolically and thereby grounds the possibility of humanistic existence as a conundrum for other May Fourth writers. Likewise, his brother and literary critic, Zhou Zuoren, didactically calls for a "humane literature" based on his iconoclastic attack on Confucian and Daoist writings because they are "a hindrance to the growth of human nature; they are things that destroy the peace and harmony of mankind; they are all to be rejected."³⁰ While Zhou Zuoren's humanistic attack on traditionalism as all that is "unnatural" could be easily deployed by "scientific" discourses that view renyao as a sign of nonhuman social pathology, I will illustrate the ways Yu Dafu's literary representation of the renyao figure work against the assumption of nonhumanity by questioning what constitutes a human subject, narrated from the perspective of a young male who embraces feminine qualities. I now turn to Yu Dafu's literary inflection of renyao in his Romantic writing style, to examine the complex crisscrossing of femininity and transgender representations, which paves the way for critical recitations of the renyao embodiment in the rewriting and adaptation of the *Legend* by Li and Cao at the end of the twentieth century.

"Renyao" ("Human Prodigy") is a short story written in 1923 by Yu Dafu that has received limited scholarly attention.³¹ The story reveals his deep fascination with the ambiguous dimensions of the erotic and the feminine. In other words, "Renyao" is one of the rare texts within the canon of May Fourth literary humanism that deals with the theme of gender ambiguity and transgender embodiment as well as their complicated relations to the trope of the feminine. The question of what constitutes a proper human subject is often one that May Fourth writers ask in addition to their rebellion against feudalism, traditional notion of filial duty, and all the "vices" they associate with the "old society." Their search for a new modern human subject was deeply embedded within a larger concern about the geopolitical situation of China at the peak of its encroachment by foreign (both Western and Japanese) imperial powers. Yet it is the gender-ambiguous body that the very question of the human is brought forth in the story. Departing from Republican discourses on renyao as a sign of social and nationalist disorder and Pu Songling's subjugation of the feminine, Yu's story opens up the field of possibility in embodying femininity and offers what Judith Butler calls "a critical perspective on the norms that confer intelligibility itself."[32] Specifically, the 17- year-old male protagonist (very likely Yu himself) protests against his mother's decision to ground him due to his recent health condition. Using internal dialogue, the young man protests, "If I can't go out, how come you people get to go out? Unless you are human, and I am not?"[33] This interesting question about the humanness of the protagonist himself can be contextualized within the Republican discourse on renyao that began to pathologize gender-ambiguous subjects as not fully human because of their assumed sexual perversity. Thus, the very title of "human prodigy" on which the story is based signals the young man's "transgendering" of himself as someone who is situated at the threshold of humanity. The story further describes his reaction to his oppression under the supervision of his mother (another sign of the repudiation of the feminine?) and his exclusion from the social world at large.

This transgendering of the male subject and the conundrum of humanism is further represented through the narrator's self-portrayal of his own gender-ambiguous body, which is later projected onto another feminine transgender subject whom he desires. For instance, the third-person narrator describes the young man's body in feminizing terms: "Maybe because of the warm sunlight, his lips today are pitifully redder than he normally is . . . he sits on the rickshaw and driven into the city, the pedestrians walking north, whether they are men, women, old, or young, not one passes by him without giving him a few stares."[34] This passage provides a crucial glimpse into the representation of eroticism and the role of gender-crossing desires in Yu Dafu's work, given that most criticisms on the Romantic dimension of his work focus on his erotic representation of women in heterosexual terms and juxtapose them against homosexual "deviance." For example, Leo Ou-fan Lee, in situating autobiographical aspects of Yu's writing, states factually, "Confronted by foppish young men from rich urban families and repulsed by homosexuality among his classmates (Kuo Mo-jo indulged in it in his high school years), Yu again sought escape in books and poetry."[35] Lee's contextualization of Yu's career frames his creative productivity as an "escape" from forms of nonheterosexual transgressions. However, in "Renyao" the male protagonist is depicted and eroticized with the kinds of representational conventions that are traditionally reserved for heterosexual femininity: red lips and subjection to the gaze of others.

Moreover, the gaze that structures the scene is open for all genders: men, women, old, and young. Male embodiment of the feminine here is inseparable from his goal of repudiating the traditionally construed feudal femininity: his rebellion against his mother by riding into the city.

Yu's representation of femininity in the story then, is not a simple subjection or repudiation of the feminine in moralizing frames (as in Feng's and Pu's texts); rather, it projects feminine self-representation onto the male body as something ambiguous yet desirable at the same time. The story's intentional staging of the feminine in a transgender light is made even more evident in another example: the protagonist's obsessive stalking of an actress whom he encountered in the opera house. Is it possible that the opera actress is in fact a biologically male dan character cross-dressed in female form? The narrative offers no decisive clue. The actress's gender is only hinted in the following description: "From her movement, the size of her limbs, it is a perfect balanced creation. Body is not too long or too short; not too fat or too thin, it is as good as his own."[36] Shortly after, the story ends with the young man chasing after the "woman" in a rickshaw while never seeing her (or "his") true face. The story therefore infuses Yu's conventional erotic depiction of (heterosexual) femininity with embodiment beyond male or female, a body that is "a perfect balanced creation." Although it is highly problematic to read Yu as celebrating transgenderism wholeheartedly by depathologizing the renyao figure, we can at least appreciate the complexity of renyao transgender embodiment as inextricably attached to the configuration of the feminine. The feminine here is not reducible to cosmological Confucian subjugation of femininity; nor is the renyao figure fully pathologized in the language of Republican-era sexology, which, according to Howard Chiang, emerged in the cultural apparatus of "epistemic modernity" that translated a new "style of reasoning" from the West.[37] On the contrary, the story assigns the feminine a bifurcated significance: as the upholder of the old social values (his mother), on the one hand, and as a nonfulfilled, rebellious, sexualized self (his own desire and the desire he channeled toward the actress) on the other. This construction of renyao as the contested terrain of femininity will be critically taken up by Li Bihua in her queer rewriting of the *Legend*, a project that construes female sexuality as multiply crossing among heterosexual, homoerotic, and gender-ambiguous desires, especially in the green snake character Ching Ching's simultaneous pursuit of sex with her sister Bai, Xu Xian, and Fai Hai.

III. Perverse Femininity and Sexual Multiplicity: Li Bihua's *Green Snake*

Li Bihua's novel, *Green Snake*, presents a critical recitation of cosmological gender worldview and feminine subjections as found in Feng's text, by imagining the fluid mapping of sexual bodies that conform to neither the division between the human and the demonic nor the binary possibility of the heterosexual and homoerotic. Let me begin by situating the question of femininity in transgender studies and queer theory before analyzing Li's "perverse" vision of femininity. In the 1990s, as queer theory began to mature, it offered a powerful analytical framework for questioning the stability of anatomical sex and the assumed core-essence of gender. Nevertheless, some lesbian scholars have taken issues with the ways in which lesbian femininity and sexuality tend to get relegated to the background while "gender crossing" representational forms such as cross-dressing and drag queen embodiment tend to be discussed as more queer. In *Femininity Played Straight*, Biddy Martin writes, "Too often, anti-determinist accounts that challenge feminist norms depend on the visible difference represented by cross-gender identifications to represent the mobility and differentiation that 'the feminine' or 'the femme' supposedly cannot."[38] That is to say, the coincidence of the institutionalization of gay and lesbian studies as a legitimate field of study and queer theory as an emerging theoretical tool all too often relies on the gay male figure as the preeminent example of cross-dressing and embodying visible forms of crossing in gender and sexual terms, almost always based on the assumption that the feminine is the ground that needs to be challenged. Worst still, the lesbian femme becomes barely visible. Martin here outlines two crucial interventions in queer theory, transgender studies and feminist politics. First, she questions the neat separation between gender/sexual crossing, with sexuality often assumed to be the domain of the "new" queer theory, versus feminist politics, which is typically framed around the question and subject of "woman." Second, Martin asks why certain trans figures, including the cross-dressers and the drag queen, are fetishized to be the ultimate subjects of crossing whereas femininity is posited as the final success (look how real he looks like a woman!) or some unfortunate modes of gender embodiment to be crossed away from (the drag king looks like a real man).[39]

Building on Martin's critique, I argue that Li's novel posits the narrational and psychical subjectivity of Ching Ching, the green snake, as someone who embodies dual components of the human and the nonhuman and whose expression of sexual desires often troubles normative categorization of gay, lesbian, heterosexual, or homoerotic. In other words, following Martin's call to rethink the role of femininity in queer and transgender studies, I will show that Ching's embodiment of multiple sexual desires centers the feminine as a subject of sexual-crossing insofar as she does not forsake the ground of femininity. From the start, the reader is fully aware of Li's subversion of the third-person narrative convention, which assumes an omniscient moralist tone: the narrator is a snake. Ching narrates, "I forgot to tell you, I am a snake. I am a green snake."[40] These two simple lines actually emphasize a cumulative mode of difference, where Ching asserts her difference from traditional narrator as the human but reemphasizes her unique positionality as a "green" snake. In doing so, she foreshadows a difference of her feminine and nonhuman subjectivity from any other snake's, especially her sister's.

This dual mode of difference and the complexity of Ching's femininity is further represented through the characteristic contrast between the older, wiser, more heterosexually driven white snake sister (the original female protagonist of the story), and herself. While the story begins in 1986 Hong Kong, when Ching is already 1,300 years old, it quickly flashbacks to 800 years ago, in the Song dynasty, before Bai and Ching decided to incarnate in human forms. In an intimate dialogue between the sisters, Ching asks Bai, "What exactly is a man?" The white snake replies by citing a poem about Su Xiao Xiao, a talented female poet from the Southern Qi dynasty. Bai describes, "Xiao Xiao wrote a poem once: 'A young woman rides in a painted carriage, a young man rides a virile horse. Where do they confess their hearts? Just under the pine tree in West Lake.' " Ching, upon hearing this obscure answer to her question about the male gender, bursts into a great laugh: "Hahaha! Even though you got your training earlier than me, you still don't know what exactly a man is!"[41]

This unique dialogue between the two nonhuman subjects to "know gender" can be read in two ways. First, it highlights the specific "non-gender" (or "a-gender") quality of both snakes in the sense that while both of them assume female forms, they still "lack" a knowledge of human gender-division; thus, the whole narrative is structured around the desire to cross from the nonhuman to the human world of cosmological gender hierarchy where they will get a first taste of what it means to be a woman, especially a heterosexual woman. The crossing aspect may be "queer" in this sense; but as Martin's critique implies, this kind of reading risks reducing the story to an empty metaphor of gender-crossing where the question of the feminine is unexamined. A second reading suggests a complicated demarcation of Ching's feminine subjectivity from Bai even in their nonhuman sameness.

The trajectory of Ching's multiple routes of desire considerably troubles normative understanding of sexual object choice. On the one hand, she seems to be inseparable from Bai in that her relationship with the white snake exceeds the language of sisterly bond or friendship. Before they descend into West Lake, where they will first meet Xu Xian, Ching adores Bai's exquisite clothing and her human beauty. Bai responds, "One woman dresses up for another woman to contemplate, what is the point? One woman won the praise of another woman, what is the pleasure?" To this, the green snake is shocked: "You don't like me anymore?" Bai says, "I do, but are you tired yet?"[42] This dialogue gives the reader the impression that Bai is Ching's proper object choice based on erotic sameness; in this regard, one might even call Ching a "lesbian" in the modern sense of the word. Yet, Bai refuses to be the object of Ching's homoerotic gaze on the basis that she is "tired" of it. Is this the literary framework of Li's conception of desire in her rewriting of the legend? Is heterosexuality presumed to be a new form of desire, whereas the underlying desire that saturates the novel is really intensely homoerotic? While the reader is tempted to follow this simple binary logic of reversal, further plot development confounds any neat division of sexual object choice along the hetero/homo binary axis.

After Bai successfully "seduces" Xu and begins their relationship, Ching is literally excluded from this heterosexual matrix and relegated to the status of an outsider. Ching angrily confronts Bai: "'Actually, maybe because I am jealous. You don't love me anymore!' Bai is shocked: 'You want me to not love him and love you only?' After a while, Ching tries to persuade her, 'Sister, Xu Xian is not a good man.' Bai replies, 'Why are you saying things that you don't even believe in?' " This dialogue mode shifts back to the viewpoint of the first-person narrator—Ching—and concludes, "She loves him, I also love him. Even though he is not perfect, we haven't met someone better than him."[43] This confession by Ching seems to confirm the traditionally heteronormative narrative of lesbian desire as that which confirms the pleasure of the male subject. Another event seems to support this view. After several twists and turns of the plot, Xu was literally shocked to death by Bai's demonic snake form when Bai failed to preserve her human form after drinking the "Xiong Huang" wine that is used to drive away demons.[44] Bai risks her life by stealing magical grass from the heavenly palace while Ching takes back the grass to save Xu. After Xu wakes up, Ching seizes the moment and has steamy sex with him. Ching narrates, "Human and snake are reduced to the most basic animals . . . I won't let him go."[45]

Yet, if the reader were to believe that Ching indeed turns from a lesbian subject to a heterosexual female who is jealous of her sister, this turning of desire remains unstable. As the story unfolds, it turns out that Ching cannot have Xu because Bai is already pregnant with Xu's child. Angry again at being excluded, Ching tries to seduce her enemy, Fai Hai, the monk who aims to suppress both Bai and herself. Asking if the monk desires her, Fai Hai replies affectionlessly: "'There is nothing good about you, you are not what I want. What kind of thing!' Ashamed of being called a thing, Ching confronts him: 'So, what do you want?' He perversely smiles at her and confesses: 'What do I want? I want Xu Xian!' "[46] While Ching's failure of seducing Fai Hai and the monk's confession that he homoerotically desires Xu Xian seem to recenter the male subject as the ideal form of beauty and confirm what historian Wu Cuncun finds to be the idealization of male beauty in the late imperial period,[47] I am more interested in how the constant fluctuation of Ching's multiple sexual subjectivities and her unstable object choices actually trouble the cosmological hierarchy of gender that originally structures Feng's text in the Ming dynasty. *Green Snake* then, paints a world where desire has no orderly flow, where whatever sexual transgression can be possible, and where a perverse utopia of subversion seems too powerful to be true. Indeed, this multiple sexual possibility is reflected in the advertising strategy on the back cover of the novel. It summarizes seductively to the potential reader: "A story about 'seduction': Bai Suzhen seduces Ching, Suzhen seduces Xu Xian, Ching seduces Fai Hai, Xu Xian seduces Ching, Fai Hai seduces Xu Xian . . . Song dynasty legend's ridiculous truth." Echoing the advertising strategy by Li Bihua and Cosmos Publishing, critic Ann L. Huss also contemplates the complexity of sexual positions in the text. Huss writes, "But imagine for a moment Qingshe and Xu Xian, or perhaps Xu Xian and Fai Hai. Never elaborated for the reader, each of these relationships nonetheless does exist mired within the textual 'blankness' which seems to be Li Bihua's trademark."[48] If everyone in this rewriting of the original *Legend* is caught within a "web of seduction," the implication is that it becomes relatively irrelevant what kind of sexual subject is being seduced, or the specific gendered embodiments of the seducer and the seduced.

In a different context, transgender theorist Jacob Hale analyzes an ad in which a fag boy is looking for a "daddy" in a cruising section of *Venus Infers*, a quarterly magazine for leatherdykes, and points out that this ad in which a feminine gay boy is looking for a masculine transgender butch or FTM (female-to-male) reveals the complexity of actual erotic possibility within trans communities (or even within the domain of human sexual desires). Hale writes, "Simple classification of sexual activity between this handsome fag boy and an FTM as heterosexual, gay, or lesbian fails. Categorizing any of this as *bisexual* misses the crucial cultural-situatedness of these practices; they are intelligible within sites of overlap between dyke, fag, leatherqueer, and trans communities."[49] Hale's argument that sexual practices and desires often exceed the assumed demarcations among the heterosexual, homosexual, lesbian, gay, and transgender points to the very potentiality of sexual fluidity and the erotic possibilities offered by sexual perversion and pleasures. Framed in this way, Ching's feminine perversion and the multivalence of erotic object choices make Li Bihua's adaptation of the *Legend* a peculiar allegory for sexual transitivity, meaning sexuality always in the state of transition. Even though it does not designate any explicit FTM, MTF (male-to-female), and cross-dressing representations that are often regarded as appropriate objects of inquiry within transgender studies, *Green Snake* provides multiple angles for thinking about femininity as a site of perverse pleasure without repeating the logic of feminine subjections found in Feng's text, which polarizes femininity as either heterosexually alluring or demonically destructive.

IV. Visualizing the Transgender Femme in Female Masculinity: The Politics of Cross-dressing in the *New Legend of Madame White Snake*

If Li Bihua's politics of rewriting troubles the demonic designation of the feminine by imagining a perverse femininity that is nonapologetic and multidirectional in its erotic possibility, Cao Jingde's *New Legend of Madame White Snake* (新白娘子傳奇), I argue, presents female embodiment of masculinity that retains close proximity to femmeness. Unlike femininity or the feminine, which is understood more generally as the proper social norms and conventional roles associated with the female sex, femmeness is defined more specifically here as the counterpart to butchness in the theorization of lesbian dynamics and figurations. My reading is that Cao's adaptation of the *Legend* allows for a fairly flexible notion of female gender-crossing that does not exclude femmeness from representations of the transgender butch; it illustrates how these varying degrees of transgendered subjectivities are intertwined with lesbian eroticism.[50] *New Legend* is a 50-episode TV series funded by Wanda production firm (萬大傳播), which was screened to TV audiences through Taiwan Television Enterprise (TTV), the main Taiwan television channel. It reinvigorated the classic story as a modern TV favorite in 1992–1993 among Sinophone viewers. The series was first screened from November of 1992 till January of 1993 to rave reviews. In the same year, the series was also screened in Hong Kong channel Asia Television Limited (ATV) and China Central Television (CCTV) in mainland China. The series was so popular at the time that in early 2009, there was news that some production firms are considering a remaking of the series. When asked what she thinks about a remake, Yip Tung (葉童), the Hong Kong actress who cross-dresses to play the role of Xu Xian, replies, "Some classics can never be outdone."[51] However, the 1992 version is also a "classic" in the sense that Yip's performance of masculinity "can never be outdone." Before analyzing Yip's masculine performance in the role of Xu Xian, it is useful to define female masculinity, butch-femme aesthetics, and what I see as strikingly new about Yip's embodiment as well as its distance and proximity to more femme expressions of femininity.

In *Female Masculinity*, Judith Halberstam contends that despite our ongoing attempt to theorize masculinity, female embodiment and performance of masculinity in forms of butchness and FTM subjectivities have been underexamined. She writes, "If what we call 'dominant masculinity' appears to be a naturalized relation between maleness and power, then it makes little sense to examine men for the contours of that masculinity's social construction."[52] Claiming that "female masculinity seems to be at its most threatening when coupled with lesbian desire,"[53] Halberstam is careful in avoiding universal claims of transgression and utopianism by qualifying that "not all butch masculinities produce subversion. However, transsexuality and transgenderism do afford unique opportunities to track explicit performances of nondominant masculinity."[54] Of course, Halberstam's point about the ways in which female masculinity expresses its most subversive potential in lesbian and queer representations raises the question of what role this alternative masculinity plays in butch-femme aesthetics. In her theorization of butch-femme relationships, Sue-Ellen Case builds on Joan Riviere's concept of womanliness as a masquerade: "If one reads them from within Riviere's theory the butch is the lesbian woman who proudly displays the possession of the penis, while the femme takes on the compensatory masquerade of womanliness."[55] While Case's designation of the butch as "possessive" of masculinity and the femme as "compensatory" is productive in theorizing some lesbian relationships, it risks separating masculinity as the naturalized domain of the butch and femininity as that of the femme. In my reading of Yip's embodiment of female masculinity, what I find striking is that her playing of Xu's role still exerts a great degree of femmeness. What is utterly queer about Yip's acting is that her presentation of female masculinity still retains a close proximity to femininity; I coin this specific presentation of female masculinity as the "transgender femme." The more colloquial understanding of transgender femmeness may be the soft butch figure.

Representations of female masculinity in the *New Legend* occupy various vexed relationships to femmeness and femininity. The series requires complex reading of femininity because unlike Li's politics of rewriting, the plot here tends to humanize the yao, the demonic white snake (played by Angie Chiu/Zhao Yazhi 趙雅芝), while still visualizing the green snake (played by Maggie Chan Mei Kei 陳美琪) as more demonic. Of course, the humanization of Bai risks relegating her in traditionally heterosexual feminine roles as virtuous mother, sacrificial wife, and Buddhist follower. Indeed, the last episode ends with her perseverance to Buddhism under the Pagoda and her son Xu Shilin's filial tie to her, which moves the bodhisattva Guanyin (the Goddess of compassion in East Asian Buddhism) so much that she orders Fai Hai to release Bai. Yet, while the linear development of the series follows a Buddhist trajectory and cosmological Confucian lijiao gender roles, its characterization of Yip's performance of transgender femmeness and Chan's transgender butchness simultaneously envisions transgender masculinities and femininities, which queer the original text by Feng in the late Ming dynasty.

Female masculinity embodied by the green snake character is seen as a sign of the demonic that needs to be tamed constantly throughout the episodes. In the opening episode, the green snake accompanies five little devils to steal money from the local treasury. In obeying the order of the green snake, the devils actually refer to "her" as "big brother." In fact, Maggie Chan's voice sounds almost not her own, possibly dubbed over by a biologically male voice. This vocal effect thus stresses the green snake character as closer to the transgender butch that Halberstam theorizes. Before her transition into Bai's maid, the green snake embodies a martial art fighter body, easily outdoing the *yamen* (local bureaucrat) officer Lee, who is also the brother-in-law of Xu Xian. Bai intervenes and starts a fight with the green snake. The green snake explodes the earth and shatters Bai's surrounding. The green snake at this moment transforms from the masculine body into the demonic snake form to scare Bai. Bai decides that she needs to punish this *yaoguai* (demonic spirit) and warns her/him: "You only have several years of training, but you are already so arrogant and uncontrollable; if I don't get rid of you today, you will cause much trouble in the future." When Bai is about to kill the green snake, he/she pleads for life, and Bai let him/her live. At this moment, the green snake returns Bai's kindness by offering to follow the white snake as a maid, thus transfiguring into a female body with green dress and green ribbons decorated on her hair. This narrative of transgender embodiment then marks the green snake's transition from a "big brother" into a female maid, from a more butch embodiment of female masculinity into supposedly "proper" femininity in which her demonic nature is linked to her claim to masculinity. If this politics of transgenderism humanizes Bai to the extent that it still adheres to the ren/yao division in the Ming text through the dehumanization of the green snake's yao quality (in the form of butchness instead of transgressive femininity this time around), Yip's cross-dressing performance as Xu Xian can also be read cross-historically. Specifically, it cites ideal model of feminine masculinity popular in the late imperial period, which both Feng's text and the TV series adhere to; yet, this citationality of late imperial ideal masculinity as feminine also productively performs a second queer function by troubling the assumed binary of butchness and femmeness and the division of T/Po identities within 1990s lesbian and queer Taiwan cultures as well.[56]

In her path-breaking book on male homoerotic sensibility in the Ming and Qing periods, Wu Cuncun finds that "in the late Ming dynasty men had begun to play down their masculinity, a feature that is evident in the 'scholar-beauty' (*caizi jiaren*, literally 'gifted youth and virtuous maiden') fiction."[57] In another study, Wu finds that "in late imperial China a feminized male appearance was generally accepted as the ideal of male beauty."[58] Feng's version obviously reflects Xu Xian's feminized beauty as he is often rendered as fragile and in need of saving by Fai Hai when confronted by the demonic white snake. So, one can argue that the choice of casting a female actress to play an originally feminized male character in the late imperial context is a modern attempt to remain faithful to historical accuracy of gender ideals.

Yet, to have Yip Tong *fanchuan* (反串/cross-dress) and play Xu's role appears to be an adventurous decision as well. Indeed, Yip herself seems to be fully aware of the novelty and alternative appeals of her fanchuan quality and collaborates with Chinese fans across the world to host a site called *Yip Tung's Fanchuan World*.[59] On the web site, there are numerous archives of media interviews, newspaper clips, and other sources devoted to the Angie Chiu/Yip Tung, feminine/transgender femme (soft butch) pairing of the TV series. Specifically, in an interview with Star TV (Satellite Television for the Asian Region), a transnational Asian TV network headquartered in Hong Kong, Angie Chiu commented on both Yip's and her performances of femininity in *New Legend*. Chiu responded to the interviewer's question of how she acts Bai's role: "Because Bai is a snake turned human, so in movement techniques, I especially express her to be softer and mellower; and also because my partner Xu Xian is played by female *fanchuan* (cross-dressing/role reverse), I must feminize her even more." Then the interviewer turned to Yip and she responded: "Since I started my acting career, I never act *fanchuan* roles. Then I was thinking: should I exaggeratingly act a masculine role? Then I felt like it shouldn't be like that; I should act it naturally."[60]

In this sense, Chiu's and Yip's specific techniques in manifesting the hyperfemininity of Bai and the nonexaggerating fanchuan female masculinity of Xu provide a queer citationality of the beauty ideal of feminized masculinity in late imperial China, to which Feng's text faithfully literalizes. However, the idealized gender roles here are obviously altered or queered by both Chiu's and Yip's choices of acting and the representation of desire within the series. In a different context, Judith Butler argues that performativity of gender should not be simplified as free choice actions that are fully agential; if there is any agency, it must be located through the complicated processes in which representation and practices of gender variance recite previous gender norms. Put differently, agency can both recircumscribe and challenge gender normativity only within the terrain of existing gender norms and histories of injury. Theorizing performativity as citationality, Butler writes, "What Lacan calls the 'assumption' or 'accession' to the symbolic law can be read as a kind of *citing* of the law, and so offers an opportunity to link the question of the materializing of 'sex' with the reworking of performativity as citationality."[61] Thus, the citationality of late imperial ideal of feminized masculinity in Yip's performance of the transgender femme acquires meanings within both heterosexual and homoerotic imaginaries in ways that both confirm historical accuracy of male beauty and depart from that faithful citationality for queer viewing pleasures.

This kind of queer citationality is especially evident in the eleventh episode. Xiao Ching, the green snake, is angry with Bai for spending so much time to help Xu establish his herbal medicine business and neglecting their goals of training and achieving nirvana statuses. To summarize the plot briefly, while exiled in Suzhou, Xu and Bai's success in opening the herbal business causes animosity from other doctors. The doctors decided to falsify to the court that Xu killed an old lady by poison. Bai—to save the old lady and rid Xu of the charge—chases the old lady's dead spirit, fights with the guards from the underworld, and restores the spirit in the old woman. When confronted by Ching that she has neglected their common goals, Bai explains, "Ching, our time together in nirvana will be long, yet my time with Xu on earth will be temporary. So I hope you can open your heart and accept him." Obeying Bai, Ching shockingly confesses, "Sister, actually I like Xu Xian a lot too." Bai is utterly speechless. Ching then covers up her erotic desire for the feminized masculinity of Xu and restates her desire: "I mean, I like his honesty, which makes him admirable." Bai repeats Ching's logic of desire by calling Xu "adorable." As Bai was missing when Xu tried to find her, at this moment he intrudes the scene (figure 5.1). Here Xu/Yip is dressed in a gray gown, in contrast to the more martial arts fighter gown

Figure 5.1 Production still from *New Legend of Madame White Snake*. From left to right: Maggie Chan as green snake, Yip Tung as Xu Xian, and Angie Chiu as Madame Bai the white snake. Reprinted with permission from TTV.

worn by Ching in the first episode. This moment generates a complex configuration of female homoeroticism in the sense that viewers are fully aware that Ching and Bai are declaring their love for Xu, a fictional male character played by the biologically female actress Yip. Yet, within the visual imaginary, this erotic triangle here also implies that Ching and Bai prefer the alternative feminine form of female masculinity, namely transgender femmeness, which Yip/Xu embodies. This visual representation accentuates a specific form of female masculinity that still hinges upon a flexible degree of femmeness for its erotic appeal. Reading this scene's pairing of high femmeness (Chiu and Chan) with transgender femmeness (Yip) also corresponds to the need of theorizing more complex notions of lesbian desire in 1990s queer Sinophone cultures.

Specifically, Josephine Ho, in an essay titled "T/Po Transgender Blues," points out the complexity of lesbian femininity and masculinity, and the need to theorize within and beyond the butch/femme division. Ho argues, "Secondly, lesbian self-expression is not always an either T or Po mentality, lesbian interactive models do not only have T/Po kinds; therefore, T/Po cannot be the only universal model for thinking lesbianism."[62] Building on Ho, we can frame Yip's performance of female masculinity as embodying a T identity that still retains Po expressions. Furthermore, Fran Martin, in her study of representations of queer cultures in 1990s Taiwan, points out that queerness hybridized into multiple identity politics that demonstrate the heterogeneity of *tongzhi* culture there. Martin writes, "Thus, neologisms like *tongzhi*, *ku'er*, and *guaitai* emerged in 1990s Taiwan as examples of glocalization in the domain of sexual knowledge: critical, selective appropriations and reworkings of terms and concepts that originated elsewhere."[63] Obviously, T/Po identities are part of the hybridization of Euro-American gay and lesbian identities that emerged in 1990s queer Taiwan cultures. Framing Yip's performance of the transgender femme figure within this cultural context can complicate Sue-Ellen Case's point that the femme occupies a strictly "compensatory masquerade"; rather, Angie Chiu's performance of high femmeness, Maggie Chan's performance of female masculinity, and Yip's acting out of transgender femmeness show that the critical translation of butch/femme aesthetics into T/Po in Taiwan operates through relational terms that are highly intersubjective; T subjects can claim Po-ness as Po can claim T-ness in their playful expressions of butch/femme identities. Consequently, Yip's cross-dressing act signals a transgender femme subject position in which female masculinity plays femme.

V. Touching "Transgender" Representations Cross-historically

In following the binary relational trope between the human and the feminine-as-nonhuman and the embodiment of the transgender renyao figure from Feng's text in the Ming dynasty, to Pu Songling's narrative of sex change as "restoring" gender, to Republican sexology discourse on gender variance as national pathology, to Yu Dafu's imagination of ambiguous femininity as the ground for questioning humanism, to Li Bihua's perverse utopia of femininity, and finally to the intertwined relationship between femmeness and female masculinity in Cao's 1992 TV series, this chapter has traced how the vexed relationship between femininity and transgender embodiment mutates across different historical contexts. By encompassing texts that range from literary, visual, to new media sources and placing them within the more historically situated understanding of renyao as a modern pathological category, we can examine more closely how sexological/nationalist discourse in early twentieth-century China and current public condemnation of Thai transgender bodies in Sinophone contexts are linked to literary representations that seek to reinforce bodily division based on the subjugation of transgressive femininity. Furthermore, if femininity has never fallen outside but crucially anchors transgender embodiment, then it makes sense that modern rewritings and adaptations of the *Legend* necessarily engage with the interplay between femininity, sexual transitivity, and female masculinity.

This cross-historical approach to questions of transgenderism and femininity can be understood in Sandy Stone's use of the term "posttranssexual" as a call to move beyond representations and transgender narratives that all too often fetishize perfect transitions from male to female and female to male. Therefore, instead of categorizing transgender or transsexual as simply a "third" gender that can fit all that escape male or female, Stone constitutes transsexuality as "a *genre*—a set of embodied texts whose potential for *productive* disruption of structured sexualities and spectra of desire has yet to be explored."[64] In my reading of Li's novel, I emphasize moments of productive disruption in Ching's embodiment of perverse femininity rather than assuming that her disruptive power simply results from her anger against heterosexual neglect by Xu Xian. In *New Legend*, the complex figurations of femmeness in Maggie Chan's and Yip Tung's performances of female masculinity show that transgender does not stand in for a perfect taking over of maleness by biologically female subjects; rather, it depends on certain embodiment of femmeness for its desirability and queer recitation of the Ming-dynasty masculinity ideal even when more explicit butchness in the green snake is still demonized as the yao, the demonic.

While recent studies in transgender history have shed light on how the possibility of sex change first emerged in the 1910s and 1920s German sexology and later received sensational public discussions in the American presses from the 1930s through the 1950s, my inquiry here is not an attempt to revise the origin story of the category of the transgender.[65] Nor am I trying to neatly distinguish different figurations of renyao as stable categories of transgender in different periods of Chinese history. My heuristic approach, following Benjamin's historical materialism, aims to blast certain forgotten minor figures such as the renyao "out of the continuum of history" to understand how this transphobic Sinophone term touches on earlier histories of feminine subjections in literary narratives.[66] I further reveal how modern literary and media adaptations in Sinophone cultures significantly revise earlier literary trope of the feminine as demonic in critical directions of visualizing perverse femininity and transgender femmeness as possible sites of pleasure. While a transhistorical approach more often presumes the continuity of certain identity and practice across a wide span of historical divides, a cross-historical methodology undertaken here acknowledges the radical impossibility of accurately retrieving sexual identities and practices in the past as "they really were." Instead, a cross-historical heuristic to theorizing transgender Chinese cultures embraces messiness as the necessary condition of possibility in both a text's faithful citation of the past and its various queer recitations, its unpredictable *afterlife*. It is in this spirit that I hope my analysis of the various configurations of femininity in their demonized, ambiguous, perverse, femme, hyperfemme, and masculine forms in relation to transgenderism can broaden the ongoing discussions of transgender politics in different Sinophone contexts that forge intricate relationality between the past and the now.

Notes

1. Wu Cuncun, "Beautiful Boys Made up as Beautiful Girls: Anti-masculine Taste in Qing China," in *Asian Masculinities: The Meaning and Practice of Manhood in China and Japan*, ed. Kam Louie and Morris Low (London: RoutledgeCurzon, 2003), 19–40.
2. Helen Hok-Sze Leung, "Unsung Heroes: Reading Transgender Subjectivities in Hong Kong Action Cinema" in *Masculinities and Hong Kong Cinema*, ed. Laikwan Pang and Day Wong (Hong Kong: Hong Kong University Press, 2005), 81–98.

3. Tze-lan D. Sang, "The Transgender Body in Wang Dulu's *Crouching Tiger, Hidden Dragon*," in *Embodied Modernities: Corporeality, Representation, and Chinese Cultures*, ed. Fran Martin and Larissa Heinrich (Honolulu: Hawaii University Press, 2006), 98–112.
4. Walter Benjamin, "Theses on the Philosophy of History," in *Illuminations* (New York: Schocken Books, 2007), 253–264 and 263.
5. Han ten Brummelhuis, "Transformations of Transgender: The Case of the Thai *Kathoey*," in *Lady Boys, Tom Boys, Rent Boys: Male and Female Homosexualities in Contemporary Thailand*, ed. Peter A. Jackson and Gerard Sullivan (New York: The Haworth Press, 1999), 124.
6. Feng Menglong (馮夢龍), *Jing Shi Tong Yan* (警世通言) [1624] (Hong Kong : Gu dian wen xue chu ban she, 1970), 420–448 and 445. All translations of original Chinese sources in the body of the text are my own unless noted otherwise.
7. By Sinophone, I meant to track the transformations of the tale and discursive meanings of renyao in different Chinese-speaking and non-Mandarin based communities across time and space in Ming- dynasty China, Republican China, and 1990s Hong Kong and Taiwan. Here, I further develop Shu-mei Shih's foundational definition of the Sinophone as "a network of places of cultural production outside China and on the margins of China and Chineseness" by showing how adaptations of the tale outside the People's Republic of China change the way we read the "original" Chinese premodern tale. See Shu-mei Shih, *Visuality and Identity: Sinophone Articulations Across the Pacific* (Berkeley: University of California Press, 2007), 4.
8. Tani E. Barlow's work exemplifies this approach of thinking categories such as "history" and "context" in open, speculative, and future anterior ways. Specifically, she draws on Gayatri Spivak's use of the term catachresis, which refers to "a concept-metaphor without an adequate referent." She contends that while it is important to theorize what women had been in modern Chinese history, it is equally important to read their heterogeneous desire for the future and their diverse goals and motivations within their particular time in history, namely to ask the question of "what women will have been." Barlow writes, "A history written in the future anterior, in other words, would not simply note the existence of a future encoded in every present, but would focus particularly on the capacity of this kind of present imagining to upset the sequence of past-present-future." See Tani E. Barlow, *The Question of Women in Chinese Feminism* (Durham: Duke University Press, 2004), 16–17. See also Dipesh Chakrabarty's theorization of History 2 as embodying nonsecular forms of history and human diversity that are "constantly interrupting the totalizing thrusts of History 1." History 1, in his study, refers to historicist narration of Western modernity that denies the coevalness of non-Western modernities. Dipesh Chakrabarty, *Provincializing Europe: Postcolonial Thought and Historical Difference* (Princeton: Princeton University Press, 2000), 66.

9. Carolyn Dinshaw, *Getting Medieval: Sexualities and Communities, Pre- and Postmodern* (Durham: Duke University Press, 1999), 1.
10. Wai Chee Dimock, "Literature for the Planet," *PMLA* 116.1 (January 2001): 173–188 and 174.
11. Pan Jiangdong (潘江東), *Bai She Gu Shi Yan Jiu* (白蛇故事研究) (Taipei: Taiwan xue sheng shu ju, 1981), 3. [Pan Jiangdong, *White Snake Story Research Compendium*]
12. Pan Jiangdong, *Bai She Gu*, 11.
13. Whalen Lai, "From Folklore to Literate Theater: Unpacking *Madame White Snake*," *Asian Folklore Studies* 51 (1992): 51–66 and 56.
14. Feng Menglong, *Jing Shi Tong Yan*, 422.
15. Feng Menglong, *Jing Shi Tong Yan*, 422.
16. For a discussion on the ideal of companionate marriage that first fostered in the coastal cities in the Jiangnan region in Ming dynasty, see Dorothy Ko, *Teachers of the Inner Chambers: Women and Culture in Seventeenth-Century China* (Stanford: Stanford University Press, 1994), 179–185.
17. Feng Menglong, *Jing Shi Tong Yan*, 438.
18. Feng Menglong, *Jing Shi Tong Yan*, 441.
19. Feng Menglong, *Jing Shi Tong Yan*, 440.
20. Kwang-Ching Liu and Richard Shek, "Introduction" in *Heterodoxy in Late Imperial China*, ed. Kwang-Ching Liu and Richard Shek (Honolulu: University of Hawaii Press, 2004), 1–25 and 4. Tani E. Barlow has similarly pointed to the discursive and material construction of women as *funu* who occupy specific protocols according to their subject positions as daughter, mother, etc. in the eighteenth-century China. See Tani E. Barlow, "Theorizing 'Women,'" in her *The Question of Women in Chinese Feminism*, 37–63.
21. Feng Menglong, *Jing Shi Tong Yan*, 445.
22. Pu Songling, "Renyao" in Pu Songling (蒲松齡), *Liao Zhai Zhi Yi* (聊齋志異) [1680] (Hong Kong: Shang wu yin shu guan Xianggang fen guan, 1963), 693–694.
23. Charlotte Furth, "Androgynous Males and Deficient Females: Biology and Gender Boundaries in Sixteenth and Seventeenth-Century China," in *The Lesbian and Gay Studies Reader*, ed. Henry Abelove, Michele Aina Barale, David M. Halperin (New York: Routledge, 1993), 479–497 and 492.
24. Wenqing Kang, *Obsession: Male Same-Sex Relations in China, 1900–1950* (Hong Kong: Hong Kong University Press, 2009), 34.
25. Recently, Howard Chiang revised Wenqing Kang's emphasis on Republican male same-sex relations as continuing, interacting with, and renewing local indigenous sexual vocabularies in previous Chinese dynastic history through mutual encounter of the Chinese and Western discourses. Instead, Chiang argues that the Republican period, through the uneven translations of Western scientific

discourses on psychology and sexology by experts, ushers in a new style of reasoning about homosexuality that has epistemological consequences on both personal and national levels. See Howard Chiang, "Epistemic Modernity and the Emergence of Homosexuality in China," *Gender and History* 22.3 (2010): 629–657. For previous scholarship on the translation of Western sexological terminologies from the West, to Japan, and back to China through a translingual model, see Tze-lan D. Sang, *The Emerging Lesbian: Female Same-Sex Desire in Modern China* (Chicago: University of Chicago Press, 2003), 99–126; on how modernizing Chinese elites reacted negatively to this translation of homosexuality and sexology during the Republican period and explained it as "an acquired aberration," see Frank Dikötter, *Sex, Culture and Modernity in China: Medical Science and the Construction of Sexual Identities in the Early Republican Period* (Honolulu: University of Hawai'i Press, 1995), 145.
26. Kang, *Obsession*, 34.
27. Michel Foucault, *The History of Sexuality Vol. 1* (New York: Vintage Books, 1990), 3–35.
28. For a more in-depth discussion of the different takes on humanism polarized between May Fourth intellectuals who generally viewed Confucian traditions as inhumanity and a neohumanist group, *Critical Review*, that argued for blending the greatest traditions of Eastern and Western civilizations to reinvent a new humanism that is neo-Confucianist in form, see Lydia H. Liu, *Translingual Practice: Literature, National Culture, and Translated Modernity—China 1900–1937* (Stanford: Stanford University Press, 1995), 239–258. Through a slightly different orientation, Shu-mei Shih argues that because of China's semicolonial condition and the lack of a total colonization by Western and Japanese powers, there emerged a bifurcation in the ways May Fourth intellectuals adopted Western influences. On the one hand Occidentalists such as Lu Xun and Hu Shi generally call for complete Westernization and antitraditionalism, while neohumanists (what Shih calls neotraditionalists) are more cosmopolitan in spirit in their selective reinvention of Chinese local tradition and reception of Western self-critique after World War I in the new humanism of Irving Babbitt. See Shu-mei Shih, *The Lure of Modern: Writing Modernism in Semicolonial China, 1917–1937* (Berkeley: University of California Press, 2001), 157–158. In another study that focuses on the persistence of inhumanity and monstrosity in the historical and literary writings of Chinese modernity, David Der-wei Wang argues that the very act of writing history depends paradoxically on the negative accumulation of monstrous memory and inhumane violence. See David Der-wei Wang, *The Monster That Is History: History, Violence, and Fictional Writing in Twentieth-Century China* (Berkeley: University of California Press, 2004), 187.

29. Lu Xun, "A Madman's Diary" (1918), in Lu Xun, *The Complete Stories of Lu Xun*, trans. Yang Xianyi and Gladys Yang (Bloomington: Indiana University Press, 1981), 1–12 and 12.
30. Zhou Zuoren, "Humane Literature" (1918), in *Modern Chinese Literary Thought: Writings on Literature 1893–1945*, ed. Kirk A. Denton (Stanford: Stanford University Press, 1996), 151–161 and 157.
31. Yu Dafu, "Renyao" (1923) in Yu Dafu (郁達夫), *Dafu Zhong Pian Xiao Shuo Ji* (達夫中篇小說集) (Hong Kong: Zhi ming shu ju, 1950), 580–589.
32. Judith Butler, "Doing Justice to Someone: Sex Reassignment and Allegories of Transsexuality," *GLQ* 7.4 (2001): 621–636 and 634.
33. Yu Dafu, "Renyao," 581.
34. Yu Dafu, "Renyao," 583.
35. Leo Ou-fan Lee, *The Romantic Generation of Modern Chinese Writers* (Cambridge: Harvard University Press, 1973), 85.
36. Yu Dafu, "Renyao," 585.
37. Chiang, "Epistemic Modernity."
38. Biddy Martin, "Sexualities Without Genders and Other Queer Utopias" in her *Femininity Played Straight: The Significance of Being Lesbian* (New York: Routledge, 1996), 71–94 and 73.
39. For an in-depth study and archive of drag king embodiment and subcultural practices, see Del Lagrace Volcano and Judith "Jack" Halberstam, *The Drag King Book* (London: Serpent's Tail, 1999).
40. Li Bihua (李碧華), *Qingshe* (青蛇) (Hong Kong: Tian di/Cosmo Books, 1986), 2–3.
41. Li Bihua, *Qingshe*, 8.
42. Li Bihua, *Qingshe*, 14.
43. Li Bihua, *Qingshe*, 83–84.
44. See Yi-Li Wu, "Ghost Fetuses, False Pregnancies and the Parameters of Medical Uncertainty in Classical Chinese Gynecology," *Nan Nü* 4. 2 (2002): 170–206 and 185.
45. Li Bihua, *Qingshe*, 110.
46. Li Bihua, *Qingshe*, 149–150.
47. Wu Cuncun, "Beautiful Boys"
48. Ann L. Huss, "*Qingshe*: A Story Retold," *Chinese Culture* 38 (1997): 75–94 and 90.
49. Jacob Hale, "Are Lesbian Woman?" in *The Transgender Studies Reader*, ed. Susan Stryker and Stephen Whittle (New York: Routledge, 2006), 281–299 and 286.
50. *New Legend of Madame White Snake* (新白娘子傳奇), produced by Cao Jingde (曹景德) (Taiwan: Wanda Production, 1992).
51. "Yip Tung Dresses Elegantly for an Event, Not Supportive for Re-making New Legend of Madame White Snake," *News Sina*, October 31, 2009, http://dailynews.sina.com/bg/ent/hktwstar/sinacn/20091031/2331828697.html (accessed November 11, 2009).

52. Judith Halberstam, *Female Masculinity* (Durham: Duke University Press, 1998), 2.
53. Halberstam, *Female Masculinity*, 28.
54. Halberstam, *Female Masculinity*, 40.
55. Sue-Ellen Case, "Toward a Butch-Femme Aesthetic," in *The Lesbian and Gay Studies Reader*, ed. Henry Abelove, Michele Aina Barale, David M. Halperin (New York: Routledge, 1993), 294–306 and 300.
56. T/Po refers to Taiwanese lesbian identification of the more masculine partner as "T" and the more feminine partner as "po." Po is a generic term that can refer to women of different ages.
57. Wu Cuncun, *Homoerotic Sensibilities in Late Imperial China* (London: RoutledgeCurzon, 2004), 164.
58. Wu Cuncun, "Beautiful Boys."
59. *Yip Tung's Fanchuan World*. http://www.yehtong.com (accessed November 11, 2009).
60. Entertainment Octopus Special Interview, first broadcast 1993 by Asia TV, reprinted and reuploaded at *Yip Tung's Fanchuan World*. http://xinbai.yehtong.com/xbinterview.htm (accessed November 11, 2009).
61. Judith Butler, *Bodies that Matter: On the Discursive Limits of "Sex"* (New York: Routledge, 1993), 14.
62. Josephine Ho (何春蕤), "T/Po Transgender Blues," (T婆的跨性別籃調詩) in *Trans-Gender* (跨性別), ed. Josephine Ho (Taiwan: Center for the Study of Sexualities, National Central University, 2003), 377–384 and 378.
63. Fran Martin, *Situating Sexualities: Queer Representation in Taiwanese Fiction, Film and Public Culture* (Hong Kong: Hong Kong University Press, 2003), 23. *Tongzhi* means "comrade" and serves as a common identity marker for organizing gay and lesbian communities in transnational Chinese cultures; whereas *ku'er* (cool kid) and *guaitai* (strange fetus) are local rearticulations of queer theory that circulate among queer academics and communities in 1990s Taiwan. See also Ji Dawei (記大偉), ed., *Ku er qi shi lu : Taiwan dang dai queer lun shu du ben* (酷兒啟示錄: 臺灣當代 Queer 論述讀本) (Taipei: Meta Media, 1997), 10.
64. Sandy Stone, "The *Empire* Strikes Back: A Posttranssexual Manifesto," in *The Transgender Studies Reader*, ed. Susan Stryker and Stephen Whittle (New York: Routledge, 2006), 221–235 and 231.
65. For the historical emergence of sex change surgeries in Germany, see Joanne Meyerowitz, *How Sex Changed: A History of Transsexuality in the United States* (Cambridge: Harvard University Press, 2002), 21, and Susan Stryker, *Transgender History* (Berkeley: Seal Press, 2008), 39–41. For sensational discussions on the possibility of sex changes in 1930–1950s American popular presses, see Meyerowitz, 14–50, and in Republican Chinese vernacular culture, see Howard Chiang,

"Why Sex Mattered: Science and Visions of Transformation in Modern China" (PhD dissertation, Princeton University, 2012), Chap. 4. For the emergence of transgender studies in 1990s American academia, see Susan Stryker, "The Transgender Issue: An Introduction," *GLQ: A Journal of Lesbian and Gay Studies* 4.2 (1998): 145–158.

66. Walter Benjamin, "Theses," 261.

PART III

Trans Locations of Culture

CHAPTER 6

Begin Anywhere: Transgender and Transgenre Desire in Qiu Miaojin's *Last Words from Montmartre* (蒙馬牠遺書)

Larissa N. Heinrich

> *If this book should be published, readers can begin anywhere. The only connection among chapters is the period in which they were written.*
>
> *Qiu Miaojin*, Last Words from Montmartre

What is the relationship of gender to genre in literary form? In his study of Leslie Feinberg's *Stone Butch Blues*, the ambivalently autobiographical "story of a transsexual who...like Feinberg hirself, halts her transition through surgery and hormones to found an embodied transgendered subjectivity," Jay Prosser observes that the book also "produces an alternative generic form—a trans-genre: a text as between genres as its subject is between genders."[1] In *Stone Butch Blues*, Prosser seems to suggest, the radically embodied nature of the protagonist's transsexuality demands the production of an equally radical literary form; form follows content as the text moves to accommodate the story's "embodied transgendered subjectivity" (and not the other way around). But what happens when a literary work inverts the relationship of form and content so that the *writing itself* becomes a site for expression of transgender identity, an end in itself? In other words, what happens to autobiographical form when writing functions not reflexively, as a means of narrating transgender subjectivity, but generatively, as a means of creating and even embodying it?

Last Words from Montmartre, by the Taiwanese author Qiu Miaojin 邱妙津 (1969–1995), is a semiepistolary, memoirlike experimental novel that may be situated within the transnational mid-1990s *belle époque* of queer "testimonial" or "confessional" novels. The body of the text consists of a series of letters from the author-narrator to her lover in Taipei and to friends in Tokyo and elsewhere in Taiwan. It opens with the death of a beloved pet rabbit and closes with an ominous expression of the narrator's resolve to kill herself. In-between, we follow Qiu along the streets of Paris to mail letters; into descriptions of affairs with both men and women, French and Taiwanese; into rhapsodic musings on the works of Angelopoulos and Tarkovsky; and into wrenching and clear-eyed outlines of what it means to exist not only between cultures but also between and among genders.

Last Words from Montmartre has often drawn comparisons with works by Yukio Mishima.[2] This is not only because of the novel's densely layered modernist and homoerotic sensibilities, nor is it because both Mishima and Qiu erased formal distinctions between art and life when they ended their lives with gruesome suicides and literary last testaments. It is because in the novel's nonlinear, looping structure we find an inspired restructuring of the novelistic and autobiographical forms. *Last Words from Montmartre* explodes anything resembling a structure—it is a novel of antistructure, repetitive, oneiric, at times rhapsodic—a mindful acknowledgement of an epistolary model that has existed in Chinese literature since the late imperial period (such as Shen Fu's novel of letters to his wife called *Six Chapters of a Floating Life*) mixed with a self-conscious appropriation of, and dialogue with, works by modernists from Woolf to Mishima, Genet to Murakami. In *Last Words from Montmartre* we see themes present in the author's celebrated groundbreaking queer novel *Crocodile's Journal*, which chronicled the life of a university student who bore a conspicuous resemblance to the author in her university years, but here matured into experimentalism: where the highly original *Crocodile's Journal* may still be considered a novel, *Last Words from Montmartre* challenges the limits of any genre.[3]

Among its many innovations, the blending of both transgenre and transgender desire in *Last Words from Montmartre*—its use of transgender aspects of the narrator's identity to reinforce, to mirror, to model, and to construct what is also a transgenre literary *form*—stands out. Just as genres of autobiographical confessional, fiction, and philosophical exploration blend to form what is already a new formal entity, in *Last Words from Montmartre* we see also a refiguring of gender that—evolving under the reader's very eyes—points finally to the deep-structural connections between gender and genre at large. The text forges an implicit connection between experiments in (and explosions of) gender heterogeneity and genre heterogeneity; the breakdown of gender and genre happens with the episodic eruption of desire within the text, so that language, form, and familiar binary gender codes are destabilized all at once. This chapter therefore aims to achieve three modest goals: First, it aims to give a brief introduction to an important Taiwanese author whose work is only just starting to be translated into English.[4] Second, it aims to provide a basic introduction and context for Qiu's experimentalism in her last and most formally challenging work. Finally, in investigating the manifestation of transgender and transgenre desire in the work, this chapter aims to add to transgender studies by giving a concrete example of what the "literary transgender" might mean for Sinophone as well as for other transgender literatures. In *Imagining Transgender* (2007), David Valentine discusses how "the development of transgender studies has been crucially predicated upon the premise that 'gender' and 'sexuality' are ontologically distinct categories across time and place, and that the analytical orientation and focus of transgender studies on 'gender' alone obscures more than it illuminates the complexity of the lived experiences of those people who scholars might identify as 'transgender figures.'"[5] This chapter will argue that Qiu's novel—in line with Valentine—resists any attempt to enforce ontologically distinct categories of gender and sexuality on the narrator, just as it defies readers to impose formal order on a piece whose foundational directive is, after all, to reject formalism entirely and "begin anywhere." In short, this chapter will argue that one of the great contributions of Qiu Miaojin's genre-bending *Last Words from Montmartre* is that in its simultaneous explosion of generic conventions and gender figurations, it successfully exposes the mutually constitutive relationship of gender and genre—the deep-structural correlation between form and content—that informs not just transgender memoir but ultimately all memoir.

Brief Biography of the Author

Qiu Miaojin is one of Taiwan's best-known lesbian authors, but is also widely considered a literary national treasure. Although she committed suicide in Paris at the age of 26, she left behind a body of works that are now considered classics not only among lesbian subcultures but in many other contexts as well. Her works have been taught in high schools and universities in Taiwan, have been reprinted numerous times, inspired a number of tribute novels and memoirs, and become a literary model for many aspiring writers of the last decade. She has a kind of cult following.

Qiu grew up in Southeastern Taiwan and graduated from the premier girls' high school in Taiwan in 1987. She majored in psychology at National Taiwan University in Taipei, and began writing short stories that were serialized in local daily newspapers, one of which won the *Zhongyang Times* short-story prize in 1989. Her piece "The Lonely Crowd" won the Lianhe Literary Prize for novellas in 1990, and in 1991, Qiu published her first collection of short stories, "The Revelries of Ghosts."[6] Qiu worked as a journalist in 1992, and later worked in a teahouse while concentrating on *Crocodile's Journal*. Her breakout novel, the book won great acclaim and eventually (though posthumously) also the prestigious China Times Honorary Prize for Literature in 1995. From 1993 to 1995, Qiu studied French at the Sorbonne, the Alliance Française, and the Institut Catholique in Paris. It was here that she killed herself, reportedly with a knife to the heart.

Last Words from Montmartre is the work she left behind. Written as a series of letters, the novel chronicles the last months of Qiu's—or the narrator's—life in Paris and her careful plans both for the novel and for her death. It is not clear whether copies of the letters were ever actually sent to their declared recipients, and the identity of the various figures in the book has itself been a topic of much speculation.[7] But most readers come to the book already aware of Qiu's suicide, and read this text as a heavily autobiographical chronicle of her last year of life. In fact, to the degree that readers approach the book already knowing its outcome (her well-publicized suicide) and the circumstances of its production (letters left behind, with instructions to publish), this publicity must also be acknowledged as an important part of the book itself.[8] Moreover, since the 2007 publication of Qiu Miaojin's simultaneous "real" diaries of the same period, we need no longer question the deliberate structure of *Last Words*; the diaries make it clear that Qiu conceived of her work as a novel separate from her personal journals and intended to publish it.[9]

Basic Introduction and Context for Qiu's Experimentalism

Given her popularity not only as a queer author but also as a Taiwanese author whose work has been taught in high schools and discussed in college classrooms, Qiu Miaojin is in many ways Taiwan's (revered) prodigal son. Her work exposes the uncomfortable truce between public and private expressions of sexual identity in 1990s Taiwan. Thematically, her attention to lesbian relationships and explicitly erotic content make her work an unexpected contender for national recognition in a newly postnationalist Taiwan, embodying a side of Taiwanese cultural identity that resists sanitization (i.e., it misbehaves by countering larger idealist narratives of Taiwanese democracy or Western-style liberalism). Stylistically, meanwhile, her use of psychoanalytic lyricism and her deliberate engagement with modernist and postmodernist masters such as Kobo Abe, Jean Genet, Andre Gide, Derek Jarman, Yukio Mishima, Haruki Murakami, and Andrei Tarkovsky, take her works beyond the boundaries of Taiwan and Sinophone literature and into a more global dialogue. As the cultural studies scholar and Taiwanese queer literature expert Fran Martin has written of Qiu's work, "Qiu's unique literary style—mingling cerebral, experimental language use, psychological realism, biting social critique through allegory, and a surrealist effect deriving from the use of arrestingly unusual metaphors—is strongly influenced by both European and Japanese literary and cinematic modernisms."[10]

Structurally, *Last Words from Montmartre* is a volatile hybrid of epistolary, journalistic, and confessional genres, interspersed with quotes or lyrics in French and English. Just after the dedication, a note from the author informs us: "If this book should be published, readers can begin anywhere. The only connection among chapters is the period in which they were written." Individual letters sometimes open by addressing a specific person ("Yong," or "Xu," for example), but as the novel progresses in its received order, the chapters sometimes begin only with a date ("May 11th") and a location ("Clichy") or a genre ("case"; "record") or nothing at all. One of the chapters is empty, except for a parenthetical statement about where the lovers are located geographically ("The period of tender love: Xu is in Taiwan, Zoë is in Taiwan," plus a couplet poem), and two of the chapters (15 and 19) are presented as letters written by the narrator's ex-lover Xu, although it is impossible to say if they were written by someone else, or if they are merely the narrator talking to herself in her alternate persona of Zoë, or for that matter how they came to be included in the text.[11] The book "ends" with Qiu's recollection of a seminal scene from Angelopoulos's Oedipal holiday of a film *O Megalexandros*, or "Alexander the Great," in which the great warrior, having returned from battle, sees the blood-stained wedding-dress of his beloved mother, whom he had married, and greets it with the words: "Femme, je suis retourné" ("Wife, I have returned"). Not one to run from melodrama, the narrator remarks in the final lines of the text: "And so it goes. I long to lay down quietly by the banks of a blue lake and die...and when I'm dead for my body to be consumed by birds and beasts, saving only the bone of my brow for Xu...like Alexander, loyal to an everlasting love."

Stylistically, meanwhile, the text uses a looping, repetitive language to build a novelistic sensibility on an armature of intimate everyday vernacular. Readers of the original Chinese are struck for instance by the way Qiu Miaojin "worries" small phrases—simple structures, multiply repeated, drive the text in an almost poetic, and certainly somewhat compulsive, fashion. Note the opening of Chapter (or Letter) #11:

> My soul is lonely, lonely in a lonely way that I'm unwilling to express to you. How can I describe the depth of my loneliness to someone who cast away my soul, cast away my life, trotted me to the brink of death without compunction, someone able to, without noticing or caring, cause me such catastrophic suffering, and to cruelly condemn me to live all by myself, in another country far from home. I can hate you a little less now. But there is still this profound, profound loneliness.

What makes the work unique as a whole is that, like the embedding of geometrical motifs in art, such repetitions—"loneliness," "trashed," "profound"—vary in density and complexity over the course of the novel, building momentum while accumulating references to other books, films, popular cultures, and literary traditions. These linguistic motifs are the scaffolding upon which layers of detail, hours of meditation, and endless streams of raw obsession are built, even as readers try to impose a chronological structure on the novel (against Qiu's express orders at the "beginning" of the novel) by inevitably trying to sort through the many dates, times, and locations she defies us to ignore. These details are, of course, a red herring. In spite of the author's injunction that readers should "begin anywhere," in *Last Words from Montmartre* we see the emergence of distinct and persuasive micronarratives—but we discover that these narratives are built not on any kind of chronology but on the correspondence of linguistic and thematic motifs. And we discover also that what these motifs in essence describe is not the constructive promise of a narrative at all, but rather the connections among the death of a relationship, the disintegration of self, and crucially, the dissolution of any unified notion of genre itself to the point where nothing else exists, both within the confines of the novel and, ultimately, beyond the text.

Transgender and Transgenre Desire

The deliberate fracture or annihilation of an individual narratorial subject—that is, the undermining of the possibility of "autobiography" itself—could be said to be a staple of experimental literary forms across many linguistic and cultural platforms (not to mention a foundational aspect of certain genres of Buddhist scripture). In *Last Words from Montmartre*, gender transformation plays an important role in this dismantling of a unified authorial persona. Announcing her agenda for total transformation early in the novel, the narrator addresses her confidante and former lover Yong, asking: "[D]on't I have to change? I don't know how I'll change. I want to become someone else... I know that I have to change my identity, live under an assumed name... I have to live by transforming myself into someone else." (我需要改變，不是嗎？我不知道要如何改變，我想要變成另外一個人...我知道我得改換一種身分，變成一個名字活著...我得變成一種人生活著). Here the narrator's declaration reverberates with repetitions of, and variations on, words for "to change" or (in a more recent idiomatic usage that is curiously well-suited to morphemic translation from the Chinese) "to trans": words like "change" (改變), "to change or transform" (變成), "to become" (also 變成), "to exchange" (改換).[12] Later, before a major shift in gender self-imagining, the narrator declares plainly:

> At first I decided to forget you, to transform myself into someone entirely different from my old self: a vital personality. Suddenly it seemed so easy, so entirely possible to picture. It would be so easy to slough off all the defining features of my old self that I hadn't been able to get rid of or gloss over before.[13]

In another early letter, the narrator directly addresses the woman who broke her heart: "If you don't want me," she writes, "I'll devote my body and life to someone else and I'll develop a healthy and full life of pleasure and creativity. But my soul is determined to belong to you. She is determined to keep loving you and to stay in conversation with you."

According to the narrator's vision, change is all or nothing, though it may never include the soul; total transformation (and total emancipation from the ex-lover Xu) is only possible through complete emancipation from the self, and the soul may or may not follow. The narrator continues, "If my soul and my flesh can never be integrated—if I can't reconcile the desires of my soul and flesh in one body—that will be my tragedy" (如果未來我的靈肉不能合一，不能在同一個人身上安放我靈與肉的慾望，那也是我的悲劇). Form follows content: as the structure and style of the letters begin to diversify and open out, the momentum of the narrator's inevitable self-destruction builds, and various chapters begin to incorporate French or Chinese alter egos and shifts in perspective such that the reader often has to relearn, several pages later, who the narrator is, and to whom she—or he—is referring. The groundwork for this gradual transition is laid early on, in the novel's resistance to committing to any explicit assignation of gender to the narrator. One way the novel accomplishes this resistance is by exploiting the "gender anonymity" allowed by first-person narration: like the narrator of Jeanette Winterson's 1992 *Written on the Body*, the narrator of *Last Words from Montmartre* avoids explicit references or commitments to gender or sex (apart from the above reference to a female-pronoun "soul"). Thus despite the assumptions readers might make based on what they know about Qiu or on intratextual references to (for instance) the narrator's membership in Parisian women's and lesbian groups, there is no reference to the narrator's "self" using a gendered pronoun, at least at first.[14] As readers, we are forced to confront our own investment in reading the narrator as female (an investment that the narrator also faces and describes later in the text, in a passage I will discuss shortly).

In a similar fashion, the text also avoids assigning gender pronouns to animals and animal-analogies, both of which play an important role in the narrator's projection of self vis-à-vis the ex-lover Xu. For instance, in the very beginning of the book we are introduced to the pet rabbit and affective object with the gender-nonspecific name Bunny ("兔兔"), whose demise and proper burial cause the narrator great anxiety and reemerge later to stand in to some degree for the tragedy of the relationship with Xu as a whole. While in English a reader might find it awkward to refer to a beloved pet as an "it," in modern written Chinese the gender-neutral "animal" pronoun "it," or 牠, is commonly used, and while the Chinese reader may at some point (even early on) wonder whether the rabbit is male or female, the writer would have to elaborate specifically on whether the rabbit was a buck or a doe. Qiu does not elaborate. Instead she maintains the neuter pronoun "牠" until the very end of the novel, long past the point at which readers might finally wish to know what gender or sex to assign to a pet so important in the narrator's life that it is elsewhere described as something the death of which the narrator may not survive; only in the last few pages is it revealed that the rabbit was a male.[15] Likewise, in an extended analogy between the narrator and a "dependable ox" that Xu is so callously willing to cast aside, the narrator once again leaves the gender-neutral animal pronoun unclarified, in spite of the intimacy that the analogy is meant to convey. The narrator observes:

> I am willing to be your ox, so you just have to make a comfortable place for it [牠] to stay, okay? You may be cruel, but could you bear to drive away the ox that you have loved, the one who has loved you for three years? Could you bear to drive it away, never to return, never to exist again?...Is this ox just any old beast? Tell me, if you feed and nurture an ox that has already proven itself, won't it produce for you the kind of livelihood, life, and love that you want? [16]

Though the ox in this passage—a passage which actually extends to most of a page, and the central analogy of which comes up elsewhere in the text—is invoked as a sort of "transmigration" or object-identification of the narrator in relationship to Xu, it too—like the rabbit and the narrator—remains gender-nonspecific.

In Chapter 2, moreover, Qiu begins to inscribe on this tabula rasa of narratorial gender the possibility of the narrator's masculinity. Describing the narrator's intense anxiety leading up to the stealth burial of Bunny in a public park in Paris, the narrator remarks:

> This morning I was stressed about burying Bunny. I had promised you I would bury Bunny in the ground, not in the water, so that you could visit the grave. But my friends all said I'd never find a good spot. And the pet cemetery was too expensive. Camira even went so far as to suggest throwing the body in the garbage. The body had been sitting there for two days already. If I put it off any longer it would start to decay and I would fail to fulfill your wishes. This afternoon I finally resolved to just pull myself together and put Bunny peacefully to rest. Then you wouldn't have to worry about either of us. Daddy would take care of Bunny.[17]

In this passage the narrator creates a snapshot of a brief burst of anxiety and the determination to resolve it, a microromance of the expression of a problem, the process of investigating the problem, and its happy resolution. If the narrator's problem is an intrusive anxiety, the solution here is to become "Daddy": to pull oneself together and, in "put[ting] Bunny peacefully to rest," to bury not only the body of the dead pet rabbit but also the narrator's own attachment to the past. In this example, the narrator manages to introduce a masculine symbolic iconography without resorting to gendered pronouns, but the gendered masculinity introduced into the text is relational rather than implicit: the narrator becomes "Daddy" in relation to the object of the letter, the other "parent" of Bunny, the one whose wishes must be fulfilled and whose imagined/projected parental concerns it is "Daddy's" responsibility to take care of. At the same time, however, Qiu's contemporaries would not necessarily have read this reference to "Daddy" as an explicit challenge to, or contradiction of, the assumption that the narrator is female, nor would they necessarily have interpreted it as a definitive sign of the narrator's "trans" gender. Queer communities in Taiwan in the mid-1990s regularly deployed what Martin has called the "dimorphous lesbian genders of T/po, comparable but not reducible to the English terms butch/femme," and "Daddy" falls comfortably, or at least legibly, under the "T" umbrella.[18] As both Martin and Helen Hok-Sze Leung observe, moreover, T/po gender categories were not only widely in play at this time, but also the subject of heated controversy about gender roles where Qiu's writing often figured prominently for its "T" narrators.[19] In a public, or published, sense, therefore, Qiu's "Daddy" narrator at this point would still have been read not as transgendered but as lesbian.

But then the novel introduces the character Zoë (spelled in roman letters in the text), a gender-indeterminate and intermediary transformation of the original autobiographical voice—a kind of alter ego—that takes on an increasingly important role as the novel progresses, in proportion to the gradual disappearance of the assumed gender of the narratorial "I," or "我," in the novel as lesbian or female. At first, at least, this new iteration of the authorial voice has no gender, implied or otherwise; it has only its definition of self in relation to the lover Xu, in contrast to whom it is brought to life. Addressing Xu, and expressing a recurring theme of the book, the narrator declares:

> So it's you, just you. There can never be anyone else in the deepest reaches of my body and soul. Even if you don't want me anymore, don't love me anymore, and don't belong to me anymore, I will still tell you loud: No love can ever replace the love that we shared, our mutual belonging, what we gave to each other, how we were open to each other, the communication we achieved between bodies and souls. What I want to tell you is that you are the person who accepted Zoë's body and soul the most. And you once were the one who loved and understood me, body and soul, the best. It's precisely because you are the only person to have loved me and accepted me like this, to have understood my songs, that you had Zoë truly and completely on fire in the palm of your hand.[20]

In this passage, Qiu once again exploits the syntactical plasticity of written Chinese and first-person narrative to avoid specifying gender or third-person pronouns for long stretches of text, carefully avoiding assigning this new character Zoë with either a gendered pronoun (他 or 她), *or* a gender by nature or association as with the figure of the ox and the self-naming as "Daddy." Nor does the narrator overstate the connection between Zoë and the narrator as previously presented, although Qiu makes it clear that "Zoë" and "I" ultimately have the same referent ("you are the only one ever to love me like this, accept me").[21] Rather what happens here is that Zoë is introduced as a new and genderless third-person iteration of the original first-person voice—a radical enough tactic of splitting and reuniting narratorial identities even without the complexities of gender identification added on.

In this sense, *Last Words'* Zoë bears a meaningful resemblance to the Greek concept of "zoē" that Giorgio Agamben elaborates in *Homo Sacer: Sovereign Power and Bare Life*. In Agamben's iteration, *zoē* represents "bare life": inherently nonpolitical, or prepolitical, zoē is a state of raw existence of life that contrasts with the inherently relational or political *bios*— "qualified" or "particular" life—from which zoē is always already excluded.[22] That Qiu was aware of—and deliberately using—such nuanced understandings of zoē is suggested by a passage in Chapter 16, when the narrator tries to explain to a Greek classmate, a would-be suitor, that zoë prefers women's bodies. The classmate objects, protesting instead that "a body is just a body" regardless of sex, and that the problem is that Zoë has never experienced raw, unmediated desire. "Zoë," he declares, "perhaps you don't understand the pleasures of raw carnal lust. You've never known Dionysus" (Zoë, 或許你不懂得單純肉欲的美好, 你從來沒經驗過酒神戴奧尼索斯是什麼). Revealingly, the classmate then adds: "Zoë, doesn't the word 'Zoë' in Greek mean "life" (生命)? Do you really understand Zoë?" (Zoë, Zoë 這個字不是希臘文〔生命〕的意思嗎? 你真懂得 Zoë?).[23] Assuming then that Qiu (if not Zoë) was well aware of the significance of Zoë, it is therefore possible to read this initial literary persona as a kind of allegory for gender: Zoë as "bare" or raw gender, not biologically determined and as yet gender-unsocialized, excluded from political (relationship) life even as he/she is completely defined by it. The critic Wang Haowei 王浩威 might call this Zoë "pre-Oedipal"; but for our purposes we might call it "pre-gender," a gender blank.[24]

Zoë materializes, then, as an alter ego of the narrator who exists between genders and in a purely relational or *potential* state: Zoë exists only in relation to Xu ("you are the only person to have loved me and accepted me") but, like the literary equivalent of a stem cell, Zoë has the radical textual potential to become either or any gender. Qiu explores all of these possibilities. In a passage from the long third chapter, after berating the ex-lover Xu for becoming someone unrecognizable—the recognition of the other, and her complementarity, being a condition of Zoë's own self-definition and recognition—the narrator then switches to the first explicitly third-person description of "himself" as Zoë in the text. He writes,

> Xu, it's not that you no longer love Zoë or need Zoë anymore. On the contrary, it's precisely because you tried constantly to satisfy him [他] and could never satisfy him that you were crushed and frustrated. Initially when you were completely open with him and could thoroughly love him, you did your best. Later, when you were completely shut down and couldn't thoroughly love him, you still did your best to satisfy him but you were too worn out, too frustrated, so you chose to abandon him. But in truth you had no way of completely getting rid of him, because after you accepted his love there was never a moment when you stopped loving him, stopped bonding with his spirit, there was never a moment when you could truly extricate your fate from his, and you never really stopped doing your absolute best to satisfy him, your very best to grow closer to him.[25]

Here, the assumed 她 ("she") of the narrator is at last countered with 他 ("he"), just as the first-person narrative voice has splintered into the third-person autobiographical voice of Zoë. Needing a relational object to define him, Zoë settles on his lover Xu and emerges as masculine; since Qiu consistently avoids the gender pronoun in earlier passages, its repetition here is conspicuous. As the novel progresses, moreover, Zoë's understanding of gender and sexuality as relational becomes even clearer. Regarding masculinity, the narrator recounts for example his initial distress upon receiving a letter from his sometime-lover Yong, living in Tokyo, whom he mistakenly believes has "foreclosed [the narrator's] sexual desire for [Yong] due to this problem of 'male vs. female' bodies." In fact, however, it turns out to have been a misunderstanding; Yong wanted to express not only her recognition of, but also a desire for, the narrator's own brand of masculinity. With relief, the narrator concludes:

> But the reality was not what I thought. In fact it was the opposite. Yong only later had the chance to clarify for me what she meant by "male." In the end it wasn't a physical thing so much as a personality thing, a matter of will, a sort of spiritual "masculinity." And what she

meant by "male" was me. It was precisely the strength of "maleness" in me and that other person she loved that enabled her desire, while blocking her desire for others.[26]

His perception of his own masculinity reaffirmed, for one brief moment—the only one in the novel—Zoë experiences the bliss of an integrated and socialized gendered self. "In the end," the narrator concludes, "she and I were in tune, our love and our sex reciprocal, symmetrical. The depth of her passion was what I'd needed all along. I honestly think it was the love and sex [Yong] gave me that sustained me this time." Inasmuch as the narrator finds a certain fleeting integration of his persona when in a masculine aspect or mode, his record of the experience of "transitioning" to female, on the other hand, is one of the most harrowing episodes of experimental "self transformation" in the novel. Here, the narrator theoretically must face (according to him) not only the unfamiliarity of learning to be in the "passive" or "receptive" mode sexually but, at last, discovering the means to achieving exactly what he had hoped for: a total forgetting of, and separation from, his ex-lover Xu (and thus by extension a forgetting of himself, a successful self-annihilation). Upon returning from a visit to Yong in Tokyo, the narrator elaborates:

> Ever since returning from Tokyo, I could feel the nature of my sexuality changing, gradually, a tectonic change so mysterious and personal that I didn't know what to make of it, or even what the factors were that had brought me to this point. I could feel myself "becoming a 'woman'" (the crude sort of definition of "woman")—or perhaps just becoming a "woman."[27] My period became extremely regular. One morning I was dreaming about you and I woke up with a start. I thought I'd gotten my period—and in fact I had, right on time, it felt like a mysterious connection. I also dreamed I had long hair, and it looked "feminine," and in the dream I was aware that I was enjoying my looks and that my face was becoming beautiful (a "feminine" sort of beauty). One day, Qingjin was looking intently at my face and told me I was very beautiful, but beautiful in a way that could be attractive to both men and women, and I could actually sense that my facial features and my behavior were becoming more feminine [女性化] My sexuality also began to take on a more "receptive" quality to it. I still fantasized about you, but the way I had loved you and gave love to you now seemed to me more of a desire for you to love me and give love to me.[28]

If the narrator's sexuality has been relational so far, now a shift in genders also signals a shift in desire. Channeled through the body, what is elsewhere in the novel a "spiritual masculinity" gives way to what the narrator identifies as the various physically manifest stigmata of femininity such as menstruation, long "feminine" hair, a certain vanity or concern with looks, and a "receptive" sexuality. This receptive sexuality in particular causes the narrator's fantasies about Xu to shift, but crucially, it also allows the narrator to envision for the first time what it might be like to "become a 'woman' through and through." The narrator observes:

> I felt that I was capable of sexual relationships with men (the sexual part, at least). Or perhaps I should say, I was starting to mis/understand [以為] that a perfect sexual relationship could be possible with a warm, sincere man (someone with a quality of "pure" masculinity about him, like Eric, from the doctoral program). The possibilities multiplied exponentially in such a short time that I couldn't handle it. I scared myself silly at the thought that an intellectual and spiritual man like Eric might materialize and find me attractive and then I'd "become a 'woman'" through and through. It was entirely possible. The person I had become was entirely capable of this. I was scared to death because it was a way, the perfect way, to escape totally from both my erotic and my romantic desires for you. What frightened me wasn't the lure of lust or of betraying you, so much as the lure of leaving you, the lure of silently and without taking a breath, taking leave of your life and disappearing forever in a kind of eternal self-cancellation [一種永遠 "取消" 自己], the lure of making it so you could never find me again.[29]

Who is Zoë? If gender is relational and Zoë successfully "becomes a 'woman,'" does the novel end? Formally speaking, if Zoë successfully "disappears" from Xu's sight by transforming into a "woman" in relationship with a "man," does Zoë then disappear from the narrative entirely, that is, does the narrative end? For it is here, at the point of desire, that the narrator's identity splits definitively. If *Last Words from Montmartre* is a new genre, then one of its defining characteristics is its attempt to create a literary portrait of the process and effects of a transition from one gendered, desiring subject into another: to experiment with one subject and multiple gendered voices, and with the effects of this particular multiplicity on literary form. In *Last Words*, it seems, there is a blank space upon which gender is written, and—if we take the author's injunction at her word—it is an inscription that can occur in any order, on an ectoplasmic perceiving body that reorganizes itself several times throughout the course of the novel without finding a home. When the narrator observes that a failure to "rest the desires of soul and flesh in the body of the same person" will be the narrator's own "tragedy," in other words, there is a certain ambiguity, since it could refer equally to the consequences of failing to love and sexually desire the same partner, but also to the consequences of failing to merge physical and metaphysical desires in the narrator's own body.

Writing as Desire, Writing as Oasis

For Qiu's narrator, one of the means of reconciling the various genders, selves, and loves, and indeed one of the only areas where perfect unity was at least theoretically achievable, was in writing. In writing, and in the imagination, the narrator could find her/his own perfect voice, the ideal union of spiritual and corporeal desires, the cleanly integrated home of all aspects of his, and her, identity. "What I really want," the narrator remarks, "is to experience the depths of life, to comprehend people and life, and to express all this through the creative practice of my art and scholarship" [我藝術與學習的創作]. *All my other accomplishments mean nothing to me. Only if I can create a masterpiece that achieves the goal I've fixed my inward gaze on over the course of my journey through art, will my life not have been wasted.* [italics in original].[30] If the narrator of *Last Words from Montmartre* cannot achieve a consciously integrated subjectivity, perhaps the text can. If the chapters of *Last Words from Montmartre* represent a true record of the narrator's absolute introspection, then in articulating the narrative "I," all apparent contradictions—including revolutions in gender—may be resolved.

No wonder, then, that at the point in the novel where the narrator offers us an image of an idealized, imaginary Zoë—a buoyant and invulnerable Zoë, a Zoë of "perfect" (and perfectly indeterminate) gender—it is an image infused not only with the trappings of both more dimporphic genders as defined within the novel, but also with references to writing. In a passage labeled only "Case" (檔案), a married woman and love-interest called Qingjin proposes a romantic trip to the coast of Normandy. The narrator contemplates Qingjin's proposal, and in imagining their rendezvous, fantasizes about surprising Qingjin with a fully-realized "transmigration" or "reincarnation" (轉世) of the Zoë-identity, a kind of apotheosis of Zoë as a fully-articulated lover, complete with dashing personality and romantic writing habits. Once again completely avoiding use of a gendered third-person pronoun, the narrator describes how:

> [Qingjin] had always wanted to travel through Europe with me. I said yes. We also agreed to go to Deauville/Trouville for a weekend in July when she got back...But she had no idea that I was biding my time,

waiting for these two months, preparing for her, preparing to "reincarnate" into a new identity, as Zoë [准備 "轉世" 的另一個 Zoë 的身分]. In July I want to present her with a Zoë who smokes cigarettes, who has long hair, who rides a bicycle, who is engrossed in learning the violin, who has returned to the novel and who is starting to write poetry on a regular basis, who can remain locked in the office and finish the thesis, whose French is catching up with hers, whose social life is extensive, who has a belly-laughing, easygoing, freewheeling [瀟灑] personality, a Zoë who is handsome, and beautiful…She had no idea that I was yearning to learn from her about life and work, two areas in which she would always be a leader and a teacher…She had no idea that once I gave her my soul, I would love her body passionately too, which was precisely the great secret about myself that I couldn't bring myself to say out loud…And on the beach at night in Deauville/Trouville, if my "reincarnation" was successful, she wouldn't see my kiss coming…She would have no idea of any of this.[31]

As in the earliest appearance of Zoë, here the narrator once again carefully avoids the use of gender pronouns, stringing together long adjectival clauses. Interestingly, the verb for change or transformation used to describe the process of transforming into the ideal Zoë in this passage—轉世, or "transmigration"—is a term tied directly to historically Buddhist notions of incarnation and transformation, or an idea of "incarnation" (化身) that can be translated both as a verb that means "to change" or "to exchange" (化) the body (身)—to transform but to trans/form, that is, to take on a new form by reconfiguring the same substance—or as a noun that indicates the final product of this transformation, the "embodiment" or personification of the new form. In both cases, a nuance of the term is to emphasize the transient and illusory nature of the material world. For the ideal Zoë, neither masculine nor feminine is enough. Any determination of gender represents only the insubstantial trappings or illusory imaginings of a material life. Thus the ideal Zoë is "both handsome and beautiful," both masculine and feminine. The ideal Zoë has long hair (for Qiu, in this and other works, a complicated emblem of femininity) but smokes cigarettes.[32] Zoë belly laughs and is expansive, engages in social life but is the consummate romantic.

But most important of all, the ideal Zoë is creatively engaged on all levels, a self-conscious agent of textual production: perfecting a second language, producing a thesis, writing poetry, and finishing a novel. At the beginning of the first full "letter," the pretransitional narrator addresses the ex-lover Xu and articulates what could be as much a description of Qiu's utopian vision of writing as it is a statement of purpose for the novel itself. First, the narrator equates writing itself with desire, noting that suppressing desire for Xu in the painful period since their breakup has meant suppressing writing itself: "I haven't... been able to pour my heart out to you in writing like I used to do, because as I've told you, the letters I write to you are themselves a fierce form of desire." But then the narrator gathers resolve. Having declared the intention to write Xu a set of letters "like the ones I wrote to you at the end of [last] year, a perfectly unrestrained symmetry of words smoldering with love," the narrator concludes the chapter by describing the potential of writing to give Xu (and the narrator him/herself) "a center":

> I can't stand the thought of you walking in the desert. I want to give you a little patch of solid ground to stand on, or at the very least some small green oasis you can look at in the distance, to keep you from drifting away from reality, from escaping back into your mind. It's all my fault! I missed my chance. But let me see if—using these words as a little plot of land and my life as a cornerstone—I can build you a center. Alright?

In *Last Words*, writing thus begins as letters addressed to a lover, an oasis of desire earmarked for Xu ("a little plot of land"); quickly spills out over these generic boundaries to become something more; and finally ends as an oasis for the narrator, a dream, a utopian vision where many-layered selves and genders (a fully transmigrated "Zoë" identity) integrate at last to engage in multiple forms of textual production and expression.[33] In this sense *Last Words* can hardly be considered the melancholic last testament of a life cut tragically short. Rather the book is a chronicle of transition and aspiration, the enactment of a meditation on the utopian potential of writing to liberate, and integrate, multiple potentialities of self in a concrete, "embodied" textual form. As such, form itself in *Last Words from Montmartre* not only acts as a means of transcending the usual constraints of gender and genre, but also as a medium for immortality.

Notes

Special thanks to Fran Martin, for inspiring me to engage with Qiu's works on a deeper level, Susan Stryker, for her key comments on an early draft of this essay, and Rosalie Z. Fanshel, for her commentary on style. I am also very appreciative of Howard Chiang's rich, constructive editorial insights and suggestions.

1. Jay Prosser, *Second Skins: The Body Narratives of Transsexuality* (New York: Columbia University Press, 1998), 178, 191 (chapter

entitled "No Place Like Home: Transgender and Trans-Genre in Leslie Feinberg's *Stone Butch Blues*").
2. For general discussions of Qiu Miaojin in English, see Fran Martin, *Situating Sexualities: Queer Representation in Taiwanese Fiction, Film, and Public Culture* (Hong Kong: Hong Kong University Press, 2003). Martin's introduction gives an excellent snapshot of Taipei's remarkable queer scene in the late 1980s and early 1990s. See also Tze-lan Deborah Sang, *The Emerging Lesbian: Female Same-Sex Desire in Modern China* (Chicago: University of Chicago Press, 2003). For a biographical timeline in Chinese, see *INK Literary Monthly* [印刻文學生活誌] Issue 22, Special issue on Qiu Miaojin, (June 2005): 81.
3. "Crocodile's Journal" is *Er'yu shouji* (鱷魚手記) (Taipei: Shibao chubanshe, 2003). On genre in this and other works, besides Martin's introduction to *Situating Sexualities*, see for example Liu Liangya, "愛慾，性別，與書寫：邱妙津的女同性戀小說" (Desire, gender, and writing: Qiu Miaojin's lesbian fiction), 中外文學 303 (1997). In terms of genre and style, one might draw a fascinating contrast between Qiu's novel and the highly accessible story "A Chinese Woman in Paris" (一个流落巴黎的中国女子) by the Hong Kong writer Huang Biyun (黄碧云), which also features first-person narration of queer tension between Chinese women protagonists in Paris in the 1990s, but in a style that might be considered subversively sentimental rather than experimental. The story appears in the collection: Huang Biyun (黃碧雲), *Tashi nüzi, woyeshi nüzi* (她是女子，我也是女子) [She is a woman and I am a woman too] (Taipei: Maitian, 1994].
4. Fran Martin has translated the short story "Platonic Hair" in *Angelwings: Contemporary Queer Fiction from Taiwan* (Honolulu: University of Hawaii Press, 2003), 51–73; and Chapter 11 from *Last Words from Montmartre* has been translated by Howard Goldblatt as "Letters from Montmartre," in *The Columbia Anthology of Modern Chinese Literature*, ed. Joseph Lau and Howard Goldblatt (New York: Columbia University Press, 2007), 455–69. My own translation of the complete *Last Words from Montmartre* is forthcoming from New York Review Books; all quotes in this chapter are drawn from the working draft of this manuscript translation and may differ slightly from the final published version of the book.
5. This quoted observation is by Howard Chiang from an editorial e-mail exchange on April 9, 2011.
6. Qiu Miaojin, *Jimo de qunzhong* (寂寞的群眾) [The lonely crowd] (Taipei: Lianhe wenxue chubanshe, 1995); Qiu Miaojin, *Gui de kuanghuan* (鬼的狂歡) [The revelries of ghosts] (Taipei: Lianhe wenxue chubanshe, 1991).
7. See for example discussions among contributors to *INK Literary Monthly* (印刻文學生活誌) 22 (June 2005): Special issue on Qiu

Miaojin, as well as multiple easily-searched online published discussions and interviews with Qiu's executor Lai Hsiang-yin ever since the publication of Qiu's "actual" diaries in 2007. Qiu Miaojin, *Qiu Miaojin riji* (邱妙津日記) [The diaries of Qiu Miaojin], 2 vols. (Taipei: INK, 2007).

8. See Fran Martin, *Situating Sexualities: Queer Representation in Taiwanese Fiction, Film, and Public Culture* (Hong Kong: Hong Kong University Press, 2003), 231. "[T]he common reading of Qiu's writing as 'self portrait' or 'almost-autobiography' is likely prompted by the style of the writing itself as much as by the fascination of the reading public with the circumstances of Qiu's death."
9. Qiu Miaojin, *Qiu Miaojin riji*.
10. Fran Martin, "Stigmatic Bodies: The Corporeal Qiu Miaojin," in *Embodied Modernities: Corporeality, Representation, and Chinese Cultures*, ed. Fran Martin and Larissa Heinrich (Honolulu: University of Hawai'i Press, 2006), 177–194.
11. Qiu Miaojin, *Mengmate yishu* (蒙馬特遺書) [Last words from Montmartre] (Taipei: INK, 2006).
12. See for example Susan Stryker, Paisley Currah, and Lisa Jean Moore, "Introduction: Trans-, Trans, or Transgender?" *WSQ: Women's Studies Quarterly* 36, nos. 3–4 (2008): 11–22.
13. Qiu, *Mengmate yishu*, 103.
14. On Winterson, see for example Susan Lanser, "Narration and Gender: The Role of the First-Person Narrator in Jeanette Winterson's *Written on the Body*," *Narrative* 3, no. 1 (1995): 85–94; and Ute Kauer, "Narration and Gender: The Role of the First-Person Narrator in Written on the Body," in "'I'm telling you stories': Jeanette Winterson and the Politics of Reading," ed. Helena Grice and Tim Woods, *Postmodern Studies*, vol. 25 (Amsterdam: Rodopi, 1998).
15. Of course, this discomfort around specifying the gender of the rabbit becomes even more obvious in translation, since in English as we personify our pets we usually can't tolerate referring to a beloved pet as "it," forcing us to assign or explicitly avoid masculine or feminine pronouns in translation.
16. Qiu, *Mengmate yishu*, 15.
17. Qiu, *Mengmate yishu*, 21.
18. See Fran Martin, "The Legacy of the Crocodile: Critical Debates over Taiwanese Lesbian Fiction," *International Institute for Asian Studies Newsletter* 29 (November 2002): 8.
19. Martin writes:
    Thematically, much of Qiu's fiction deals with lesbian subjects, particularly with relationships structured around the dimorphous lesbian genders of T/po, comparable but not reducible to the English terms butch/femme...It is the thematic concern with T identity and desire that has catalysed

much of the critical controversy. At least three different and contradictory approaches to Qiu's focus on T narrators can be discerned. First, particularly since the publication of The Crocodile's Journal, Qiu's writing has functioned as a point of identification for her young lesbian readership: metaphorical references to crocodiles and coded usage of the nick-name of The Crocodile's Journal's protagonist, Lazi, were ubiquitous in mid-to-late 1990s lesbian magazine and Internet subcultures. Second, however, the response to Qiu's fiction in the early-to-mid 1990s by academics, influenced in part by Euro-American lesbian-feminism, was fairly harsh. Some critics worried that Qiu's T narrators reproduced oppressive, patriarchal gender relations. These critics sometimes ascribed the psychic anguish of Qiu's narrators to the fact that their author was unacquainted with feminism and the organized tongzhi movement, thus censuring Qiu's fiction for perpetuating 'negative images' of lesbians. But third, just a couple of years after this, there emerged a new tendency to discuss Qiu's writing from the perspective of local efforts to recover the histories of Taiwan's T/po lesbian cultures which, it was sometimes argued, had been suppressed by the intellectual feminists' critique of their purportedly sexist structure. This third movement, in turn, effected a dialogue with the Euro-American rise of studies of butch/femme and transgender identities in lesbian and gay studies at about the same time. Martin, "The Legacy of the Crocodile: Critical Debates over Taiwanese Lesbian Fiction." See also Helen Hok-Sze Leung, "Thoughts of Lesbian Genders in Contemporary Chinese Cultures," *Journal of Lesbian Studies* 6, no. 2 (2002): 123–133.

20. Qiu, *Mengmate yishu*, 21.
21. Lydia Liu writes in *Translingual Practice: Literature, National Culture, and Translated Modernity* (Stanford: Stanford University Press, 1995) about the history of the gender-division of "ta" (她/他) in modern Chinese.
22. Giorgio Agamben, *Homo Sacer: Sovereign Power and Bare Life* (Stanford: Stanford University Press, 1998).
23. Qiu, *Mengmate yishu*, 144.
24. Wang Haowei 王浩威, "書寫, 死亡, 性倒錯: 從邱妙津〔蒙馬特遺書〕說起" (Writing, death, and paraphilia: Starting from Qiu Miaojin's *Letters from Montmartre*), *Lianhe wenxue* (聯合文學) 13, no. 4 (1997): 70–74.
25. Qiu, *Mengmate yishu*, 33–34.
26. Qiu, *Mengmate yishu*, 104–105.
27. In the text: "我感覺到我〔在變成一個"女人"（一個庸俗般的"女人"的定義），或可能變成一個"女人"〕"

28. Qiu, *Mengmate yishu*, 103–104.
29. Qiu, *Mengmate yishu*, 103–4.
30. Qiu, *Mengmate yishu*, 49 (italics in original)
31. Qiu, *Mengmate yishu*, 45–46.
32. Martin, "Platonic Hair."
33. See Chapter 5 of the novel for one of the more explicit examples of self-referentiality in the text; the narrator describes how by "the tenth letter this manuscript had taken on a life of its own, with its own style, thesis, and aesthetic...an abstruse, high-density excavation, an extremely pure work about one very tiny subset of a young person's life," and in Qiu, *Mengmate yishu*, 90.

CHAPTER 7

Trans on Screen

Helen Hok-Sze Leung

BEGINNINGS: MOVING TARGETS

Autumn, 2001. While leafing through the catalogue of the Netherlands Transgender Film Festival, one of a handful of film festivals in the world with an explicit aim to "encourage visibility and positive representations of transgender issues,"[1] I was surprised to find that *Swordsmen 2*, an old Hong Kong martial arts blockbuster starring Jet Li and Brigitte Lin, had made it into the program.[2] The 1992 film was well known to me. The casting of actress Brigitte Lin as the indomitable Dongfang Bubai, a swordsman who practices a form of martial arts that requires self-castration, was considered to be a homophobic erasure of gay content in much of the burgeoning queer film criticism emerging in Hong Kong during the 1990s. The film's inclusion in a *transgender* film festival almost 10 years after its release was certainly provocative. It prompted me to see that what seems problematic from gay/lesbian perspectives can have a significantly different meaning when viewed through a transgender lens.

Spring, 2002. I was invited to give a lecture on Asian cinema at *Inside Out*, Toronto's Gay and Lesbian Film Festival. Inspired by *Swordsman 2*'s resurrection as a "transgender film," I suggested a similar rereading of *Portland Street Blues*, a 1998 triad film starring Sandra Ng in an acclaimed role as Sister Thirteen, a butch woman and a gang leader. In the film, Sister Thirteen has sex with other women but reserves her fiercest loyalty and affection for men.

This characterization has prompted many critics to question whether she is an authentic lesbian character. In my lecture I argued that both films, when viewed from a transgender perspective, become much more interesting. For instance, the casting of Brigitte Lin in *Swordsman 2* challenges audience' presumption that they can tell the difference between transsexual and nontranssexual femininity. Likewise, the affection between a butch woman and a man in *Portland Street Blues* does not necessarily signify heterosexual desire but rather a *homoerotic* attraction between two masculine figures that are commonplace in triad gangster films.[3] Not surprisingly, my audience in Toronto was not entirely convinced. Some lesbian members of the audience feared that my "transgender reading" serve as an apologia for heteronormativity, whereas transgender members of the audience thought neither of the films represent "real" transgender people. Not only do the audience's misgivings show me, once again, that transgender and gay/lesbian interpretations can often be at odds, they also remind me that strong audience investment in "realistic representation" and "positive image" often places an undue burden on both queer and transgender characters to be positively representative of whole communities.

Almost a decade has passed since those early conversations. During this time, several important developments have widened the possibilities of how transgender can be considered in relation to cinema. First, there has been an exponential growth of scholarly, artistic, and activist works on transgender issues that are produced by and for the interests and well-being of transgender people. The cinema, in particular, has seen an explosion of independent works—most prominently in the documentary genre—that are explicitly made by and for transgender communities.[4] At the same time, there is a critical tendency in theoretical discourse to go *beyond* the nominal understanding of transgender as an identity and as the naming of a specific group of people. In a recent special issue on "Trans-" in the *Women's Studies Quarterly* edited by Susan Stryker, Paisley Currah, and Lisa Jean Moore, the editors argue that "the time is ripe for bursting transgender wide open," and in so doing articulate the questions raised by transgender subjectivities and embodiments in relation to the crossings of other categorical differences:

> A fundamental aspect of our editorial vision is that neither "-gender" nor any of the other suffixes of "trans-" can be understood in isolation— that the lines implied by the very concept of "trans-" are moving targets, simultaneously composed of multiple determinants.

Furthermore, the editors argue for the deployment of "trans" as a verb and a critical practice that is comparable to, but distinct from, that of "queering":

> "Transing" in short, is a practice that takes place within, as well as across or between gendered spaces. It is a practice that assembles gender into contingent structures of association with other attributes of bodily being, and that allows for their reassembly.

The notion of "transing" also enables intersectional work in which diverse forms of trans processes that transform or realign boundaries between self and other can be considered together. An example is the research collaboration between transgender studies scholar Susan Stryker and researchers such as Nikki Sullivan (who studies cosmetic surgery, tattooing and branding, as well as other modificatory practices) and Samantha Murray (who studies the discourse around bariatric surgery and other medical surgical interventions into obesity).[5]

Second, the rapid growth in queer Asian scholarship has resulted in the development of critical frameworks that eschew simply "applying" LGBT frameworks to non-Western phenomena of sexual and gender variance. For instance, Peter Jackson's formulation of "pre-gay, post-queer" in the Thai context draws attention to historical formations of sexual and gender variance that predate the advent of LGBT identities, thus crisscrossing and/or overlapping contemporary gay and transgender identities and embodiments.[6] More recently, in a special issue of the *Journal of Inter-Asia Cultural Studies* on "Trans/Asia," Josephine Ho and Fran Martin demonstrate the importance of the "specificity of place" in shaping local articulations of transgender identities, cultures, and communities.[7] In cinema studies, Song Hwee Lim's analysis of cross-ethnic casting in transnational Chinese cinema through insights culled from transgender practices explores the relation between various forms of "transing" on screen.[8]

In light of these critical developments, the study of transgender issues in Chinese-language cinema can be more fruitfully considered as an exercise in locating moving targets. In other words, it needs not be fixated on a singular notion of what constitutes transgender on screen. It must not limit itself—nor, however, should it remain indifferent—to representational politics. Instead, issues concerning representation are best explored in relation to or alongside wider questions about how embodied difference (of gender and beyond) is constituted, guarded, permeated, and reconstituted on screen. In this chapter, I will explore three interpretive models of reading trans on screen. I am by no means suggesting that these three are the only, or even the best, kind of approaches. I simply want to show the varied and creative critical possibilities that the notion of trans has enabled.

The first model, the most conventional but nonetheless important, focuses on gender variant characters and their cultural meanings. In mainstream cinema, in particular, characters who disrupt the normative alignments presumed between sex assignment, gender presentation, and gender identification seldom emerge as fully articulated subjects. More often, they are displaced symbols of cultural anxiety over, or fascination with, various forms of boundary crossings. Jay Prosser's critique of *Silence of the Lambs* for representing the "somatic trouble" of the transsexual as trouble for the social corpus;[9] Judith Halberstam's analysis of the ways transgender characters are punished for their "inflexible" gender identity in *Boys Don't Cry* and *The Crying Game*;[10] as well as John Philips's study of the ambivalence underlying depictions of transgender in Hollywood films[11] are examples of a critical model that exposes the ideological workings of such displacement. Like Hollywood cinema, Chinese-language cinema is replete with examples that would benefit from such critique. An implicit—at times explicit—imperative behind such critical works is the advocation for a *different* kind of representation, one that is less harmful for the communities represented.

The second interpretive model approaches transgender not as an identity but rather as a term of relationality. For example, Judith Halberstam's reading of the masculine bonding between butches in *By Hook Or By Crook* or my reading of homoeroticism between a butch woman and male gangsters in *Portland Street Blues* illustrate the gendered dimensions of desire, love, and friendship that are rendered unintelligible by hetero as well as homonormative narratives.[12] Furthermore, Halberstam has pointed out that the use of "transgender" as a broad umbrella term denoting all cross-gender identifying subjects has at times blurred the difference between diverse forms of embodiments and presentations. For Halberstam, approaching "transgender" as relationality also allows us to *specify* how people place themselves in "particular forms of recognition" to signify how they relate to others within an intimate bond or a community.[13] The films of queer auteurs Cui Zi'en and Zero Chou especially warrant such an approach as they explore how relational bonds, particularly between queer subjects, can be transformed by unexpected modes of gender presentation and recognition.

The third critical model is perhaps the most adventurous. It turns its attention to what Nikki Sullivan calls "trans practice"—a broad notion that denotes various modification practices that transform bodily being.[14] Sullivan is writing about practices such as piercing, branding, tattooing, and cosmetic surgery in addition to sex reassignment surgeries. In the context of Chinese-language cinema, the example of martial arts and myriad forms of theatrical, acrobatic, athletic, and spiritual training come to mind. Paying attention to the modification practices—rather than primarily to issues of identity and relationality—uncovers trans articulations in unlikely and provocative places. It is from this angle that I would like to revisit *Farewell My Concubine* (1992). The film has raised all kinds of problems for critics concerned with issues of gender and sexuality because it depicts a brutal process of enforced feminization while associating it with homosexual desire. It has also been critiqued as a national allegory that views modern China as a feminized victim. Following Sullivan's ethical imperative, I propose a reading that foregoes judgment on whether the film's depiction of transgender constitutes positive or negative representation. Rather, I am interested in what its depiction of Beijing opera training as a "trans practice" shows us about the negotiation between self and otherness.

1. Looking at: Trans Others

Gender variant characters have been repeatedly projected on screen as figures of alterity, much like the way sexual, ethnic, and racial "others" have been represented on screen. Their gender variance—whether in the form of intersexuality, transsexuality, cross-dressing, or any form of transgender embodiment and presentation—is visibly exoticized but the "back story" of their gender history is seldom made clear. Furthermore, these characters are most often found in films with supernatural elements such as ghosts, demons, and magical martial arts. It is thus seldom possible for audience to recognize these characters within the terms of realism. In other words, none of these characters fits into the narratives of contemporary identity categories. Whether demonized as a symbol of monstrosity or idealized as a paragon of perfection, they appear not as fully articulated subjects, but as objects of fantasy. A range of displaced investments—from anxiety and fear to fascination—underlie these representations.

A good example can be found in *A Chinese Ghost Story* (1987), a popular retelling of a well-known story from the eighteenth-century collection of supernatural tales, *Strange Tales from a Chinese Studio*. The film tells the story of a beautiful ghost, Xiao Qian, who is imprisoned by a malevolent tree spirit with a monstrously long tongue.

Known simply as Madam, the spirit pimps out beautiful ghosts to lure unsuspecting men to her lair so she could feed on their yang energy. While the script does not include any mention of Madam's gender history, the casting of male actor Lau Siu-ming in the role uses the audience's nondiegetic recognition of a male body to suggest a discrepancy between male body and feminine presentation.[15] This implicit suggestion of gender variance in the character is further amplified by the way she talks in an alternately male and female voice. Neither Madam's gender history nor her self-identification is available to the audience who only sees the titillating sight of her gender ambiguity as a physical manifestation of—indeed even a short hand for—her monstrosity.

A more complex example appears in *Swordsman 2* (1992) and its sequel *The East Is Red* (1993). In this loose adaptation of Jin Yong's martial arts novel, the arch villain Dongfang Bubai castrates himself to practice a lethal form of martial arts to dominate the world and, in the process, turns into a formidable villain and beautiful woman. I have argued elsewhere that the casting of Brigitte Lin—in contrast to the cross-gender casting of Madam—actually honors certain aspects of transsexual subjectivity because the audience's nondiegetic recognition of Lin as a beautiful woman actually matches the diegetic ambition of the character to appear precisely as just that.[16] Even so, Dongfang Bubai's transsexuality is explicitly figured in the film as evidence of the character's ruthless ambition, destructive power, and monstrosity. By intimately linking Dongfang Bubai's will to dominate the world with the transformation of her body from male to female, the film has displaced anxiety about totalitarian rule onto the sex-changed body, which it portrays to be both dangerously seductive and violently destructive.

When not depicted as monstrous villains, gender variant characters are idealized as tragic figures of obsessive or sacrificial love. For example, in Wong Kar-Wai's meditative martial arts film *Ashes of Time* (1994), brother and sister Murong Yin and Murong Yang—played, once again, by Brigitte Lin—turn out to be the same person: a "wounded soul behind two identities," as described by the narrator Ouyang Feng's voice-over. Murong's split personality is symptomatic of the character's traumatic experience of unrequited love. When she cross-dresses as the masculine Yang, an alternative persona has taken over her consciousness. This "alter" plots the murder of the lover who jilted her thereby resolving the trauma of the victimized woman. In Yim Ho's *Kitchen* (1997), a film based on Banana Yoshimoto's novella, the protagonist Louie explains that his gentle, loving mother actually used to be his father, who raised him after his mother's death while "keeping his dead wife's spirit alive in her new, female body." In Yonfan's over-the-top erotic thriller *Colour Blossoms* (2004), a real estate agent Mei-Lin becomes haunted by a ghost—played alternately by transsexual Korean actress Harisu and Japanese diva Keiko Matsuzaka—who tells the story of how in her youth she changed her sex "to protect the love" she felt for a lover. In these films, all cases of gender variance result from obsessive love. In *Ashes of Time*, Murong's cross-dressing is a symptom of her mental trauma. In both *Kitchen* and *Colour Blossoms*, the characters' transsexuality is not a result of their gender self-identification, but evidence of the lengths they would go to in order to sacrifice for the person they love, be it an orphaned son or a lover. From the point of view of representational politics, all of these films fall short of providing any viable mode of recognition for transgender audience. In *A Chinese Ghost Story* and the *Swordsmen* films, the visual recognition of gender variance leads directly to monstrosity while in *Ashes of Time*, *Kitchen*, and *Colour Blossom*, the narrative of gender variance—whether in the form of cross-dressing or transsexuality—leads only to pathological obsession.

More realistically realized transgender characters do exist, although quite rarely and only in a marginal capacity. Interestingly, the two examples that come to mind both focus on issues of *work*. This singular interest may be due to the perception that transgender visibility is associated with the presence of what legal scholar Robyn Emerton calls "transgender specific professions," which are far more prolific in the entertainment industries of Thailand and the Philippines or in the bar culture of Japan than in Hong Kong, Taiwan, or mainland China.[17] The critically acclaimed *Whispers and Moans* (2007)—a docu-drama that fictionalizes ten days in the lives of a group of sex workers—includes a layered portrayal of a transsexual woman, her working life, and her relationship with her boyfriend. Zero Chou's melancholic *Splendid Float* (2004) spotlights a lesser-known profession through the character of a gay Daoist priest who conducts funeral rituals by day and performs in drag for a dance troupe at night. These, however, are rare exceptions amongst a much larger body of films in which gender variant characters are neither fully fleshed out subjects nor agents of their own actions. Their gender expressions do not result primarily from their self-identification. Rather, they are stand-ins for some notion of "difference," whether construed as villainous monstrosity or sacrificial obsession. They sustain a fantasy through which audiences can channel their own anxiety or fascination.

When we look at these characters, we are looking at everything *but* transgender subjects, who are nowhere to be found amongst the monsters, victims, and ghosts.

2. LOOKING ASKANCE: TRANS RELATIONS

A different critical strategy does not try to look at transgender characters per se, but rather look *askance* at issues of relationality. It focuses on the transing of relational bonds: the ways in which the crossings of gender realign desire, affection, and affinity between people, in a manner that is unpredictable within hetero or homonormative narratives. Here I will focus on films by queer auteurs, by which I mean out queer filmmakers whose stylistic signature involves markedly queer aesthetics and/or themes.[18] I count amongst others Stanley Kwan, Tsai Ming-Liang, Yonfan, as well as Cui Zi'en and Zero Chou—the two younger filmmakers whose works I will discuss—as queer auteurs. Cui's and Chou's films provide what Halberstam calls a "mode of recognition" that is consciously meant for queer audiences: each film "universalizes queerness" within its specific cinematic space without ever returning the audience to a heteronormative gaze.[19] In the two films that I will discuss, there is conscious attention paid to the complex gendered dynamics of intimacy between queer bodies and how transing practices can be constitutive of unique relationship bonds.

Cui Zi'en is one of very few out gay directors working in mainland China. In his films, he has consistently explored the dynamics of gay life while showing a deliberate indifference to representational realism or conventional aesthetics. Until his most recent documentary *Queer China, Comrade China*, which is uncharacteristically intended for a more mainstream audience, all of Cui's films have adhered to his principal concern with "deconstructing all the traditions in filmmaking"[20] or, as Cui puts it more starkly in Chinese, "raping cinema."[21] *Enter The Clowns* (2004), the film from Cui's ouevre that deals most prominently and explicitly with transgender themes, is also especially representative of this aesthetic choice. The film's self-styled "rigid, rough, sharp, tedious cinematic language"[22]—evident in its long shots with little depth of field, its abrupt and rapid panning shots in place of cuts, and its muted, claustrophobic lighting—disorients and destabilizes audience expectations.

Through this demanding aesthetic, the film attempts to explore the queerness of kinship by "transgendering" all major relations in the family. Short vignettes are staged around the character Xiao Bo: a death bed scene in which his dying mother, who turns out to be either a transvestite or a preoperative transsexual woman, asks to suckle him with sperms in place of breast milk; a fight scene between Xiao Bo and his transsexual girlfriend who frets about losing Xiao Bo's attention after her transition; and a domestic scene in Xiao Bo's violence-tinged household where his birth mother, now a trans man, still lives with his hot-tempered ex-husband. The film's highly symbolic register clearly is not meant to portray realistic transgender lives. Rather, as its tag line "We are all transgender" suggests, it attempts to denaturalize the gendered dynamics of kinship relations—in the same way that its cinematic language denaturalizes aesthetic conventions—while rendering all family relations queer and unpredictable. Cui's interest lies not so much in representing the fact of transgender lives but in unsettling the audience into different ways of looking. By deploying its harsh cinematic language that destroys the seemingly "natural" ways of cinematic viewing, the film also compels us to give up the heteronormative ease of viewing and forging relational bonds. It suggest that only by looking queerly could we begin to see bodies and relations that kinship norms have kept obscured from view.

The melancholic and lyrical style of Taiwanese filmmaker Zero Chou cannot be aesthetically further apart from Cui Zi'en's austerity, but the two share a similar commitment to exploring queer themes in complex and original ways. Chou's *Drifting Flowers* (2008) is a film that provides one of the most original treatments of "trans relations" in queer cinema. Moreover, the film breaks the mold of queer cinema's predominantly urban and middle-class focus by portraying queer lives in Taiwan's small towns and poorer communities. Divided into three distinct but subtly interlinked time periods, the film tackles a theme rarely explored in-depth in queer cinema: friendship. The film is replete with beautifully executed examples of queer friendship in its finest nuance. In each instance, an intriguing form of transgender practice is shown to be fundamentally constitutive of the specific dynamic of the friendship. The best example takes place in the film's second section, set in the characters' twilight years. The story portrays a convoluted "trans relation" between Yan and Lily, a gay man and a lesbian woman who in their youth had gotten married for appearance, but have not seen each other again until old age. By then, Lily is suffering from Alzheimer's disease and often forgets that her long-time lesbian lover Ocean is already dead. Yan, depressed by his HIV status and string of failed lover affairs, goes to visit his old friend. Lily, in her illness, misrecognizes Yan and treats him as though he is Ocean. When Yan dresses up in a shirt and tie, Lily tells him not to go out in such masculine clothes and with such flattened chests because she

Figure 7.1 Yan and Lily sitting together contentedly. Zero Chou, *Drifting Flowers*, 2008. DVD Still.

worries it is not safe for a butch to be so blatant. She then dresses Yan in women's clothes and the two spend their days together like two contented grannies. Even though Yan is a feminine gay man, he is not transgender in identification. In these scenes, he dresses as a woman not out of identification but rather out of kindness for his friend. Likewise, Lily's request for Yan (whom she takes to be Ocean) to dress in women's clothes comes from a concern for her butch lover's safety. Yet, what results from her misunderstanding and Yan's compliance is a touching and mutually dependent feminine friendship that is very much built on the accidental transing of their relation (figure 7.1). Thus, while there are no transgender-identified characters per se in the film, locating trans relationality amongst its characters illuminates the film's nuanced and highly original treatment of queer friendship.

3. Looking Amidst: Trans Practices

Finally, I want to offer a preliminary exploration of an interpretive framework that focuses on "trans practices."[23] Putting aside issues of identification or relationality, it is also instructive to examine actual somatic processes that modify bodily boundaries. In what may look like a counterintuitive choice, I turn to *Farewell My Concubine*, which stars the late Leslie Cheung as fictional Beijing Opera actor Cheng Dieyi. Despite Cheung's own clever public discussions of the film and his subsequent (especially posthumous) iconicity as a queer figure,[24] the film has often been criticized for what is perceived to be a homophobic portrayal. Two thematic elements, in particular, are deemed objectionable. First, the film spends a great deal of screen time depicting the coercive and physically demanding training actors have to go through to become accomplished stage performers. In particular, Dieyi's training to become a dan—the female role-type—appears to involve an abusive and involuntary inculcation of femininity in the young boy. Second, the adult Dieyi's obsessive devotion to both the art and to the actor who plays the male lead is perceived to be a wrong-headed portrayal of gay desire. Critics feel that the film is implying that gay desire results from the abusive and forced feminization of Dieyi during boyhood.[25]

This criticism is not inaccurate if our purpose is to locate a contemporary gay (or, for that matter, transgender) subject in the film. In that sense, Cheng Dieyi certainly falls short. It is entirely reasonable to list Dieyi alongside all the examples I presented earlier of characters whose transgender embodiments serve more to displace some forms of social anxiety than to express a transgender identity. Certainly, much has been written about the film's sweeping construction of modern national history and its figuration of the nation as a transgender, feminized, and victimized body.[26] More recently, however, there are critical efforts to redirect the focus on the film's epic and spectacular dimension to its more personalized and intimate aspects. Yomi Braester's study of the film's staging of the lost urban spaces of old Beijing is an example.[27] In a similar spirit, I want to take a more intimate look at the somatic process by which Dieyi becomes the literal embodiment of the highest ideal presented in the film: the perfection of an art form.

Furthermore, the tension in the film—between its unsavory depictions of the brutally abusive aspects of Beijing opera training and its unflinching celebration of the art form itself—is also instructive in illuminating a central conundrum in critical works on trans practices. As Nikki Sullivan shows in her survey of theoretical writings on body modification practices from sexual reassignment surgery to cosmetic surgery, there is a tendency amongst critics to make a dichotomizing and moralistic distinction between "good" and "bad" practices. Whereas early feminists such as Janice Raymond and Sheila Jeffreys infamously condemn transsexuality as monstrous, some contemporary theorists privilege "non-mainstream" modification practices such as tattooing and branding while castigating cosmetic surgery as normative and conforming. Sullivan further points out that the "intent" or active agency of the practitioner is not necessarily a good yardstick in defining good from bad practices because every subject, whether or not conscious of it, acts within institutional and ideological limits. It is presumptuous, if not downright impossible, to categorically draw a line between where agency stops and where ideology begins. Instead, Sullivan proposes that we forgo the dichotomizing impulse and regard *all* body modification processes as distinct forms of "transmogrification," which she defines as "a process of (un)becoming strange and/or grotesque, of (un)becoming other." Sullivan suggests that we regard all bodies, whether visibly going through some form of transformation or not, to be in states of becoming and unbecoming, and that we approach *any* modification practice to be potentially illuminating of those states.[28] In other words, any modification practice—however we evaluate its benefit or harm—that transforms and reassembles the body's seemingly "natural" boundaries can show us the constructedness of all bodies and, in so doing, denaturalize the line between what appears "normal" and what appears "strange."

In *Farewell My Concubine*, Beijing opera training is depicted as a historically specific form of "transmogrification": a life-long physical training that molds pliant bodies into stylized theatrical role-types. The film's focus is on Dieyi's gradual transformation from an untrained boy to the perfect embodiment of all the classic dan roles. During the first half of the film, physically transformative aspects of the training are repeatedly emphasized: from the scene when the mother of young Dieyi brutally chops off the boy's extra finger so he can train properly; the long sequences of boys arduously enduring merciless beating to achieve perfection of form and movement; and in the dramatic scene in which Dieyi, after having an opium pipe shoved in his throat, finally delivers the line "I am by nature born a girl" without a mistake. The fruition of those scenes culminate in the second half of the film, which is punctuated with long sequences of the adult Dieyi performing some of the most renown dan roles in the Beijing opera oeuvre. The entire narrative may at first sight appear to be one of "transgendering," of a boy's transformation into a female role-type. Yet, on closer look, it should more accurately be seen as a paradigmatic narrative of *gendering*, period. In other words, how Dieyi learns to become a type of stylized womanhood is not dissimilar to how other characters learn to embody other roles, both on and offstage. Dieyi's fellow trainees in the theatrical troupe, whether they are learning to be *sheng* (the lead male role), *chou* (the clown's role) or other role types, have to undergo the exact same physical process, so brutal that one boy ends up choosing suicide over his training. Dieyi's "stage-brother" Xiaolou, who later becomes successful playing lead male roles alongside Dieyi, must also inculcate his masculinity through the same kind of transformative training. Later on in the film, when opera connoisseur Master Yuan criticizes Xiaolou for taking "too few steps" in a performance, thus falling short of the regal air of a hegemon king, it is evident that a male actor's embodiment of masculinity can fall short and is itself as much a trans process as the training for female roles. More successful than Xiaolou in his training, Dieyi—as Master Yuan observes—has perfected the art to such an extent that the actor has become "the living reincarnation" of all the roles he performs (figure 7.2).

Furthermore, the brutality and coercion involved in Beijing opera training is not only paradigmatic of the process of (trans)gendering, but also of *all* processes of becoming in the film. Even though not all characters go through visible processes of transformation, the film portrays a tumultuous century of political upheavals that in effect compels everyone into constant states of becoming and unbecoming. One of the ways in which the film depicts the constant shifts in power—from the Japanese, to the regional warlords, to the Nationalist government, to Communist rule and the vicissitude during the Cultural Revolution, is by showing the characters donning clothes that would appear "correct" (from Qing dynasty era robes to Western-style suits during the Republican era to Mao jackets under the Communist regime) in the eyes of those in power. They undergo sartorial makeover much in the same way that actors change costumes

Figure 7.2 Dieyi and Xiaolou transforming into their roles. Chen Kaige, *Farewell My Concubine*, 1993. DVD Still.

from production to production. In one scene set at the height of the Cultural Revolution, those accused of having "questionable background" are paraded in "costumes" signifying their bad status while being publicly humiliated. Throughout all this, Dieyi is constantly the only character who remains out of steps and out of place. In a scene after he burns all his theatrical costumes to lament the degradation of the art form under the Communist regime, the camera follows Dieyi from the back as he walks away awkwardly, clearly a misfit, in his Mao jacket and sandals. That scene economically sums up Dieyi's unwillingness or inability to morph from what he has perfected to be his "self," not in the sense of an authentic essence, but pointedly an artistic creation forged on physical hardship, talent, and devotion. At the same time, this inability or unwillingness also becomes Dieyi's uniquely admirable trait, by which he dares to remain, in his words, "true from beginning to end" [*congyi erzhong*]. The trans practice of Beijing opera training, brutal as it is, is shown in the film to have produced both a beautiful form of artistry and an admirable character with the courage to embrace becoming strange and becoming other. In one of the most impassioned and evocative writings on transgender embodiment, Susan Stryker theorizes and performs Frankenstein's monster by embracing the rage and suffering forged from the experience of being an outcast. Stryker does not flinch from claiming the trans body as "unnatural," "a flesh torn apart and sewn together," and a body that "literalizes the violence" of a normative order that produces but shuns this body. Most importantly, Stryker shows that the trans body can be a "monstrously powerful place" from which to act, as it exposes the constructedness of the "natural" order and the foundational violence of gendering that constitutes all subjects, whether they are marked as such or not.[29] It is from this place that I would like to resuscitate Cheng Dieyi from being so often understood as merely a victim, both within the film and as a product of the director's homophobic imagination. It is possible to view him in a rather different light. The tragedy seems rather to belong to the characters around Dieyi who, unwitting of how they are being continually produced and reproduced by the normalizing regime, simply reform themselves over and over, sartorially and ideologically to fit into a norm that, in the end, always threatens to elude them. By contrast, Dieyi's unflinching embrace of his otherness—forged out of an abusive process but transformed through his artistic integrity—allows him to constitute a self on his own terms, against a "natural" order that is always trying to disrupt those terms. In this regard, Dieyi is a trans subject, not in the conventional identity sense but more provocatively in the sense that he reassembles gender and constitutes his self within the contingent structure of power that produces him.

Parting Words: Trans Looks

Whether we are looking at transgender characters, looking askance at trans relations, or looking amidst trans practices, what constitutes "trans cinema" is very much in the eye of the beholder. In other words, a trans cinema is ultimately the result of different kinds of trans looks—different ways of seeing trans. Trying to locate the "moving target" of trans on screen is thus an exercise in continuing the discussion of how we see, what compels us to look, and what eludes our sight. What the thriving works on transgender theory, politics, and culture have enabled us to do is to look more closely, creatively, and adventurously while keeping our eyes intransigently out of bounds.

Notes

1. http://www.transgenderfilmfestival.com/about/
2. http://www.transgenderfilmfestival.com/2001/_GB/article_swordsman.html
3. I develop these arguments in detail in my book *Undercurrents: Queer Culture and Postcolonial Hong Kong* (Vancouver: University of British Columbia Press, 2008), 65–84.
4. Recent examples of self-reflexive and complex autobiographical documentaries by transgender filmmakers include: *She's a Boy I Knew* (Gwen Haworth, 2007), *Prodigal Sons* (Kimberly Reed, 2008), and *Against A Trans Narrative* (Jules Rosskam, 2008).
5. Somatechnics Research Centre, http://www.somatechnics.mq.edu.au/
6. Peter A. Jackson, "Pre-Gay, Post-Queer: Thai Perspectives on Proliferating Gender/Sex Diversity in Asia," *Journal of Homosexuality* 40, nos. 3–4 (2001): 1–25.
7. Fran Martin and Josephine Ho, ed., special issue on "trans/Asia, trans/gender," *Inter-Asia Cultural Studies* 7, no. 2 (2006).
8. Song Hwee Lim, "Is the Trans- in Transnational the Trans- in Transgender?" *New Cinemas: Journal of Contemporary Film* 5, no. 1 (2007): 39–52.
9. Jay Prosser, *Second Skins: The Body Narratives of Transsexuality* (New York: Columbia University Press, 1998), 67–68.
10. Judith Halberstam, *In a Queer Time and Place: Transgender Bodies, Subcultural Lives* (New York: New York University Press, 2005), 76–96.
11. John Phillips, *Transgender on Screen* (New York: Palgrave Macmillan, 2006).

12. Judith Halberstam, *In a Queer Time and Place*, 92–96; Leung, *Undercurrents*, 77–83.
13. Halberstam, *In a Queer Time and Place*, 49.
14. Nikki Sullivan, "Transmogrification: (Un)Becoming Other(s)," *The Transgender Studies Reader*, eds. Susan Stryker and Stephen Whittle (New York: Routledge, 2006), 552–564.
15. It is interesting to note that in the 2011 remake of the film, the role is cast with a female actress instead, thus erasing the transgender implications of the original casting.
16. Leung, *Undercurrents*, 71–77.
17. Robyn Emerton, "Finding a Voice, Fighting for Rights: The Emergence of the Transgender Movement in Hong Kong," *Inter-Asia Cultural Studies* 7, no. 2 (2006): 248–249.
18. My conception of queer auteurs is influenced by Song Hwee Lim's provocative discussion in "Positioning Auteur Theory in Chinese Cinema Studies: Intratextuality, Intertextuality and Paratextuality in the films of Tsai Ming-liang," *Journal of Chinese Cinemas* 1, no. 3 (2007): 223–245.
19. Halberstam, *In a Queer Time*, 94.
20. Qi Wang, "The Ruin Is Already a New Outcome: An Interview with Cui Zi'en," *positions* 12, no.1 (2004): 181–194, on 193.
21. Cui Zi'en, "*Enter The Clowns* Rapes Cinema into Uselessness" (《丑角登場》把電影強暴得一無是處), in *Diyi guanzhong* (第一觀眾) [First audience] (Xiandai chubanshe, 2003).
22. Zi'en, "*Enter The Clowns*."
23. For a detailed elaboration of this argument, see my *Farewell My Concubine: A Queer Film Classic* (Arsenal Pulp Press, 2010), 94–106.
24. See my detailed discussion in Leung, *Undercurrents*, 91–92.
25. Zhang, Benzi, "Figures of Violence and Tropes of Homophobia: Reading *Farewell My Concubine* between East and West," *Journal of Popular Culture* 33, no. 2 (1999): 101–109; Sean Metzger, "Farewell My Fantasy," *The Journal of Homosexuality* 39, nos. 3–4 (2000): 213–32.
26. Jenny Lau, "Farewell My Concubine: History, Melodrama, and Ideology in Contemporary Pan-Chinese Cinema," *Film Quarterly* 49, no. 1 (1995): 16–27.
27. Yomi Braester, "Farewell My Concubine: National Myth and City Memories," in *Chinese Films In Focus: 25 New Takes*, ed. Chris Berry (London: BFI, 2003), 89–96.
28. Sullivan, "Transmogrification: (Un)Becoming Other(s)," 561.
29. Susan Stryker, "My Words to Victor Frankenstein Above the Village of Charmounix," in *The Transgender Studies Reader*, ed. Susan Stryker and Stephen Whittle (New York: Routledge, 2006), 244–256.

CHAPTER 8

Writing the Body

Carlos Rojas

> A symbol appears in my art in the form of the character "Fen/Ma Liuming," and specifically the graceful face of a woman on the body of a man. The performances created by this union of the feminine with the masculine have given structure to a new form of language.
>
> Ma Liuming

> I tried my best to pull down the museum—a symbol of modern civilization—but my body, in return, was pulled back by it. The body is a proof of identity and also a kind of language. Other forms of communication are too far removed.
>
> Zhang Huan

In one of the most evocative self-portraits from China's late imperial period, Ren Xiong 任熊 (1823–1857) depicts himself standing erect, a cloak draped loosely over one of his shoulders (figure 8.1). This undated full-body image is nearly life-size—the hanging scroll is 177 × 79 cm and the figure is about 160 cm (5' 3"), which may very well have been close to height of the artist, who is described as having been of modest stature.[1] Beyond its actual dimensions, the portrait's strategic use of foreshortening would have made the figure appear even taller than it actually was. As the viewer's gaze is drawn upwards from the figure's disproportionately large slippers and lower pants legs to his

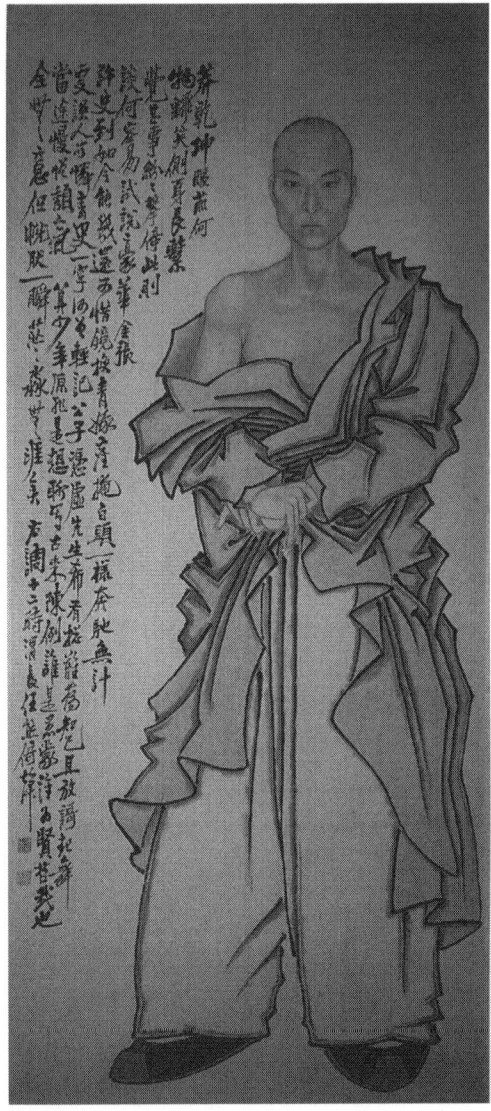

Figure 8.1 Ren Xiong, "Self-portrait" (undated, mid-nineteenth century).

midsection, however, it is suddenly arrested by the sight of what art historian Richard Vinograd describes as a

> torso and bust [that] are rendered with light flesh colors that model the muscles precisely and bring out vividly the tense cords of the neck,

the high cheekbones, gaunt face, and penetrating, narrowed eyes. The head is nearly smooth-shaven and is quite without any pretense of gentility or cultivation.²

In the context of a Chinese portraiture tradition that tended to place much more attention on a subject's attire and physical setting than his or her physical body, Ren Xiong's emphasis on his own bare flesh is rather startling. As a result, his body projects a seemingly self-evident immediacy, while at the same time inviting the viewer to reflect on what precisely the body signifies in the first place.

Ren Xiong's evocatively mimetic depiction of his body conveys a sense not only of immediacy but also of alienation. The dramatic verisimilitude of the subject's face and upper body, for instance, is accentuated by the schematic appearance of his cloak, which consists of little more than an outline drawn with thick, black calligraphic strokes. The resulting juxtaposition of lifelike flesh and textlike fabric yields the impression that the artist, as anthropologist Angela Zito has observed, "is in the very process of emerging naked from the tangle of markings and traces that make the boundaries of Qing life."³

Originally from a poor family near Hangzhou, Ren Xiong may well have intended the portrait's emphasis on his physical body to serve as a critical response to the literati privileging of abstract signifiers of social status. The resulting sense of *ressentiment* is articulated in the work's colophon, which begins with a plaintive series of queries:

> In the vast world, what lies before my eyes? I smile and bow and go around flattering people [in hope of] extending connections, but aware of what affairs? In the great confusion, what is there to hold on to and rely on? How easy it is merely to chat about this!⁴

The colophon then proceeds to describe the artist's acute awareness of his own mortality, together with his regret that common people such as himself are generally elided from the sorts of historical narratives that might preserve his memory:

> If we should try to talk comparatively about the extravagant noblemen [of Han times] like Jin, Zhang, Xu, and Shi—how many like them are left now? What is more pitiful is that even though the mirror shows my black eyebrows exchanged [for white] and worldly dust covering my white head, I am still like a racing steed without plans. What is even more of a pitiable impediment is that the historians have not recorded even a single, light word about me.⁵

In this description, the artist's sense of alienation from his actual mirror image ("the mirror shows my black eyebrows exchanged [for white])" is juxtaposed with his alienation from the abstract mirror of history ("historians have not recorded even a single, light word about me"). In the process, the portrait reflects not so much the artist's own self-perception, but rather his *failure* to recognize himself within the normative schema of social validation. The work is positioned at the limits of conventional representation, wherein the materiality of the artist's body is translated into a kind of virtual language that is then used to interrogate the semiotic systems within which the artist himself is positioned.

Ren Xiong's self-portrait emphasizes the artist's position at the margins of not only orthodox systems of social validation, but also of the artistic traditions and conventions through which the work is itself produced in the first place. While the artist's cloak is sketched with brush strokes that bear a distinct resemblance to Chinese calligraphy, the mimetic rendering of the artist's bare flesh, by contrast, is the product of a set of Western representational techniques that were still relatively rare in mid-nineteenth-century China. In fact, Ren Xiong himself was one of the early pioneers in adopting these sorts of Western artistic techniques, and was one of the founders of an art movement, known as the "Shanghai school," that promoted a hybrid technique synthesizing Chinese and Western artistic elements. The striking mimeticism of the artist's self-portrait, therefore, functions not merely as a transparent depiction of his physical appearance, but also comments self-referentially on the work's own representational technique.

In more general terms, Ren Xiong's painting poses questions regarding the underlying significance of the body itself. Through the work's strategic juxtaposition of flesh and text, Ren Xiong is essentially asking: What is the language of the body? How may subjects use their bodies to challenge the representational regimes within which they are embedded? What is the role of these semiotic systems in demarcating the systems' own conceptual limits? In the following discussion, I take Ren Xiong's self-portrait as a starting point for reflecting more generally on the semiotics of corporeality. What, in other words, is the relationship between the physical body itself and the bodies of sociocultural signification that are projected or inscribed onto it? What is involved in trying to read the significance of the body and—conversely—what would it mean to try to write, or rewrite, the language of the body?

To address these questions, I examine a handful of mid-nineteenth- and late twentieth-century texts that implicitly grapple with the relationship between gender and sexual difference. One of the key theoretical contributions of second-wave Western feminism concerned the conceptual distinction between sex, which was believed to be firmly rooted in biology, and gender, which was perceived as the product of a complex set of contingent sociocultural forces. While this distinction provided a useful response to essentialist assumptions about sexual difference, it did so precisely by contrasting the socioculturally inflected sphere of gender with an ostensibly stable ground of biologically determined sex. More recently, however, Judith Butler has critiqued this dichotomy between gender and sex by arguing that biological sex actually does *not* occupy a space categorically outside sociocultural construction, but rather that sex—like gender—is necessarily mediated through discourse. Her point is *not* that there are no aspects of sexual difference that are biologically determined, but rather there is no autonomous sphere of biology that is structurally separate from that of discourse.[6] This argument has implications that are both theoretical (in the sense that the very act of designating something as lying outside the purview of discourse is itself necessarily a discursive gesture in its own right) as well as practical (in that anatomical, hormonal, genetic, and other biological indicators of sexual difference are sometimes at odds with one another, and the question of how to make sense of the resulting ambiguities or contradictions is one that science alone cannot answer).

One of Butler's central arguments is that both gender and sex are the product of an iterative performative practice. The Chinese texts I examine here all center on themes of transgendered performance, and unlike the focus of contemporary trans studies on subjects who adopt a new gender or sex because they do not identify with their putative (corporeal) sex,[7] the transgendered performances in these Chinese texts are explicitly located within the sphere of cultural production. Whether in the service of traditional Chinese opera or avant-garde performance art, the transgendered personas that are produced through these performative practices are often quite stable and may persist for many years, even coming to assume a virtual life of their own. Even as these texts appear to assert the possibility of fashioning a (trans)gendered persona that would be functionally independent of the embodied sex of the actual performer; however, they simultaneously reveal a complicated ambivalence about the semiotic status of the body itself. My focus here, therefore, is on the ways these texts interrogate the relationship between a semiotics of performance and a language of corporeality.

Gender

In the early 1990s, a number of young artists began moving to the rundown neighborhood of Dashanzhuang in northeast Beijing. Like Ren Xiong, many of these artists were positioned at the margins of their corresponding social regimes, and even their adopted neighborhood—which they affectionately dubbed Beijing's East Village—was starkly emblematic of this marginality. As the art critic Karen Smith describes, the neighborhood was located

> in the shadow of the metropolis[, where] many of the village's indigenous population scrape a living by collecting and sorting rubbish. Waste accumulates by the side of small ponds. This pollutes the water, generating noxious fumes in the summer. Raw sewage flows directly into the water. Slothful, threadbare dogs roam the narrow lanes between the houses.[8]

While the artists initially moved to this underdeveloped area in search of cheap rent, they soon began using their dilapidated surroundings as a backdrop for a variety of performances designed to articulate their position at the margins of contemporary China's overlapping political, cultural, and economic orthodoxies.

Two of the most influential figures to emerge from this community were Ma Liuming 馬六明 (b. 1969) and Zhang Huan 張洹 (b. 1965). Like many of their East Village colleagues, Ma and Zhang were originally trained in oil painting, but began shifting their attention to performance art shortly after moving to Dashanzhuang in 1993. Ma, with his svelte physique and long straight hair, had a distinctly feminine appearance, and became known for a series of performances in which he appeared as a feminine persona that he dubbed *fen-Ma Liuming*. Zhang, on the other hand, had a compact, muscular physique and very short hair (which he subsequently shaved bald), and proceeded to develop an influential body of work in which he would positioned himself in starkly masochistic situations that strategically accentuated his own masculine appearance.

The East Village community's interest in performance art is frequently traced to a pivotal encounter in September of 1993, when the British performance artists Gilbert Proesch and George Passmore (known as "Gilbert and George") came to Beijing to host a month-long show. Widely known for their "living sculpture" performances, Gilbert and George were already international icons by the time they arrived in China, and consequently the East Village artists were both flattered and apprehensive when the British guests accepted their invitation to come see their studios. Ma Liuming recalls being anxious before the visit, concerned that he and his colleagues would not have anything substantive enough to show the guests, and as he was lying in bed agonizing over what to do, he noticed a crack in his ceiling:

> I got up on the bed to touch it: the panels of the ceiling were soft. I decided to place a plastic bag full of liquid red paint in the ceiling. I moved the furniture, the scene played out in my mind. I looked for appropriate music and I found "The Wall" by Pink Floyd…The next day, when the small group arrived, I turned on the music. Everybody was looking at me, a little intrigued. I had asked another artist, Zhang Huan, who has since made other performances, to help me. I got up on a chair, raised my finger toward the ceiling and pierced the sack that was hidden there. The red liquid began to run down my arm, over my hair and chest. I had taken off my clothing save only for a pair of black pants…in order not to make a mess of my clothes! I stayed still like that, keeping the pose for a few minutes. The blood trickled down and the applause exploded. I was filmed and a number of pictures were taken. Those few minutes had a profound effect on me, but perhaps more so on the East Village and its inhabitants.[9]

A now-famous photograph of the resulting performance, which came to be known as "Dialogue with Gilbert and George," shows a visibly agitated Ma Liuming flanked by his two impassive British guests (figure 8.2). Ma is partially nude and covered in a bloodlike fluid, while Gilbert and George are both wearing their trademark three-piece suits.[10] Like the juxtaposition of flesh and text at the heart of Ren Xiong's self-portrait, this contrast between the half-naked Chinese artist and his formally dressed British guests raises complicated questions regarding the relationship between corporeal subjects and the complicated networks of national, class, and gendered signification within which they are embedded.

One consequence of the strategic emphasis, in "Dialogue," on Ma's partially naked body is that it invites a variety of sexualized interpretations. Some critics, for instance, have suggested that the red liquid dripping from the crack in the ceiling is symbolic of hymen blood, implying that the performance as a whole may be seen as Ma's "first 'intercourse' with his audience."[11] Alternatively, the liquid may be viewed as symbolic of uterine blood, thereby making the performance a dramatization of Ma's figurative "birth" as a performance artist. To paraphrase de Beauvoir, however, the transgendered persona for which Ma would subsequently become famous was not *born*

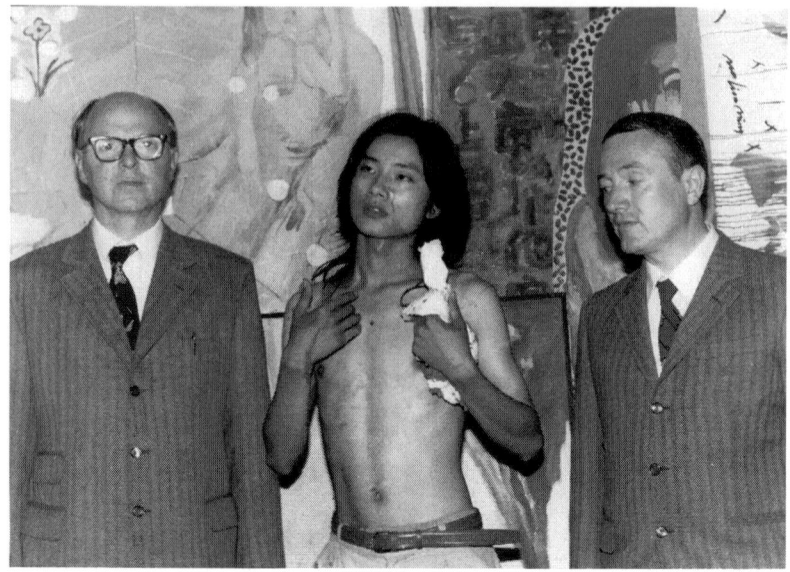

Figure 8.2 Ma Liuming, "Dialogue with Gilbert and George," (1993). Reprinted with permission from Ma Liuming.

as it much it was a result of a process of *becoming*—a product of a series of performances wherein he strategically fashioned the alter ego on which his professional reputation was established.

The next critical step in the constitution of Ma Liuming's transgendered performative persona took place a few days later, as Ma Liuming and some of his friends were amusing themselves by trying on women's clothing and jewelry. Ma recalls how, when he saw his own reflection in a mirror, he was

> shocked to see that my appearance had changed. I wanted to take this further and therefore swapped clothing with one of the women. I found myself in a dress, very awkward. The entire group was stunned by my feminine side.[12]

The identificatory logic of this scene resembles that of Lacan's mirror stage, wherein an infant develops its sense of self as a result of a process of projectively identifying with the external reflection it sees in a mirror.[13] Just as Lacan argues that an infant's self-conception is a product of its (mis)recognition of its external specular imago, Ma suggests that it was precisely his alienated recognition of his own mirror image that provided the inspiration for the transgendered persona that he would subsequently adopt as his performative alter ego.

Given Ma Liuming's emphasis on this moment of specular misrecognition, it is ironic that one of his most salient concerns was that his transgendered persona might be misunderstood by his audience. As he explains,

> A few days later, while looking at the pictures that had been taken of me that night, I told myself that I could use this tool in my art. But women's clothing could create contradictions, *making me appear as a transvestite, which I am not in real lif*e. I wanted to maintain better control over my reception, and therefore decided to perform without clothing so that people could see my male body.[14]

The irony here is acute. Ma claims that his concern was not so much with the possibility that he might be mistaken for a woman, but rather that he might be perceived as a "transvestite." Therefore, he decided to dispense with clothing altogether, allowing his male genitals to provide a strategic counterpoint to his feminine performance. As a result, his works came to emphasize not so much the performance of gender as such, but rather the strategic performance of *trans*gender.

In one of his early performances, Ma Liuming invited a small audience to join him in a make-shift outdoor kitchen he had set up in the East Village neighborhood ("Fen-Ma Liuming's Lunch," 1994). Appearing nude and in his feminine persona, Ma cooked a fish, shared it with his audience, and then returned the remainder to the original pot. He paused at one point during this process to sit on the ground, and began sucking on a plastic tube affixed to his penis. Drawing on traditional Chinese medical notions, Ma later explained that the plastic tube component of the performance symbolized the circulation of the qi through the body, signaling the conceptual interdependence of feminine yin and masculine yang. This dramatization of the circulation of qi within the artist's body was, in turn, mirrored by the circulation of fish meat within the performance as a whole, with the audience's literal consumption of Ma's fish mirroring their scopic consumption of his performance itself. Ma's quasi-onanistic gesture of sucking on the tube, therefore, reproduces in miniature the spectatorial dynamics that underlie the overall performance, suggesting that the resulting work is a product of a symbiotic relationship between performer and audience.

Ma Liuming's efforts to "maintain better control over [the] reception" of his performances (to quote his explanation for why he originally decided to start performing naked), together with his parallel attention to the audience's role in helping realize his performances, entered a new phase in the late 1990s. During a 1998 performance in the Netherlands, for instance, he began inviting audience members to join him onstage as he performed nude in his feminine persona, with some of the guests choosing to remain fully clothed while others joined Ma in varying states of undress. In this way, the audience literally became part of the performance, symbolically underscoring their role in shaping the significance of the performance itself.

During a trip to Indonesia three years later, Ma Liuming introduced yet another twist on this theme of audience participation by taking a sleeping pill before going on stage to pose naked, so that it would be his unconscious body with which volunteers from the audience would be posing (figure 8.3). In this way, Ma's earlier wish *to maintain control over* the reception of his work is transformed into a deliberate act of *relinquishing control over* his own body during the performance itself. Ma essentially refashions this "live" performance into an anticipation of the way in which *representations* of his performances circulate within a broader cultural sphere far beyond the artisti's immediate control. In presenting his unconscious body for the audience's virtual consumption, therefore, Ma is simultaneously underscoring the constitutive role played by the audience in shaping the meaning and significance of his works in general.

Appropriately enough, it was precisely around this time that Ma Liuming—by now already in his thirties and no longer as slender

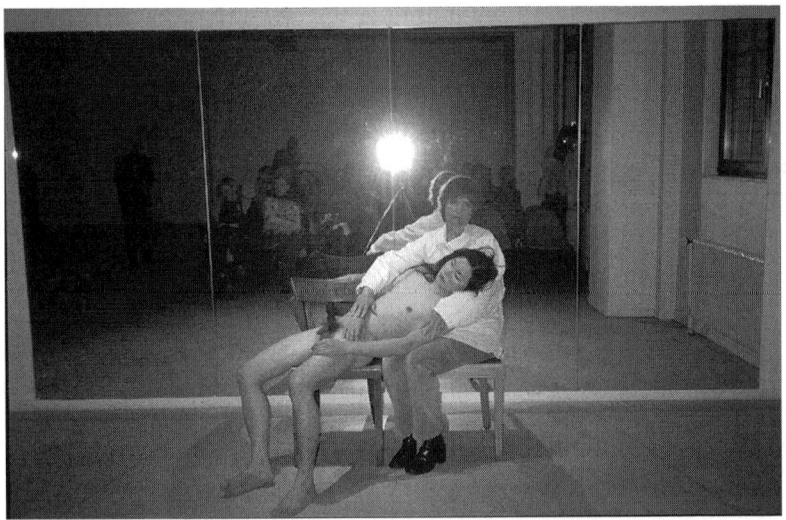

Figure 8.3 Ma Liuming, "Fen-Ma Liuming in Düsseldorf," (2000). Reprinted with permission from Ma Liuming.

and effeminate as before—began moving away from live performance and focusing instead on coordinating exhibitions of photographs and video recordings of the performances he had already completed, in effect treating these visual reproductions of his performance as material equivalents to his own unconscious body. As Ma began discontinuing his popular transgendered *fen-Ma Liuming* performances in the early 2000s, he returned to his earlier interest in oil painting, and many of his works from this period feature variations on a visual theme of the adult artist with an infant's body—suggesting the artist's own symbolic "rebirth" as an oil painter.

To the extent that Ma Liuming's return to imagery of infancy in the early 2000s constituted a tacit admission of the inherent limits of his ability to control the reception of his works (or even the physical appearance of his own aging body), it also serves as a useful reminder of the limits of his control over the legacy of his original 1993 "Dialogue" performance itself. In fact, the same naked and bloody iconography that provided the catalyst for Ma's subsequent interest in transgendered performance also appears to have helped inspire his East Village colleague Zhang Huan to develop a parallel series of performances works featuring not a *trans*gendered, rather a *hyper*gendered, fictional persona. That is to say, in contrast to Ma's strategic performance of a feminine persona, Zhang instead performs an exaggerated version of his "own" masculinity.

Like Ma Liuming, Zhang Huan began developing an interest in performance art around the time of Gilbert and George's visit in September, 2003. After helping Ma Liuming prepare his "Dialogue" performance, Zhang then proceeded to stage a strikingly similar intervention on the front steps of Beijing's National Gallery the following month. Zhang and some of his classmates at the Central Academy of Art had been invited to exhibit some of their oil paintings in Beijing's National Gallery, but just before the exhibit was scheduled to open Zhang stripped down to his underwear in front of the gallery, opened an urn containing a dismembered doll floating in red paint, and dumped its contents over his head (figure 8.4). He then collected the doll parts, reassembled them, and carried them into the gallery, where he strung them up in front of a piece of black canvas. He was fined ¥1000 (equivalent to about $170 at the time) for his actions, and the exhibit was immediately cancelled.[15]

Although Zhang has suggested that he intended for this National Gallery performance, known as "Weeping Angel," to function as a critique of the role of China's one-child policy in forcing young women to have abortions,[16] in the context of his artistic career the

Figure 8.4 Zhang Huan, "Weeping Angel," (1993). Reprinted with permission from Zhang Huan.

performance may instead be viewed as an allegory of his own symbolic (re)birth as a performance artist. His nearly nude, blood-soaked appearance in this performance, furthermore, directly anticipates his trademark abject, naked performances for which he is now best known.

Precisely a week after Zhang Huan's October twenty-sixth intervention on the steps of National Gallery, the East Village-based photographer Rong Rong 榮榮 (b. 1968) visited him in his studio. Rong Rong recalls that the studio contained

> parts of a great number of plastic dolls—heads, torsos and limbs—all in various positions and combinations. Some were hung from the ceiling while others were installed on top of beer bottles. "This is my work," [Zhang Huan] said. "I picked them out of the garbage dump nearby."
>
> Zhang Huan began telling me his life. He was married before he came to Beijing. Now divorced, he came here to study painting and enrolled in the Oil Painting Department at the Central Academy of Fine Arts.
>
> He lit a cigarette. Smoke slowly rose and surrounded the plastic dolls behind him, creating an alien world.
>
> Looking at Zhang Huan and his room with this fascinating array of objects, I asked: "Can I take some photographs of you in front of this background? Some different pictures?"
>
> "In what way different?"

"Without your clothes on—like the dolls."
"Sure. That's exactly what I would like to do," he replied willingly.
I found a piece of canvas, put it on the dirty floor, and asked him to lie on top of it.[17]

While this account of this session is recounted from the perspective of the photographer Rong Rong (who, by the time he recorded this account, had already had a bitter controversy with Zhang Huan over who owns the photographs that he took of Zhang's early performances), the emphasis on Zhang's comparative passivity here is rather striking. Zhang, in his account, is manipulated by Rong Rong, his photographer and audience. Uncannily reminiscent of the conclusion of the "Weeping Angel" performance a week earlier, Zhang appears almost doll-like as he lies naked on the canvas—a second-order simulacrum of the human form.

Rong Rong recalls how, at one point during this informal photography session, he grabbed a prosthetic leg that was lying around the apartment and tossed it to Zhang, who proceeded to "fix it onto his body" (figure 8.5):

Now the three-legged Zhang Huan rolled around in an increased state of craziness in front of my camera.

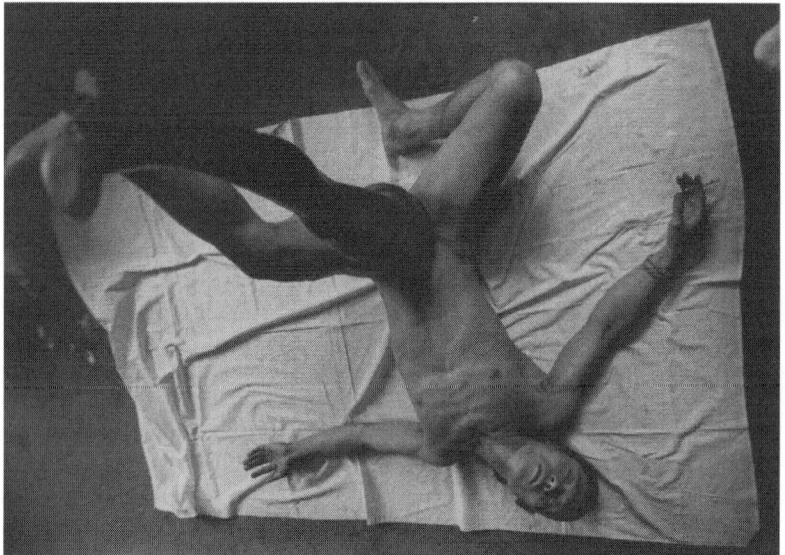

Figure 8.5 Zhang Huan with prosthetic leg. Photographed by Rong Rong (1993). Reprinted with permission from Chambers Fine Art Gallery, New York.

> While we were both absorbed in our collaboration, Zhang Huan's girlfriend, Binbin, walked in without knocking. She couldn't help bursting into laughter as Zhang Huan held the fake leg and ran to her.[18]

To the extent that Zhang's dolls may be seen as symbols of corporeal fragmentation, the prosthetic leg that he had lying around his apartment embodies a logic of displacement and circulation. In placing the artificial limb over his crotch, Zhang was simultaneously obscuring and exaggerating his genitals, and in the process underscoring the fundamentally contingent relationship between the anatomical member and the abstract phallus which it ostensibly signifies.

In psychoanalytic terms, the prosthetic limb in this performance may be seen as an example of what Jacques Lacan calls a "partial object," or an *objet petit a*. For Lacan, an *objet a* is a psychic entity that becomes figuratively disassociated from the subject and enters into circulation within a liminal realm where it functions as an abstract "cause of desire":

> The *objet a* is something from which the subject, in order to constitute itself, has separated itself off as organ. This serves as a symbol of the lack, that is to say, of the phallus, not as such, but insofar as it is lacking. It must, therefore, be an object that is, firstly, separable and, secondly, that has some relation to the lack.[19]

Just as the phallus *qua objet a* is a symbolic entity that is necessarily separable from the subject, the prosthetic leg in this photo session functions as a paradigmatically separable organ symbolizing both the artist's anatomical penis as well as his abstract phallus. The prosthesis is literally a substitute for a corporeal appendage, and derives its significance from its interstitial position between the body and the symbolic matrix through which the body is rendered intelligible.

Over the next several years, Zhang Huan developed a distinctive body of performance work in which he acted out a sense of social marginalization against the backdrop of his dilapidated East Village neighborhood. In one of his best-known works, for instance, he smeared his body with a honey- and fish-oil mixture and then sat naked in a filthy outhouse for forty minutes as his body became covered with flies ("12 Square Meters," 1994), while in another he suspended himself, naked, with chains for a ceiling and allowed his blood to drip through a catheter onto a hot stove on the table below ("65 Kg," 1994). In these and similar works, Zhang placed his muscular and well-toned body in a state of ritualized abjection, presenting his body as a sort of debased "partial object" that derives its significance from its symbolic circulation within a field of performance and spectatorship. He was, in effect, treating his body as if it were one of the discarded dolls he recovered from nearby trash heaps—a vestigial remnant of the fractured societal and representational structures from which they originated.

In late 1998, Zhang produced a work consisting of three staged photographs, in which he appeared naked from the waist up and either covered in black writing, holding a hollowed-out pig's ribcage in front of him, or both (figure 8.6). The text that appears on his face and torso in two of the three images consists of a seemingly random assortment of words and short phrases, including phrases for emotional attributes (e.g., "very honest," "too much fury"), Chinese medical terms for parts of the body (e.g., *dantian*, which literally means "the region where the *qi* resides," appears just below his navel, and *xintai*, "heart/mind," appears across his right breast), Roman letters (the letters *A*, *B*, and *C* appear along his right arm and *x*, y, z along his left), together with the occasional Chinese

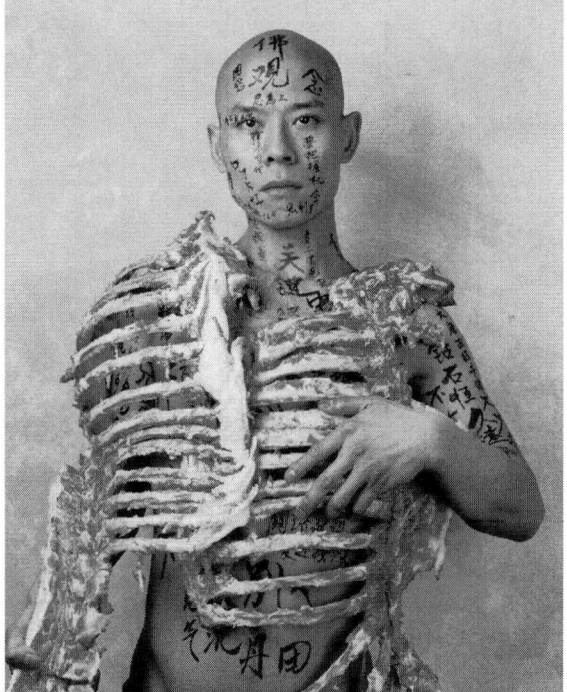

Figure 8.6 Zhang Huan, "1/2," (1998). Reprinted with permission from Zhang Huan.

transliteration of a Western name (*Kafka* [ka-fu-ka] is written along his torso). These various inscriptions invite us to approach Zhang's body as a virtual text, even as they underscore the inherent limits of the body's ability to signify in its own right. This audience-generated text illustrates the inherently collaborative relationship between the artist and his audience, and specifically the audience's ability to render the significance of the artwork legible in the first place.[20]

Zhang's lean upper body, shaved head, and gaunt expression in these images resemble Ren Xiong's appearance in his self-portrait a century and a half earlier—but while Ren's self-portrait appears to posit a binary opposition between text and flesh, Zhang's photographic triptych instead presents a tertiary relationship between the artist's naked body, the text that is literally inscribed on his skin, and the (pork) flesh with which his figure is juxtaposed. The implication is that the artist's body is not simply opposed to a semiotic sphere of textual signification, but rather is positioned *between* text and flesh, deriving its significance from their dialectical interrelationship.

The juxtaposition of text and flesh in this 1998 work provides a useful way of conceptualizing the more general relationship between gender and sex in Zhang Huan's and Ma Liuming's performance works. Both artists use a strategic combination of bodily performance and physical setting to communicate a set of gendered connotations—either a delicate femininity or a hard-edged masculinity. Both artists, furthermore, use their nude bodies to convey a set of meanings that either appear to corroborate (Zhang Huan) or strategically undermine (Ma Liuming) the gendered connotations of the overall performance. Just as "1/2" presents the significance of the artist's body as a product of a dialectical relationship between the textual writing or the animal flesh with which it is juxtaposed, Zhang's and Ma's 1990s performance works similarly use corporeality, and specifically male genitalia, as semiotic elements that are closely imbricated with the other fields of signification with which it is juxtaposed.

Desire

In their 1990s performances, Ma Liuming and Zhang Huan found inspiration not only in the work of foreign artists such as Gilbert and George, but also presumably in indigenous Chinese cultural institutions. In particular, Chinese opera traditionally included only male actors, who were responsible for performing both masculine and feminine roles, for which they deployed an elaborate set of codified conventions. Here, I will consider two novels that both examine issues of gender performance and sexual identity in the context of late imperial Shanghai's *kunqu* opera culture. The first work, Chen Sen's 陳森 1849 novel *Pinhua baojian* 品花寶鑒 (Precious mirror for evaluating flowers), revolves around a pair of romances between two (male) opera patrons and two (male) opera performers specializing in feminine roles (dan 旦), while the second is a 1996 rewriting of Chen Sen's novel by contemporary Taiwan author Wu Jiwen 吳繼文, which takes the original novel's theme of same-sex romance and reimagines it within the context of the surge of literary interest in queer themes in 1990s Taiwan.

Although Chen's work is regarded as the first full-length Chinese novel to focus on issues of same-sex desire, the text itself insists that the actual sex of the lovers is less important than the desire that brings them together. In one frequently quoted passage from near the beginning of the work, a character remarks, "What I find most incomprehensible is why contemporary people regard love for a woman to be common and love for a man to be unusual. After all, since both are instances of passion, what need is there to distinguish between man and woman?"[21] The main plotline of the novel takes this rhetorical question at face value and generally treats its transgendered protagonists as straightforwardly feminine, though the work also contains an assortment of subplots that present a more complicated attitude toward the relationship between gender and sex. While the romances between the two pairs of protagonists are presented in idealized and platonic terms, for instance, the secondary characters who surround them engage in a wide variety of sexual practices that are described in graphic detail. Despite the novel's ostensible disinterest in "distinguish[ing] between man and woman," the work's various subplots reveal a fascination with sexual difference combined with a residual anxiety about the significance of anatomical sex characteristics.

In an otherwise inconsequential vignette near the end of the work, for instance, a minor character by the name of Li Yuanmao asks a seamstress to mend a garment for him, then hires her to stay on to perform some additional services. Yuanmao's friend, Sun Sihui, secretly observes the entire scene, and the next day he follows Yuanmao's example with the same woman. When Sihui then tries to pay the seamstress the same 400 cash he had seen her accept from Yuanmao, however, she replies indignantly:

> "This is for me? Tze, Tze, Tze! This is some offer! And you call yourself a "lord" (*laoye* 老爺)? This is not my price."
>
> When Sihui heard this, he answered, "But I saw you accept this price yesterday; I haven't underpaid you. How is it not four hundred cash?"

...Then [Yuanmao] heard the seamstress say, "Quick, quick! Pay up! Don't waste my time!"

Sihui answered, "Why is this? I am the same kind of person as him. So why do I have to pay extra?"

The seamstress replied, "The same kind of person? He is an ordinary person, but you are a lord! And furthermore, yesterday we didn't even take off our clothes, but today I have had to go to two or three times as much trouble. And you have the gall to only give me four hundred cash? As a lord, you're a joke!"[22]

Sihui asks how she knew he is a "lord," indicating that he is willing to pay the price she is asking if she can correctly identify which portions of his body are "precious" (*zhugui* 主貴). She responds that the precious part of his body is his "cock" (*jiba* 雞巴), but then immediately specifies that his member is "covered in swollen blotches" (*manmian de zao geda* 滿面的糟疙瘩).[23] Either impressed by the prostitute's flattering attention to his member, or perhaps humbled by her decidedly unflattering focus on its disfiguring blotches, Sihui quickly agrees to pay the elevated price she is demanding.

In this passage, the significance of Sihui's physical member is mediated through the blotches that appear on its surface. Like the calligraphic outline of the cloak in Ren Xiong's contemporary self-portrait, these unexplained blotches on Sihui's penis underscore not only the organ's underlying corporeality (given that they are likely the result of venereal disease), but also its symbolic significance (given that they are explicitly used here to corroborate Sihui's social status as a "lord"). Just as the seamstress successfully parlays her identification of Sihui's phallus into a demand for higher compensation, it is precisely the ability of the phallus to circulate within a symbolic economy that effectively grounds its perceived value as a token of social worth. The phallus, in other words, functions as a paradigmatic *objet a* that, like a Marxian commodity, derives its value from the process of circulation and exchange.

This focus on anatomical sex attributes in response to an overt emphasis on gender performance is taken a step further in the 1996 debut novel by Taiwan-based publisher Wu Jiwen. Entitled *Shijimo shaonian ai duben* 世紀末少年爱讀本 (*Fin-de-siècle* reader of young love), the novel retells parts of Chen Sen's original work from the perspective of a servant of one of the protagonists, granting particular attention to issues of identity, status, and subjectivity. One particularly interesting sequence, for instance, centers around an opera performer by the name of Lin Shanzhi. Lin appears in Chen Sen's original novel as a sort of spectral double of one of the work's main opera performances, Du Qinyan—in that Shanzhi's original master eventually traded him and used the proceeds to purchase Qinyan, thereby making Qinyan the mirror image of Shanzhi. The sequence in *Fin-de-siècle Reader*, meanwhile, explores similar issues of substitution and exchange, though in relation not to Shanzhi's original master but rather Lord Hua, the patron who subsequently purchases him.

In Wu's novel, there is a detailed first-person description of Shanzhi's reaction to having been purchased by Lord Hua, focusing in particular on how the actor's initial reservations about the prospect of physical intimacy with the older man are assuaged by the sight of the patron's flaccid member:

> In the deepest recess of that thick mass of pubic hair, at first I couldn't believe what I was seeing, thinking that it was my blurred vision or an optical illusion in that deepest mystery of mysteries, there was his purplish-red member. It was listlessly laid out there on display, like the viscera of some animal.... It looked like a unripe pear, exceedingly ... comical. Perhaps when it is standing tall it might assume a different appearance altogether, but by this point I already had no interest in knowing.[24]

It is precisely the "comical" appearance of the patron's member that permits the actor to identify with it. As Shanzhi explains, "I loved him because I had the power to pity him, because I knew that in the end we were equal, because I knew that he, too, had his own fears" (201). In a curious twist on the logic of Lacan's mirror stage model of subject formation, the recently purchased and figuratively emasculated Shanzhi identifies with an external imago in the form of his patron's limp member—thereby taking a figure that is symbolic of his patron's loss of virility and transforming it into a paradoxical ground for his own self-conception.

A similar logic of displaced identification is developed in the remainder of the passage, as Lin Shanzhi describes how it was his ability to pity his new patron's flaccid penis that led him to try to restore it to its former glory:

> I tenderly used an ointment to cover his member, and that formerly limp and cold thing was gradually restored to its former vitality. My hand could feel its reawakening, together with the warmth occasioned by that reawakening. After passing through my hand, that warmth permeated my entire body....
>
> [His member's] enormity vastly exceeded what I could have imagined, and the base was so thick that it could not be grasped with a

single hand. Enormous, hard, and burning hot, its color changed from date-red to purplish black, and the ointment made it resemble the blinding reflection given off by a polished bronze ornament....

This was the first time I was able to carefully observe and touch a body that was completely open to me and receptive to my pity, and which could use love to respond to my love.... I let my hand move faster, and felt as though the person lying there was myself, and as though it were my own member I was holding in my hand.[25]

In reanimating his patron's member, Shanzhi simultaneously revitalizes himself ("after passing through my hand, that warmth permeated my entire body"), and in the process rediscovers his own identity ("I felt as though the person lying there was myself"). He perceives own subordinated status reflected in his patron's dephallicized member, and it is precisely through this process of (mis)recognition that he is then able to affirm his own positionality.

Lin Shanzhi suggests that it is precisely his perception of his new master's dephallicized penis that grants him the ability to "love" and "pity" the older man. Lin combines the characters *ai* 愛 ("to love") and *lian* 憐 ("to pity") in the adverbial phrase *lian'ai de* 憐愛地 ("tenderly"), when he describes how he "*tenderly (lian'ai)* used an ointment to gently cover his [master's] member." We find this same character, lian 憐 ("to pity"), in Ren Xiong's lament that, "What is even more of a pitiable (*kelian* 可憐) impediment is that the historians have not recorded even a single, light word about me." In both instances, the feeling of "pity" is initially inspired by the subject's own sense of disempowerment and symbolic exclusion from a matrix of social orthodoxy, even as it is precisely this same act of expressing "pity" that allows the subject to assert his new identity. To the extent that lian connotes empathy and, by implication, the possibility of vicarious identification, the sense of (self-)pity that Lin Shanzhi and Ren Xiong feel as a result of their socially marginalized positions is translated into a sense of empathy for their own displaced status, thereby enabling a process of projective identification with the systems of identity from which they felt excluded in the first place.

Chen Sen's and Wu Jiwen's novels both juxtapose a focus on gender performance with a complicated exploration of corporeal semiotics. Anatomical sex attributes such as the penis function, accordingly, not as a concrete ground for sociocultural notions of gender difference, but rather as a product of processes of signification in their own right. Not only is gender conceived as a semiotic matrix that is figuratively inscribed onto the physical body, the body itself is also understood to be a product of a similar sort of symbolic economy.

Coda

The Chinese word used to refer to the male member in the passages from Wu Jiwen's novel cited above is *fenshen* 分身. Consisting of two characters meaning "partial/parted" and "body," respectively, this binome is borrowed from a Buddhist term referring to the separation and reduplication of the body of the Buddha (*ātmabhāva-nirmita*, in Sanskrit),[26] and it also happens to be a direct inversion of the standard Chinese term for "identity."[27] Used in Wu's novel to refer to the male genitals, the term underscores an understanding of the phallus as a partial object—which, to function as a locus of identity, must be figuratively separated from the subject and circulate within a broader symbolic economy. The fenshen, therefore, may be seen as the ultimate Lacanian *objet a*, its function as a material ground of sexual difference necessarily predicated on its status as an autonomous symbol.

A similar emphasis of separation and circulation may also be found in the name Ma Liuming coined for his transgendered persona—*fen-Ma Liuming*, which simply consists of his actual name preceded by the character *fen* 芬. This character literally means "fragrance," but its use here also suggests its homophonous lexical root, fen 分, or "partial/parted." Just as a fragrance literally consists of olfactory molecules that have been separated from the object emitting them (for instance, a fragrant plant) but which just retain the ability to convey a memory of this absent origin, Ma Liuming's performative person is distinct from the artist, but is nevertheless directly reminiscent of him. Ma Liuming's use of the name *fen-Ma Liuming* to refer to his fictional persona, therefore, suggests that his performative identity is positioned in a partial/parted relationship to the artist, just as the fenshen/phallus is positioned in a partial/parted relationship to the subject.

One of the most memorable associations of the term *fenshen* within Chinese popular culture concerns the ability of the legendary Monkey King (Sun Wukong), the irascible protagonist of the Ming-dynasty classic novel *Xiyou ji* 西遊記 (Journey to the West), to take hairs from his body and transform them into miniature replicas of himself. Positioned at the very margins of the physical body, hair can be literally separated (cut, plucked, etc.) from the body with miniscule effort, yet it is also one of the aspects of the body that contributes most directly to how a person is perceived and remembered.

A suggestive exploration of some of these implications of hair as a paradigmatic partial object, or *"fenshen,"* can be found in a 1995 performance on which Ma Liuming and Zhang Huan collaborated with the photographer Rong Rong. Rong Rong describes how one day he happened to be looking through some pictures he had taken of the East Village artists,

> and found that the most interesting ones are of Zhang Huan and Ma Liuming. Zhang Huan is bold, tough and masculine. Ma Liuming, on the other hand, is elegant and feminine. With shoulder-length hair and a slim body, he is a man without masculinity. Their performances are antithetical in every way.[28]

With this gendered contrast in mind, Rong Rong proposed a joint photography session, for which the artists undressed, shaved, and brushed their teeth, and then "'purified' themselves in front of the mirror."[29] Ma shaved Zhang's head bald, except for a small tuft of hair in the back, and even cut their pubic hair. The two men then climbed into a bathtub together, where they posed naked for the camera, their bodies partially covered with Zhang's cut hair (figure 8.7).

Known as "Third Contact," this performance strategically contrasts the gendered connotations of Zhang's and Ma's respective

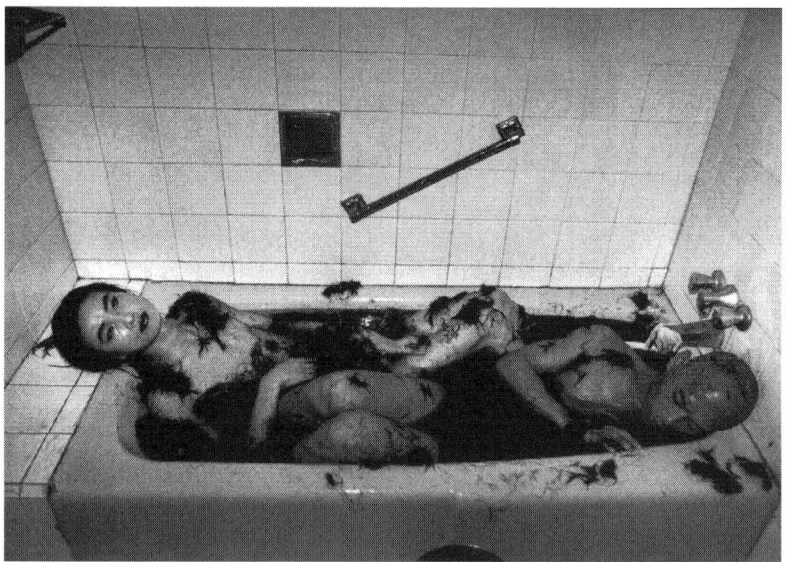

Figure 8.7 Ma Liuming and Zhang Huan, "Third Contact." Photographed by Rong Rong (1995). Reprinted with permission from Chambers Fine Art Gallery, New York.

performative personas, while drawing attention to the distinct ways in they each incorporate their male anatomy into his works. The image of Ma and Zhang lying in the bathtub together is distinctly reminiscent of the Taoist yin-yang symbol, which itself suggests the intimate interpenetration of masculinity and femininity within the body, and in the environment as a whole. This Taoist symbol is frequently compared to a pair of fish, and given that several of Ma's performances had featured fish that were apparently being used as miniature symbols of the artist himself, it is therefore particularly fitting that in this 1995 performance he and Zhang Huan were put in a position visually and conceptually reminiscent of a pair of fishes.

The most striking aspect of this staged performance is the abundance of cut hair. Hair, as suggested above, is a paradigmatic example of a Lacanian partial object, symbolizing the contested liminal zone where the body's dual status as a corporeal entity and a semiotic construct collide. It is, in other words, a quintessential fenshen—symbolizing both the artists' ability to fashion performative personas that—in the form of photographs, videos, and narrative descriptions—have the ability to be reproduced ad infinitum and circulate widely (like Monkey's use of his hairs in *Journey to the West*), as well as their use of their anatomical members to either corroborate or strategically counterpoint their gendered performances (as Lin Shanzhi does in his treatment of his master's "*fenshen*" in Wu Jiwen's novel). Just as Zhang Huan's hair clippings cover both Zhang's and Ma's bodies in the "Third Contact" performance without conveying a unitary and unambiguous significance of its own, the male genitalia that appear prominently in many of the artists' works from this period similarly lack a unitary and autonomous significance independent of the broader context in which they appear. Rather than being irreducibly corporeal counterpoints to the artists' gendered performances, their male genitalia are, instead, performative artifacts in their own right, and they own derive meaning and significance through process of sociocultural inscription.

Notes

1. James Cahill, "Ren Xiong and his Self-Portrait," *Ars Orientalis*, 25 (1995): 119–132 and 124.
2. Richard Vinograd, *Boundaries of the Self: Chinese Portraits 1600–1900* (Cambridge: Cambridge University Press, 1992), 128.
3. Angela Zito, "Silk and Skin: Significant Boundaries," in *Body, Subject, and Power*, ed. Angela Zito and Tani Barlow (Chicago: University of Chicago Press, 1994), 103–130 and 124.

4. 莽乾坤，眼前何物？翻笑側身長系，覺甚事，紛紛攀倚。此則談何容易！ Translation adapted from Richard Vinograd, *Boundaries of the Self*, 129.
5. 試說豪華，金、張、許、史，到如今能幾？還可惜，鏡換青娥，塵掩白頭，一樣奔馳無計。更誤人，可憐青史，一字何曾輕記！
6. "There is an 'outside' to what is constructed by discourse, but this is not an absolute 'outside,' an ontological thereness that exceeds or counters the boundaries of discourse; as a constitutive 'outside,' it is that which can only be thought—when it can—in relation to that discourse, at and as its most tenuous borders," Judith Butler, *Bodies that Matter: On the Discursive Limits of "Sex"* (New York: Routledge, 1993), 8.
7. See, for instance, David Valentine, *Imagining Transgender: An Ethnography of a Category* (Durham: Duke University Press, 2007).
8. Karen Smith, "Rong Rong, Records of the Observer" (1998), unpublished manuscript, cited in Wu Hung, *Transience: Exhibiting Experimental Art at the End of the Twentieth Century* (Smart Museum of Art: University of Chicago, 1999), 107.
9. Caroline Puel, "Concerning "Fen-Ma Liuming," http://www.taikangtopspace.com/exhibitions/12_ma_liuming/texts02.htm, translation modified.
10. See Thomas Berghuis, *Performance Art in China* (Hong Kong: Timezone 8, 2007), 102–103.
11. See, for instance, Yuko Hasegawa, "Ma Liuming: The Politics of Non-differentiation," in *Fen/Ma Liuming* (Beijing: Cheng Xindong Publishing House, 2004).
12. Caroline Puel, "Concerning "Fen-Ma Liuming."
13. Jacques Lacan, "The Mirror Stage as Formative of the Function of the I," in *Écrits: A Selection*, trans. Alan Sheridan (New York: W. W. Norton & Co., 1977).
14. Caroline Puel, "Concerning 'Fen-Ma Liuming," emphasis added.
15. Wu Hung, *Rong Rong's East Village: 1993–1998* (New York: Chambers Fine Art, 203), 50. Yu Yeon, however, reports the amount of the fine to have been 2,000 RMB. See Yu Yeon Kim, "Intensified Corporeality," in *Zhang Huan, Kunstverein in Hamburg*, ed. Yilmaz Dziewior (Germany: Hatje Cantz, 2003), 26–29
16. As Zhang Huan remarks, "You could not keep your child when your girlfriend was pregnant...Girls of my generation have to go through many abortions; some have done it twice or three times, some five or six times. Many unborn babies died. This is the situation of the nineties. I am not clear about the seventies and eighties. But I know my own generation well." Quoted in Wu Hung, *Transience*, 105.
17. Wu Hung, *Rong Rong's East Village*, 53–54.
18. Wu Hung, *Rong Rong's East Village*, 53-4.

19. Jacques Lacan, *Four Fundamental Concepts of Psychoanalysis* (New York: W.W. Norton and Co., 1998), 103.
20. Zhang Huan returns to this theme of textual inscription in one of the most influential works he produced after leaving China in 1998: "Family Tree" (2001), which consists of nine photographs in which Zhang Huan's face is increasingly covered with a dense palimpsest of Chinese text, until the final panel where his face and head appear completely black.
21. Chen Sen 陳森, *Pinhua baojian* (品花寶鑒) [Precious mirror for evaluating flowers] (Beijing: Renmin Zhongguo chubanshe, 1993), 135. The following section is adapted from Chapter 3 of my book, *The Naked Gaze: Reflections on Chinese Modernity* (Cambridge: Harvard Asia Center, 2008).
22. Chen, *Pinhua baojian*, 582–583.
23. Chen, *Pinhua baojian*, 582–583.
24. Wu Jiwen 吳繼文, *Shijimo shaonian ai duben* (世紀末少年愛讀本) [*Fin-de-siècle* reader of young love] (Taibei: Shibao wenhua chubanshe, 1996), 201.
25. Wu, *Shijimo shaonian ai duben*, 201–202.
26. For instance, this term can be found in "The Emergence of the Treasure Tower," Chapter 11 of *The Lotus Sutra* (precise origins unknown; first translated into Chinese in AD 255), where it is used to refer to the "various Buddhas who are emanations of my [the Buddha's] body." See Burton Watson, *The Lotus Sutra* (New York: Columbia University Press, 1994), 172.
27. The binome *shenfen* 身分 (identity) may also be written with alternate character for "*fen*": 芬.
28. Wu Hung, *Rong Rong's East Village*, 128.
29. Wu Hung, *Rong Rong's East Village*, 128.

CHAPTER 9

Performing Transgender Desire: Male Cross-Dressing Shows in Taiwan

Chao-Jung Wu

> *Cross-dressing is a true masquerading, an anatomy of oneself, an emersion of one's heart, and double sides of a unity.*
>
> Lin Chilong, the stage designer of *SWET* (2006)

> *Bodies and minds are not two distinct substances or two kinds of attributes of a single substance but somewhere in between these two alternatives.*
>
> Elizabeth Grosz, *Volatile Bodies* (1994: xii)

I. Introduction

Cross-dressing performances, particularly female impersonation, have a long tradition rooted in Chinese and Taiwanese culture. Two of the best-known examples are the *jingju* (Beijing opera) in China and *zidixi* (junior theatre) in Taiwan.[1] While these traditional examples of male cross-dressing performance are generally dying out, a new form of male cross-dressing entertainment, the *fanchuanxiu* (cross-dressing show), emerged and swept across Taiwan's theatre culture in the late 1990s. Among many fanchuanxiu troupes, *Hongding Yiren* ("Redtop Arts"), established in 1994 in Taipei, was the most popular in Taiwan's cross-dressing entertainment industry in the nineties. Although members of Redtop Arts claimed that their performance was the modern version of the traditional cross-dressing art, their shows represented a middlebrow, commercialized entertainment genre, which was distinct from the highbrow art form of the traditional theatre. Fanchuanxiu usually consisted of approximately 20 skits. Selected from around the world, the sources for their drama, dance, and music materials came from cultures local and global, Eastern and Western, and traditional and contemporary. The fanchuanxiu embodied the aesthetic characteristics of pastiche and hybridity. Male cross-dressing performance (especially the ones showcased by Redtop Arts) became so popular that it was generally perceived as a new cultural phenomenon in Taiwan.[2]

Taking a different approach from previous studies that have examined the performance of fanchuanxiu through interpretations of visual and textual media, this chapter utilizes primary data collected from live performances and personal interviews with performers (mainly former Redtop Arts members), their administrators, audiences, and relevant institutions.[3] My fieldwork was conducted in the spring of 2005, two years after Redtop Arts' newly built theatre was unexpectedly destroyed and some Redtop Arts performers had formed their own troupe. This chapter concerns the cross-dressing performers of this post-Redtop Arts troupe, named *Xin shiji fanchuan meirenxiu* (the "New Century Cross-Dressing Beauty Show"), which performed daily at an amusement park in Zhanghua County in southern Taiwan.[4] I anticipate that at a later time and in a different place, former Redtop Arts members may feel more comfortable talking about the troupe and presenting themselves to outsiders more freely. My analysis reveals a concealed reality starkly different from previous reports and studies on the subject. I argue that the kind of backstage preparations that the performers undertook illustrates the performativity and construction of gender, and that their offstage lives represent an embodied battleground between government authorities, mass media, and their own "real-life" struggles with gender ambiguity and homosexual experience.

Upon my first entrance to the greenroom backstage at the New Century Male Cross-Dressing Beauty show, I found the room filled with wigs, adornments, costumes, high heels, bras, cosmetics, and props. Cross-dressing performers were busy preparing for the show: sewing evening gowns, stylizing wigs, putting props in order, or putting on corsets, stockings, and makeup. Watching the actors' preparation for gender performance, I was amazed by how they drifted across multiple boundaries—man and woman, cultural and sexual, body and mind, public and private, East and West, and traditional and modern. All of this prompted me to ask: How did these actors alter their bodies and minds to construct onstage female images and identities? What kind of physical and psychological maneuver was involved?

Fanchuan artists' sexual anatomy, social gender, and performance strategies overwhelmingly corresponded to Judith Butler's argument about gender performativity. According to Butler, the idea of performativity exposes the constructed nature of gender under a specific social system of power.[5] However, the kind of political parody and displays of subversive power found in the Western drag and lesbian/gay culture did not necessarily appear in fanchuanxiu. With the exception of the clown role, most fanchuan artists did not view their performance as mockery or sarcasm for the purposes of humor or shock value. Even though many of them admitted their homosexual inclinations, they did not identify themselves as queer or "camp," and continued to not "come out." Neither did they intend to act on the Western notion of camp, nor did they consciously convey a political message in their shows. Being aware of such discrepancies, I critically adopt Western queer theory as correlative insight and interrogative reference, which in turn provides dialogical and reflective analysis.

This chapter studies fanchuanxiu from an ethnographically informed perspective, focusing on the differences between individual performers in terms of their psychological factors, personal backgrounds, and sexual orientations. Through their storytelling and my onstage and offstage observations, I uncover the emotional routines and quotidian challenges faced by male cross-dressing performers in late twentieth-century Taiwan. These previously unavailable materials enable a systematic and comparative understanding of fanchuan artists' personal lives, as well as their strategies for coping with social norms. This chapter organizes these ethnographic data around three major lines of inquiry:[6] the performers' personal profile (including their physical attributes, sexuality, cultural and social backgrounds), backstage preparation (which involved the denaturalization of the body and the construction of a dream woman), and offstage life (which revealed their gender identity and confrontation of heteronormativity). These sociocultural, physical, and psychological dimensions of fanchuan artists' transgender performance not only reveal the fluidity of gender identity, but also exemplify an embodied process of gender construction and performativity in contemporary Taiwanese culture.

II. Personal Profile: Physical Attributes, Sexuality, Cultural and Social Backgrounds

In this section, I begin with the life stories of two fanchuan artists—Black Pearl and Manning. These two particular life stories are significant because they reflect the shift in the orientation of Taiwan's mass entertainment industry from traditional theatre to popular culture.

Black Pearl grew up in a *gezaixi* (Taiwanese folk opera) family troupe, where he learned theatrical posture and acrobatics from a young age. When his mother became ill, he stood in for her role and cross-dressed to perform in local theaters including gezaixi and the "soul guiding opera" (i.e., *qianwang-gezheng* 牽亡歌陣 and *wunü-kumu* 五女哭墓).[7] When the popularity of fanchuanxiu reached its peak in the mid-1990s, Black Pearl joined Redtop Arts for a short period of time. Later, he published an autobiography, entitled *Fanchuan yiren Hei Zhenzhu* (The male cross-dressing performer Black Pearl, 1998), revealing his homosexual inclination and erotic life stories.[8] Perhaps due to his explicit proclamation of his homosexuality and lascivious performance style, he was forced to leave Redtop. He then became a third-sex barmaid working alternatively in Japan and Taiwan.

The other fanchuan artist, Manning, began his career in cross-dressing performance when he was in elementary school (in the mid-1980s). He recalled his cultural activities in a military village where he grew up.[9] He often saw his father and other male elders from the village singing female roles in Peking opera. According to Manning, it was customary for his family to watch male cross-gender singing, and later this experience brought the family's acceptance of his occupation as a fanchuan artist.[10] In his teenage years, he disguised himself as a girl performing in a *nagashi* troupe and in an electronic entertainment float performed on the street. Before becoming a Redtop member, he had ten years of cross-dressing performance experience in restaurants, hotels, wedding ceremonies, funerals, show business, and red-envelope singing halls. Manning self-identified as gay and claimed that in his body lived a female soul.[11]

Black Pearl and Manning both had a background in the male cross-dressing tradition in traditional Taiwanese theatre. Their life stories reflected the change in vogue of Taiwan's mass entertainment form from traditional theatre to modern show business. Furthermore, both Black Pearl and Manning admitted their feminine mentality and homosexual inclinations, which existed before they joined the cross-dressing profession. They pointed out the interweaving relationship between fanchuanxiu artists, homosexuality, and the more recent nightclub business, the third-sex barmaids.

In addition to the two cases mentioned above, fanchuan artists came from a variety of career backgrounds. Due to the decline of show business in restaurants and construction sites,[12] many backup dancers lost their jobs and later chose to become fanchuan performers. Other professional backgrounds included former actors, workers of architectural shuttering,[13] hairdressers, cosmeticians, model trainers, style designers, jewelry sellers, and some college graduates majoring in dance, theatre, or arts. Among them, hairdressers, cosmeticians, model trainers, and style designers were already well acquainted with women's fashion due to their former professional interactions with female clients. It is interesting to note that these types of occupation tend to be largely populated by gay men.

The fanchuan artists I interviewed included 9 actors from Redtop Arts, 8 from the New Century Cross-dressing Beauty Show in Zhanghua,[14] 4 from *Huali bianshen* 華麗變身 (Top Arts Entertainment) in Taichung,[15] 3 from *Hongpai yiren* 紅牌藝人 (Top Artists) in Taipei, 3 from *Tiantang-niao* 天堂鳥 (The Bird of Paradise) in Taichung, 2 from *Baixue zongyi jutuan* 白雨綜藝劇團 (Snow White Entertaining Troupe) in Taipei, and 1 from *Jinling hongfen juyi gongzuo fang* 金陵紅粉劇藝工作坊 (Blushing Diva Troupe) in Taipei. The age of those interviewed ranged from 24 to 42 years old.

An actor usually had more than one motivation for taking up cross-dressing and one factor may weigh in more than others, depending on individual situations and personal needs. Below I give a detailed discussion of these factors.

Economic Need

According to a governmental survey reported in *Scoop Weekly Taiwan*, men who took up cross-dressing performance as their profession did so purely for economic reasons.[16] On a website constructed for gay users, a viewer discussed his impression of fanchuan artists as follows: "I believe that if not for the sake of money, why would any man wear make-up like this?"[17] If a fanchuan artist denied any homosexual inclination (as was the case with the initial reaction of members of Redtop Arts), the general public tended to use other reasons (usually economic ones) to rationalize their behavior. Such surveys and reports reveal that the general public's impression of male cross-dressing performers had not changed much from the distant past when the majority of male dan were either born into theatrical family

Table 9.1 Some *fanchuan* artists' personal profiles[i]

Stage name	Birth Year	Education	Occupation other than cross-dressing performance	Height & Weight	Distinguishing feature in Performance	Gender/sexual ID[iii]
A-xiong 阿兇/阿雄	1957	HS[iii]	Backup dancer, dance instructor	174 cm/60 kg	Male dancer; old woman; androgyny	Gay
Little Tsai Qin 小蔡琴	1960	HS	Minor singer	168/60	Professional singer in woman's tone quality	Gay
Niu-Niu 妞妞	1963	HS	Backup dancer	168/60–70	grotesque androgyny	Gay
Zhou Xiang 周紅瑄/周湘	1964	MA (major in Chinese music and theatre)	Male *dan*; manager for actors	165/50	Well trained in singing and acting in traditional Chinese operas; hyperfemininity	No answer
Sheng Honglong 沈紅龍	1964	HS (Violinist)	TV backup dancer	170/60	Lifelike femininity (impersonates old women); the only "male star" in the Redtop[iv]	Gay
Ong Hongwen 翁紅文	1964	HS (dance)	TV backup dancer and dance teacher	174/55	Hyperfemininity (elegant style)	Gay
Angela 安琪拉/徐偉程	1964	HS	Troupe leader of the Top Artists, actor, singer, and dancer	163/50	Live singing; Hyperfemininity	Straight
Jinmei 晉梅	1970	HS	Third-sex barmaid; now housewife	165/52	Hyperfemininity (elegant style)	Post-op TS
Manning 曼寧	1971	BA (accounting)	Singer and dancer	167/52	Hyperfemininity (traditional Chinese lady)	Id. w/ F[v]
Maria 馬利亞	1971	HS (AD design)	Embroiderer	175/87	Marilyn Monroe; parody	Id. w/ F
SongtianWanzi 松田丸子	1972	MA (theatre)	Broadcasting DJ, SWET troupe leader	165/52	Hyperfemininity (angle like; mixture of lovely & sexy)	Gay
Bai Bingbing 白冰冰	1972	HS (dancing)	Backup dancer	171/75	grotesque androgyny	Gay
Romansa 羅曼莎	1973	BA	Third-sex barmaid	175/65	Hyperfemininity (elegant style)	Bisexual →Gay
Lai Weijiong 賴鬱炅	1974	BA (dress design)	Dress designer, member of *Jinling hongfen juyi gongzuo fang* [Blushing Diva Troupe] and SWET	172/70–80	grotesque androgyny	Gay
Linda	1974	HS	Performer	167/56	Hyperfemininity (sexy style)	Inter-sexual TS

Name	Year	Education	Occupation	Height/Weight	Style	Identification
A-Gui 林紅貴	1975	HS (major in singing)	Singer and backup dancer	176/65	Hyperfemininity and grotesque androgyny	Gay
Yalan 陳亞蘭	1977	HS (TV)	Baker; porter	173/61	Hyperfemininity	Id. w/ F
Lin Yilian 林憶蓮	1977	College	Third-sex barmaid, headwaiter	170/57	Hyperfemininity (traditional Chinese lady)	Id. w/ F →gay
Tianli 阿桃/田麗	1980	HS (chemical engineering)	7–11 counter; office staff	178/61	Hyperfemininity (elegant style)	Id. w/ F
Shuqi 舒淇	1982	HS (theatre)	Third-sex barmaid	173/59	Hyperfemininity (Sexy, spicy girl Hollywood style)	Id. w/F →gay[vi]

Note: What motivated these men to pursue a career in cross-dressing performance? Based on my informants' responses to my survey, I gathered four major motivating factors:
(a) Economic need
(b) Wider fame
(c) Psychological fulfillment (expressing hidden characteristics; A conscious alternative personality)
(d) Personal interest, art, and commercialism

In Zhou Xianggeng's MA thesis on the study of Chinese traditional male dan, he sums up four mindsets for male dan devoting themselves to the profession. Zhou Xianggeng, "Qiandan yianjiu" (Research on the female impersonator in Chinese opera) (MA thesis, Nanhua University, 2002), 70. The result of my own survey on the modern fanchuan yiren shows a telling correspondence with Zhou's finding, yet with nuances of difference

[i] This table is a list of effective cases who have accepted my extensive interview. From them, I also gathered other fanchuan artists' personal information, which expands my discussion base. Except for Jinmei, who had a complete sex change, got married, and retired from the *fanchuanxiu* business, all of them listed here are still performing on stage.

[ii] This is the interviewee's self-identification regarding gender and sexual orientation.

[iii] HS stands for High school.

[iv] In a fanchuan show, the female impersonator is always the focus of gaze and applause, and male dancers are supporting roles. Hong is well-known for his impersonation of old women, including the Qing Empress Dowager Cixi and an old Japanese woman who had experienced the vicissitudes of life in the World War II period, and was waiting for her military son to return. In order to make a sharp contrasting effect (woman/man; old/young; weak/powerful—all performed by the same person), Tsai Tou designed a program to show off Hong's manfully energetic dancing skills, immediately following Hong's old woman skit. This skit was the only one in which a male dancer plays the main role.

[v] "Id w/ F?" means psychologically identified with female, psychological TS (transsexual), but not willing to have a sex reassignment surgery.

[vi] Shuqi and Lin Yilian identified with females earlier in their careers, but they later switched to a gay identification.

troupes or bought from poor families. The assumption of monetary incentives denies the possibility of transgender inclination, simplifies the multifluidity of desire, and ignores diversified transgender subjectivities. It further reflects a hegemonic interpretation of cross-dressing based on a rigid heteronormative structure of reasoning, which creates and reinforces an unfavorable environment for the transgender community.

According to my surveys, the families of fanchuan artists were not limited to the poor or lower-middle classes; rather, they were spread widely among lower-middle, upper-middle, and well-to-do social classes. Some fanchuan performers, along with the changing socio-economic contexts (e.g., the introduction of capitalism after World War II in particular), had been rather well educated (college graduates or higher), and their families were fairly prosperous. Quite a few came from elite families and held Master's degrees.

Nevertheless, monetary incentives presented an important, though not exclusive, motivating factor for becoming a cross-dressing performer. For male cross-dressing actors in particular, to possess economic mobility often meant having the option to be independent and self-sufficient. A crucial reason for fanchuan artists' economic need lay in their "atypical" sexual identity (see table 9.1 under the category of "Personal gender and sexual ID").[18] While the pressure to have a family loomed large, many homosexuals chose to break away from their parents or moved out of their parents' place to conceal their sexual orientation or get rid of parental pressure altogether.[19] Economic independence also allowed them to have greater freedom in their sexual preference and practice. For those in poverty or without a college education, fanchuan was a good option for making money. These fanchuan artists from lower-middle class families told me that their families disliked their occupation at first, but later acquiesced for two major reasons: at least the job was not illegal, and the actors contributed a large portion of their salary to support their families.

Wider Fame

Before becoming a fanchuan artist, the majority of the performers that I interviewed either received theatrical/performance training or had years of performing experience in the show business.[20] Many of them graduated from arts high schools and majored in singing, dancing, theatre, television, or cinema. Some felt that it was too difficult to achieve success in relevant competitive professional environments, and therefore considered fanchuan a good way to gain fame and money. After evaluating their physical attributes (the combination of a slim and slender body mass and soft facial shape being the ideal), they often decided to enter this profession with the anticipation that they would become famous more easily.

Angela, one of the earliest modern fanchuan artists, originally played supporting roles in movies when he was a high-school student. He considered his appearance "not good enough": "I am too short to be a top actor. In Taiwan's show business, they don't want such mediocre, unknown actors like me."[21] When he was a student in Japan, he took a part-time job washing dishes to pay for his tuition. Due to his performance background, a schoolmate introduced him to a cross-dressing nightclub, where he began his cross-dressing career. For Song Hongxun, a college graduate who majored in theater and a television actor, "Given the stagnation of the show business, there is not much opportunity from which one can advance a career. I treat cross-dressing performance as one type of acting, which is just a job for me."[22] Entering the fanchuan profession to gain wider fame was also captured in the experience of Sun Hongyi, a former backup dancer who later became a popular Redtop fanchuan artist known for his wild and sexy dance style: "I used to play the supporting roles, but now a leading role. I feel very good about this."[23]

Psychological Fulfillment

Sun's "good feeling" was not simply the result of gaining adoration and fame; it also involved certain levels of psychological satisfaction. According to other Redtop members, Sun is a transsexual—an individual who has a strong desire to undergo or simply has undergone sex change.[24] About ten years ago, Sun decided to put himself through a sex reassignment surgery (SRS), becoming one of a few fanchuan artists who have gone through this procedure. Many fanchuan performers, although psychologically identifying themselves as female (see figure 1 under the category "Gender/sexual ID"), were not willing to have SRS for various reasons. Many of them particularly enjoyed "doing" (or "being") a woman on stage and in private (without costume), yet preferred that their physical body remained functionally male for the rest of the time.[25] For many of them, cross-dressing performance was a way to express their hidden, but self-conscious characteristics. This is similar to Charlotte Suthrell's study of cross-dressing culture in the UK and India, which found that cross-dressing was "an outlet for emotions which [transvestites] perceive to be inapplicable to their own male life and character."[26]

Fanchuan artists Yalan and Manning disputed *Scoop Weekly Taiwan*'s report on their financial reasons for joining the profession: "Cross-dressing performance is our interest and we enjoy doing it. They [the public and the reporter] obviously do not understand us." Almost all of the fanchuan artists I interviewed acknowledged that they had both male and female personalities and inner states (to differing degrees). As fanchuan artist Songtian Wanzi put it: "*Bianzhuang* [cross-dressing] is a flavor enlivening my life from time to time, and it lets my soul have a fling."[27] When asked if cross-dressing had influenced his psychological development in terms of gender identification, Songtian's response also denounced the monetary incentive explanation:

> This question should be asked reversely. It is precisely because I have characteristics of both [binary] genders that I cross-dress and learn theatrical plays. Due to such a preexisting psychological state, I do cross-dressing performance. It is not because fanchuan show has become popular, and I want to do it for the money. If you want to earn money, you have many other choices.[28]

Personal Interest, Art, and Commercialism

Similar to the case of Black Pearl mentioned above, who received traditional theatrical training in female impersonation through local theatrical training, Zhou Xiang obtained systematic training in male dan from the academia. Zhou grew up in a wealthy family; his parents were both Peking opera lovers and amateur performers.[29] Due to his own interest and the support of his family, Zhou continued to learn female impersonation (*qingyi* 青衣 [mature lady] and *huadan* 花旦 [vigorous young lady]) from leading dan masters in Taiwan.[30] He joined the Redtop Arts to extend his interests in performance and to partake in another type of stage experience. Having witnessed the withering of traditional drama, the art of male dan in particular, Zhou had an ambition to create an entertainment genre that would combine artistic elements with commercialism, hoping that traditional theatre could attract a wider audience given the ways that the show business had evolved.[31]

For the past decade or so, fanchuanxiu has not been limited to the theatrical domain. It has been extended to other commercial activities. Many enterprises of different occupations have invited fanchuan performers to enhance their sales/business and to entertain their customers and employees. Songtian Wanzi once remarked on the collaboration between art circle and enterprise: "We help the enterprise in its business and the enterprise supports us financially. This is a win-win deal."[32] To give a successful fanchuanxiu and to achieve the variety of purposes mentioned above, cross-dressing actors had to go through a complex process of gender transformation and embodiment, to which we turn next.

III. Backstage Preparation: Denaturalizing the Body and Constructing a Dream Woman

> Two small children in a museum [are] standing in front of a painting of Adam and Eve. One child asks the other, "which is the man and which is the lady?" The other child answers, "I can't tell—they don't have any clothes on."
>
> Judith Shapiro[33]

This story illustrates the social constructionist view of gender, which posits that what we perceive as the category of sex is not a static condition of the body. Rather, it is assembled in heterogeneous corporeal forms presented at different times and spaces depending on multilevel factors or forces. As Lin Yulin puts it: "The body is a locus of the dialectical process of interpreting (or experiencing) a new historical set of conventions which have already informed corporeal style."[34] Without the clothes, the body-self is neutral and ungendered, until the moment it is embodied with psyches/minds to put on gendered clothes and act out gendered movement.

Similarly, fanchuan artists' onstage female performance and identities are constructed with a series of complex symbolic elements. To illustrate this, my analysis of their backstage gender embodiment will focus on five crucial elements: body and face shape, makeup, attire, body movement, and voice.[35] Needless to say, these symbolic elements are always encoded further through the representation of lighting, music, and sound effects so as to convey specific meaning and signification.

Body and Face Shape

The first thing that male cross-dressers considered before putting on any type of costume or accessories was their body shape. Contrary to the story of undressed Adam and Eve quoted above (in which body shape does not matter), to fanchuan artists, a heavy or slim Adam did make a difference. Among female gender specialist (i.e., *nü* dancers) there were two female-role types: the general female role and the clown. A fanchuanxiu troupe usually had only one or two people who played the comic role. A fanchuan artist who played the general female role needed to keep his body mass slim and slender without conspicuous muscles, to "have more sexual attraction." In contrast to the general female role, a clown-type fanchuan performer partially allowed stocky or heavyset builds with some muscles. His objective was not to "pass" as a woman, but to create androgynous style that would be comical and grotesque.

Being a fanchuan artist usually required the following set of physical characteristics: a handsome/beautiful face (oval shape being the more favorable), a small chin, a lack of facial hair,[36] a clear complexion, good physical fitness, and young age. Overall, one should give a healthy and youthful impression. Height also mattered—tall men with slim figures were preferred in the fanchuan "market" for their good body ratio, long/thin legs, and prominent stage appearance. For fat or masculine cross-dressing performers—who could never transform into Venus—the comic role would be their only choice.

During the years when the popularity of cross-dressing show reached its peak, the profession was very competitive in terms of the actors' facial/body appearance. While many cross-dressing performers insisted on keeping their original bodies, some decided to permanently modify their body through cosmetic surgery to create better images on stage. According to my interviewees, around 50 percent of fanchuan performers had undergone some kind of plastic surgery. Double eyelid folds (to create large, widely spaced eyes) were the most common procedure; other surgeries such as abdominal lipectomies, liposuction, cheek implants, augmented rhinoplasties, and chin lifts, were also popular within the fanchuan community.[37] Other common treatments include orthodontic treatment, teeth whitening, and salon crystal-nail design. An article posted on a website entitled "Have a facelift—Men are crazy about it too" written by the director of the Cosmetic Surgical Association of Taiwan, indicated an increasing number of men who had facelifts: "It shows that the number of men who have facelifts has obviously increased. Among them, many were young men; others include the third-sex barmaids and gays."[38]

According to my survey, fanchuan artists contributed greatly to this trend. A recent news broadcast (June 9, 2006) reported that the Redtop Arts' administrator, elder Tsai, encouraged his members to have plastic surgery.[39] Indeed, many Redtop Arts' members even became live advertisements for the plastic surgery clinic where they received their facelifts. While showing me the photos he took before his cosmetic surgery, the former Redtop female impersonator Shuqi said "I was once very fat (70 kg) but my face was still too thin to disguise as a beauty. I decided to have an abdominal lipectomy and transplant the lipid/fat into my cheek and chin. The results were quite satisfactory."[40]

To have more delicate skin, a small portion of fanchuan artists took female hormones that, in time, produced an effect on their sexual characteristics and their psychology. However, the practice of taking female hormones and receiving facelift should not be simply interpreted as a result of hostile competition in the fanchuan circle or abnormal conduct. As Butler remarks on the cultural construction of corporeal styles:

> The body is a material ground of cultural meanings both received and innovated. The choice to assume a certain kind of body, to live or wear one's body a certain way, implies a world of already established corporeal styles. To choose a gender is to interpret received gender norms in a way that reproduces and organizes them anew. Less a radical act of creation, gender is a tacit project to renew a cultural history in one's own corporeal terms.[41]

Viewed from this standpoint, the body-self of fanchuan artists must be seen as a canvas upon which he/she can express his/her feelings, thoughts, imagination, and experiences—a powerful articulation of body politics and body autonomy and an indirect challenge to the socially prescribed idea of gender. The ways fanchuan artists reinscribed or remodeled their bodies suggest that a sexed fe/male body (physical body), neither natural nor real, is an apparatus that reflects the social sex/gender system, as well as a particular state of mind in a specific time period. Thus fanchuan artists managed their flesh and blood, so to speak, to silently express, inscribe, and embody an unmentionable identity.

Makeup

Makeup and attire, imposed by various sociocultural systems, were perhaps the foremost signifiers of sex/gender norms. Well-delineated eyebrows, long dark-thick lashes, thick-vivid lips, and rouged cheeks were often considered to be the most important facial features of femininity.

Similar to the traditional male dan performance, making seductive eyes to woo the audience was an important acting technique.

Many fanchuan performers commented on its importance: "We cannot live without artificial eyelashes on stage." Songtian Wanzi agreed: "Artificial eyelashes are a great help for my eye expression."[42] For a better stage effect, many fanchuan artists made their own exaggerated long and thick eyelashes, which could be easily distinguished from ordinary sets for sale in the market. A-gui, a former Redtop member and now the troupe leader of the New Century, also emphasized the need for sexy lips: "We paint our lips filled out round and thick like a sexy cherry/apple which invites you to have a bite."[43] Ironically, the hyperfeminine makeup applied by male cross-dressing performers only reveals the ways by which men materialize women and fetishize them as objects of desire.

Attire

According to the medical psychologist John Money, "Since dressing is traditionally gender-coded almost everywhere on earth, cross dressing is one highly specific act of gender cross coding."[44] Fanchuan artists' attire was often designed to suit specific performance types and body shapes—various stylish wigs, customized stuffed-bras, and two to three pairs of pantyhose were the most fundamental. Wigs, often long, were decorated with shining pins: various types of updo or free hanging hair (curled or straight) fall around the shoulders or down to the waist. Their wigs (one often owns several sets) were often made out of real hair that could be cleaned and arranged into various styles.

The next important step was to hide what they called their "thing" (penis). They typically pulled their penises backwards between their thighs and then wore tight underpants. For some sexy animated skits, performers needed to wear bodysuit-like costumes; in such cases, the performers did not wear underpants but two to three pairs of pantyhose that were tight enough to hold their penises backwards. They then would put on customized stuffed-bras to create prominent breasts (not necessarily very large, depending on the type of skits they are going to play). Some performers wore foundation garments to shape their bodies prior to the suits/costumes tailored for individual fanchuan artists. For a fanchuan performer, the best costume designer was one that would make their bodies appear in "perfect" physical proportion: from an original ratio of 5:5 or 4:6 (upper torso: waist to heel; the general male figure) into the ideal 3:7. Other details, including polished nails, high heels, earrings, necklaces, bracelets, and dress gloves, were all essential symbols/icons that helped create an

Figure 9.1 Original appearance: bald, natural shape of eyebrows, single eyelid folds. Reprinted with permission from the artist and the author.

Figure 9.2 Clear foundation, dark eye shadow, well-delineated eyebrows, thick and dark lashes, double eyelid folds (painted), blush-color cheeks, and thick/vivid lips. Reprinted with permission from the artist and the author.

Figure 9.3 Concealed tattoo, underhose, and bra. Reprinted with permission from the artist and the author.

Figure 9.4 Wig (thick and healthy), necklace, earrings, pins, concealed tattoo. Reprinted with permission from the artist and the author.

Figure 9.5 Stage appearance: pantyhose, dress gloves, round hips, zipped-up bodysuit, and high-heeled boots to give the appearance of long, thin legs. Reprinted with permission from the artist and the author.

erotic female body. These visible and symbolic representations constructed by male cross-dressing performers not only reconstructed female identities, but also created a type of substitute form for male sexual desire. Finally, any scar, acne or tattoo, that may "ruin" the purity and flawlessness of "perfect" femininity, should be concealed. Figures 9.1 to 9.5 illustrate an example of the general process of male cross-dressing. Most fanchuan artists' disguise processes were slightly different from person to person. The model presented in this series of photo has neither taken female hormones nor undergone cosmetic surgery.

Body Movement (Gesture, Poses, and Actions)

Body movement was thought to be crucial to the success in "passing" as a real female character. Fanchuan performers' elegant flowing arms, graceful pelvic movements, and lovely tilted heads, all approximated the feminine, thereby enhancing the erotic fascination of their spectators. Dynamic body language was converted into sequential symbols that were essential signifiers to a display of meanings. In most cases, fanchuan artists embodied not a conventional/ordinary womanliness, but extreme femininities that were dramatized yet internalized within the cultural convention. Dr. Tsai remarked that the "refined" artistic representations of the female and the importance of feminine movements were essential to the success of a fanchuan artist:

> We don't take people who are overly feminine, for many of them carry their natural femininity into their stage performance. Yet, this "gifted" femininity very often becomes an obstacle to a further improved and refined femininity. Moreover, even when some candidates are very pretty after putting on make-up and a costume, if they do not have the talent to act and dance, they cannot transform into a real beauty on stage; they are merely dolls.[45]

For elder Tsai, a gay or an effeminate man did not necessarily possess an inherent talent in cross-dressing performance. Tsai made it clear that ultimate femininity was essentially illustrative (not inborn) and constantly replicable through conscious learning, training, and practicing.

Redtop members often learned about female body language from videotapes that documented female acting and dancing or through training with dance/modeling teachers. As mentioned earlier, many fanchuan artists were backup dancers for (female) singing stars or their own dance teachers before entering the cross-dressing profession. As such, these dancers were already well-versed in feminine gestures, poses, expressions, and behaviors. Ong Hongwen, the dance teacher and top star of Redtop, trained Redtop members how to walk elegantly with high heels day and night even during meals.[46] During Redtop shows, new members without stage performance experience would be kept in the backstage to practice makeup application and walking with high heels.

Voice

Voice was a means through which one could directly express feeling, meaning, and intention on stage. Developing a female voice was probably the most difficult skill for a male cross-dressing performer to acquire. One can easily imagine how difficult it is to train a 20-year-old male to sing/speak artistically in a stereotypical high-pitched female voice,[47] even if he was born with a high-register voice. Among the fanchuan artists I interviewed, Zhou Xiang, Angela, and Small Tsai Qin were the few who could speak and sing in female voices, and together with their fanchuan techniques, they could "pass" off as females with no obvious, detectable evidence otherwise. As I discussed earlier, Zhou was trained to sing the role of the male dan at a young age. This background made it easy for him to sing contemporary popular songs in high registers with specific soft intonations and articulation. His female singing technique made his female impersonation even more persuasive:

> On stage, Zhou Hongxuan (Zhou Xiang's stage name) wears *qipao* of the forties, curvaceously walking forward to sing the song called *Jiaodao* 郊道 [Outskirt route],[48] and the audience starts to become restless: somebody suspects that he is lip-synching. Nobody believes that a man could so skillfully impersonate a woman. Some doubt his male sexuality and suspect that he may be bisexual or a female who imitates fanchuan yiren. Later it is proven that 1) He is truly singing live; 2) He is a real man. However, if a man cross-dresses to be more beautiful than a real woman, and if his voice is also completely feminine, people will unavoidably put him under suspicion of being a renyao [human freak]. However, if we consider this suspicion seriously, then we may equally come to humiliate Mei Lanfang.[49]

Voice, as a noncorporeal signifier of the "nature" and "reality" of gender, remains a domain that external forces (including surgery) cannot easily intervene or alter. For many fanchuan artists and their audiences, voice was probably one of the most powerful elements of gender meaning and identity.[50]

The relationship between voice and power was also evident in fanchuan artists' cross-dressing performance, especially if the right to speak represents an exercise of power. Except for a few "gifted" or well-trained fanchuan artists who were able to speak and sing in female voice, the majority of them relied exclusively on recorded music and lip-synchs. In Redtop's early policy, their members were not allowed to speak in public whenever they appeared with makeup and female dress, whether on stage, the media, or television programs. This intentional "speechless policy" bolstered Redtop artists' concealment of their true identity in public interviews or talk shows, including their names, personal background, and sexual identities.

Here, a cursory comparison can be made between fanchuan artists and women with respect to the gendered dimension of the right to speak. Women, traditionally treated as second-class citizens in almost all societies, were often deprived of speech rights in the public sphere. An important way for men to consolidate their power over women historically has been to keep women silent. Redtop's early speechless policy exemplifies a similar situation in which the appropriation of the feminine role meant the adoption of a silent role.

More recently, the New Century Cross-Dressing Beauty Show designed a new skit in which a performer expressed femininity at first and later proceeded to talk in a low voice with male-identified manners as to reproclaim his "original" sex and "normality." By doing so, the performer aimed to bring audiences back to "reality," thereby reminding them of gender dualism. Intentional or not, the "sex change" of the performer's voice in these skits implies that in a patriarchal society, a feminine voice can only exist as a fantasy; marginal voices are silenced and erased; and only (heterosexual) male voices are legitimate. Even when fanchuan artists later became frequent guests on television talk shows and were allowed to talk in their original male voice in public, they were still often presented in a rigid binary frame: linkman versus disclosers; mainstream versus marginal groups; and heteronormative subjects versus homosexuals/sexual deviants. For Redtop members in particular, even in light of the transition in their policy to allow their female impersonators to talk on TV programs, their personal stories were almost always crafted for the purpose of maintaining the troupe's positive reputation.

The significance of fanchuan artists' speechless policy is twofold: it consolidates the orthodoxy of binary gender classification—disallowing any discrepancy between voice and appearance; and it reveals the symbolic violence of heterosexual hegemony—muffling other "noise" from disadvantaged gender minorities. The suppression of the Otherness is not limited within performance associated areas; it extends to fanchuan artists' offstage life, which I discuss below.

IV. Offstage Life: Revealing Gender Identity and Confronting Heteronormativity

Behind the Mask
Humans and animals are alike,
When dealing with different environments,
both have their own protective sheath.

> Behind the magnificent smile, there is a true feeling buried deeply in the heart.
> This secret is so deep down that it is beyond anyone's reach,
> Except for during a serene night, like a wound that is torn,
> the bleeding cannot be staunched,
> but blood constantly effuses from the body.
> It is a kind of pain that no one can understand,
> This has already become his habit.
> Such are the helplessness and sadness behind the mask.
>
> Romansa[51]

What is his secret? Why can he not reveal it? Why does this secret cause pain? What is behind the mask/masquerade? Is it yet another mask? The psychological dimension of a fanchuan artist was often hidden: it was a world that they prevented outsiders from entering. Romansa, one of my major informants, originally told me that he was heterosexual and "maybe" bisexual. He initially reacted to my survey question about sexual identity by insisting that to label him homosexual would be to humiliate him. But as we got to know each other better over time, he was able to open himself up to me and to see me more and more as a friend. When our relationship was no longer structured around the confrontational pattern of a social scientific oral interview, he willingly revealed his true sexual orientation and shared his love stories with me.[52] Beginning with Romansa's struggle with his sexual orientation, this section of the chapter will focus on the relationship of fanchuan artists to homosexuality, sexual politics, psychological constituents, and the "phantom kinship system" in Taiwan.

Fanchuan Artists and Homosexuality

In the mass media, fanchuan artists were often portrayed as no different from other "ordinary" (straight) men who had girlfriends and got married. To "prove" that they were "normal" and "healthy," many cross-dressing actors publically claimed that they were married and had children. Reporting on the correlation between homosexuality, male cross-dressing performers, and third-sex publicists, Hong Bitang, the governmental officer of social affairs, said:

> Recruits of *fanchuan* artists have to submit physical examination reports to prove that they are healthy men...According to some academic research, only 1% or 2% of male cross-dressing performers are homosexuals.[53]

According to my informants, however, no such "required physical examination report" ever existed, and the majority of fanchuan artists in fact self-identified as gay. To my question on sexual identity, my interviewees' replies included: "Out of one hundred fanchuan artists, one hundred and one are gay!" "Men who do *fanchuan* are all gay." "The majority are gay." "In my fifteen years of cross-dressing performance life, all *fanchuan* artists I know are gay."[54] Romansa's early reaction to my previous interviews may provide a clue to why Hong's research results turned out the way they did.[55]

In the world of theatrical performance, subjectivity is continuously transforming and altering along the lines of fluid and changing masquerades. The stage is where the unusual and the unreal become normal and realized, being a "safe" retreat for all types of heterodox performance. It is where cross-dressing performers can legitimately transgress the boundaries of gender and sexuality. My observations of fanchuan artists reveal that it is only through the repetition of stage performance and in the guise of being a heterosexual man that an inner "she" can reach the public through the stylized embodiment of a series of constructed female images on stage. In cross-dressing performances, gender reinvention and reproduction challenge conventional assumptions about the relationship between sex and gender, on the one hand, and represent a moment of artistic articulation by a predominantly homosexual population within the institutional confinements of a heteronormative culture on the other. In other words, given that some of the artists do not self-identify as a complete "inner she," the fanchuan stage becomes a venue for gay men to express gender fluidity and unsettle social norms of gender.

Contrary to the theatrical stage, the homosexual's private life in the real world was often considered a secret story hidden in the shadow of society. Male cross-dressing performers lived in "double marginality": to the wider public, they were freaks, outcasts, or troubled individuals with weird fetishes; in the gay community, their decision to act out their overt femininity was often looked down upon. As Small Caiqin points out:

> Within the gay community, we fanchuan artists are totally rejected. They think we are hypocritical [referring to their denial of being homosexuals in the media]. If they know you are a Redtop member, they won't further develop love or companionship with you, but merely friendship...What it means to be "homosexual" is that we are attracted to people of the same sex. It is only in relationships that are founded on deep love that we can survive these conditions.[56]

To avoid being rejected or ignored, fanchuan artists usually would not reveal their occupation upon meeting other gay men. According to another informant, Yalan, fanchuan artists stood no chance in getting involved in a romantic relationship with other gay men. He recalled that his former lover became angry after seeing his performance and asked him to take off his costume and makeup immediately after the performance. Being fully aware that cross-dressing was Yalan's job, his former lover still felt uneasy and even ashamed of dating someone who acted out femininity so overtly. This reveals the extent to which effeminophobia and transphobia, especially as directed against male cross-dressing performers, existed in the Taiwanese gay community in the 1990s, despite the various kinds of antisexual oppression and antigender discrimination social movements that came before.

Fanchuan Artists and the Politics of Sexuality

Sexual orientation and identification of fanchuan artists played an important role in cross-dressing performativity, as reflected in the power distribution within their community (table 9.2). Here, I will carefully investigate various sexual identifications of fanchuan artists and bring to light their diversity. Based on my survey of fanchuan artists, I have devised the following classification scheme of the possible sexual orientations with which they might identify:[57]

The five types of sexual identity listed below have all come up in our conversations over the course of my field work. But, in the fanchuan community, the "standard gay" and the "effeminate gay" were the most pervasive types of sexual orientation. These two types consisted of different levels of female inclination in terms of sexual orientation, self-recognition, appearance, and manner.[58] The effeminate gay included those who were clearly feminine, were sexually submissive, or identified themselves as females with no intention to undergo sex reassignment surgery.[59] For example, apart from Sun Hongyi, who I mentioned above, there was one other interviewee who also insisted on covering his breasts with a Turkish towel backstage.[60] The "masculine gay" type and straight men were rarely seen in the community. If the effeminate gay was the most common gender orientation in the fanchuan circle, the transsexual type (including preoperative and postoperative transsexual) was the major gender type in third-sex nightclubs.

Table 9.2 A feasible typology of male cross-dressing performers' sexual orientation

Type	Original Chinese character	Roman script transliteration	Literal English translation	Colloquial English translation	Percentage[1]
Masculine Gay	一號	yi hao	Number 1	Dominant sexual role	Perhaps do not exist in the male cross-dressing community
Standard Gay	標準的同志 ("雙修"／可一可零)	biaozhun de tongzhi/shuang xiu—kie yi kie ling)	Standard gay/double major (can be either number 1 or number 0)	Either sexually dominant or submissive	Approximately 20% of the community[2]
Effeminate Gay	零號/娘娘腔	ling hao/ niangniang qiang	Number 0/girlish speech	Submissive sexual role/ effeminate man	Approximately 80% of the community[3]
Transsexuals	變性人	bianxing ren	Transsexuals	Transsexuals	Few in the community
Straight Men	異性戀	yixing lian	Heterosexuals	Heterosexuals	Rarely exist in the community

[1] Percentage measured here is based on the information provided by A-gui, the former member of Redtop troupe and currently the troupe leader of New Century Cross-Dressing Show. Most of the performers I interviewed (20 people) tended to agree with this assertion.

[2] In the "standard gay" type, to be sexually dominant or submissive is flexible depending on the particular sexual situation/position with which he feels more comfortable. In other words, if his counterpart is stronger or more masculine, then he will be the submissive and vice versa. Among Taiwan's gay community this type is called "double major" (here I call it Standard Gay Type) to distinguish it from the "masculine gay" type (gays who prefer to be in the dominant sexual role) and "effeminate gay" type (gays who prefer to be sexually submissive).

[3] In the gay community, effeminate gays are rejected and some even think they should not be included in the community.

The above categorization should not be considered rigid or static. Rather it existed in a fluid and changeable gender/sexual spectrum. Within one single type of standard gay and effeminate gay, there existed nuances and gender variances. The data I collected also show that a man may switch from one type to the other. For example, Yilian regarded herself as a female since childhood, but later changed his mind and appearance in his twenties—the situation I mark as "Id w/F → gay" in table 9.1, under the category "Gender/Sexual ID." Yilian's life story well exemplifies the fluidity of psychological gender:

> The reason that I changed is for the sake of love. Before, when I was totally like a girl, my boyfriends were mostly heterosexuals. However, they truly loved "real" girls, so my love affairs were all very short. Gradually, I have realized that what I really want is the feeling of a "man-and-man together," rather than a "man-and-woman relationship." This is the real gay's state of mind. Hence, the first step is to change my appearance, because a gay won't want to love someone who has a feminine look. If so, he would rather choose a real woman.[61]

Interestingly, male cross-dressing performers' sexual orientation and identification played an important role in the power distribution within their community. There seemed to be a tendency for those who self-identified as the standard gay to be in charge of administrative work and prioritized as the more important members of the community, while the effeminate gays were more frequently followers and played supporting roles. Redtop Arts members selected to represent the group in the media in their male appearance were often those who self-identified as standard gay. These were performers who did not display an overly effeminate mannerism in public, but instead could present a "healthy," manly image that conformed to gender dualism and heteronormativity. The effeminate gays, however, were usually asked to appear in the media solely in their female impersonation attire.

The uneven distribution of power makes it evident that male cross-dressing was a process at once empowering and disempowering. Following the Lacanian psychoanalytic notion of sex, we may read male cross-dressing performers' assuming of the feminine sex (at least onstage) as a practice of "symbolic castration."[62] The finding that most of fanchuan artists were homosexuals and willing to "self-castrate" might allow us to unsettle, or at least provoke anxiety about, heterosexist patriarchy. However, Redtop members' claiming to cross-dress as a profession (not as sexual inclination or practice) and initial denial to any link to homosexual behavior (making alliances with heterosexual hegemony) somehow constituted a safeguard against social condemnation and escape from contempt for their symbolic castration. Knowing the true meaning of their false public declarations, we come to understand why male cross-dressing was only allowed on stage. If a fanchuan artist claimed himself to be a "sissy," always bearing the stigma of symbolic castration, he would never be able to gain power through cross-dressing performance. His play then becomes no different from a female masquerade.

Recall that to the Tsai brothers, fanchuan artists who psychologically identified as females have relatively less potential to improve their female impersonation techniques. This presumption of gendered performance ability reinforces the idea that fanchuan performers are not representing an original female; inborn femininity is not the prime essence of their aesthetic concern. A-gui (the "standard type"), the third generation of Redtop and a frontline star, still maintained this presumption when he was recruiting for his own troupe:

> There was a mother who brought her son to me. She asked me if I could train her son to be a performer for this reason: "People who love to perform won't become degenerates." I then examined the young man and felt that he was not suitable for this profession. I was told that he liked to wear female dresses on the street in daily life. This kind of mindset is not right because performance is different from having the psyche of being a female. If he is an *ordinary boy* with a delicate and pretty figure, then he will advance greatly in performance. If he loves to be the female part and has done it since he was young, then no.[63]

Not surprisingly, cross-dressing performers' psychological state and sexual politics directly reflected their appearance. One obvious example of this gender embodiment was hair treatment—another gender signifier. While many fanchuan artists of the standard gay type refused to trim their eyebrows and armpit hair to maintain their manly appearance, those of the effeminate gay type preferred to have thin, trimmed eyebrows, and some of them kept growing their hair long to enhance their feminine appearance. Manning, who identified as a female and sexually subdominant in the gay community, described his position in the troupe as follows:

> I was assigned to make my public appearance on the third day of entering Redtop due to my previous cross-dressing performing experience. However, I played a servant girl in the beginning and had remained at the same rank through the end [of the Redtop]. Leading roles require tall man, so that they can be more visible to the audience. I am much sought after for third-sex cabaret, but not on the stage. Dr. Tsai likes

manly types who can make great contrast after putting on make-up: a manly man transforms himself into a charming and gorgeous woman. When confronted with decision/policy making, we need someone who is stronger and can stand out and speak for us. If I were in charge of this, I would panic when someone tries to exploit us.[64]

Within the all-male cross-dressing community, there existed a profound hierarchy of power relations and manipulation. A-gui's use of term "ordinary boy" in his talk to distinguish himself (standard gay type) from the "feminine gay type" exemplifies this idea. This distinction of power reinforced a form of gender hierarchy that is surprisingly similar to the social relations of gender in a heteronormative society. Does this, as a nearly identical phenomenon, tell us about the very nature of power relations and people's instinctive need for it? It at least suggests that the Tsai brothers' presumptions and politics exemplify how a heterosexual hegemony and prejudice are maintained, penetrate, and affect even those who are doubly marginalized.

Psychological Constituents

What kind of psychological process does a male cross-dresser experience in transforming from a "he" (offstage primary gender) to a "she" (onstage secondary gender)? Fanchuan performances entailed a host of repeated gender codes and conventions and deeply rooted psychological activities. Most fanchuan performers agreed that, perhaps due to their homosexual inclinations, they were more sensitive than straight men. Besides their "gay nature," all of them agreed that stage acting more-or-less had affected their movements and attitudes in daily life, even on a psychological level. Clearly, gender was not an article of clothing that could be put on or taken off at volitional will.[65]

Following the previous categorization of fanchuan artists' sexual identifications and based on Butler's concept of gender performativity, I would suggest that the innate psychological processes of fanchuan artists' cross-dressing could be generally divided into two types. For the "standard gay" type and "straight men" type, they could "enter" their assigned secondary (or stage) sex from the symbolic domain through the self-imaginary process of being a woman (or "castration" on a psychological level). For them, cross-dressing is "doing" (which is distinguished from "being"), as a kind of performance, and requires certain psychological adjustments. Shen Honglong, who belonged to the standard gay type, admitted that it was difficult for him to play female roles when he was a Redtop dancer. He recalled that the first time Tsai Tou invited him to impersonate the Qing Empress Dowager Cixi, Tsai teased him:

"you look like a T!"⁶⁶ "The toughest part," Shen conceded, "was not to imitate the feminine look, but to capture the inner spirit of women. It's difficult to express innate femininity."⁶⁷ A-gui, also the standard gay type, described his psychological "switch" as linked to the attire:

> After I complete my fanchuan process, there reside two characters within me. After putting on make-up, I still cannot enter the female character. We still talk loudly with our legs wide open and smoke like men. Only at the point when I put on my costume and high heels do I feel that I have transformed into an elegant lady.⁶⁸

However, not every male cross-dressing performer had this sense of transgender identity. The second type of psychological process is associated with the effeminate gay type of cross-dressing performers. Many of them stressed that they were not "doing" (or acting) the female role, but that they "were" truly female. Only on the public stage could they enjoy "being" themselves or expressing another side of their inner selves, however temporarily. After the performance, they would have to put on the clothes that are deemed more "socially acceptable" to their biological sex again. When asked "During what stage in the process of your female construction do you feel that you are switching into a female role?" Manning responded:

> I have difficulty answering this question. It is because I always consider myself female. Since I was little, I have been a girl [psychologically] both onstage and offstage. I'm always a sissy, feminine, and my eyes are watery and shining—I *am* a woman inside out.⁶⁹

Many male cross-dressing performers did not consider themselves as imitating females or specific female characters. How they looked onstage was actually closer to who they were than their offstage appearance. As Tianli put it, "When I'm performing, I feel I'm presenting myself. I'm not a 'wannabe' trying to imitate anyone; instead I am only expressing that inner part of me."⁷⁰

The Phantom Kinship System

For most fanchuan artists, family was the first social institution with which they must battle. Family is understood here as a microcosm paralleling the macrocosm of Chinese society and state, as an embodiment of the kinship system. To persuade their family to accept their cross-dressing profession was already a difficult task, let alone if the fanchuan performers had an atypical gender orientation. Some of the effeminate gay types had clear memories of their childhood, during which if they revealed their unconventional gender inclination, most of them were forced to erase or "stamp out" their nonnormative behaviors and thought. Tianli recalled:

> I have two sisters: one is a T and the other is normal.[71] I remember that when my parents took us to a toy shop, I picked up a Barbie doll and my T sister took a super robot. I did not have second thoughts about this, but my parents told me it was abnormal. I grew up in a traditional family, within which I seldom talked about myself, especially to my father. Later, my parents got divorced. Perhaps because of this event my mother was more willing to listen and communicate with us. Over time, I gradually revealed and explained my sexual identification and my profession to her. She understood, but still could not completely accept this situation. She even tried to push me into marriage: "you are quite old already; you should get married. I've prepared three hundred thousand dollars for you to get a bride,[72] so that you can fulfill your duties to our ancestors."[73]

Some fanchuan artists did not have the courage to let their parents know about their real occupation. Yalan— the only son of his family—felt anxious about revealing his occupation and gender orientation to his father (a retired soldier), who always got annoyed and cursed whenever he saw male cross-dressing performance or reports of it on television. Yalan figured out his true gender orientation when he was transferred to a high school in Taipei. At a gay bar, he unexpectedly learned that a man could turn into a beautiful woman and attract the male gaze: "When I see the male audience gaze expressing 'you are so beautiful,' this fulfills the part of me that is unfulfilled...I am satisfied." He secretly started his cross-dressing career by joining the New Century Cross-dressing Beauty Show. He then carefully thought through his situation and the way to justify it to his parents:

> Before, there were many television programs that interviewed cross-dressing performers. I hid myself and avoided talking. I was afraid that my family would recognize me. Now I've prepared what to say if my parents find out: 1) in the past, female roles were performed by men in the theatre; 2) I'm not stealing or robbing; 3) I'm born to be a homosexual, and you are the person who gave me the personality and sexual/gender inclination—If I do not complain to you, how can you blame me for this? 4) Every month I send money home; I contribute to my family the most; 5) If you tell me you are afraid of neighbors recognizing your son as a cross-dressing performer, I'm even more

afraid than you to let others know about my job; 6) What's wrong with male cross-dressing performance? I'm merely performing it. I don't behave the same way offstage. I'm still healthy; my thing [penis] is still there; 7) Do you know the mercy Buddha whom you pray to everyday, is originally a male? Do you think that he is actually a female? No! He is also doing the same thing that I'm doing now—playing the female role [transforming into a female image]!⁷⁴

This passage speaks for many fanchuan performers. Regarding the earlier story of a mother bringing her son to learn cross-dressing performance, A-gui went on to say:

If the mother knows that male cross-dressing performers are all homosexuals, she won't ask me to train her son. I even heard parents who said, "If my son does this type of occupation, I'll kill him." Until now, my mother only knows that I'm a fanchuan yiren, but doesn't know that I'm gay. I have known my sexual orientation since I was in kindergarten. It's my fate; it is not Redtop that made me gay.⁷⁵

The former Redtop Arts' member Yilian made a simple but clear assertion about why a heterosexual man cannot take up the male cross-dressing profession:

Men who can become fanchuan yiren are gay with almost no exceptions. There should be no ordinary [heterosexual] men within this circle. We gays are free. Ordinary men need women and need to have kids. They have a traditional path to follow. It's impossible for them to take up the profession. Even for economic need, it could not possibly last long. In those years [ten years ago], the family of his girlfriend or wife would not be happy to see him in such an occupation.⁷⁶

It is true that in modern Taiwan, family is still considered to be the most important building block of society. Single mature men and women are usually under great pressure to form their own families. In fact, this is the most difficult social norm that most homosexuals continue to face.

While most of fanchuan artists expressed in confidence that they would never marry (a woman), there were still a few who may submit to the socially established practice and their family's expectations. There was one performer who indicated that in a couple of years, if his parents were still alive, he may consider getting married to make them happy. The male-to-female transsexual Linda also mentioned that if her parents were still alive, she would not have undergone SRS. This unbearable "family phantom" hovering over the transgender (including fanchuan) community was found in another unusual example. The postoperative transsexual Jinmei was a former fanchuan artist of the Paradise Bird Troupe, a former third-sex barmaid, and now a married woman.[77] Since her parents did not agree with her sexual identification and plans for surgery, she had to find a quick way to earn money—to be financially independent and to be able to fulfill her dream. After she completed her SRS at 20, her parents silently accepted her sexual identity.[78] However, marrying into another family meant to walk away from one type of pressure to another: her mother-in-law suspected her original sex and questioned her about her menstruation cycles. Under the pressure of her mother-in-law, Jinmei was forced to make notes to track her ovulation period.[79] Ironically, the mother-in-law, who was once the oppressed object in a traditional Taiwanese family when she was young, here holds a phallic scepter to assume the (pseudo) power of patriarchy and enforces sexual oppression upon her daughter-in-law (a "pseudo woman"). Jinmei's lack of menstrual blood, which has long been a symbol of "filth" and "odor" in traditional patriarchal society, facilitated her mother-in-law's sexual oppression.[80] Under the converging attacks of patriarchy and hierarchically-structured family politics, the transsexual occupies a social status that falls well below an ordinary woman.

V. Conclusion

Through personal profile documentation, and backstage and offstage observations, this chapter has explored the reasons why some men take up cross-dressing performance as a profession and the ways in which fanchuan artists construct their bodies and minds that enable their onstage female images and identities. My ethnographic data show that economic need, wider fame, psychological fulfillment, and personal interest are the major factors that motivated some men to pursue cross-dressing performance as a serious profession. Fanchuan artists' complex process of gender transformation is a sociocultural, physical, psychological, and power struggle. Their backstage preparations illustrate the performativity and the constructedness of gender and, by extension, the fluidity of gender identities. Their offstage lives further embody the battleground between government authorities, the mass media, and the performers' "real-life" experiences with gender ambiguity and issues of homosexuality. Fanchuan artists' life stories reveal that compulsory heterosexuality is produced by the kinship system (a historical social mechanism), which consists of particular sex/gender norms.[81] To insure marriage and offspring (patriarchal modes of reproduction), every member in society is further engendered and forced to behave heterosexually. In late twentieth-century Taiwan, women and sexual minorities were manipulated by similar sources of sexual oppression for the purposes of reifying certain social mechanisms.

Notes

1. See Siu Leung Li, *Cross-Dressing in Chinese Opera* (Hong Kong: Hong Kong University Press, 2003).
2. Before the establishment of Redtop Arts, there had been some individual professional male cross-dressers performing in Taiwanese show business.
3. Chang Ai-Zhu, "Xingbie fanchuan, yizhi kongjian yu hozhimin bianzhuang huangho de wenhua xianji" (Gender cross-dressing, heterotopias and the cultural want-to-be-ness of postcolonial drag queens), *Zhongwai wenxue* [Chinese and foreign literature] 29, no. 7 (December 2000): 139–157; Lin Yu-ling, "Jiedu Taiwan zongyi jiemu fanchuanxiu de xingbie wenhua" (Decode the gender culture in fanchuanxiu in television programs), in *Kua xingbie* [Transgender], ed. He Chunrui (Taipei: National Taiwan Central University, 2003), 173–220; Tsai Shih-tsong, *Hongding yiren* [Redtop Artists] (Taipei: Redtop Culture, 2000); Tseng Yung-I, "Nanban nüzhuang yu nüban nanzhuang" (Female and male impersonation), in *Shuo xiqu* [On Chinese music drama] (Taipei: Lianjing Chubanshe, 1983), 31–47; Yen Yu-Feng, "Dianshi tanhuaxing zongyi jiemu yu xingbie fanchuan zaixian" (An analysis of transvestites on TV talk shows) (MA Thesis, Tamkang University, 2001).
4. In fanchuanxiu, the female roles are far more important than the male roles. This chapter only focuses on the study of male cross-dressing performers.
5. Judith Butler, *Gender Trouble: Feminism and the Subversion of Identity* (New York: Routledge, 1990), 139.
6. A fourth line of inquiry is about the performers' interaction with audiences is discussed in another chapter in my dissertation. See Chao-Jung Wu, "Performing Postmodern Taiwan: Gender, Cultural Hybridity, and the Male Cross-Dressing Show" (PhD Dissertation, Wesleyan University, 2007).
7. Information taken from Black Pearls's autobiography, which was transcribed by Huang Huo from an oral account. See Huang Huo, *Fanchuan yiren Hei Zhenzhu* [The male cross-dressing performer Black Pearl] (Taipei: Haujiao, 1998), 154, 174. "Soul-guiding operas" refers to a ceremonial performance by a professional troupe that takes place at a funeral. It usually consists of a "red-helmeted" master/

director and three female chanters. There is a troupe/ceremony called *wunü-kumu* (五女哭墓) [Five daughters crying in front of the tomb], performed by women or male cross-dressing performers.
8. Huang, *Fanchuan yiren*.
9. When the Nationalist Party and army lost the civil war and fled to Taiwan in 1949, military men and their dependents built up their home villages and communities throughout the island.
10. His family runs a *teppanyaki* restaurant. Manning reported to me that he does not like to smell the cooking oil and smoke, but prefers to dress up and put on makeup as a lady to perform. This job simply is less toilsome compared to restaurant work.
11. In gay circles in Taiwan, a person who has a male body but with a female soul is not considered gay. However, here I simply follow my interviewees' self-declaration/identification.
12. In Taiwan, some restaurant owners and constructors may invite television or movie stars to give a show of singing and dancing to enhance their business.
13. Workers of architectural shuttering include those who are "a building worker," "builder," or "a construction laborer." Among cross-dressing performers I interviewed, there was one who once worked as a construction laborer. He told me that "cross-dressing performance is an easier job" for him.
14. A county located in mid-southern Taiwan.
15. A city located in mid-Taiwan.
16. Hong Bitang (洪碧堂), "Tongxinglian zhe, nanban nüzhuan fanchuan zhe, disanxing gongguan—xiangguan wenti de tantao" (同性戀者、男扮女裝反串者、第三性公關─相關問題的探討) [Homosexuals, male cross-dressing performers, and third-sex publicists—a discussion of relevant issues], *Shehui fuli* (社會福利) [Social welfare] 136, no. 6 (1998): 58–69, on 67.
17. An online discussion/chat about a fanchuan beauty contest held in a nightclub in 2005 Taipei. See http://club1069.topfong.com/board/replay.php?id=170169 (accessed January 20, 2006).
18. More information will be discussed in the later subsection "Offstage Life: Revealing Gender Identity and Confronting Heteronormativity."
19. Luo Ching-Yao, "Wenhua zhuanzhe zhong de kuer yuejie: jiuling niandai Taiwan tongzhi lunshu, shen/ti zhenzhi ji wenhua shijian (1990–2002)" (Queering across the border at the crossroads: The queer discourse, body/voice politics and cultural practices in Taiwan, 1900–2002) (MA thesis, National Chiao Tung University, 2005), 109.
20. A few actors, on account of their outstanding appearance (suitable for cross-dressing), had their performance training after entering the troupe.
21. Personal interview on June 17, 2005.
22. Wang Er (王鄂), "Nanren huali bianshen meinü fenmuo dengchang Taiwan fanchuanxiu yangming guandao" (男人華麗變身 美女粉墨登場 台灣反串秀陽明關島), *TVBS Weekly* 49 (10–16 October 1998):

91. Song was known in his former acting career for his role as police officer. He learned dance from Tsai Tou, who persuaded him to be pursue fanchuan yiren.
23. Sun comes from an elite family, as his father and brothers are medical doctors. Sun is multi talented—he was once a successful interior designer. Information about Sun is from an interview with fanchuan yiren Ong Hongwen and A-gui.
24. This is an extreme example, but not rare to find among fanchuan yiren. Sun's Redtop colleague A-gui recalled: "Sun was unhappy about his hairy legs. He disliked and was angry about his man thing (penis). Backstage, most of us walked around with only underpants. Sun did not. He felt that he was a woman" (personal interview on January 12, 2006). Upon the end of my fieldwork, (to my knowledge) there were four namable fanchuan yiren who had completed SRS.
25. There is an overlapping area between the definitions of transsexual (TS), transgender (TG), cross-dresser (CD), and fanchuan yiren. In practice, sometimes the distinction is blurry. For example, there are some TS who refuse to have SRS and some CD who take female hormones. Therefore, self-identification among fanchuan circles varies. I will discuss these distinctions later in the section on " Offstage Life."
26. Charlotte Suthrell, *Unzipping Gender: Sex, Cross-Dressing and Culture* (New York: Berg, 2004), 4.
27. Quoted from his 2006 stage production *Drag Queen*.
28. Personal interview on April 6, 2006.
29. When he was in elementary school, he joined the Peking opera community and learned to play the role of *xiaosheng* 小生 [Civilized young man]. At his graduation ceremony from elementary school, a girl who played the role of mature lady was unable to perform. The instructor assigned Zhou the female role to replace her.
30. Zhou's interest is not limited to Peking opera. He is also familiar with female singing/acting techniques of other local Chinese theatres, including *chuanju* 川劇, *kun-qu* 昆曲, *huangmeidiao* 黃梅調, *yueju* 越劇, and *gezaixi*. He performed male dan on Taiwan's TV programs and abroad by the invitation of Ministry of Foreign Affairs, Ministry of Education, Government Information Office, and Council for Cultural Affairs Taiwan. Besides his academic training from the Chinese Theatre Department of Chinese Culture University, Zhou plays several traditional Chinese instruments such as the *qin* [the 7-stringed Chinese zither], *zheng* [the 21-stringed Chinese zither] and *pipa* [the 4-stringed Chinese lute].
31. Personal interview on April 7, 2005.
32. Personal interview on May 13, 2006.
33. Judith Shapiro, "Transsexualism: Reflections on the Persistence of Gender and the Mutability of sex," in *Body Guards*, ed. Julia Epstein and Kristina Straub (New York: Routledge, 1991), 248–279, on 248.

34. Lin Yulin, "Jiedu Taiwan," 250.
35. Kimberly J. Devlin's article "Pretending in 'Penelope': Masquerade, Mimicry, and Molly Bloom" has a major impact on the following section. My lists of signifiers are mostly inspired by her analysis on Molly Bloom's femininities: appellative, verbal, sartorial, proprietorial, and gestural. Kimberly Devlin, "Pretending in 'Penelop': Masquerade, Mimicry, and Molly Bloom," *A Forum on Fiction* 25, no. 1 (Autumn 1991): 71–89, on 72.
36. Too much facial hair will make it difficult to put on makeup.
37. Former Redtop members Ong, Shuqi and Manning reported to me that there are about 5 out of 10 members who had double eyelid fold surgery.
38. See http://www.dr-tsao.com.tw/04-20.htm (accessed July 18, 2006).
39. See http://www.bg1.com.tw/news_content.asp?id=26 (accessed July 18, 2006).
40. Personal interview on November 11, 2005.
41. Butler, *Gender Trouble*, 131.
42. Personal interview on May 13, 2006.
43. Personal interview on October 16, 2005.
44. John Money, *Gay, Straight, and In-Between: The Sexology of Erotic Orientation* (New York: Oxford University Press, 1988), 102.
45. Phone interview on July 23, 2005.
46. He had taken lessons from female model at a professional training institute.
47. Female impersonators in Peking opera performance usually started their training at a very young age.
48. A popular song of the 1940s in Taiwan.
49. Zheng Zhijie, "Bi nüren geng nüren de nanren" (A man more feminine than a woman), *China Times Weekly* (11–17 June 1995): 14–22, on 17.
50. I was surprised to hear fanchuan artists talking with feminine intonation and articulation in backstage. This seems to indicate that they are into their female roles even backstage. But outside of the performance area, I seldom observe this phenomenon.
51. Romansa's poem put in his own website named *Huali de maoxian* 華麗的冒險 [Splendid adventure]: http://spaces.msn.com/lica732188/PersonalSpace.aspx?_c11_BlogPart_blogpart=myspace&_c=BlogPart&_c02_owner=1 (accessed February 20, 2006).
52. I attended his performances, took photos, and gave him my feedback. At the time of having interview with Romansa, he was a college student. As a university lecturer, I gave him advice on his college career. Through in-person contact and frequent e-mail exchange, I gradually developed our friendship and his trust in me.
53. Hong Bitang, "Tongxinglian zhe, nanban nüzhuan fanchuan zhe, disanxing gongguan—xiangguan wenti de tantao" (Homosexuals, male cross-dressing performers, third-sex publicist—a discussion

on relevant issues), *Shehui fuli* [Social welfare] 136, no. 6 (1998): 58–69, on 67. Hong's assertion has been accepted by other scholars without question.

54. During my interview, I tried to urge my interviewees to recall if any fanchuan yiren they know are heterosexual, and there was only one interviewee who could provide me a specific name. Upon the end of my fieldwork, there are only three namable fanchuan yiren who are married (to females), and among them only one is still involved in cross-dressing performance. However, some interviewees reminded me that even if you see one or two fanchuan yiren get married, it does not mean they are heterosexual. They may do it just to fulfill the expectations of their family and society—for the purpose of having a son to carry on the family name.

55. According to some of my interviewees, they have ill feelings toward interviewers from the media as well as academia for their stigmatizing and aggressive tactics of representation and depriving fanchuan artists of their dignity and privacy.

56. Personal interview on August 23, 2005.

57. On the survey form, I also give free space to my interviewees for the possibility of refusing to identify themselves with any type (deidentify). Except one, all of them consciously gave me clear answers on their gender/sexual identification.

58. As the Redtop Arts' deputy-leader Shen Honglong points out: "as a *fanchuan yiren*, if he does not have certain level of female identification, and only 'auto-hypnotizes' to be a woman, then his performance won't be successful." However, these fanchuan yiren are asked to show a "male disposition," when facing the media.

59. A large portion of this group had thought about having SRS, but most of them gave up because of difficult circumstances and various considerations, such as family, cost, older age, and post SRS syndrome.

60. Due to his gender identification, he had a painful experience during compulsory army duty. He told me that up to now, he still could not take off his towel in front of other men, or take a shower or sauna with other men like other gays love to do.

61. Interviewed on February 20, 2006. Similar to Yilian's personal experience, Shuqi also switched from the "effeminate type" to "the standard type" (both psychologically and physically) for the same reason of being a "real gay" in order to gain "true love" in the gay community. They grew up in families that did not condemn their "feminine games" during their childhood. Out of curiosity and for economic reasons, they were once third-sex barmaids in high school. Both Shuqi and Yilian described their previous appearance as "a beautiful woman without breast": slim with long hair, thin eyebrow, makeup, skirt, and high heels. Shuqi even took female hormone to have better feminine look. When the general business of third-sex bars and fanchuan show turned down, both Shuqi and

Yilian started to reconsider their profession and life styles. They turned for other jobs and later figured out that they would like to have the "man-man" relationship rather than "woman-man" type with their lover. They started to adjust their mind, gain fat, have butch haircuts, and not trim their eyebrows. Shuqi even went to have swimming lesson to gain some muscle. But he told me that perhaps because of the female hormones he took when he was young, his breasts are still soft now. Luckily, Shuqi's family knew his sexual orientation and did not blame him for it. Yilian still keeps this secret from his family.
62. Jacques Lacan, *Écrits*, trans. Alan Sheridan (London: Routledge, 1977), 1–7.
63. Personal interview on June 5, 2005, emphasis added.
64. Personal interview on February 7, 2006. The "manly type" Manning mentions here again refers to both outlook and behavior conforming to the gender dualistic norm. But one should not ignore the fact that several performers who are hyper-effeminate or even TS also have excellent performance skills. Many of them do not agree that their sexual identification would impede their professional success.
65. This therefore corroborates Butler's argument that gender is performative and not a performance.
66. "T" stands for tomboy, referring to masculine lesbian. Personal interview on June 10, 2005.
67. Personal interview on June 10, 2005.
68. Personal interview on September 14, 2005.
69. Personal interview on September 29, 2005.
70. Personal interview on September 29, 2005.
71. He uses the term "normal" to refer to heterosexual without a second thought.
72. Here his mother means to "buy" a woman from a Southeast Asian country. This kind of "trade bride" has become a common practice in Taiwan for the past 20 years among lower-middle classes, or men who are old or physically disabled.
73. Personal interview on October 13, 2005.
74. Personal interview on June 16, 2005.
75. Personal interview on June 5, 2005.
76. Personal interview on November 3, 2005.
77. Jinmei's husband is a heterosexual office clerk. They met each other at a friend's tea party, before Jinmei had undergone surgery. Therefore, her husband knew everything about her transsexual past, but avoided mentioning it after they got married.
78. In Taiwan, SRS is expensive, involving complicated requests and strict preclinical/psychological examinations. Moreover, both parents (if alive) need to sign a letter of consent regardless of the patient's age. In order to have the surgery done, many TS simply go to Thailand to have the surgery and return to Taiwan to have a

physical diagnosis and get their ID changed. Jinmei had her "lower part" done in Thailand and "upper part" in Taiwan, which cost two hundred and twenty thousand NT dollars in total.
79. Even though she plans to adopt children, government policy states that only female-to-male postop transsexuals can adopt children.
80. On the gendered meanings of blood in Chinese history, see Charlotte Furth, "Blood, Body and Gender: Medical Images of the Female Condition in China," *Chinese Science* 7 (1986): 43–65.
81. For a theoretically rich elaboration of the sex/gender norms, see the classic essays by Gayle Rubin: "The Traffic in Women: Notes on the 'Political Economy' of Sex" and "Thinking Sex: Notes for a Radical Theory of the Politics of Sexuality," both can be found in Gayle Rubin, *Deviations: A Gayle Rubin Reader* (Durham: Duke University Press, 2011).

CHAPTER 10

Transgenders in Hong Kong: From Shame to Pride

Pui Kei Eleanor Cheung

INTRODUCTION

Presently, we are in the midst of an emergent transgender movement in Hong Kong. While there may have been some sporadic, hidden networks of transgender individuals before the turn of this century, there were no formal transgender groups or communities in Hong Kong, let alone a transgender movement.[1]

Based on my fieldwork with the gender-variant communities in Hong Kong, this chapter offers an overview of the transformation of transgender subjectivity from shame to self-acceptance to a sense of pride against the backdrop of the development of a social movement rooted in transidentity in Hong Kong.[2]

Before we go into the details of such a transformation, I would like to say a few words about the pronouns and the meaning of the word transgender as they are used in this chapter. When third-person pronouns are used to refer to my informants, I use the ones that reflect how they identify their gender (at least to me). For example, the female pronouns (i.e. she, her, and hers) are used when referring to an informant who identifies herself as a woman notwithstanding whether she was assigned as male or female at birth. Some informants' gender identifications, however, are not so straightforward, so it would be rather inappropriate to use the binary gendered pronouns (e.g. she, he, him, her etc.) to refer to them because they define their gender expression as, for example, neither male nor female, very ambiguous, genderqueer, the third gender, no gender, half male and half female, so on and so forth. I therefore use the pronouns coined by Kate Bornstein in *Gender Outlaws* (1994) when referring to those who do not identify themselves simply as male or female. In Bornstein's system of gendered neutral pronouns, the subject is "ze", the object and possessive adjective is "hir", the possessive pronoun is "hirs", and the reflexive is "hirself."[3]

From my fieldwork, I noticed that many of my informants, especially those who have been involved in their communities for quite a long time, used the term transgender (especially its argot, "TG") to refer to someone who is "more than" a cross-dresser but not quite a transsexual because ze experiences gender dysphoria and may, to varying extents, identify hirself as a gender other than hir birth-assigned gender and expresses (or wants to express) that identity, and ze may be waiting for sex reassignment surgery (SRS) or ze may not intend (or circumstances would not allow hir) to undergo SRS. However, as the influence of the transgender movement is becoming stronger in Hong Kong, more people have begun to use the term "transgender" as "an umbrella term including many categories of people who are gender variant," ranging from cross-dressers to intersexed people to transsexuals.[4] I adopt this latter definition of transgender throughout this chapter, but the emphasis of my analysis will be on those who were about to, or had already undergone, SRS at the time of the interview.

Methods

The data analyzed in this chapter is drawn from fieldwork (which included participants' observations and casual conversations) and formal interviews conducted with gender-variant people in Hong Kong between 2005 and 2012.

Formal interviews were conducted with 18 informants; some were interviewed more than once, over more than two years' time, or as they progressed along their gender journey. They are all ethnic Chinese residing in Hong Kong, between 19 and 54 years old at the time of the interview. Informed consent was obtained from each informant, and confidentiality and anonymity were ensured.[5] Informants were also told that they could decline to respond to any question or withdraw from the study at any time without negative consequences.

Many of my informants were recruited using snowball sampling. At the very beginning of this study, I was introduced to a few key informants through some lesbian, gay, bisexual, transgender, and queer (LGBTQ) community leaders when I first started this study.

After getting to know these key informants on a more personal level, I was invited to participate in various social gatherings and activities organized by people in the gender-variant communities, such as hospital visits (for SRS or related conditions), parties for the New Year celebration or birthdays, cross-dressing photo shoots, and even a memorial gathering for a transwoman who had committed suicide. Through these gatherings, my list of informants snowballed a great deal as I was introduced to more and more individuals of the communities.

Apart from snowball sampling, I also adopted the strategy of convenience sampling (also known as opportunity sampling) to help me find informants for this study. Through my voluntary work and involvement in the LGBTQ communities in Hong Kong (e.g., hotline volunteer for Queer Sisters, facilitator for Nutong Xueshe gender workshops, and volunteer for Transgender Equality and Acceptance Movement [TEAM] and Transgender Resource Center [TGR] etc.), I often had the opportunity to encounter people who were gender variant. I recruited some of them to participate in my study because they were readily available.

For most of the interviews (except the earliest ones which were unstructured as they acted as a pilot), an interview guide was used focusing on informants' gender identity formation, but unlike an interview schedule (where questions have to be asked verbatim), the former merely served as a checklist of topics for informants to speak freely in their own terms and share experiences and concerns that they felt were significant to them, supplemented by appropriate probing and request for further clarification or explanation of certain ideas or experiences. Each interview usually lasted for about 90 minutes to 2 hours, but a few of them lasted considerably longer, for about 5 to 6 hours, as those informants had a more substantial list of things that they would like to share with me. All formal interviews were voice recorded and later transcribed, in their original dialect (i.e. Cantonese), for data analysis to preserve their original meaning for analysis as much as possible.

This study follows the constructivist paradigm of grounded theory as advocated by Kathy Charmaz, which aims to construct a reality amidst multiple realities by seeking the meanings of both the informants and the researcher.[6] Qualitative software NVivo 8 was used to analyze all the interview transcriptions and field notes following the grounded theory techniques as a tool. All the texts were subjected to initial coding, also known as open coding, by comparing incident to incident. After the emergence of some hunches or themes, more interviews were then conducted according to the principle of theoretical sampling, that is, sampling that is based on emerging concepts and by varying the situations to maximize differences.[7] The new data were subsequently analyzed. During or after the phase of initial coding, the initial codes were then classified into major categories and subcategories.

Transphobia and Shame

Many transgenders I have met used to, or still do, find their gender identity/expression very shameful, and this can be attributed, to a certain extent, to the public perception of gender-variant people (especially that of transsexuals) in Hong Kong. According to a pathbreaking survey of 856 Hong Kong Chinese participants using the Chinese Attitudes toward Transgenderism and Transgender Civil Rights Scale, Mark King found that the term that was most commonly used (54.2% responses) when referring to transgender was *jan-jiu* (人妖),[8] which is a derogatory term meaning human monster literally.[9] The second most commonly used term (16.6% responses) by King's participants was *naa-jing* (乸型), which refers to men who are sissy or effeminate.

There are three things worth noting from King's study with respect to the commonly used terms to describe transgenders in Hong Kong. First, about half of the typical terms named by King's participants are derogatory, and since jan-jiu and naa-jing were the most common and yet derogatory, we can infer from them that the popular terminologies that are available to describe transgenders are generally quite negative and that they reflect the people's general sociocultural attitude toward transgenders in Hong Kong.

Second, there are about 4 (including jan-jiu and naa-jing) out of the 13 terms named by King's participants that refer to those who are birth-assigned males, whereas only 1 (*naam-jan-po*, 男人婆, "manly woman") refers to those who are birth-assigned females, and the rest being fairly gender-neutral terms. This seems to suggest that there may be much more prejudice and disapproval against birth-assigned males who do not conform to the male gender norms, whether through their gender expression (as in the case of jan-jiu and naa-jing) or through their nonheterosexual practice (i.e. being gay), than against their birth-assigned female counterparts. Indeed, King's qualitative interviews "suggest that FtM TG do not receive the same degree of pathologization, stigmatization, and delegitimization."[10] Another possible reason for such discrepancy in the terms that reflect transgenders' birth-assigned gender may be that transwomen are much more visible in Hong Kong than transmen (probably through the popular "*jan-jiu* shows," i.e. cabarets featuring transwomen, that are shown in Thailand as well as their touring cabarets in Hong Kong).[11]

Third, King found that "Hong Kong Chinese people often conflate transgenderism with effeminate homosexuality."[12] This confusion was made evident by his participants when naming various terms relating to homosexuality in reference to transgenders. This indicates that Hong Kong Chinese people still had not grasped the categories that are used by (or are used to understand) sexual and gender minorities very well.

Despite the use of derogatory terms when referring to transgenders and the absence of an appreciation of the labeling politics of gender and sexual minority groups, it is nevertheless encouraging to learn from King's study that "Hong Kong Chinese people generally do not hold very negative attitudes towards TG/TS people and are generally supportive of transgender civil rights."[13] King's conclusion was echoed by another survey conducted by Sam Winter's research team in 2008 in which Hong Kong undergraduate students' attitudes toward transgenders were measured using the Genderism and Transphobia Scale, and the overall score was found to be toward the tolerance side even though the Hong Kong sample seemed to be more transphobic than Darryl Hill and Brian Willoughby's 2005 Montreal sample.[14]

Since the studies on Hong Kong people's attitudes toward transgenders are very recent, we do not have solid social scientific data on their attitudes in earlier periods. Therefore, we can only infer from the prejudice and discrimination some transgenders had personally experienced in the past to get a glimpse of the public perception of transgenderism over the years. According to the anecdotes I collected from some of my informants, it is apparent that the cultural context for transgenders was much more hostile in the past. For instance, about two to three decades ago, it was not uncommon for passerby to swear and shout out derogatory words such as jan-jiu, in public places, at the person whom they believed to be a transwoman. Nowadays, if a transwoman is being clocked (i.e., being found out that she was transgender) in public places, she might be stared at or her gender identity questioned (perhaps out of curiosity rather than hostility) by a passerby. However, if transwomen were clocked in female public toilets, it is quite likely that toilet users would report them to the police or security guard out of concerns that they were perverts trying to get into the female toilets. As a matter of fact, two of my informants had the firsthand experience of being reported to the police or security guard because they used the female toilets.

Even though nowadays the attitudes of Hong Kong Chinese people, especially younger people or those with higher levels of education, are found to be not very negative and may be becoming more tolerant,[15] many of my informants have been experiencing emotional distress and traumas, some of which could find their origins in the prejudice and discriminations that they have encountered over the years. This is akin to the "sexual minority stress" that Meyer identified in the lesbian, gay, and bisexual populations because social stressors such as stigma, prejudice, rejection, and discrimination "create a hostile and stressful social environment that causes mental health problems";[16] I prefer the concept of "gender minority stress" when discussing similar kinds of stress as experienced by the transgender populations.

I have also noticed that informants who are older tend to be under greater social pressure to conform with the gender norms as their sociocultural environment seemed to be much more hostile in the past during the time when they were growing up; and as a result, some seemed to suffer more from gender minority stress. Below are a few examples to illustrate how transphobic the sociocultural environment was like in Hong Kong during the earlier days and how my informants, who were often filled with shame and/or fear, reacted to such an environment.

Maria, a male-to-female informant, was bullied at school because of her feminine demeanor. It happened around the early 1960s in Hong Kong. Perhaps as a means to avoid others' bullying and questioning, Maria was a loner and avoided playing with others at school:

> When I was very little I was already very quiet and did not like to speak, but at that time I did not identify myself as a man or a woman etc. In any case, some classmates laughed at me, and those classmates and the teacher seemed to be saying to me all the time, "why are you like this? Why are you so girlie?" etc. But at the time I did not have any specially strong feeling that it was a gender identity issue... I did not find it a very big problem that I did not like to play with others. However, some people consider it a problem. For example, some classmates shouted out loudly in public [at Maria] words such as "effeminate." [Maria; male → close to being a female in terms of psychological state; 52; preoperative][17]

Apart from social pressures from one's peers, the media have also played a role in perpetuating these kinds of rigid gender norms, and this particular agent of socialization is even more powerful as many transgenders have internalized these kinds of norms and felt shameful about their gender identity/expression. For example, around 1980s, Sema came across some health and agony aunt type of columns in the newspapers that very harshly criticized men who cross-dressed, so ze was led to think that men who wore women's clothes were bad:

> When I was twenty-something, I felt that CD, that is men wearing women's clothes, was an evil thing. That is to say, there were shame and guilt, and it was judged as wrong. From then on, I tried to have some self-healing through self-correction by not looking at women's clothes any more. Instead, I joined some very macho friends to do some very macho things. [Sema; male → very ambiguous, a mild sex change inclination; 46; nonop]

Indeed, this kind of transphobic environment prompted many transgenders to hide their strong need/desire to be the other gender. Similar to Sema, Joanne also found hir gender issue shameful and did not want others to know about it:

> As I became older, I found that there was a problem when I thought about changing sex and the like. I began to feel that I should not let others know or discover it. I felt very ashamed and found this abnormal, I therefore began to hide it. (Joanne; male → transgender [i.e. neither male nor female] or genderqueer; 44; preoperative)

Similar to Sema's intentional "self correction," Joanne tried very hard to hide hir feminine traits and make hirself more masculine:

> Those [feminine gender expressions] exist intrinsically, but they have been hidden...I remember when I looked at photos of me that were taken when I was a few years old, I was still very sissy—I was folding my arms and my legs with a very shy look in the pictures. But from my teens onward, I would very consciously attempt to hide these things. I would, for example, use a chest expander and a handgrip etc. to build my biceps as I hope to be more masculine and tough. In addition, [I also hoped that] my hobbies were more inclined towards masculinity, but back then I was not too inclined [toward masculinity]. Nevertheless, for instance, at the beginning when I was little, I knew how to knit, but gradually I did not knit. I used to play with dolls, but I then stopped playing. I gradually adjusted those things that were inclined towards femininity such that they won't be so extreme, as I feared that others would discover it... [Joanne continued to hide hir feminine gender expression as well as hir cross-dressing behaviours

as ze grew older] I was getting very nervous as I feared that others would discover it. What was I fearful of? Any minute sign, whenever others had anything to say about me, I would immediately correct it. I therefore did a lot of things to remind myself not to do it again. Far as I remember, as this continued to develop, I had become very nervous for all this time and many people had told me that I was being defensive when making new friends. When I began to know someone, I dared not disclose anything because I was fearful that I would reveal something. One time it was very obvious, I remember when I was 20, I was graduating from [tertiary education].[18] I remember clearly that our male classmates went out together after we graduated and we took a group photo together...After the photo was taken, I was being laughed at by a classmate, and he laughed about it for a very long time. He laughed at me as I sat with my knees kept together. He said, "only girls sit like that! Which guy would sit like that?" I did not deliberately sit like that, but it just got revealed like that. Since then, I reminded myself never to sit like that anymore...I had to sit with my legs apart deliberately. It's only until the last few years when I did it the other way round, to return to my old way... So I continued to train myself. From the age of 20 till I was about 40, I had often been told by others that I was being macho, and nobody ever noticed any problem in me...I would act more masculine, such as by the way I walked, my posture, my manner and speech. I remember clearly that each time I watched a movie, especially Tom Cruise' movies, and every time after watching a movie, I wanted to imitate closely the impression that the hero conveyed to people, like how he walked etc. It was interesting to note that when I showed my photos to my friends, some of those photos look very much like Leon Lai.[19] Indeed, at that time I also felt that I really wanted to act like Leon Lai. [Joanne; male → transgender (i.e. neither male nor female) or genderqueer; 44; preoperative]

Joanne's prolonged effort to hide hir secret and the way ze upheld the view that it was abnormal had eventually taken their toll on hir mental health. The ongoing and intense nervousness that Joanne used to experience exemplifies what I call gender minority stress.

While there have been more social pressure upon birth-assigned males to conform to masculine gender norms, and gender transgression of birth-assigned females are relatively more tolerated in Hong Kong (cf. the TB phenomenon),[20] discrimination against female-to-male sex changers was still high during the time when another informant, Edward, was struggling with his gender identity (even though he was born in the mid-1970s). During his late teens, Edward made do with the homosexual label because he found that there was less discrimination against homosexuals than against transsexuals, and hence he found it easier to come out to others as a homosexual instead of a transsexual:

> By the time I started working, the people around me...had begun to be more accepting of homosexuals as the internet became more available. So, at that time, I absolutely did not mind to admit [that I was a homosexual]...Meanwhile, however, I had no choice and was merely being forced to admit that I was a homosexual. Someone said to me, "hey, you fucking asshole, you freak, are you a tranny?" So, I resisted a great deal as soon as people talked about sex change or freaks because I was very scared—it's like my skeletons in the closet were being dug out by others. Although people started to accept homosexuals at that time, if you tried to tell them that you were a transsexual, I feared that they would chase after me for several blocks and beat me up with some metal stools... [Edward therefore resisted the notion of sex change a great deal] because back then people would find you very strange... because for some unknown reason an equal sign was added between sex change and abnormality. If you think back to the earlier years, the older generations always equated sex change with abnormality, and for some unknown reason only abnormal people would go for sex change...So, the first time I read those words [when Edward happened to learn the news on Hong Kong's first FTM sex change from a newspaper]—I am talking about junior secondary school—I actually was not really clear what sex change was about. I only knew that I did not like having such a gender and that something could be done about it. I only thought about it in my own head and gathered that it was those *jan-jiu* (human monster) in Thailand! From my own perspective, I could only see that sex change was equated with *jan-jiu*, and for some unknown reason *jan-jiu* was equated with abnormality. Given the lack of information, sex change equaled *jan-jiu* which was then being equated with abnormality were the only linkages I could think of as I found that the *jan-jiu* in Thailand had always been criticized as abnormal, neither male nor female, and nonsense blah blah blah. Thus, even if I felt that I had that condition, I would not dare to tell anyone. It's like being a thief. [Even with school social workers] I wouldn't tell at all! Of course, it's their business if they were able to find out, but I definitely wouldn't tell them. However, I knew myself. Remember, there are two different components to this mixed feeling: I did not admit that I was a transsexual (back then I still did not), but I also felt that I was like a guy. [Edward; female → male; 32; postoperative]

As mentioned earlier, the sociocultural context for transgenders was much more hostile in the past. Conversely, nowadays there are more trans people who feel more able to express their preferred gender overtly. For example, Hannah, who was born in the late 1980s, was able to insist on her gender expression and go against her mom's disapproval for many years:

> For example in the past I had some jewellery or just a few feminine items, and [my parents] were very unhappy about it... In fact, I had manicure since I was young... When I was very little my mom used to cut my fingernails, but the thing is she could not control me afterwards. In fact, my nails have been like this [long] since I was little. My mom has always told me to cut them. Actually I do not mind whether or not my nails are cut short, because many women have short nails; those who have manicure may have very long nails... However, [my mom] said one thing that I minded very much, so I decided not to cut them. She said, "why as a boy you grow your nails so long?" I found what she said very repugnant! If she tried to ask me to cut them by saying that long nails can be broken easily and that they are inconvenient etc.—if she had articulated those reasons—I would be fine with it, I would accept this kind of reasoning. Sometimes I also found them inconvenient and would cut them all. But as soon as she said "why as a boy you grow your nails so long?" I would have the feeling to go against it. As you think men should not have their nails grown so long, I would grow them out for you to see. This is not necessarily rebellious. If she used other reasons, I might have accepted it. I was only directed against her reasoning [regarding gender], not merely about that particular event. [Hannah; male → female; 19; preoperative]

As shown in my informants' testimonies above, the oppressive environment has an impact on transgenders insofar as they tend to internalize transphobia and feel shameful about their gender identity. However, as the environment is becoming less hostile, there seems to be more transgenders feeling confident in expressing their gender and reacting against other people's disapproval (for example, Hannah's reaction against her mom's disapproval). This confidence and reaction against others' disapproval may help one affirm one's gender identity, and for some transgenders it even leads to a sense of pride.

Pride

Despite the shame and/or fear many of my informants, especially the older ones, had experienced, many reached the "Self-Affirmation/ Equilibrium Stage" of the GIFT model sooner or later—where they could affirm or make peace with their gender identity.[21] Nevertheless, by affirmation or making peace, I do not mean that all birth-assigned male informants would necessarily affirm or make peace with a female gender identity. Nor do I necessarily mean that birth-assigned female would affirm or make peace with a strictly defined male gender identity. Rather, they have come to accept their gender identity (or the changes/evolution of their gender identity) which may or may not fit the conventional male or female category.

While some informants managed to reach (or tried to reach) a sense of equilibrium insofar as they made peace with their gender identity, some informants also found the process of coming out (whether to oneself or disclosure to others) a self-affirming experience as they were liberated from the sense of shame they used to have. Jo, for example, found her process of coming out to be greatly facilitated by her "Exploration Stage" (cf. the GIFT model) in which she networked with other gender-variant people:

> [Prior to knowing any people in the transgender community] I very much hid myself because I felt that I was a monster. I hid myself from everyone and would not show anything. After I got to know some friends in this community, I realised that there was actually a big group of people in the world who were like me—I don't mean abroad but within Hong Kong! I had also met some of them who had already received the operations, but I did not find them very strange. They might have encountered more difficulties in life, but I found out that they could at least live their lives and be a normal person. So, getting to know the community and making friends with them had a great impact on me. I began to have confidence as I knew that "you are not alone!" This sense of "you are not alone" was very strong!
>
> Moreover, [knowing them] was quite encouraging, for example, at the beginning I was very timid and shy at times, I dared not go out in women's clothes. After knowing some of these friends, and some of them were more daring [than me], perhaps some of them were not TS but pure CD... and they did not pass either. After I got to know them, together we went out cross-dressed. So, it had given me the confidence and I had the guts to come out... to liberate myself. In the past all my female thinking and behaviour etc. were hidden away. After knowing them, I could liberate myself, for example, I gradually allowed my family and friends to know that I had such a need. [Jo; male → 100% female; 45; postoperative]

Although Jo has been able to liberate herself from feeling ashamed about her gender identity, she and many others like her prefer to live in stealth after their SRS so that they can blend into the world as an ordinary man or woman. On the contrary, Joanne was probably the first in Hong Kong who has gone a step further in taking pride in her transgender identity:

Right now I very much accept being called a transgender...I hope to accept this identity of mine such that I could affirm myself with self-respect and confidence. This is called transgender pride...Some trans people advocate for being proud of the fact that they have lived half their lives as male and half their lives as female. I hope to be proud of my previous experience and not to hide my past...[Nevertheless, Joanne did not affirm hir transgender identity in the past because] I was unsure whether or not I could pass and whether I would be pointed at by other people all the time when I went out. If that were the case, I would rather bear with it and live as a man than go for the operation even though I would feel more comfortable after the operation. In other words, I still did not accept my trans-identity about a year to a year and half ago. It has developed very rapidly within the last year or so. That is to say, I could accept myself to go through a sex change, and then it was suddenly developed into a state where I could accept myself as a trans—being neither male nor female, even after the operation I would continue to accept myself as a transgender. [Joanne; male → transgender (i.e. neither male nor female) or genderqueer; 44; preoperative]

As mentioned earlier, Joanne used to try very hard to suppress hir femininity, but hir female psychological state continued to come out such that for many years ze was very much tormented by these two polarized extremes. Nevertheless, as Joanne continued hir "Exploration Stage" through networking with those within the CD, transgender, and lesbian[22] circles as well as coming out to more friends around hir, ze began to obtain more insight about hirself and hir gender condition. The watershed moment came at the beginning of 2007 when ze suddenly decided to accept newspaper and magazine interviews with hir name and photos published whereby ze came out in public as a transgender:

When I began coming out to friends, I found out that it was no big deal. Of course there were some setbacks that made me want to commit suicide, but anyway that's the past. Actually, it came a phase during the process of coming out that, apart from the hurt, each time I came out to someone I was able to get to know myself even more. I then arrived a phase when I wished to tell my mom about it but did not know how.

You remember I accepted an interview last year. Actually, my main wish was to let my mom and others around me know that I have this condition...[because] I had reached a state in which I felt that I could not bear with it anymore—I could no longer hide myself, I wanted the whole world to know about it, the people around me to know about it, and to accept this condition of mine—whether or not they accepted it, I hoped to be seen in a status that I felt comfortable. So, I accepted the interview, and this actually had quite a big impact on me because I had suddenly come out to everyone such that I no longer feel too frightened that other people would find out about my identity. It does not matter even if they find out as I've already accepted the interview, and everyone in my office knew about it, my whole family knew about it, and many people in my church knew about it...As such, I have become more feminine in my everyday life. In the past, I dared not go to work with my hair permed like this. It did not matter at home, but at work I feared about my colleagues' reaction as they did not know about it. After the magazine interview was published and everyone knew about it, I had become brazen, and I go to work with my hair permed like this. This [coming out publicly] had led me to walk forward more bravely in making myself more feminine in my everyday life. This was, in fact, a very important step for me. [Joanne; male → transgender (i.e. neither male nor female) or genderqueer; 44; preoperative]

Joanne's decision to come out publicly shows that ze transformed from not accepting hir transidentity to embracing and affirming it. However, Joanne's transformation did not come out of the blue, rather, during hir "Exploration Stage" (cf. the GIFT model), ze had already obtained a great measure of insight (including seeing pride in hir transidentity) from exploring different LGBT and CD communities for several years and from the process of coming out to some friends at an earlier phase, and when such an insight was coupled with the unbearable state that Joanne had eventually reached in which ze felt that ze could no longer hide hir femininity, ze had both the insight and impetus for the transformation, namely, to shed hir male identity and embrace hir transidentity.

THE EMERGENCE OF TRANSGENDER MOVEMENT IN HONG KONG

Since the decriminalization of male homosexual conduct in Hong Kong in 1991, many lesbian and gay organizations have been established out in the open, and many of them have the mission to promote equal rights for gays and lesbians in Hong Kong.[23] Meanwhile, although there has never been any law in Hong Kong that criminalizes transgenderism per se, there was no registered organization that focused its service for the transgender community and fought for transgender rights until 2002, when Jessica Park, a transwoman, and a few like-minded people established Transgender Equality and Acceptance Movement (TEAM). The group consisted of both Westerners and Chinese. Around the same time, another group (predominantly Chinese), CD Family, that also serves gender-variant people was established; but unlike TEAM, it does not focus on political activism, rather, it has been the longest running group that creates the social space (both online and offline) for cross-dressers in Hong Kong.

During the early days, TEAM organized regular social gatherings for transgenders in Hong Kong, and it had "taken only a few cautious steps towards activism,"[24] such as their effort, around 2003, to request the Immigration Department to remove the "B" code on the identity cards of postoperative transgenders as it was a giveaway that the cardholder was a postoperative transgender.[25]

TEAM was spurred into a series of political activism after the suicide of Louise Chan and Sasha Moon, both transwomen, within the span of three days in September 2004. Their decisions to end their lives may partly be attributed to the discriminations they had suffered from their transidentity. Their deaths sent shockwaves across the transgender communities in Hong Kong, and, in turn, had helped build solidarity among people in the communities. "Following Louise and Sasha's death...TEAM made its first press announcement as a group, and it took up a place on the government's Sexual Minorities Forum, its first step towards political activism."[26] As a reverberation of Louise's and Sasha's suicide, various transgender groups, including Gender Concerns (性？無別) and Lazy Workshop (蛇王工作室), were subsequently founded to raise awareness of transgender rights.

As a researcher and activist for LGBT rights, I have noticed a gradual increase in awareness and inclusion of transgenders within the LGBT communities and within the curriculum of gender/sexuality courses at various universities in Hong Kong along with the progress TEAM had made on political activism. This has been greatly facilitated by a number of transgender individuals (most of whom participated in TEAM some years ago), who are willing to share their personal experiences with the public, and this ranges from speaking to students about their experience during university courses to sharing with participants of related workshops/seminars at community centers or other venues to appearing in interviews for media publicity (including television, newspapers, and magazines).

Among these individuals, Joanne is one of the key persons today who vigorously promotes the transgender movement in Hong Kong (figures 10.1 to 10.3). Joanne has been involved in LGBT activism since 2006, and,

Figure 10.1 Photo of Joanne on the International Human Rights Day in Hong Kong (2010). Reprinted with permission from Joanne Win Yan Leung.

Figure 10.2 Photo of the International Day Against Homophobia and Transphobia in Hong Kong 2012. Reprinted with permission from Joanne Win Yan Leung.

Figure 10.3 Photo of Joanne speaking at a gender seminar hosted by TGR (Transgender Resource Center). Reprinted with permission from Joanne Win Yan Leung.

as mentioned earlier, ze came out publicly as transgender (through the printed media) in 2007. Since then there is no turning back for hir, and Joanne has become the most vocal and dedicated transgender activist in Hong Kong. In mid-2008, Joanne and several like-minded friends established Transgender Resource Center (TGR). Its mission includes promoting Hong Kong's transgender movement through education, providing the public and the transgender community information and resources, raising society's awareness of transgender issues, and providing supports to and fighting for the rights of transgenders. Since its inception, owing to the effort of Joanne and fellow transgender volunteers, TGR has participated in over 100 sharing of transgender's lived experience at lectures, talks, and workshops with numerous universities, colleges, and other organizations. They have also been interviewed many times by different media.

Apart from public education, TGR has also played a very important role in supporting its members (currently its Facebook membership is over 900 people). As if to take up what TEAM had left off, TGR has been hosting monthly social gatherings for transgenders and their allies since the beginning of 2011; these gatherings are usually packed (with several dozen participants, and sometimes close to a 100 if it is a special event), and this indicates that gender-variant people's need for a safe social space is huge. It is fair to say that TGR has the largest transgender membership in Hong Kong, and it has helped support most of the transgender cases (e.g., referring gender-variant people to transfriendly medical personnel, providing peer counseling, dealing with the immigration department when individuals were denied the service to change the gender marker on their identity cards, etc.).

If the tragedy of Louise and Sasha was the impetus for TEAM to develop into a serious activist group, the origins of TGR's unprecedented and full engagement in the transgender movement can be traced to W's court case. To understand W's case, it will be necessary to discuss briefly the legal status of transgenders in Hong Kong. Currently, anyone who has undergone SRS can change the gender marker on hir Hong Kong identity card. The identity card is the official identity document necessary when applying for other documents (such as passports and driving licenses), for employment and all other activities that require residents' proof of identity; and the law requires all Hong Kong residents to carry their identity cards at all times. Nevertheless, one's legal gender remains the same as that stated on one's birth certificate (which is the same as one's birth-assigned gender) regardless of what is stated on one's identity card, and this applies to the case of marriage. Around 2009, a postoperative transwoman, known as "W," applied for a judicial review regarding whether a postoperative transwoman may marry a man in Hong Kong. Both the Court of First Instance (in 2010) and the Court of Appeal (in 2011) have rejected W's application and subsequent appeal because the court regarded W's application for marriage as same-sex marriage that is not permitted in this Special Administrative Region.[27]

When W lost her court case the first time, TGR mobilized, probably for the first time in such a visible manner (as most transgenders in Hong Kong prefer to live in stealth, especially after their SRS), several transgenders to appear in public through the media to voice out the transgender issues. The politically correct term for transgender in Chinese (跨性別—"*kwaa-sing-bit*") has even begun to enter the public lexicon. Prior to that, the media rarely used this term to describe those who were transgender, rather, they tended to use the derogatory term jan-jiu (人妖; human monster) or the less derogatory one, *bin-sing-jan* (變性人; sex/gender changed person), to describe those who might undergo or have undergone SRS.

As W's case gained wide media coverage, Joanne felt that they could utilize the momentum of W's case to strengthen the transgender movement:

> That's why each time in an interview [with the media], I would mention something related to the direction of the movement. For example, last time in an interview, when W had lost the appeal, I had also mentioned that this was the "first wave" to push for Hong Kong's transgender movement... For all these times, I have actually been integrating many different things together. Actually, today I dare say to others that this is a movement! I think that was how Hong Kong's transgender movement began. [Joanne; male → transwoman; 48; postoperative]

If we compare today's Joanne with what ze was like, say, 20 years ago, we would notice a drastic transformation that ze had undergone with respect to hir sense of self: from finding hir gender issue shameful such that ze had to hide and "correct" it to leading the largest transgender group in Hong Kong with a vision to push forward a social transgender movement in full throttle. Indeed, hir personal testimony attests to the idea that it was the earlier phase of "shame" and pain ze went through, coupled with hir knowledge that many people like hir continue to suffer from social stigma, that drives hir unshakable dedication to the transgender movement:

> I think being a sex-changer myself, I have experienced the complete transgender psychology... [I know of] too many difficulties when no one can help, and there isn't any resource from society whatsoever to care for this group of people. I think as a person who has gone through it and experienced so much, I do not wish any latecomer to experience this painful process any further. I have personally known two [transgender] friends who have committed suicide already,[28] and I do not want to have a third one. Yet there is no one in society who

can give them a little understanding and inclusion, so I feel that I must be an active participant of this movement so as to cultivate a better and fairer understanding of this group of people in society. I wish to have more inclusion and acceptance in society. [Joanne; male → transwoman; 48; postoperative]

Currently, TGR is busy liaising with the medical professions, scholars, and LGBT activists to challenge the medical hegemony as there is a newly added requirement imposed upon FTM transgenders to undergo some stringent and unreasonable SRS procedures if they wish to change the gender marker on their identity cards.

As of the time of writing for this chapter, we do not yet know the outcome of this case, but the activist works by TGR as well as other transgender activists suggest that transgenders in the current era are much more confident in fighting for their rights, and this, I believe, has a lot to do with the shifting of their own self-concept as seen in the personal experiences of some of my informants discussed in this chapter—from seeing their transgender identity as shameful to seeing it as something they can accept and even be proud of. However, instead of waiting passively for the public perception of transgenderism to change in society, transgenders have to continue to collaborate with solidarity to educate the public about gender diversity and to strive for transgender rights.

Notes

1. I use "communities" as opposed to "community" to highlight the plurality and diversity among those who are gender variant.
2. The term "gender variant" is used as an umbrella term to refer to a wide range of individuals whose gender identity/performance is, in various ways and to different extent, discordant with their birth-assigned gender.
3. Kate Bornstein, *Gender Outlaw: On Men, Women, and the Rest of Us* (New York: Routledge, 1994).
4. Arlene Istar Lev, *Transgender Emergence: Therapeutic Guidelines for Working with Gender-Variant People and Their Families* (New York: Haworth Clinical Practice Press, 2004), 399.
5. During the earlier stage of this study, most of my informants were not "out" to the general public. Thus, it has been vital to protect the identity of my informants. However, during the writing of this chapter, the transgender movement is developing rapidly in Hong Kong, I therefore have discussed this anonymity issue with one of my informants, Joanne Leung, who has become a leader of the transgender community in Hong Kong, and we think it is appropriate to

use her real name in this chapter especially given how "out" she currently is in Hong Kong. I have checked with her the contents of our previous interviews that are published in this chapter to ensure that she is comfortable with the use of her real name when citing those contents.
6. Kathy Charmaz, *Constructing Grounded Theory: A Practical Guide through Qualitative Analysis* (Thousand Oaks, CA: Sage, 2006).
7. Anselm L. Strauss and Juliet M. Corbin. *Basics of Qualitative Research: Techniques and Procedures for Developing Grounded Theory*, 2nd ed. (Thousand Oaks: Sage, 1998).
8. Cantonese pronunciations are used for all the transliteration of the Chinese words mentioned in this article. My transliterations are based on the scheme of phonetic symbols for standard Cantonese published by Wong Shik Ling (黃錫凌). Please note that Wong's scheme of phonetic symbols are based on the International Phonetic Alphabet, thus, for example, the phonetic symbol "j" in Wong's scheme is pronounced as "y" (e.g. the phonetic symbols "jin" is pronounced as "yin"). Cf. the electronic resources based on Wong Shik Ling's "A Chinese Syllabary Pronounced according to the Dialect of Canton" created by the Chinese University of Hong Kong: http://humanum.arts.cuhk.edu.hk/Lexis/Canton/
9. Mark Edward King, "Transprejudice in Hong Kong: Chinese Attitudes towards Transgenderism and Transgender Civil Rights" (PhD thesis, University of Hong Kong, 2008).
10. King, "Transprejudice in Hong Kong," 262.
11. "Jan-jiu show" is a very popular activity among Hong Kong tourists when visiting Thailand, and these shows were also very popular when they toured in Hong Kong. For example, when the Bangkok Golden Dome Cabarets came to perform in Aberdeen on Hong Kong island in 2005 and 2006, it was reported on the news that Aberdeen residents complained about serious traffic problems caused by the shows because they attracted "thousands of mainland tourists a day." Paul Tsang, "Feathers Fly as Residents' Woes Dog Transvestite Cabaret," *South China Morning Post* (6 January 2006), City 4.
12. King, "Transprejudice in Hong Kong," 238.
13. King, "Transprejudice in Hong Kong," 294.
14. Sam Winter, Beverley Webster, and Pui Kei Eleanor Cheung, "Measuring Hong Kong Undergraduate Students' Attitudes towards Transpeople," *Sex Roles* 59, nos. 9–10 (2008): 670–683; Darryl B. Hill and Brian L. B. Willoughby, "The Development and Validation of the Genderism and Transphobia Scale," *Sex Roles* 53, nos. 7–8 (2005): 531–544.
15. King, "Transprejudice in Hong Kong."
16. Ilan H. Meyer, "Prejudice, Social Stress, and Mental Health in Lesbian, Gay, and Bisexual Populations: Conceptual Issues and

Research Evidence," *Psychological Bulletin* 129, no. 5 (2003): 674–697, on 675.
17. To help readers relate the essential background information of the informants when a quotation is cited, a quotation identifier (put inside a pair of square parentheses "[ ]") is used at the end of an informant's quotation to indicate the informant's name or pseudonym, birth-assigned gender, informant's own description of gender identity at the time of the interview, age at the time of the interview, and status in relation to SRS.
18. Name of the institution deleted to protect informant's privacy.
19. Leon Lai is a Cantonese pop-singer in Hong Kong.
20. TB refers to "an identity adopted by many masculine lesbians in Hong Kong." Although the term is commonly used within the lesbian community, it is also very popular among students at all-girls schools in Hong Kong. Indeed, according to Lai Yuen Ki, from the 1960s onwards, "girls from girls' schools extracted 'TB' from the term 'tomboy' and used 'TB' to represent girls who were masculine and fell for girls." From my own observation within the lesbian community in Hong Kong, a TB may or may not have a gender identity of a male, and some of my informants regarded their gender identity as TB. In other words, for some people, TB is a gender category. Lai Yuen Ki, "Lesbian Masculinities: Identity and Body Construction among Tomboys in Hong Kong" (MPhil thesis, Chinese University of Hong Kong, 2004), 2–3.
21. The GIFT model stands for the model of Gender Identity Formation and Transformation of Gender Variant people in Hong Kong. It consists of five dimensions (Body Identity, Psychological Identity, Gender Expression and Role, Gender Priority, and Sexuality) and seven stages (Earliest Memories and Childhood Signs, Confusion and/or Noticing it as a Problem, Exploration/Transitory Identification, Struggle, Escalation, Transformation/Trigger, and Self-Affirmation/Equilibrium). See Pui Kei Eleanor Cheung, "Gender Variant People in Hong Kong: A Model of Gender Identity Formation and Transformation" (PhD thesis, University of Hong Kong, 2011).
22. Through networking with the lesbian community, Joanne came to understand that ze was a trans-lesbian, i.e. a MTF transgender who is attracted to women.
23. On the decriminalization of male homosexual conduct in Hong Kong, see Phil C. W. Chan, "The Lack of Sexual Orientation Anti-Discrimination Legislation in Hong Kong: Breach of International and Domestic Legal Obligations," *The International Journal of Human Rights* 9, no. 1 (2005): 69–106.
24. Robyn Emerton, "Finding a Voice, Fighting for Rights: The Emergence of the Transgender Movement in Hong Kong," *Inter-Asia Cultural Studies* 7, no. 2 (2006): 243–269, on 244.

25. The "B" code signifies the fact that the details (e.g. one's sex) stated on one's identity card is different from one's birth certificate, and those who know what those codes stand for may be able to tell that the cardholder is a postoperative transgender.
26. Emerton, "Finding a Voice," 244.
27. Cf. W v Registrar of Marriages, Court of First Instance [HCAL 120/2009, August 9 and 10, 2010, October 5, 2010] and W v Registrar of Marriages, Court of Appeal [CACV 266/2010, October 12 and 13, 2011, November 25, 2011].
28. One of them was Louise and the other one's suicide may be attributed partly to the rejection from her family and significant other.

PART IV

Afterword

CHAPTER 11

De/Colonizing Transgender Studies of China

Susan Stryker

As the historical research of this volume's editor, Howard Hsueh Hao Chiang, makes clear, in recounting the introduction of "transsexuality" to China, concepts originating in Western discourses informed by sexological science have a way of travelling transnationally, as part of broader patterns of Eurocentric imperialism and colonization and as part of the global accumulation and transfer of capital. This has certainly been the case with transgender, a term that emerged in Anglophone North American gender-variant communities in the mid-twentieth century, and which experienced a meteoric rise in usage in the early 1990s as a critical, political, and identitarian label for any expression of gender that contests the familiar dichotomy of "man" and "woman." But as Chiang's work and the work of his colleagues collected herein makes clear as well, how such concepts as "transsexual" and transgender are variously resisted, adopted, creatively transformed, and critically redeployed frustrates any simple narrative of a coercive imposition by the West on the rest of the world of foreign epistemological and ontological constructs of personhood. In the contact zone of incommensurable cultural differences, across asymmetrical relations of power, de/colonized subjects, societies, and scholars have found opportunities for agential action not only through the rejection of concepts and categories of Western origin, but also through their appropriation, translation, hybridization, and dubbing.

The works collected in this volume adopt several different strategies for imagining what a "transgender China" might look like, and what Chinese "transgender studies" might do. Pui Kei Eleanor

Cheung's "Transgenders in Hong Kong" is perhaps the most methodologically straightforward: there are people called (by themselves and others) transgenders, and we can study them, as we would study any other object in the material world. Daniel Burton-Rose, in surveying Daoist and Buddhist thought across long stretches of Chinese history to recover information that might call into question currently dominant ideas about what makes a woman a woman and a man a man, also conducts transgender studies in a fundamental vein: he pays critical attention to phenomena that disrupt or denaturalize our *attribution* of normative linkages between biological sex, gendered self-perception, kinship status, social role, and sexual expression.

Chao-Jung Wu's study of Taiwanese fanchuan theatrical gender impersonation points to one of the most fertile possibilities for transgender studies to refigure existing bodies of scholarship. Ritualized cross-gender performance in socially sanctioned spaces for socially recognized ends is a pervasive practice across many cultures, including China, and it is the subject of an extensive ethnographic and interpretive literature that typically asserts either the homosexuality or heterosexuality of the performers; transgender studies offers a new analytical perspective on theatrical cross-dressing, not necessarily by asserting a transgender identity for the performers of such acts, but rather by reframing the homo/hetero binary itself. Similarly, Zuyan Zhou and Carlos Rojas both explore culturally and historically specific constructions of gender ambiguity, androgyny, and admixtures of masculine and feminine styles or identifications, in, respectively, the genre of caizi-jiaren (talented scholar/youthful beauty) romances and in the work of contemporary Beijing conceptual artist Ma Liuming. Such phenomena are not transgender in a nominal or identificatory sense, and yet their interrogation foregrounds the contingency and specificity, rather than the ontological giveness, of such categories as man, masculine, feminine, and woman—which is precisely what transgender studies aims to do.

Larrissa Heinrich's chapter on Qiu Miaojin's novel *Last Words from Montmartre* takes up a well-established heuristic in transgender studies (the often-contentious boundary between queer and trans) to make a characteristic move (a shift toward antifoundationalist poststructuralist theory that undermines and recasts the initial categories of analysis), which works as well in Sinophone as in Anglophone contexts. Helen Hok-Sze Leung's "Trans on Screen," which engages with self-styled transgender studies literature more explicitly than any other work in this volume, offers a compelling example of what can be accomplished by decentering the Anglophone and Eurocentric biases that characterize the first iteration of the transgender studies field: in her hands, transgender as a mode of analysis is itself transformed and reworked through its application to the interpretation of Chinese cinema.

The two remaining contributions to this volume, by Alvin Ka Hin Wong and Howard Hsueh Hao Chiang, both grapple, at least indirectly, with two emerging problematics in the current iteration of transgender studies that place it in the mainstream of contemporary interdisciplinary critical scholarship. Wong, in his account of how *The Legend of the White Snake* has traveled transhistorically through a variety of performance venues and produced different "transgender effects" in each spatiotemporal location, calls our attention to an understanding of "transgender phenomena" that resonates with recent work in science studies, such as Karen Barad's materialist feminist quantum physics, that posits phenomena, rather than objects, as the fundamental units of being—with a phenomenon always being determined by a particular configuration of observer, experimental apparatus, and process of registering events. Transgender, in other words, is context-dependent: it is always (partially and nonexclusively) in the eye of the beholder. Finally, Chiang's work on the intersection of Western discourses of psychopathological transsexuality with Chinese traditions of court eunuchism point us in the direction of biopolitics. If we accept the basic proposition that gender is part of a regulatory apparatus of statelike powers that—as described by Foucault, Agamben, Hardt, Negri, and others—individuates embodied subjects while aggregating them as members of a conglomerate body-politic, then any analytically rigorous conceptualization of *trans*gender necessarily depends on the concrete, material, and historical arrangements that must be "crossed" in a given biopolitical context: Chinese transgender, in the transit from eunuchism to transsexuality, is specific to itself.

This volume makes an important contribution both to Sinophone studies and to transgender studies, but it nevertheless represents only the beginning of a complex conversation about how concepts and categories travel transnationally from Anglophone scholarship to Chinese culture, society, and history. In titling his introduction "Imagining Transgender China," Chiang invites the work collected here to be contextualized by David Valentine's influential book, *Imagining Transgender: An Ethnography of a Category*. In the remarks that follow, I accept that invitation, and use Valentine's work as a jumping-off point for imagining what a (post) colonial, de/colonial, and anticolonial transgender studies—including Chinese transgender studies—might look like. Much of what I say here is drawn, in somewhat revised and condensed form, from texts jointly authored with Paisley Currah and Aren Aizura, with whom I have worked, respectively, to launch a new journal of transgender studies and to publish a second volume of the *Transgender Studies Reader*, and in which we addressed precisely these questions as part of framing the ongoing development of the field. I thank them both for their conversations and contributions without necessarily attributing to them the viewpoint or opinions I express below.

Valentine's work can be read as hostile to the project of a "transgender studies," to the extent that such a project is imagined *only* as a conceptual export of the global west and north that is being spread to the global south and east, or that begins *only* in elite academic settings from which it trickles down to a street that finds it irrelevant. Valentine argues that the category "transgender" itself is often imagined as a superior modern form that advances itself at the expense of old-fashioned, premodern, traditional, or "local" non-Western understandings of sex, sexuality, embodiment, gender, and identity. This is a progress narrative in which transgender, through a reverse discourse, positions itself as even more modern than the increasingly shopworn categories of "gay" and "lesbian," with their rigid, fixed, outmoded concepts of man and woman, and their complicities in homonationalist and consumerist forms of citizenship.

Particularly within the discipline of anthropology, Valentine contends, "transgender" increasingly supplies the conceptual scaffolding that organizes and interprets cross-cultural variations in embodied personhood; but in doing so, he suggests, it extends the trope of modernization and inappropriately deploys Eurocentric ontological categories. One implication of this conceptual move is that the academic institutionalization of transgender studies—which advances a goal of transgender social legitimization through the development of an expertise structured by the foundational preconditions of transgender's intelligibility—risks deploying a kind of Cartesian grid on the world of human diversity and mapping it in ways that relentlessly orient it, in indubitably imperialist fashion, toward Anglophone and Eurocentric standards and measurements.

In directing our attention to those ways in which transgender activism and advocacy themselves can become complicit with the globalizing logic of neoliberalism, with the concomitant risk of transgender studies scholarship becoming the (un)witting ideological accomplice of this (un)stated politics, Valentine offers an important caution against naïve liberationist and progressivist transgender discourses, and usefully points out their racial, class, nationalist, and linguistic biases. When transgender is understood to include all gender variant practices and identities rather than being understood as an analytical stance vis-à-vis the refigurable interrelationality of sex, gender, and identity, transgender studies does indeed risk erasing violent colonial histories of knowledge-production about embodied difference. After all, cataloguing divergences from modern Eurocentric understandings of sex, gender, sexuality, embodiment, and identity in different cultures or classes, assigning meaning and moral weight to such "abnormalities," and exploiting or fetishizing that difference according to the developmental logic of colonialism and capitalism, have all been central features of Euro-American societies for over 500 years. Understanding the dissemination of transgender as a category that originated among white people within Eurocentric modernity thus necessarily involves an engagement with the political conditions under which that term was produced and within and through which it now circulates.

What kinds of questions and practices, then, can transgender studies offer that advance an anticolonial, de/colonial, or (post) colonial agenda, and that resist the subsumption of non-Western configurations of personhood into Western-dominant frameworks?

At the very least, it would involve careful attention to the movement of transgender phenomena, knowledge, and practices across regions, nations, and rural-urban spaces, and it would acknowledge that the relationship between highly mobile medicalized categories such as transsexual, and culturally specific terms that travel shorter distances is not a monolithic one in which the purity of an ethnic practice is polluted and diminished by the introduction of a standardized modern import: in any site, the uptake of an imported term makes it as local and as indigenous as it is foreign and invasive. Such a transgender studies would also concern itself with how various forms of personhood in locations around the world imagine their own relationship to those things that transgender can be made to evoke, such as modernity, metropolitanism, Eurocentrism, whiteness, or globalization. It would explore the adaptive reuse of the category itself—whether transgender is experienced as a form of colonization, as an avenue for alliance-building or resource development, as a means of resistance to local pressures or transnationalizing forces, as an empowering new frame of reference, as an erasure of cultural specificity, as a countermodernity, as an alternative to tradition, or as a mode of survival and translation for traditional cultural forms that are unintelligible within the conceptual double binary of man/woman and homo/hetero associated with the modern West. Transgender studies should also acknowledge that transgender sometimes functions as a rubric for bringing together, in mutually supportive and politically productive ways, marginalized individuals and communities of people in many parts of the world who experience oppression because of their variance from socially privileged expressions of manhood or womanhood.

Furthermore, when academic researchers in the Anglophone global north and west investigate communities, identities, practices, institutions, and statuses elsewhere that look "transgendered" to contemporary Eurocentric observers, the work of the transgender studies field necessarily involves an ethicocritical assessment of whether or how the phenomena toward which the researcher is oriented and invested in either can or cannot, or should or should not be apprehended through the optics of transgender studies. It involves attending to the implications of either including or excluding such phenomena from consideration. Moreover, it calls for reflexive self-consciousness on the part of researchers as to why they themselves desire to include or exclude various phenomena from being considered transgendered, why they might seek to name it as something else, and what their own stakes are in seeking particular identifications or disidentifications with the phenomena they study. In addition, what holds true for research across cultural boundaries today holds equally true for historical and speculative research across the boundaries of time: we should be very careful not to impose presentist categories of sex and gender on the unruly strangeness of the past or the unfathomable future yet to come.

Finally, the field of transgender studies should not imagine that knowledge flows in one direction only—extracted from the bodies of the subaltern, the underclass, the colored, the colonized, the uneducated, the unsophisticated, the deviant, and the improperly socialized—for the benefit of a privileged elite for whom that knowledge becomes an instrument or technique for the profitable management of difference. Ideally, the field of transgender studies is a site where a critical gaze can be turned back by Others toward the scene of normativity's engenderment, and where those othered within Eurocentric modernity can produce counterknowledge for projects of their own.

Transgender China takes important steps in that direction.

Contributors

Daniel Burton-Rose completed his MA in Asian Studies at the University of Colorado, Boulder and is currently a PhD student in East Asian Studies at Princeton University. His master's thesis is entitled "Integrating Inner Alchemy into Late Ming Cultural History: A Contextualization and Annotated Translation of Principles of the Innate Disposition and the Lifespan (Xingming guizhi 性命圭旨) (1615)." He is the author of *Guerrilla USA: The George Jackson Brigade and the Anticapitalist Underground of the 1970s* (2010) and the editor of *Creating a Movement with Teeth: A Documentary History of the George Jackson Brigade* (2010). Among numerous articles he contributed a piece on "Queering the Underground" for the activist-oriented anthology *That's Revolting: Queer Strategies for Resisting Assimilation* (2004).

Pui Kei Eleanor Cheung is a researcher and activist for LGBT issues in Hong Kong, and her PhD thesis (University of Hong Kong) was on gender identity formation of gender variant people in Hong Kong. She has lectured on gender and other subjects at the University of Macau.

Howard Chiang received his PhD in the History of Science Program at Princeton University and is currently Assistant Professor of Modern Chinese History at the University of Warwick, where he is also affiliated with the Global History and Culture Centre and the Centre for the History of Medicine. He is completing a manuscript on the historical and epistemological transformations of sex in twentieth-century China, entitled *Sex Off Center: Science, Medicine, and Visions of Transformation in Modern China*.

Larissa N. Heinrich is Associate Professor of Literature at the University of California, San Diego. She is coeditor with Fran Martin of *Embodied Modernities: Corporeality and Representation in Chinese Cultures* (2006), and author of *The Afterlife of Images: Translating the Pathological Body between China and the West* (2008). Her translation of Qiu Miaojin's *Last Words from Montmartre* is forthcoming from New York Review Books.

Helen Hok-Sze Leung received her PhD in Comparative Literature from the University of Wisconsin-Madison and is currently Associate Professor of Gender, Sexuality, and Women's Studies at Simon Fraser University, Canada. She has published widely on queer cinema and queer cultural politics. She is the author of *Undercurrents: Queer Culture and Postcolonial Hong Kong* (2008) and *Farewell My Concubine: A Queer Film Classic* (2010).

Carlos Rojas is Associate Professor of Chinese Cultural Studies at Duke University. He is the author of *The Naked Gaze: Reflections on Chinese Modernity* (2008) and *The Great Wall: A Cultural History* (2010). He is the coeditor (with David Wang) of *Writing Taiwan: A New Literary History* (2007) and (with Eileen Chow) of both *Rethinking Chinese Popular Culture: Cannibalizing of the Canon* (2007) and *The Oxford Handbook of Chinese Cinemas* (forthcoming). He is also the cotranslator (again with Eileen Chow) of Yu Hua's novel *Brothers* (2009) and is the sole translator of Yan Lianke's novel *Lenin's Kisses* (2012). He is completing a manuscript on discourses of corporeality and disease in modern China, entitled *The Sick Man of Asia: Diagnosing the Chinese Body Politic.*

Susan Stryker is Associate Professor in the Department of Gender and Women's Studies and the Director of the Institute for LGBT Studies at the University of Arizona. She earned her PhD in United States History at University of California-Berkeley in 1992, and later held a Ford Foundation/Social Science Research Council postdoctoral research fellowship in sexuality studies at Stanford University. She has held visiting faculty positions at Harvard University, University of California-Santa Cruz, and Simon Fraser University in Vancouver. From 1999 to 2003, she served as Executive Director of the GLBT Historical Society in San Francisco. She is the author of *Transgender History* (2009) and the coeditor (with Stephen Whittle) of the Lammie-winning anthology *The Transgender Studies Reader* (2006).

Alvin Ka Hin Wong received his PhD in the Cultural Studies section of the Department of Literature at the University of California, San Diego, and is now a Mellon Postdoctoral Fellow in both Comparative Literature and Gender Studies at the University of California, Los Angeles. His research interests cover the fields of modern Chinese literature, Sinophone studies, transnational Chinese cinema, and queer studies. His dissertation examines the interregional queer representations in literature and cinema of mainland China, Hong Kong, and

Taiwan within an East–East comparative approach. He has published an article in the *Journal of Lesbian Studies*.

Chao-Jung Wu is an Assistant Professor in the Chinese Music Department at the National Taiwan University of Arts. She received her PhD in Ethnomusicology from Wesleyan University.

Zuyan Zhou obtained a PhD in Chinese and Comparative Literature from Washington University in St. Louis in 1996 and is currently Professor of Comparative Literature and Languages at Hofstra University. His research interests cover Chinese literature of the late imperial period, Taoist philosophy, gender studies, and modern Chinese cinema. He is the author of *Androgyny in Late Ming and Early Qing Literature* (2003) and *Daoist Philosophy and Literati Writings in Late Imperial China: A Case Study of The Story of the Stone* (forthcoming).

INDEX

a-gender (also non-gender), 141
Abe, Kobo, 165
adaptation, 11, 188; of the *Legend of the White Snake*, 127–158
aesthetic, 10–11, 100–101, 145, 150, 157, 190–191, 226, 250
alchemy, 68, 77, 81–86, 94
anatomy, 33, 43–44, 46, 140, 203, 212, 215–216, 218, 221, 227
andric, 99, 102, 106, 109, 111–116
androgyny, 7, 10–11, 230–231, 236, 288; androgynous ideal, 97–125; gendered androgyny, 67–95
archive, 26–31, 38–39, 41, 48, 55, 59, 148, 156
area studies, 12
asexual, 69
Ashes of Time, 188–189
autobiography, 52, 138, 161–164, 167, 170, 172, 179, 197, 228, 256
autonomy, 5, 106, 111–114, 203, 219, 221, 237

Ba Jin, 136
Beijing's National Gallery, 209–210
Beiyang Army, 52
Benjamin, Walter, 128, 152
berdache, 11
biology, 7, 25, 32–33, 43–45, 68, 80, 84, 139, 146, 150–151, 171, 203, 252, 288
biomedicine, 24, 28, 33–44, 51
bisexuality, 144, 230, 243, 245, 264, 268
blood, 46, 49, 86, 133, 165, 205–206, 209–212, 237, 245, 255

body, 7, 10–11, 24, 27–28, 33–44, 47, 49–50, 52, 55–56, 68, 69, 72–73, 79, 81–87, 94, 98–99, 108, 120–121, 128–133, 137–139, 146–147, 162, 166–176, 188–189, 193–196, 199–223, 227–228, 233, 235–244, 245, 289
body modification, 11, 185, 193. *See also* trans practice
breast, 86, 191, 213, 238, 247
Buddhism, 7, 26, 67–95, 113, 129, 133–135, 146, 167, 176, 219, 288; Buddha, 70–73, 83–84, 219, 254; Tibetan Buddhism, 74–76
butch, 5, 17, 128, 130, 144–152, 170, 183–186, 192
Butler, Judith, 3, 9, 10, 138, 148, 203, 227, 237, 251

caizi, 10, 97–125
calligraphy, 100–101, 202
castrated civilization, 23–24, 28, 42, 44, 56
castration, 11, 23–66, 88, 108, 183, 249–251; self-castration, 45, 48, 50–51, 183, 249; voluntary castration, 48–51, 55. *See also* eunuchism
Chen Duxiu, 136
Chen Sen, 214–216, 218
Cheung, Leslie, 192–193
China Times Honorary Prize for Literature, 164
Chinese Attitudes toward Transgenderism and Transgender Civil Rights Scale, 266–267

A Chinese Ghost Story, 187–190
Chou, Zero, 186, 189, 190–192
chronology, 7, 68, 166
cinema, 11, 128, 165, 183–198, 232, 289
citationality, 147–148
civil rights, 5, 266–267. *See also* Chinese Attitudes toward Transgenderism and Transgender Civil Rights Scale
civil service examination, 24, 104, 106, 112
Cixi, Empress Dowager, 231, 251
Classicism, 7, 67–95, 97
colonialism, 23, 35, 37–39, 56, 128–129, 155, 256, 289, 291
colonization, 155, 287–292
Colour Blossoms, 189
Coltman, Robert, 33–37, 42–43, 47, 50–52
commerce (also commercialism), 38, 99, 102, 226, 231, 234–235
concubine, 99, 104, 107, 113, 116, 117, 119, 135
Confucianism, 7, 24, 44, 68, 80, 97, 105–107, 111–113, 116, 121, 129, 133–139, 146, 155
corporeality, 10, 28–29, 32, 37–38, 42–43, 50, 52, 54, 58, 130, 133, 153, 175, 202–203, 205, 212, 214, 216, 218, 221, 235, 237, 243
cosmology, 39, 77, 84, 129–130, 133–135, 139–141, 143, 146
Crocodile's Journal, 162, 164
cross-dressing, 8–9, 76, 98, 103, 120, 128–130, 135, 139, 140, 144–150, 187–189, 225–262, 264–265, 269, 273, 276, 288. *See also* transgenderism; transvestism
Cui Zi'en, 186, 190–191
Cultural Revolution, 195–196

da zhangfu, 107–111, 114, 116–118, 121
daddy, 143, 169–171

dan actors (also *huadan*), 8–9, 100, 127, 136, 139, 193–194, 215, 229, 230–231, 234, 237, 243
Daodejing, 80–81
Daoism, 7, 26, 67–95, 111–112, 137, 189, 288
de Certeau, Michel, 37
defeminization, 24. *See also* femininity
demon, 128–129, 132–134, 136, 140, 142, 144, 146–147, 150, 152, 187
depathologize, 139
Derrida, Jacques, 39
desexing, 69
desire, 5, 29–30, 33, 45, 68, 70, 116–118, 121, 129, 138–139, 141–145, 148–152, 161–181, 184, 186–187, 190, 193, 212, 214–218, 225, 232–233, 238, 241, 269, 292
diaspora, 25
discourse, 8, 12, 24–25, 28–29, 38–39, 52, 55, 69, 80, 107, 116, 136–138, 151, 184–185, 203, 287, 289–290
drag, 3, 140, 189, 227
Drifting Flowers, 191–192
dyke, 144

emasculation (also demasculinization), 24–25, 29–30, 33, 45, 51, 70, 136, 217. *See also* masculinity
embodiment, 6–7, 9–10, 23, 25, 27–28, 35, 38, 43, 48, 51, 54–56, 98–99, 102, 120, 129–151, 161–162, 165, 176–177, 184–187, 193–196, 203, 212, 226–227, 235, 237, 242, 246, 250, 252, 255, 289–291
enlightenment, 35, 71, 74, 112
Enter the Clowns, 190
epistemology, 3, 5, 7, 11, 17, 27, 33, 39, 41, 43–44, 47, 55, 155, 287
epistolary, 162, 165
eunuchism (also eunuchs), 11, 23–66, 70, 104, 108–109, 289. *See also* castration

fag, 143–144
family, 24–25, 27, 30–31, 34–35, 44–45, 48, 50, 52–54, 97, 102–103, 111, 113, 120, 132, 138, 190–191, 201, 228–229, 232, 234, 252–255, 273, 275–276
fanchuan, 9, 147–148, 225–262, 288
Farewell My Concubine, 187, 192–197
fashion, 24, 80, 100–101, 229
female hero, 105–106, 118
female impersonation, 100–101, 225, 231, 234, 237, 243–244, 249–250
female literacy, 102
female masculinity, 3, 25, 129–130, 144–152
femininity, 5, 10, 24, 68, 71, 74–75, 80–81, 97–102, 104–106, 108, 111–114, 118, 128–152, 173–174, 176, 184, 187–188, 192–193, 199, 204, 206–209, 214–215, 220–221, 228, 230–231, 238, 241–252, 268–269, 272, 274, 275, 288. See also defeminization; feminization; gender
feminism, 3, 5, 12, 24–25, 69, 104, 140, 193, 203, 289
feminization, 99–102, 105–106, 114, 129, 138, 147–149, 187, 193
femmeness, 128–130, 140, 144–152, 170
Feng Menglong, 102, 128, 131–135
feudalism, 136–137, 139
flesh, 38, 54, 167, 174, 189, 196, 201, 202, 205, 214, 237
footbinding, 23–29, 50, 52, 55
Foucault, Michel, 56, 59, 60, 62, 136, 289
free love, 24, 136
Freud, Sigmund, 33
FTM, 144–145, 266, 271, 281

Gan Bao, 78–79
gangster, 186
gay, 3, 5–6, 8–9, 140–141, 144, 150, 183–185, 189–193, 227–231, 236, 242, 246–255, 268, 275, 290

gay and lesbian movement, 3, 5
gay and lesbian studies, 9, 140
gender: ambiguous (ambiguity), 49, 68, 129, 137–139, 151–152, 263, 269; anonymity, 168; classification, 70–71, 77, 80, 87, 144, 244; crossing, 11, 105, 113, 119, 135–141, 144, 184–185, 190; dichotomy, 67–70, 76, 87, 99, 121, 135, 194, 203, 287; dimorphism, 4, 6, 69, 170; discrimination, 8, 71, 247, 267–268, 270, 276; disruption, 69, 77–80, 151, 186, 288; division, 87, 97, 99–103, 136, 141, 147, 150; fluidity, 7, 10–11, 69, 99–103, 104, 106, 120–121, 140, 227, 246, 249, 255; gender-bending, 67, 81; gender-indeterminate, 170; gender-neutral, 68, 168–169, 266; non-gender (also a-gender), 141; oppression, 24–25, 69, 99, 247, 255–256, 272, 292; performativity, 3, 9, 10, 148, 203, 205–206, 221, 226–227, 247, 251, 255; representation, 5, 7, 9–10, 76, 85, 99, 127, 129–131, 135, 137, 139, 140–141, 144–146, 148, 150, 151–152, 176, 183–187, 189–191, 241–242, 250; variance, 3, 5, 7, 11, 67, 127–130, 148, 151, 185–189, 249, 263–266, 273, 276, 279, 287, 291–292. See also embodiment; femininity; feminization; identity; inversion; masculinization; masculinity
Genderism and Transphobia Scale, 267
Genet, Jean, 162, 165
genre, 7, 10, 11, 97, 99, 101, 104, 106, 110–111, 114–115, 119–120, 127, 132, 151, 161–181, 184, 226, 234, 288. See also transgenre
gestation, 79, 85–86
gezaixi, 228
Gide, Andre, 165

GIFT, 8, 272–275
god, 72, 81–84, 132
goddess, 74, 86–87, 146
Guanyin, 74, 146

hegemony, 10, 12, 27, 39, 101, 115, 118–119, 195, 232, 244, 249, 251, 281
heterogeneity, 6, 12, 38, 130, 150, 163, 235
heteronormativity, 3, 10, 142, 184, 190, 191, 227, 232, 242, 244–255
heterosexuality, 129–130, 136, 138–144, 146, 148, 151, 184, 244–256, 266, 288; heterosexual matrix, 142
Hirschfeld, Magnus, 3
Hobson, Benjamin, 46
homoeroticism, 8, 25, 100, 139–143, 147–148, 150, 162, 184, 186
homonormativity, 186, 190
homosexuality, 5, 9, 68, 100, 136, 138, 144, 187, 226–232, 244–256, 267, 270–271, 275, 288
Hong Kong, 6, 8, 128–129, 141, 145, 148, 183–198, 263–284, 288
Hongding Yiren (Redtop Arts), 9, 225–262
hormone, 161, 237, 241
Hu Shi, 136
Hua Mulan, 105
human, 6, 24, 28, 33, 54, 67, 75, 78–79, 81, 83, 97–98, 104, 106, 115–119, 121, 127–152, 211, 243–244, 266, 271, 277, 280, 290

identity, 5–12, 28, 38, 44–45, 56, 68, 87, 97–98, 104–108, 110–111, 113–114, 117–119, 121, 128, 133, 147, 150, 152, 161–162, 164–165, 167, 171, 174–177, 184–188, 193, 196, 199, 215–216, 218–219, 227, 232, 235, 237, 241, 243–247, 252, 255, 263–281, 287–292
imperialism, 42, 287
Inside Out, 183

International Day Against Homophobia and Transphobia, 277
International Human Rights Day, 277
intersexuality, 7, 68, 187, 264
inversion, 5, 100, 102, 161, 219

Jarman, Derek, 165
jiaren, 10, 97–99, 104, 106, 114–115, 120–121, 147, 288

kinship, 105, 190–191, 245, 252–255
Kitchen, 188–189
knifer, 30–31, 46–48, 50
kunqu, 101, 215

Lacan, Jacques, 33, 148, 206, 212, 217, 219, 221, 249
Last Words from Montmartre, 161–181
law (also legal), 25, 33, 46, 48, 69–70, 189, 232, 275, 279
leatherdyke, 144
leatherqueer, 144
Lee, Ang, 128
Legend of the White Snake, 11, 127–158
lesbian, 3–6, 9, 140–150, 163, 165, 168, 170, 183–184, 191, 227, 264, 268, 274, 275, 290
Li Shizhen, 70
Li Yu, 100, 103
Lianhe Literary Prize, 164
literary humanism, 136–137
literati, 10, 97–125, 127, 201
lithograph, 45–47, 50
Liu Jin, 104
longyangjun, 99
Lotus Sutra, 72, 74
Lu Xun, 136–137

Ma Liuming, 10, 199, 204–209, 214, 219–221, 288
Mao jacket, 195–196

marriage, 24, 44, 51, 78, 99, 102, 114, 119–120, 132–134, 165, 175, 191, 210, 231, 245, 253–256, 279
martial arts, 103, 128, 146, 149, 183, 187–188
masculinity, 3, 10, 24–26, 32–37, 43, 51, 75, 98–99, 106–121, 129–130, 144–152, 169–170, 172–174, 195, 209, 214, 220–221, 269; female masculinity, 3, 25, 129–130, 144–152; spiritual masculinity, 174. *See also* emasculation; gender; masculinization
masculinization (of women), 102–103
masquerade, 105, 108, 118–119, 145–146, 150, 245–246, 250
Matignon, Jean-Jacques, 35–39, 42–43, 46–47
May Fourth, 24, 55, 129, 136–137
meditation, 68, 71, 81–87, 166, 177, 188
Mencius, 106–109, 112
menstruation, 86, 174, 255
merchant, 102
missionary, 24, 29, 33–42, 46, 50–52
modernity, 39, 129, 136, 139, 291–292
Money, John, 238
monstrosity, 79, 187–196, 266, 271, 273, 280
Murakami, Haruki, 165

Needham, Joseph, 81
neither male nor female (also neither man nor woman), 68, 70, 74, 263, 269–271, 274–275
neo-Confucianism, 116, 121
Netherlands Transgender Film Festival, 183
non-female, 69–71
non-gender (also a-gender), 141
non-male, 69–71
nonhuman, 128–151
nüzhong zhangfu, 105–106, 121

official history, 77
Orientalism, 12, 29
Other, 29, 68

Pacific War, 26
Paris, 162–164, 168–169
passing, 5, 242
pathologize, 129, 136, 138–139
Peking opera (also Beijing opera), 8–9, 127, 136, 187, 192–197, 225, 228, 234
Peking University, 34
photography, 27, 36–42, 43, 46, 205, 209–214, 220–221; medical photography, 36–42, 43, 46
Pinhua baojian, 215–216
political marginality, 108, 112–115
Portland Street Blues, 183–186
post-transsexual, 151
postmodernism, 4, 165
pride, 8, 263–284
prostitution, 99, 100, 103, 136, 216; male prostitution, 100, 136
psychiatry, 5
psychoanalysis, 4, 33, 165, 212, 249
psychology, 54, 75, 87, 98, 102, 112, 120, 155, 164–165, 227, 231, 233–234, 237–238, 245, 249–252, 255, 268, 274, 280
Pu Songling, 77, 129, 135, 137, 151
Pure Land, 71–74
Puyi, 26, 52–54

qi, 79, 81, 83, 86, 98, 105
Qianlong emperor, 45, 48, 49, 53
Qin Liangyu, 103
qing (sentiment), 10, 24, 99–101, 115, 118–121
Qing dynasty, 10, 26, 31, 39, 41, 42, 44, 46–55, 68, 80, 97–125, 127, 129, 135, 147, 195, 201, 231, 251
qingyi, 234
Qiu Miaojin, 161–181
Qu Yuan, 105

queer, 3–4, 6, 9, 12, 25, 67, 130–131, 139–141, 144–150, 152, 162, 164, 165, 170, 183–186, 190–193, 215, 227, 263–265, 269–270, 274–275, 288; studies, 3–4, 6, 12, 141
Queer China, Comrade China, 190

rebellion, 103, 105, 137, 139, 272
reformer, 24
reincarnation, 71, 84, 175–176, 195
relationality, 25, 130, 150–152, 171–174, 186–187, 190–192, 291; trans relations, 190–192
religion, 77, 80, 82, 102, 110, 112–114
Ren Xiong, 199–202, 204, 205, 214, 216, 218
renyao, 128–130, 132–133, 135–139, 151–152, 243; "Renyao" (Yu Dafu's short story), 137–139
reproduction, 33, 43, 44–52, 79, 209, 246, 256
revolutionaries, 24
Rong Rong, 210–212, 220–221

scholar-beauty romance, 10, 97–125, 147
School of the Mind, 107, 113, 116
Semiotics, 10, 202–203, 214, 218, 221
sex, 3–5, 12, 23–25, 43, 55, 67–74, 78, 80, 98–99, 102–103, 112, 129–130, 135–136, 139, 140, 143–144, 148, 151–152, 168, 171, 173, 183, 186–189, 203, 214–216, 218, 227–231, 233, 235–237, 244–247, 249–250, 252, 254–256, 264–265, 269–271, 280, 288, 290–292; sex-alteration, 55 (*See also* third sex); sex assignment, 186; sex change, 68, 71–72, 74, 78, 80, 129, 135, 151–152, 188, 231, 233, 244, 269–271, 274, 280; sex reassignment surgery (also SRS), 4, 187, 231, 233, 247, 254–255, 264–265, 273, 279–281; "sex wars," 5

sexology, 3, 5, 129, 136, 139, 151–152, 155, 287
sexual crossing, 140, 141
sexual fluidity, 144
sexual identity, 5, 10, 104, 152, 165, 215, 230–231, 232–233, 243, 245–247, 249, 251, 253, 255
sexual orientation, 5, 68, 87, 136, 227, 230–231, 232, 245, 247, 248, 249, 254
sexuality, 5–7, 12, 26, 55, 67–69, 74, 100, 128, 131, 133, 136, 138–140, 142, 144–145, 151, 155, 161, 163, 172–174, 187–189, 193, 227, 228–235, 243, 244–255, 267, 276, 287–291
shame, 8, 23, 28, 54, 56, 118, 143, 247, 263–284
Shanghai School, 202
Shijimo shaonian ai duben, 216–218
Shijing, 76
Sick Man of Asia, 23, 38
Sinophone, 19, 26, 55, 66, 130–131, 145, 150–152, 153, 163, 165, 288, 289
snowball sampling, 264–265
social construction (also sociocultural construction), 145, 203, 235
social worker, 67, 271
species, 73, 108
spiritual masculinity, 174
Splendid Float, 189
Stanley Kwan, 190
Stent, G. Carter, 28–31, 32, 35, 37, 42–43, 46–49
structure of feeling, 24
subject, 5, 8, 10, 24–25, 29, 37–39, 42–43, 45–46, 48, 51, 55, 71, 78, 87, 97, 106–115, 118–119, 121, 127–130, 132–139, 140–144, 145, 150, 151–152, 161–162, 167, 170, 174–175, 184, 186–190, 193–194, 196, 201, 202–203, 205, 212, 216–220, 226, 232, 244, 246, 263–265, 287–289

Sun Yat-sen, 52
Surgery, 31, 32 , 34, 36, 42, 48–50, 161, 185, 187, 193, 215, 231, 233, 236–237, 241, 243, 247, 255
Swordsmen (and/or *Swordsmen 2*), 183, 189

T/Po, 147, 150, 170
Taipei, 162, 164, 225, 229, 253
Taiwan, 6, 9, 56, 83, 129, 145, 147, 150, 162–165, 170, 189, 191, 215–216, 225–262, 288
Tang Bohu, 98
Tarkovsky, Andrei, 165
TG, 264, 266–267
The East Is Red, 188
theatre, 9, 225–226, 228–234, 253
theatrical, 8–9, 25, 100–101, 187, 194, 196, 228–234, 246, 288
third sex, 4, 12, 23–66, 70, 228–231, 236, 245, 247, 250, 255. *See also* sex
trans practice, 186–187, 192–197
trans relations (in Hong Kong cinema), 190–192
transcendence, 7, 12, 33, 67–95, 109, 115, 177
transformation, 8, 11–12, 24, 26, 33, 37, 39, 42, 50, 74–75, 78–79, 82–87, 121, 132–133, 135, 147, 167, 170, 173–174, 176, 185–188, 194–196, 208, 217, 219, 235, 236, 242, 246, 251–252, 254–255, 263, 275, 280, 287, 289
Transgender Equality and Acceptance Movement (TEAM), 265, 276, 279
Transgender Resource Center (TGR), 265, 278–281
transgenderism: as a heuristic device, 11, 127–158; Chinese conflation with effeminate homosexuality, 267; in Hong Kong cinema, 183–198; literary transgenderism, 136, 161–181; public perception in Hong Kong, 266–267, 281; as

a rubric of historical experience, 24; in Taiwan's *fanchuan* profession, 225–262; transgender butch, 128, 144–146; transgender femme, 128–130, 144–150, 152; transgender movement, 69, 263–264, 275–281; transgender studies, 3–7, 9–12, 68, 87, 130–131, 140–141, 144, 163, 185, 287–292; transgender(ed) subjectivity, 8, 25, 45, 128, 129, 141–142, 161–162, 188, 263. *See also* cross-dressing; transvestism
transgenre, 11, 161–181
transing, 185, 190, 192
transmen, 267
transmigration, 169, 175–177
transmogrification, 194
transnationalism, 127–158, 162, 185, 287, 289, 291
transphobia, 128, 152, 247, 266–272, 277
transsexuality (also transsexualism), 26–27, 55–56, 128, 145, 151, 161, 184, 186–189, 191, 193, 231, 233, 247, 248, 254–255, 264, 266, 270–271, 287, 289, 291
transvestism, 3, 5, 69, 105, 191, 207, 233. *See also* cross-dressing; transgenderism
transwoman, 265, 267, 275, 276, 279–281
Tsai Ming-Liang, 190
typology, 70, 248

unofficial history, 110

van Gulik, Robert, 100
vice, 110, 137, 248
virgin, 112–114, 120
virility, 44, 99, 106, 108–109, 111–112, 115–121, 141, 217

Wang Dulu, 128
Wang Gen, 117

Wang Yangming, 104, 110
Wei Zhongxian, 104, 110
Wen Zhengming, 101, 113
Whispers and Moans, 189
womanhood, 102, 194, 292
women's movement, 3
writing, 42, 104, 116, 118–119, 137, 139–146, 151, 161–181, 193, 196, 199–223
Wu Jiwen, 215–218, 219–221
Wu Zetian, 73

Xie Zhaozhi, 100
Xiyou ji, 219
Xu Wei, 103, 105–106

yang, 78, 81–82, 85–86, 101, 104, 106–111, 112, 188, 207, 221
Yangzi Delta, 78
yin, 10, 78, 81–82, 85–87, 99–101, 104–111, 112, 121, 207, 221
Yonfan, 189, 190
Yu Dafu, 129, 136–138, 151
Yue opera, 9
Yukio Mishima, 162, 165

Zhang Huan, 10, 199, 204–205, 209–214, 220–221
Zhou Zuoren, 137
Zhu Yuanzhang, 107
zidixi, 225